MAKE IT COUNT

COURTS, CLASSROOMS & THE CASTRIES NORTH PLAYBOOK

Marcellus Bax Stiede

Disclaimer

Make It Count blends reportage, personal recollection, and opinion. Statistics and policies reflect the best information available at the time of writing and may change. Views and interpretations are the author's own and should not be taken as statements of fact unless expressly identified as such. Mention of individuals, organizations, parties, or companies does not imply endorsement or affiliation. Some names and identifying details have been changed, combined, or omitted to protect privacy.

If you believe a factual error appears in this work, or if you have a rights or privacy concern, please contact the publisher at BookContactPress@ gmail. com so we can review and, where appropriate, correct in a subsequent printing or digital update. Trademarks and service marks remain the property of their respective owners. This book does not provide legal, medical, or financial advice.

CONTENTS

Author's Note

I wrote this because too many of us have been made to feel like petitioners in our own community – lining up for crumbs, clapping for ribbon cuttings that never turn into maintenance, and hearing speeches where results should be. That ends here. The promise of this book is simple and testable: representation is a service job, not a coronation. It must be done in daylight, with names, dates, budgets, and before and after photos the whole community can check.

I'm running as an independent to work without permission slips, to publish what I ask for and what we get, and to be held to a scoreboard you can see – not a slogan you can sing. I said it on a platform and I mean it in print: We are not beggars; I am not a king.

WHY THIS BOOK, WHY NOW?

Because Castries North deserves a different standard – one built on steady delivery, not political theatre. This isn't a manifesto to be admired; it's a playbook you can use to track the work: clinics that open on time, study halls that raise scores, small works that make a big difference, and a weekly rhythm that tells you what moved and what didn't. The tools, letters, and checklists in these pages exist for one reason: to turn promises into operations.

You'll see that I treat service as a craft – like sport, where you win by doing the small things right, over and over. Close out. Box out. Make the extra pass. In public life that means: show up, listen, get into the details, and then close – be present when the crossing is chalked, walk the drain from upstream to downstream, call the head nurse to confirm deliveries and escalate if the shelf is still empty.

This moment calls for less drama and more method. That's why the book anchors a Covenant & Scoreboard – plain language pledges on a wall you can read, tied to open dashboards and a cadence of updates that keep everyone honest.

WHAT I OWE YOU

Presence and plain talk. An open office with set hours, regular town halls, and messages written in human language – not fog. When something slips, you'll hear it from me first, with the fix attached.

Names, dates, budgets. Every week starts with a Works Board and a short list: what we're tackling, who's responsible, when it finishes. Every quarter we'll say not only what we did, but what we stopped because it wasn't working. Politics can hide in spin; communities thrive in sunlight.

Execution, not theatrics. I care less who gets credit and more whether the walkway is flat and the drain runs. Close the job; publish the proof. Finish is a sacred word.

Respect for your time. Sometimes service is a text reminder, a thank you note, or a five minute call that unblocks a student's application. Representation is service, not a throne – even in the little things.

You shouldn't need insider gossip to know whether your community is moving. **We'll make the score visible:**

- **Weekly Scoreboard (public):** four simple charts on the wall and online – small works completed vs. scheduled, clinic "uptime," scholarship pipeline steps, and study hall attendance. Walk in on Monday, see the numbers; on Tuesday, see the letters and calls in motion to fix what's off.

- **The Castries North Covenant (posted):** wall readable goals with deadlines and named owners. If it slips, it says so in public – and adjusts with your input. Living pledge, steady values.

- **Open files, open requests:** the projects we ask central government to fund – line by line – so you can see the "yes," the "no," and the "not yet." Information is the new asphalt.

- **Stop–Start–Scale reviews:** every quarter we publish what we will stop, what we will start, and what we will scale based on results – not vibes.

- **Scholarship pipeline trackers:** checklists that move a student from talent ID to degree – passport, transcript, SAT dates, coach calls – logged and reviewed weekly.

These are not abstractions. They are how we make it count week by week, so that five years from now we can point to outcomes, not adjectives.

The work we do must start close to home, because dignity lives where feet touch pavement. Our fixes begin where you live and walk — from Vigie to Vide Bouteille, La Clery to Sunny Acres and Summersdale, Choc to Bisee, and up through Union Hilltop and Blackstone — the crossings, drains, walkways, lights, and clinic hours that turn a day from frustrating to decent. None of this needs a throne; it needs a list, a budget path, and a representative who treats finish like a sacred word.

You'll see Small Works That Matter catalogued and tackled in order: the zebra crossing by the school, the relined drain with mesh baskets, the bus stop that finally blocks rain, the clinic opening early twice a week so working people can check blood pressure and still make town. You will help us rank the hotspots and then watch us work down the list – explaining deviations in plain view.

Starting close to home doesn't mean thinking small. It means proving a model: when a community sees steady service with accountability, it becomes the new normal. Quietly, many want to lead this way; they just need an example and a little cover. Let's provide it.

This book is not an argument for me; it is a contract with you. Hold me to the words on these pages. Publish the schedule; finish the job – that's our culture now. If we live it, the politics will have to catch up.

– *Marcellus Bax Stiede*

Part I – Roots, Reason & the Promise

1

We Are Not Beggars;
I Am Not a King

The first time I said it out loud on a platform, a few people laughed, a few clapped, and one elder woman at the back just nodded. She didn't move, didn't smile – only nodded, as if to say, "At last, somebody willing to call a thing by its name." I said it plainly: We are not beggars; I am not a king.

I grew up among people who went to work early, came home late, and stretched a dollar past the end of the week. Nobody in La Clery or Vide Bouteille waited for a letter from a minister to fix a leaking roof. You borrowed a ladder. You found a cousin with a hammer. You made a plan. But politics, somewhere along the road, taught us the opposite: line up, bow your head, wear a colour, beg a favour. That is how dignity evaporates – one small ask, one long wait, one "come back next week" at a time.

Representation is not feudalism. It is not a patron with a basket of bread. It is a job description: show up, know your people, fix problems you can reach, and fight like hell for the ones you can't. It is a public service role, clear as a nurse's shift or a teacher's timetable. And if you can't point to what you fixed – on the ground, in daylight – you're not representing; you're rehearsing.

Castries North is home to more than ten and a half thousand people, spread across communities each with its own heartbeat — Vigie, where the sea breeze meets the runway fence; Vide Bouteille, climbing its hills with schools and shortcuts; La Clery, proud and unbowed by years of neglect; Sunny Acres and Summersdale, steady and growing; Bisee and Choc, buzzing with commerce and commuters; Union Hilltop and Blackstone, quiet on the ridgeline. Each has a handful of simple fixes that would make life work better — a light replaced, a drain cleared, a walkway leveled. None of it takes a royal decree. Just a plan, a budget that moves, and a representative who answers the phone and shows up until it's done.

I'm running as an independent for a reason. Not because red and yellow never did good – plenty of good people live inside both tents. I'm running independent because I want to serve without permission slips. I want to ask for things on the basis of need and merit, not based on how loudly we clap at a rally. I want to publish what I ask for, what we get, what we didn't get, and why. I want a scoreboard you can hold me against, not a slogan you can sing at me.

WHAT WENT WRONG (AND HOW TO PUT IT RIGHT)

We allowed politics to become performance: a polished speech, an entourage, and a week of giveaways before an election. We mistook motion for progress – ground-breakings without ground works; ribbon-cuttings without maintenance plans; Facebook posts standing in for a site visit. We stopped asking the most basic questions: Who owns this? When does it finish? Where is the budget? What's next?

Putting it right starts with returning the office to its owners. The constituency office belongs to you. It must be open at predictable hours – hours that make sense for people who work. It must answer calls, return messages, and log problems. It must have a map of our communities on the wall and a live list of works on the desk. If we can't show you the sheet – what's scheduled, what's in procurement, what's waiting on a ministry – then we're asking you to trust vibes. Vibes don't pour concrete.

Here is the framework I owe you:

• **Service** – The small things done quickly: drains cleared, sidewalks patched, crossings painted, lights repaired, school fences fixed, clinics resupplied, after-school spaces opened.

• **Accountability** – The public record kept tidy: budgets requested and received, contractors listed, dates promised and dates met, with photographs and names responsible.

• **Visible delivery** – Results you can point to: before-and-after you can show your neighbour and say, "Yes man, look."

Those are not theories. They are habits. And habits, once built, carry across governments.

THE DIGNITY TEST

I keep a simple test for every action from the rep's office: Does it lift dignity? If a resident – let's call her Ms. Joseph – walks into the office about a blocked drain near her house in Vide Bouteille, the wrong response is, "Leave your number; we'll see." The right response is to pull out the ward map, mark the drain, ask for a photo on her phone, and log it with a ticket number. Give her a date we'll inspect, a date we'll clear, and the name of the works supervisor. Post the job on the weekly "Small Works That Matter" board. Then – this matters – call Ms. Joseph the day after the job and ask if water is moving. If it isn't, we return.

That is dignity. Not because we did her a favour, but because we treated the complaint like a public task. Nothing secret. No strings.

If your son needs a letter for a scholarship, you don't need to find me at a podium or a party. You need a staffed desk that can translate your need into forms, deadlines, and calls to coaches or admissions officers. You need standards – what the office promises to do within 48 hours, one week, or one month. If you're chasing a meeting for weeks, the system is broken. If you're bringing me a hamper list near Christmas, the system is broken twice.

I believe that independence matters. Being independent is not an attitude. It is a set of choices about where you sit, who you answer to, and how you budget time. When you're free of a party whip, you can vote with your constituency first. You can collaborate with whoever brings value to Castries North without checking colours. You can negotiate publicly and you can say no publicly. Independence lets you build alliances project by project – health with one member, sports with another, local works with a third – without the nonsense of "enemy" and "ally." In a small country, everybody's your neighbour. We cannot afford pretend wars.

But independence also puts pressure where it belongs: on the representative. There's no party brand to hide behind. If something doesn't move, you can't point to a party conference. The road is either paved or it isn't. The clinic is either stocked or it isn't. Independence sharpens the blade of accountability.

When I say I reject the red-vs-yellow game, I mean it. The only colours I care about in office are the yellow of a freshly painted speed bump outside a school, or the green of a well-kept park. Independence means I can invite everyone to the table – whether they wore red, yellow, or neither on election day – and give them a job to do for their community without someone higher up whispering that I shouldn't work with so-and-so because of party lines. We've seen enough of that divisiveness. It's time for an approach that says: if you have hands and heart, you're welcome to help. In Parliament, I'll vote with my conscience and my constituency – full stop. If Government proposes something that benefits Castries North, I'll support it and push to improve it; if they neglect us or try to railroad something harmful, I'll oppose it loudly. Some will call that naïve, say that one independent voice can't sway a government. I say, watch us. A truth spoken plainly, backed by the people and illuminated for all to see, carries weight. And if one voice can't sway them, then I'll make it a chorus by working with other MPs who care about their communities more than their party bosses. Quietly, many of them want to act this way – they just need an example and a little cover. We in Castries North can provide that example.

The scoreboard is how you will judge me, and I work well with a scoreboard. Ours will be simple, public, and updated weekly. A large sheet on the office wall, mirrored online. Think of it as the community's dashboard. We'll track:

- **Local Works:** number of jobs planned / in progress / completed (drains, sidewalks, crossings, retaining walls, street lights). Each job with a location, budget, contractor, and finish date.

- **Education & Youth:** after-school spaces open, teachers/tutors engaged, SAT prep cohorts, scholarships facilitated, internships placed.

- **Health:** clinic uptime (hours actually open vs scheduled), basic meds in stock, wait times for common services, community exercise programs running weekly.

- **Safety & Public Spaces:** parks and courts refurbished, functioning lights in known dark corridors, clear signage around schools.

- **Response Time:** average time to return a call; average time from complaint to site visit; average time from site visit to action on small works.

I don't need a consultant to tell me what a good week looks like. A good week is when the "Completed" column grows and the phone rings less about the same old problem.

WHAT VISIBLE DELIVERY LOOKS LIKE

Let's be concrete. Picture these ten scenes, each one a small, visible promise:

- **Vigie Crossing** – A zebra crossing with a pedestrian refuge near the school and beach access; posts and reflective paint that don't disappear after the first rain; a sign that says "School Zone – 15 mph."

- **Vide Bouteille Drain** – Concrete relined, grated in sections, leaves and plastic kept out with a simple mesh basket at the upstream inlet. A youth crew paid stipends to clear after storms.

- **Sunny Acres Walkway** – A broken slab replaced with a gently sloped path; rails for seniors; a bench at the midpoint for catching breath.
- **Bisee Bus Stop** – A roof that actually blocks rain, a seat that isn't tilted, and a notice board with the week's schedule of works so people can see what's moving.
- **Clinic Hours that Match Life** – Open by 7 a.m. two days a week so working people can check blood pressure, refill meds, and still make it to town. Medicine stock levels published each Friday.
- **Secondary Schools' After-School Hub** – Tables, whiteboards, and two rotating tutors; a sign-in sheet; a WhatsApp broadcast list that pushes homework schedules and SAT practice links; Saturday sport that doubles as conditioning and fellowship.
- **Court Lights** – Two courts with fixed lights (not just patched wires); a maintenance rota; a community "lights captain" who checks monthly and flags faults.
- **School Fence & Gate** – Welded and painted, with a parent volunteer hour for touch-ups every term.
- **Small Business Kiosk** – A legal, clean space for a fruit vendor near heavy foot traffic; access to water and waste disposal so health officers can nod instead of frown.
- **The Works Board** – On the office wall, updated, with checkmarks beside finished jobs and dates beside promised ones.

None of this requires a throne. It requires a list, a budget path, and a rep who treats "finish" like a sacred word.

I know that service is a craft. My first profession was sport. Good teams don't win by shouting; they win by doing small things correctly, over and over. Close out. Box out. Make the extra pass. Representation is the same craft. You prepare, you show up, you listen, you get into the details, and then you close.

Closing means the rep is present when the line is chalked for the new crossing – not for a photo-op, but to check the gradient. Closing means the rep stands with the contractor's foreman and says, "Walk me through the gutter from upstream to downstream; where's our choke point?" Closing means you call the head nurse Monday morning to ask if the delivery arrived and if the shelf is still empty; if it is, you escalate before noon and you tell the public what happened.

A representative who does not close leaves citizens chasing ghosts. We've all seen it: a big promise, a whisper of progress, then silence. That silence is where mistrust breeds. We will starve it with information.

It is clear to me that information is the new asphalt. When people feel blindsided, they resist even good projects. When they feel included, they help you carry blocks. So we will tell you the plan before shovels move. We will show you the map with red dots for "hotspots" – the spots that flood first, the corners where cars clip mirrors, the places where the pavement is slick with moss. You will help us rank them. We will print the list. Then we will work down the list, explain deviations, and push ourselves for speed without sloppiness.

We will also publish what we ask from central government – line by line. If the Ministry of Infrastructure says yes to our drain package and no to our sidewalk bundle, you will see both answers. Politics can survive in spin. Communities thrive in sunlight.

Money is used to serve the people, and it must be used to serve without strings. What I mean, is that in a real way, Saint Lucia is not poor; we are poorly arranged. Money exists for small works; it often flows late or through the wrong channels or with more middlemen than masons. Our office will be a bridge. We'll bundle small jobs by zone so procurement is fair and faster. We'll favour local contractors who live with their work. We'll involve schools and churches where sensible – shared spaces get maintained because people feel ownership.

And we'll do something we've forgotten to do: close out accounts promptly. Paid on time means contractors answer the next call.

I don't care who gets the political credit if the walkway is flat and the drain runs. I care whether our elders walk without fear and our children reach home dry.

My focus is on the community, and the community must uphold its commitment to the youth. I am a son of sport, and sport taught me something that school sometimes hides: potential wears many faces. I've watched a quiet boy on a sandy court find voice, discipline, and a passport. I've watched a girl with track shoes and a stiff arm learn to talk to a room, then talk to an admissions officer, then talk herself into a scholarship. There are no magic tricks – just structure that turns effort into opportunity.

Our youth plan is not a press release; it is a pipeline:

- **Talent ID & Mentorship:** coaches and teachers noting more than times and scores; they note attitude, attendance, and the spark that says "teach me."

- **Academics & SAT Prep:** a timetable pinned to the notice board with clear weekly goals; mock tests; assistance for fee waivers; parents' sessions so the whole home is in the plan.

- **Coach Introductions & References:** honest letters – strengths, weaknesses, what support this child will need to thrive; tape shared properly; follow-ups not left to chance.

- **Scholarship Packaging:** transcripts, passport, proof of vaccinations, financial affidavits – the unglamorous stack that sinks too many dreams because nobody helped collate it.

- **Degree to Job:** mentorship continues; internship links; clear conversations about coming home with skills or supporting home from abroad.

This is #SportsEconomics: not royalty worship, but a repeatable pathway from court to campus to career. It is cheaper than crime, richer than any parade, and contagious – success makes the next success easier. When one child returns for Christmas and speaks at PDJSS(PDJSS), ten others sit up straighter.

I believe that health is a neighbourhood habit. We do not need a lecture about chronic disease to know what it is costing us. We see the amputations. We see the funerals that shouldn't be. Our clinic is the first front. But the other front is your block, your walking group, your neighbour who says, "Let's go." We will make movement easy by making it friendly. Low-cost group walks, music at the end, a water cooler and a little chart to tick off weekly steps. Simple strength sessions with resistance bands. Blood pressure checks at predictable times. This is not fancy policy; it is the everyday fight for independence – independence of body and budget.

If seniors can cross a street safely and get their pills without a three-hour wait, we are saving limbs and dollars. If thirty workers can squeeze a pre-work clinic visit at 7 a.m., we are bending the curve of a national crisis. The rep's office can't replace a hospital. But it can make the gateway strong.

I believe in listening as infrastructure. Pipes carry water. Listening carries truth. We will keep three listening tools running at all times:

- **Ward Walks** – I and a small team will walk a different pocket every week, no microphone, no convoy – just shoes and ears.

- **The 10-Minute Desk** – A fixed appointment slot every day for quick matters; you'll know the time; you'll know it's yours.

- **The "Not for Facebook" Line** – Some issues are sensitive: a youth on the edge, a family in crisis, a government service that humiliated you. We'll keep a private path where you can be heard and helped without spectacle.

Listening without the power to act is cruelty. So every listening channel must tie back to the works board. If we hear it, we log it. If we log it, we move it or we explain why it isn't moving yet.

I want to dispell the myth of the one-time big fix, and mega promises. As Lucians we love a big announcement. I love it too. It makes us feel like something historic is happening. But most of the weight of life sits on small hinges: a light at a corner, a bus shelter, a clinic line that moves, an after-school table. When these hinges fail, you feel it in your back and wallet. When they work, you stop thinking about them and start thinking about your own goals.

The myth of the big fix keeps us waiting for a king. I am not a king. I am a worker you hire for five years – renewable only if the hinges are oiled and the doors swing.

For some things we must be stubborn. I won a basketball scholarship in 1989 that took me to Kansas. That opportunity did not appear in a dream. It came because people showed up – coaches who wrote letters, teachers who pushed grades higher, a community that believed a boy from La Clery could fly farther than he'd seen. I came back to teach at Sir Ira Simmons. I built camps that brought coaches down and pushed young Saint Lucians up. I worked in corporate management long enough to learn that schedules and budgets either rule you or you learn to rule them. And I came home again because I like to see a thing done – not promised, done.

Along the way I met too many families who taught me what dignity looks like: the father who turned a shipping pallet into a front step rather than ask a politician for a favour; the mother who stood up at a meeting and said, "My son doesn't need a hamper; he needs a referee." The child who told me quietly that he'd never been called on in class, then took the ball on a cracked court and found a way to speak without words.

These people made me stubborn about service. They are the reason I can't smile and wave while a drain floods the same yard three rainy seasons in a row.

I see a future of partnership without pageantry. You see we'll need ministries, agencies, NGOs, churches, and the business community. We will welcome them – without the pageantry that wastes time. If the Ministry of Infrastructure has a crew, we will meet them on-site with the map and the list. If a church wants to partner on an after-school space, we will add tables and a tutor, and we will publish the hours. If an SME wants to sponsor SAT fees or a bench on the walkway, we will stamp their name on it and honour it as a community asset – not a campaign prop.

We will also invite the diaspora to plug in by skill, not just by wire transfer. Engineer in Toronto? Give us two hours on a Saturday for a Zoom with our secondary school science club. Nurse in New York? Walk our students through patient care careers. IT pro in London? Help build the basic data sheets that make our office run like a small firm. Skill by skill, small lift by small lift – the exact opposite of the selfie culture that exhausts everybody and builds little.

HOW YOU CAN HELP (WITHOUT A T-SHIRT)

If you're reading this because you live in Vigie, Vide Bouteille, La Clery, Sunny Acres, Summersdale, Choc, Bisee, Union Hilltop, or Blackstone, your help isn't a chant – it's a checklist:

- Tell us the three most annoying things on your street. We'll add them to the board.
- Volunteer one hour a month. Paint a bench, watch a crossing, bring your trade to a small job.

- Become a "spotter." Send geo-tagged photos of issues so the works supervisor can plan routes that save time and fuel.
- Adopt one youth. Not as a project or pity. As a neighbour. Track homework. Ask about practice. Show up once at a game.
- Hold me to the schedule. Circle dates in red. Ask why something slipped. Make me say the reason out loud.

I want a constituency that acts like owners. Owners don't wait for kings. Owners meet crews with water in a cooler and a question about the next job.

THE PROMISE AND THE EXIT

This chapter started with a sentence and ends with a promise. The sentence – we are not beggars; I am not a king – that's not a play on words – well ok, maybe it is, but more important is that it is a mirror. If you are tired of performing poverty for attention, step away from that stage with me. If you are tired of pretending your representative is a monarch or a magician, step back into the plain truth: your representative is just a worker. I am a worker.

So here is the promise in four lines:
- *I will publish what I plan to do, every week.*
- *I will tell you who is doing it, with what money, by when.*
- *I will show you when it is done, with proof you can step on.*
- *If I fail, I will say so first, out loud, with a reason and a fix.*

I want to walk down a street in Castries North where the improvements are so ordinary they barely earn a nod. Where the bus stop is dry, the crossing is bright, the clinic opens early twice a week, the court lights click on when the sun goes. Where the works board in the office is boring because "completed" is heavier than "promised."

Where a child headed to SAT class waves at me like a neighbour, not a saviour.

That future is not a throne you bestow. It's a job we do – together. You bring your eyes, your voice, your stubbornness for the things that matter. I bring my back, my team, and a refusal to accept that this island must always choose between colours to get a sidewalk. We will build a politics that steps off the stage and onto the street.

And when someone asks you, months from now, "Who is your representative, really?" you can say, "A worker. One of us. One of us." Then point to a crossing, a drain, a clinic line moving – and to a child walking home with a backpack and a plan. That sight right there is our crown. Not on my head – on our street.

We are not beggars. I am not a king. I am a servant of a community that knows its worth, sets a list, watches the work, and finishes the job. That is how Castries North will stand upright again – without bowing, without begging – by building, week after week, the ordinary, visible things that make dignity a daily habit.

2

Castries North at a Glance

I walk through Castries North with a notebook in one hand and a lifetime of memories in the other. This constituency isn't just lines on a map to me – it's home. With around 10,530 people across 4,300 households living here, Castries North is a tight mosaic of neighbourhoods, each with its own character and challenges. From the breezy coast of Vigie to the bustling streets of Vide Bouteille, from the orderly lanes of Sunny Acres to the spirited community of La Clery and the ever-growing hub of Bisee – this chapter is a journey through them all. It's a data-driven tour, yes, but also a personal one. I want to show you the people behind the numbers, the needs etched in every cracked sidewalk and flooded drain, and the practical fixes that can make life better in each corner of our constituency.

Castries North is officially one of Saint Lucia's 17 constituencies, but in truth it feels like many places in one. We have the only peninsular airport on the island, shopping centres that draw crowds from all over, and quiet cul-de-sacs where neighbours still greet each other by name. We are urban and suburban; we are dense in population but rich in community spirit. What unites us is a shared sense that every part of Castries North deserves dignity – the basic services, safety, and opportunities that make a community thrive. Yet for too long, from Vigie to Bisee, many of us have had to get by without even the basics. Our job now is to honestly look at where we stand, neighbourhood by neighbourhood, and chart a course for the future. Consider this a factual check-in with each community – a "glance" that goes beyond the surface. We'll count people and problems, but also talk solutions. Each section ends with what can be done, because a diagnosis means little without a prescription. Let's start at the water's edge and work our way inland, through the heart of Castries North.

VIGIE: PENINSULA OF PROMISE

Vigie sits at the southern tip of Castries North, a slim peninsula pointing out into the Caribbean. With just a few hundred residents (the 2022 census counted 322 people in Vigie), it might be one of our smaller neighbourhoods by population, but it looms large in importance. Vigie is home to George F. L. Charles Airport – our inter-island airport – and the beloved Vigie Beach, where families picnic on weekends and vendors set up grills under the sea grape trees. It's a place where regional travelers first touch down in Saint Lucia, and where locals go jogging in the golden morning light along the beachfront. St. Mary's College, one of the island's great secondary schools, stands on Vigie's grounds. In short, Vigie is a gateway: it links Saint Lucia to our neighbours and connects Castries North to both commerce and recreation.

Yet, talk to the residents of Vigie and you'll hear that living next to national assets doesn't guarantee local prosperity. They worry about speeding along the John Compton Highway that skirts Vigie – cars zip past the airport and beach turnoffs, making it risky for folks (especially the elderly or school children) to cross the road. Some streetlights have been unreliable, leaving stretches of the Vigie road in darkness at night. And while the airport brings economic activity, noise from low-flying planes is a daily reality for those in the flight path. Residents take pride in their neighbourhood – neat little yards along the Vigie stretch attest to that – but they also note that basic upkeep is often slow. The public restrooms by the beach sometimes go without maintenance, and during heavy rains, runoff from the main road can flood parts of the beach parking area.

The needs here are straightforward and solvable. Traffic safety is one: I've spoken with Vigie families who would like to see proper pedestrian crossings or even an overhead walk near the SMC school and airport junction. We can push for flashing crossing lights and speed-calming measures on that highway, so that the life of the community isn't cut in two by a dangerous road. Another need is beach facilities – a small investment in clean, well-maintained changing rooms, proper waste bins, and regular patrols could keep Vigie Beach safe and welcoming for everyone. The residents shouldn't feel that hosting an airport means they get less attention; if anything, it should mean more. With partnership and planning, we could arrange for the airport authority or local businesses to "adopt" sections of Vigie's public spaces – for example, sponsoring new solar streetlights along the beach road and housing area (in exchange for visible community recognition).

Imagine Vigie with a bright, continuous promenade, where evening walkers and joggers are safe under the glow of proper lighting. It's doable. It just takes representation that asks for it, that coordinates between the Ministry of Infrastructure and the local community to make sure those bulbs get replaced and those crosswalks get painted.

The people of Vigie are proud of their peninsula. They see the potential of their community to be not just an entry point for travelers but a model neighbourhood for locals. Vigie reminds us that even a small area can have big significance – and that no community's needs should be overlooked just because other eyes see it as "mostly the airport." I am determined that Vigie gets its due: respect for its residents' safety, upkeep for its public spaces, and inclusion in the broader plans for Castries North's upliftment.

VIDE BOUTEILLE: THE OLD AND THE NEW

Heading north and a bit inland from Vigie, we come to Vide Bouteille – a community that blends the old-school and the new-wave of Castries North. "Vide Bouteille" literally means "empty bottle" in Creole, a name from plantation days, but today this area is full of life. It covers a stretch from the lower hills (just above the city centre) out toward the Castries–Gros Islet Highway, including pockets like Morne Du Don and Entrepot. If you've ever driven to the big supermarkets at Choc or visited the Castries Comprehensive Secondary School (CCSS), you've been through Vide Bouteille. In fact, CCSS – one of our major public secondary schools – sits right in this community, serving students from all over the north of the island. The presence of a school means twice a day the narrow roads of Vide Bouteille see a mini-rush hour of buses and parents' cars. It's a daily reminder that infrastructure here has not kept pace with use: the junctions clog up, and without sidewalks, students spill onto the edges of the street.

Vide Bouteille's residents span generations. Many older folks have lived here for decades – they remember when the area was less developed, when you could identify every family by name. Now there are also newer homes and even a few businesses tucked in. What binds everyone together are some very concrete concerns. First, road conditions: the main Vide Bouteille Road has potholes that have gone unfilled so long they've developed nicknames. Side streets fare no better; I know one area by Entrepot where residents themselves poured gravel into a trench across the lane just to make it passable. Drainage is another persistent issue. When heavy rains fall, water rushes downhill from Morne Du Don through Vide Bouteille. With clogged drains and absent curbs, runoff often ends up in people's yards or stagnating by the roadside. Residents have been calling for a proper fix – larger culverts, regular drain clearing, maybe even a small retention pond upstream – but those calls seem to echo in an empty bottle, so to speak.

Community facilities are a mixed story here. On the one hand, Vide Bouteille is home to VBCC (Vide Bouteille Cultural Club), a community centre and sporting club that has been around since the 1960s and has given generations of youth a place to grow. On the other hand, in recent years VBCC has struggled – parts of its facility need repairs, and access has been a contentious issue (at one point the gates were literally locked due to disputes). The playing court by VBCC, once a hive of activity, has cracked pavement and hoops with rust. For a community that has produced national athletes and spirited debaters through that club, it's painful to see it underused. The same goes for Entrepot's playing field – mostly bare patches of dirt now – and a small playground near Morne Du Don which had its swings broken and never fixed.

What does Vide Bouteille need? Investment and coordination. The fixes here are practical: repave the key roads (and not with a quick tar cover that washes away, but a proper resurfacing). Install sidewalks or at least marked pedestrian lanes near the school – our children should not be walking in the road. Implement a scheduled drain maintenance program, especially before and during the rainy season, so that when the downpours come Vide Bouteille isn't the usual suspect for flash floods. These are the kinds of projects that could be financed through the Constituency Development Programme and Basic Needs Trust Fund grants – funds specifically meant for community infrastructure like drains, footpaths and local roads. Why haven't we been getting them? It boils down to representation. We need an MP who not only identifies the needs but aggressively pursues the funds and partnerships to address them.

On the community side, reviving VBCC is a top priority I see for Vide Bouteille. This isn't just about sports; it's about giving young people a constructive space. I've pledged to help unlock and refurbish VBCC – to partner with its management and perhaps corporate sponsors so that the basketball court is resurfaced, the roof is fixed, and the doors are open to kids after school once more. Imagine VBCC as it was meant to be: not a private club, but a true community hub where a student can get homework help at 4 PM, join a debate or robotics club at 5, and play some basketball at 6. We can do this. We have done it in the past – VBCC's own history shows that when community members band together (often with very little money but a lot of heart), they can create something lasting. I intend to bring that spirit back, with modern support. And on a very personal note: I started much of my own community work right here, training youth on a cracked court, hustling to find equipment. Vide Bouteille taught me early that neglect is the enemy of potential. With targeted improvements, this neighbourhood's everyday reality – safer streets, cleaner drains, an active youth centre – can finally match the pride people have in calling it home.

SUNNY ACRES

If you continue northward past Vide Bouteille, just on the inland side of the Castries–Gros Islet Highway, you find Sunny Acres. The very name suggests a place of brightness and space. Indeed, historically Sunny Acres was developed as a suburban-style residential area – moderately large yards, two-car driveways, fruit trees swaying in the breeze. Walking through Sunny Acres, you might momentarily forget you're in one of the most densely populated districts of the island. It feels like a quiet enclave. But even enclaves are not immune to the issues of the broader community.

Sunny Acres is home to Gablewoods Mall, one of the island's first major shopping centres, which along with the adjacent strip of big-box stores (like the Massy Stores MEGA supermarket at Choc) forms the commercial heart of Castries North. On a Saturday, the roads around Sunny Acres bustle with traffic from shoppers. Residents here can literally walk to do their errands, which is a convenience, but it comes with headaches: traffic congestion at the Choc roundabout, noise from delivery trucks, and lately a concern about petty crime spilling over from the busy retail area (car break-ins, etc.). The mall's presence boosts property values, yet some Sunny Acres homeowners feel overlooked – as if all attention is on keeping the highway area pretty for commerce, while the internal streets suffer neglect. Case in point: a resident showed me a streetlight that had blown in 2015 on their road and as of 2025 had never been fixed. They resorted to installing a motion-sensor light on their gate pillar for some semblance of illumination at night.

Unlike some other parts of Castries North, Sunny Acres does not struggle with poor roads – the main avenues here are paved and generally without potholes. Its issues are more subtle but equally important. Drainage is one: because Sunny Acres sits slightly uphill of the Choc area, water flows down towards the highway. If the main storm drains by the highway are clogged (which they often are), the water backs up into Sunny Acres' cul-de-sacs, flooding yards. I recall clearly the flash flood of late 2020 – it turned one Sunny Acres road into a temporary river, and a friend's ground-floor apartment was swamped, causing thousands in damage. Such floods are not annual, but when they happen, they reveal the cracks (literally) in our planning.

Another need here is community security and cohesion. Sunny Acres, being a relatively middle-income area, doesn't receive much in terms of social programs or government attention. There's no community centre, no health post, not even a public playground within the neighbourhood. It's as if planners assumed the folks here could drive elsewhere for everything. But not everyone in Sunny Acres is affluent; there are retirees on fixed incomes, single parents renting apartments, and they too crave a local support system. During my walks, I met an elderly couple who said the highlight of their week is when the mobile library van comes by (since they can't easily get to the central library). That mobile library is an NGO initiative, not a state one – proof that if we identify a need, sometimes we have to fill it creatively.

So what can we do for Sunny Acres? First, infrastructure coordination. When we fix drains at Choc, we must include the Sunny Acres outlets. I will push for a joint effort between the city council and national works department to survey every drain in Sunny Acres and ensure it links properly into the wider network. We might also explore installing a retention basin or runoff park in a low-lying area near the mall – effectively a green space that can absorb excess water during storms, doubling as perhaps a little park when dry. Second, security and community services: I propose the idea of a Neighbourhood Satellite Centre – perhaps carving out a room in Gablewoods Mall or another accessible spot to be a mini community centre. It could host a weekly nurse visit (for blood pressure checks, etc., saving seniors a trip to the main health centre) and have a meeting room for a Neighbourhood Watch or youth club. This doesn't require building a new facility from scratch; it requires using what we have smartly. I've already spoken to a business owner at Sunny Acres who is willing, in principle, to sponsor a small space if it means a safer, more engaged community – we just need to formalize such partnerships.

Sunny Acres might look on the surface like it's doing "alright," but I refuse to accept that alright is good enough. This community can be a model of balanced development – where commerce and residents coexist without one eclipsing the other. A place that is sunny not just in name, but in the everyday lives of people who feel secure, heard, and served.

LA CLERY: THE HEARTBEAT OF COMMUNITY

If I could point to the heart of Castries North – its emotional centre – it might well be La Clery. This is a community known for its vibrant spirit, sports legends, and a close-knit neighbourhood feel. It's also a place that has borne the brunt of neglect, perhaps more than any other in our constituency. La Clery is not small; it's one of our larger population centres (the broader La Clery area, including adjacent

Morne Du Don and Arundell Hill, easily has a few thousand residents). Mention the name and locals think of the La Clery playing field, the social housing area known as "Block M" or "the Blocks," the La Clery bridge and river, and the long stretch of road that connects to the Gros Islet Highway by the famous "Kiss Me" structure (a landmark building by the highway). La Clery has history and potential in equal measure. I also have deep personal ties here – many of my basketball proteges and friends come from La Clery, and I've spent countless hours on its field and streets, either in friendly rivalry or community projects.

Let's start with the people. La Clery folk are resilient and proud. This is a working-class area; you'll find many tradespeople, civil servants, vendors, bus drivers, teachers making their home here. In the mornings, you see the steady exodus – people walking out to the main road to catch buses to work, children in neat uniforms heading to schools (some to nearby Vide Bouteille Secondary, some to Anglican or RC Boys downtown). In the evenings, you smell dinners cooking and hear laughter or debate on verandas. It's a community that wants to thrive. But what's holding it back are very tangible deficiencies. Infrastructure in La Clery has been all but ignored for years. The main road through La Clery was last fully resurfaced over a decade ago; since then it's been patch jobs on top of patch jobs, resulting in a bumpy, uneven ride that torments car suspensions and pedestrian ankles alike. Several inner lanes – like those near the Blocks – have no pavement at all, just dirt and stones that turn to slush in the rain.

Then there's the matter of lighting and safety. One of the sorest points residents raise is that the lights around the La Clery playing field have been out for roughly ten years. Imagine that: an entire decade where the community's primary recreation space goes dark after sunset because the floodlights failed and were never repaired. This isn't just an inconvenience; it's a message. It tells the young footballer who'd like to practice at 7 PM that he's not a priority; it tells the women's exercise group that used to meet at dusk that they don't matter enough to have a lit safe space. And it's not just the field – numerous streetlights in the interior of La Clery (e.g., near the river road) have blown and never been fixed. Darkness invites risk. I've heard from residents who feel anxious walking home from an evening church service or coming back from work because whole stretches are pitch black. Ten years of darkness is unacceptable.

Flooding and environment: The La Clery River that runs by the community is shallow and gentle most of the year, but it has a tendency to overflow in heavy rain. Over time, debris and silt have narrowed the channel. The bridge by the main road gets clogged with branches and garbage when the river swells, causing water to back up into nearby yards. Earlier this year, we nearly had a nasty flood after a sudden downpour – only some quick self-organized community clean-up of the debris saved the worst. A proper river desilting and building of retaining walls in key spots is overdue. People remember promises of it, but few have seen action.

La Clery is also a cradle of talent – sports and otherwise. Some of Saint Lucia's well-known athletes hail from here. We talk about "Big Joe" from La Clery (Jonathan), who electrified high school basketball in the 90s. We recall community initiatives – like the youth tournaments named after local heroes (I recently gave closing remarks at the Loloy Daniel Tournament final held here). The passion for progress is here; what's lacking is infrastructure and investment to match it.

So what are the practical fixes for La Clery? Let's list them plainly:

- **Restore the Lights** – Quite literally, turn the lights back on. Reinstall proper lighting around the playing field and key dark spots in the neighbourhood. This is an easy win: it may require a budget for new fixtures or bulbs and coordination with LUCELEC (the power company), but it's not rocket science. A modern LED floodlight system for the field, with an energy-efficient timer, could be installed within months if prioritized. I commit to making this one of the first things to tackle. La Clery's evenings should be alive with activity again – safe, supervised, and in the light.

- **Roads and Drains** – Launch a dedicated La Clery Road Renewal project. It should start with re-engineering the main thoroughfare: scrape it down, grade it, and repave it entirely. No more band-aids on an open wound. Then systematically address the side lanes, even if it's a stepwise plan over a couple of years to pave or concrete them. In tandem, clean and widen the drains. The drain that runs along the Blocks, for instance, needs concrete lining and regular clearing. Community leaders have detailed knowledge of every trouble spot – as your MP I would make sure those voices guide the works teams directly (no one knows the flash flood patterns better than the families who have to move their furniture when the water rises).

- **River Defence** – Work with the Ministry of Agriculture (which often handles river management) to dredge the La Clery riverbed and shore up the banks with gabion baskets or concrete in the most erosion-prone areas. This is climate-change adaptation at the local level – we know storms will come, so let's not wait for disaster. We also will turn this into a community effort where feasible: tree planting along the banks, community clean-up drives every quarter so the river isn't choked with waste. In fact, not long ago I planned a big cleanup of the La Clery River – and interestingly, once I announced it, the current rep's team scrambled to do one ahead of us. If competition is what it takes to get action, so be it – but let's make it regular, not just election-season optics.

- **Community Centre and Services** – La Clery does have a resource centre building near the field, but it's small and often under-equipped. I would push for expanding its capabilities: maybe a second floor or an annex that can serve as a homework centre/tutoring space and a small clinic outpost. If we can't build new (budget can be tight), we can optimize: use the existing schools after hours. Sir Ira Simmons Secondary is just up the hill in Morne Du Don; why not have adult education classes or youth workshops in a couple of its classrooms at night? I'm a firm believer in using what we have. The playing field itself, once lit, could host more community events – sports, yes, but also outdoor movie nights or cultural shows that bring residents together in pride and unity.

Above all, La Clery needs consistent representation. People here tell me not that they expect miracles – they aren't asking for a stadium or an eight-lane highway. They're asking for basics: fix our roads, light our streets, listen to our calls. One elder in La Clery phrased it perfectly to me: "We not looking for handouts, we looking for a fair deal. We put in our part – we pay taxes, we mind the young ones – we just want the government to do theirs." That's it. La Clery has done its part, as I said at a meeting recently: The people of Morne Du Don (La Clery's extension) have always done their part... but what have you gotten in return? No real representation. That must change. If Castries North is a body, La Clery is the thumping heart, and it deserves a steady flow of support, not blockage and neglect. My vision is that in a few years, we can point to La Clery as a success story: a rejuvenated playing field bustling with youth at night, smooth roads where cars and pedestrians co-exist safely, a river that stays in its banks, and a community that feels seen.

BISEE AND ENVIRONS: BETWEEN COMMERCE AND COMMUNITY

Moving to the northernmost reaches of Castries North, we enter Bisee (often spelled Bisee) and its surrounding locales like Choc, Union, City Gate, and Summersdale. This zone is where the constituency blends into a larger commercial corridor – Choc Bay marks the boundary with Gros Islet to the north, and the Union areas climb into the hills to the east. Bisee itself sits just inland of the coast, a mix of residential pockets and busy roadways. If you've driven to Rodney Bay from Castries, you have passed Bisee – maybe you noticed the billboards and the big fuel station, or the turning by the Massy supermarket. Many people see Bisee as just that congested stretch near the Choc roundabout. But behind that façade, a real community lives here. In fact, the Castries North constituency office (for the current MP) is located in Bisee – a small building along the road – though ironically that office has not meant visibility or action for the people.

Let's talk people and layout. Bisee has long-standing residents who remember when the area was scrubland and farms. Now, due to Castries' expansion, it's effectively an outer suburb. Houses range from modest concrete bungalows to a few newer townhouse complexes. The population in the Bisee polling district is significant – combined with Choc and Summersdale it numbers in the high hundreds. According to the census, the immediate communities labelled Choc Bay and Summersdale/Union have small counts (51 and 209 respectively), but that belies the larger number in greater Bisee which isn't listed but is certainly a major chunk of our 10,530 residents. Many young families live here, drawn by relatively affordable land and proximity to jobs in the north.

However, basic infrastructure hasn't kept up. Roads: beyond the main highway, many side roads in Bisee/Union are narrow, winding, and in poor shape. One example is the road into Union Hilltop – folks there have complained about its condition for years (crumbling edges, no proper drainage), and it's only gotten a cursory grading once in a blue moon. Water and sanitation: Bisee doesn't have a major issue with water supply (thanks to improvements in the Beausejour water network), but sanitation is a quiet concern – there's no sewer system here, so all are on septic or pit, and with increasing density that could become a health issue if not monitored.

The big issues that are visible centre around the intersection of community and commerce: traffic and pedestrian safety. The Choc roundabout is a notorious bottleneck at rush hour. Residents of Bisee who just want to cross the highway or merge from a side street often take their life in their hands. We've had a few accidents and many near-misses with people trying to dash across to get to the mall side. There is a pedestrian crossing by the roundabout, but drivers rarely stop as they should. I strongly feel we need either a pedestrian overpass or a set of pedestrian lights there – it's a national road, yes, but it's right within our constituency and our people are the ones at risk daily. I will advocate at the national level for smarter traffic management at that junction (there has been talk of expanding it or re-engineering it, which I support, as well as adding sidewalks leading up to it from the Bisee side so people don't have to walk on the road shoulder).

Another challenge: environment and flooding. Bisee lies in the lower catchment of two streams – one coming from Union, another from inland near Grande Riviere – which converge near the coast. The lower Bisee/Choc area is low-lying, and when heavy rains come, water accumulates. We've seen flooding in the past in the yards behind the supermarket and along the road to City Gate. Part of this is due to the loss of mangroves and natural flood plains by the beach when development happened. We can't fully undo that, but we can mitigate. I propose we install additional large concrete culverts under critical points of the roads to aid water flow, and invest in small-scale drainage projects: for instance, a proper covered drain along the City Gate road which now often turns to a muddy creek in rain. The good news is that funding exists for such projects through disaster mitigation grants – we simply have to apply and argue for Bisee's case, which I will.

Community services in Bisee are thin. There's no public health facility in this part of the constituency; the nearest is the Gros Islet Polyclinic or going back to the Castries city. For a mother with a sick child in Bisee without a car, that's a long and costly trip. I believe we should consider extending hours or services of either the Gros Islet clinic for Castries North residents or set up a periodic mobile clinic station in Bisee (perhaps at the constituency office building if properly outfitted). When it comes to schools, children here usually attend those in neighbouring areas (e.g., the Grande Riviere primary or schools in town), but as this zone grows, we should plan for educational facilities as well. One bright spot: Bisee is close to the Union Orchid Gardens and the newly built St. Lucia Sports Academy in Union. Those are opportunities – I'd like to see the Sports Academy and its resources (gym, coaches) engage with local youth in Bisee, offering clinics or use of facilities to inspire the next generation.

Economically, Bisee's people benefit from the jobs at the mall and nearby businesses, but many local small entrepreneurs feel left out. For example, street vendors have often been chased from in front of the big stores due to "no vending" rules, which is understandable for traffic, but then where do they go? We can designate a small area – maybe a lay-by or lot – for a community market spot where local sellers (fruit, snacks, crafts) can safely vend without impeding traffic. This has worked in other parts of St. Lucia (like a designated spot near the Rodney Bay junction for vendors). It just takes will and a plan.

In Bisee and its environs, the practical fixes revolve around one concept: integration. Integrating the booming commercial zone with the wellbeing of residents, integrating flood control with development, integrating our community into the conveniences that surround it. Under my leadership, I would ensure that every new development at Choc or Union comes with community impact assessments – if a new store goes up, does it provide a sidewalk or a bus stop shelter as part of its permit? If a new road opens, does it help locals or just divert traffic elsewhere? Castries North's northern belt can be one of prosperity shared, but it requires a representative who constantly reminds planners and investors: people live here. We are not just passing through.

A SHARED REALITY, A SHARED HOPE

Having walked through Vigie, Vide Bouteille, Sunny Acres, La Clery, and Bisee (and the little pockets among them), one thing stands out crystal clear: the everyday reality of Castries North is one of unmet potential. In each area, people are doing their best – organizing clean-ups, mentoring kids, patching potholes with home-mixed concrete – but they shouldn't have to do it all alone. The census and statistics give us one view (like our constituency's growing voter enrolment, up from about 9,800 in 2006 to over 12,000 by 2021). But behind those numbers are individual stories. The father in Vide Bouteille who uses an old shipping pallet as a front step because the community drain project never came. The mother in La Clery who stood up in a town hall meeting and said, "My son doesn't need a welfare hamper, he needs a referee and a chance to play under lights." These are real voices – I've heard them. They all echo a simple plea: give us the basics, and we will build the rest.

Castries North at a glance is a picture of problems, yes – but also of practical solutions within reach. Every neighbourhood needs something specific, but they all need something simple: representation and resources that respond to their reality. Throughout this chapter I've outlined needs and fixes area by area. Summarizing them, you could say: better roads, safer streets, reliable utilities, places for kids, and a listening ear in leadership. These are not extravagant asks. In fact, they are the minimum. The good news? We can meet these needs with the tools already at hand – government programs, local initiative, diaspora support, and plain old hard work. The bad news? Those tools have largely been left on the shelf by those in power, while our communities languished.

I often use the phrase "Castries North can rise again." I believe it to my core. It's not a blind slogan; it's born of seeing the talent in our youth clubs, the commitment of our elders in community groups, and even the stats that show we have strengths to build on (for example, our district's unemployment is middle-of-the-pack, not the worst, and we have more business activity around us than anywhere else in Saint Lucia). The ingredients for a turnaround are all here. We just need leadership that mixes them right and turns up the heat on implementation.

As we conclude this walkthrough of Castries North, I want to emphasize a vision of each place in the future:

• **Vigie,** with a safer main road, a kept beach, and community tourism where locals benefit from every plane that lands.

• **Vide Bouteille,** with smooth roads and a vibrant reopened VBCC where the next generation is nurtured every afternoon in sports, arts, and academics.

- **Sunny Acres,** with flood-free streets and a small community centre – a neighbourhood that balances quiet living with the convenience of nearby commerce, no longer overlooked.

- **La Clery,** shining, with floodlights at night, and the sounds of youth playing and neighbours greeting each other on well-lit streets; a place moving beyond past neglect, now with even greater community pride.

- **Bisee and Choc,** with traffic tamed by smart design, where residents can cross safely, and where local enterprise has a seat at the table of development.

- **Summersdale,** with calm residential lanes, continuous sidewalks linking safely to the highway and shops, and strengthened drainage that keeps yards dry after heavy rain – quiet, connected, and safe for families.

- **Union Hilltop,** with safer hillside roads and retaining works, reliable water pressure and street lighting, and a living link to the Union playing field and Sports Academy – so after-school sport, tutoring, and transport connections are part of daily life, not luck.

- **Blackstone,** with slope-smart drainage and culverts, marked and lit footpaths to the bus routes, and a small, clean community space for meetings and homework – practical fixes that make a small upland settlement feel seen and secure.

- **City Gate,** with a proper bus bay and shelter, a safe pedestrian crossing into the commercial strip, and a small cluster of licensed vendor stalls – so commuters, shoppers, and small businesses can share the space without chaos.

- **Malabar,** with clean, clearly signed beach access, safer road crossings near the airport bend, upgraded lighting, and formalized beachfront vending—orderly, welcoming, and visibly managed for residents and visitors alike.

- **Palm Beach,** with a simple, well-kept seaside promenade, bins and restrooms that actually work, and weekend community programming—turning a beloved stretch into a reliably family-friendly public space.

This is not wishful thinking. This is planning and doing. The data guides us to where the pressure points are; the community voices tell us what's most urgent. With those in hand, Chapter 2 of this book – much like Chapter 2 of our journey – lays the groundwork. We've glanced at Castries North, but I refuse to just glance and move on. I stare unflinchingly at the problems because I intend to fix them. And I never lose sight of the people, because they are Castries North. In the next chapter, I'll step away from the statistics and dive into a personal story – one drive, one young man's future, and the lessons I drew about service and leadership. But as you read that, remember this chapter's message: every community in Castries North counts. Every child on every street, every retiree on every porch, every dream in every home – they all count, and with the right approach, they all can have a chance to shine.

3

A Drive to Park University

The engine was already running when I slid into the driver's seat, heart thumping with purpose. It was early – the kind of pre-dawn darkness that makes every streetlight feel like a lone star. I had a long drive ahead. Park University in Missouri was a few hours away by highway, and I was on a mission fuelled by equal parts hope and nerve. In the rear-view mirror, I caught my own eyes and for a moment saw a younger version of me: Marcellus the basketball kid, hustling on St. Lucian courts with a dream of making it off the island. But this drive wasn't about me. It was about a young man nicknamed Darwin whose future was folded in my pocket in the form of a few stats, and a whole lot of trust.

Malvo "Darwin" Joseph and I go way back – not in friendship, but in rivalry. Darwin is from Soufriere, on the west coast of Saint Lucia, a town known for its twin Piton peaks and hot springs, but also for tough, scrappy ballplayers. For years, Darwin and I faced off on the national basketball team. He was the wiry, relentless guard assigned to defend me every summer when I'd come home from the U.S. to play in tournaments. If I tried a crossover, Darwin's quick hands were right there; if I drove left, he was on my hip like a shadow. We were close in age, both competitive to the bone. In those days I was the one with the U.S. college experience, and he was the hometown hero trying to prove himself against me. Every matchup was like looking in a mirror that talked back – he mirrored my moves, countered my strengths, and forced me to elevate my game.

Fast forward to one summer in the early 2000s. I was in graduate school in Kansas, and I came home for the off-season as usual. We held national team training at the indoor court in Castries. Darwin showed up in better shape and sharper form than I'd ever seen. His footwork had tightened up – no wasted steps, just efficient motion. He was patient, too; the impulsive kid who used to lunge for every steal had learned to wait, to play angles and timing. I remember one sequence vividly: I gave him my signature head-fake – a little shoulder dip I used to send defenders lunging the wrong way. In the past, he might have bitten and I'd slip past. This time, Darwin didn't budge. He stayed in front of me, feet set, body low, eyes steady. I had to take a much tougher shot than I wanted. As the ball clanged off the rim, I broke into a grin. I was proud. That might sound strange – being proud of an opponent – but in that moment I sensed Darwin had levelled up.

He wasn't just playing against me; he was playing beyond me, showing qualities that any coach would kill to have on their squad.

Sometimes life gives you a glimpse, a quiet revelation. That day, watching Darwin hold his own, I had one: Darwin deserves a bigger stage. He was in his early twenties, about the same age I was when I got my break to go to college in the States. I knew what that opportunity had done for me beyond basketball – a degree, exposure, confidence, a wider world. Darwin had the game and the grades (from what I'd heard) to do the same, but no scouts were coming to tiny Saint Lucia to watch him, and he didn't have a stack of highlight tapes to send out. In fact, like many talented Caribbean players, he didn't even have formal game film; most of our local matches weren't recorded. What he did have was me – an older rival who believed in him, a friend, a fellow Lucian willing to stick my neck out.

So I made a decision that could have easily gone south: I decided not to wait for any formal process. I decided to act. I made some calls, did some asking around, and found out that Coach Claude English at Park University was known to give Caribbean players a chance if he was convinced of their potential. Coach English had a respectable program in the NAIA division and had briefly met some Saint Lucian players through a Kansas contact of mine. That was enough of a crack in the door for me to shove my foot in. I phoned him: "Coach, it's Marcellus Stiede. We met a couple years back at that tournament in Kansas – I'm the guy from St. Lucia, yes... I have a player here you need to know about." We spoke briefly; he was intrigued but non-committal, understandably. He'd want to see the player, or at least some footage. Footage. Here I was trying to sell a coach on a kid without a single proper video. Words would have to do.

A few days later, I found myself driving up the interstate towards Park University's campus. It was just me – no Darwin at my side. At the time, Darwin was still back home in Saint Lucia, and I was in Kansas; I had come up to the States to continue my grad studies. I figured, let me go plant the seed. It felt a bit crazy – like an unofficial ambassador of Saint Lucian basketball going to petition on one player's behalf – but I also felt a calm certainty. I had seen enough players and enough basketball to know Darwin had "it." And more importantly, I knew he had the character to follow through if given a chance.

The drive gave me time to reflect. Mile after mile of open road, with the Kansas plains gradually giving way to Missouri hills, I replayed scenes in my mind: Darwin boxing out opponents a good six inches taller, Darwin running suicide drills until everyone else quit but he kept going, Darwin leading kids in his town through pick-up games at the local court, acting every bit the role model without a big audience. Mentorship and duty were the words that floated up from my subconscious. Why was I doing this, really? It wasn't going to earn me any money or fame. If anything, I risked looking foolish if Coach English said "no" or if Darwin didn't live up to my pitch. But something deeper compelled me: a sense of duty to pay forward what others had done for me. When I was a teenager with raw talent, there were mentors – coaches, teachers – who stuck their necks out to get me to Emporia State. They had no guarantees I wouldn't falter, but they believed in giving me a shot. Now it was my turn. This drive was about loyalty to community – not just my immediate neighbourhood, but the broader St. Lucian community of young hopefuls. If one of us climbs a ladder, we ought to extend a hand down for the next.

And so there I was, a lone car cutting through the morning mist, thinking about how life can make leaders out of us in the most unplanned ways. I wasn't an elected official or a coach with a title. I was just a grad student with a car. Yet leadership was happening in that very ordinariness. Nobody told me to go advocate for Darwin;

in fact, a more selfish person might have thought, "Why help the guy who once tried to steal my thunder on the court?" But leadership often begins with a personal choice – to help when you're not obligated to, to speak up for someone when you could just as easily stay silent.

When I finally arrived at Park University and walked into Coach English's office, I felt strangely calm. Perhaps during the drive I had made peace with whatever outcome. I was greeted by a tall man with a firm handshake and curious eyes. Coach Claude English was a presence – a former player himself, I later learned, who understood what hunger looked like in a young athlete. I got right to the point. "Coach, thanks for seeing me. I don't have a DVD or a tape for you. All I have is a story about a player from back home." I told him about Darwin – about how he plays, but more importantly how he carries himself. "Coach, there's a player in St. Lucia who looks a bit like me, plays like me, and deserves a shot," I said, leaning forward earnestly. "I don't have a tape – but trust me on this. He's got the fundamentals, he's coachable, and he's hungry. You give this kid a chance, you won't regret it."

I could see Coach English measuring my words, measuring me. In a way, I was putting my own reputation on the line. If Darwin came and flopped or, worse, misbehaved, it would reflect on me. But I wasn't worried about that. Darwin was too grounded for foolishness; if anything, he might be too shy at first. Coach asked a few questions: Height? ("Six-one, but plays bigger.") What's his character like? ("Disciplined, quiet leader, natural work ethic.") Can he handle college academics? ("Yes, he's bright – finished his A-levels.") Coach English nodded slowly. There was a long pause. Then he said something like, "Well, if he's as you say, I might have a spot. But he's got to get here, and I'll need to see him in person." I broke into a smile and said, "Coach, if you say the word, he'll be here. I'll make sure of it." In that moment, Coach listened. That's all I could ask. He agreed to review some basic stats I'd send by email and to tentatively pencil in Darwin for a tryout at the start of the next semester. I walked out of that office feeling ten feet tall. The door hadn't swung wide open, but it was ajar now – and that's all an eager person needs.

On the drive back, I rolled down the windows. The day had turned sunny, with the kind of wide Midwestern sky that made me feel anything was possible. I allowed myself to daydream a bit: Darwin coming to Missouri, donning the Park University Pirates jersey, hitting his first three-pointer in a college game, earning a degree. None of this was guaranteed, but the mere possibility felt wonderful. There's a unique joy in acting for others. It's almost paradoxical – you expend energy, you inconvenience yourself, yet you feel recharged. As the miles ticked by, I reflected on the power of trust that had been exchanged. I had asked Coach to trust me (and by extension, Darwin), and Darwin was implicitly trusting me to not steer him wrong. I was trusting Darwin to seize the opportunity if it came. And underlying it all, I trusted that doing the right thing was worth it, regardless of immediate outcome.

A few months later, the real work began: coordinating Darwin's paperwork, helping him navigate the visa process, preparing him for what to expect in the U.S. I coached him on little things: the pace of the college game, the need to speak up in class if he didn't understand something (a challenge for a soft-spoken islander), even how to use an ATM card which he'd never needed back home. In those moments, I realized how mentorship isn't just big speeches or training sessions; it's the thousand small assurances and pieces of advice that help someone actually step through a new door. Darwin later told me that when he landed in the U.S. and felt the cold air for the first time, he heard my voice in his head: "Pack a proper jacket, you'll thank me later." It made him smile and steel himself for the journey.

Now, I wish I could say the rest was easy, but life is not a straight line. Darwin had his struggles adjusting – in his first semester, he battled homesickness and the shock of intense academic workload. On the court, he had to fight for a roster spot among players who didn't take kindly to a foreign unknown getting a look-in. Coach English gave him a fair shake, but made no promises about playing time. Through it all, Darwin kept at it. He would call me occasionally, more to talk about school than basketball: "Boy, these finance classes are something else," he'd say with a nervous laugh, or "I joined a study group, trying to keep up." I became a long-distance mentor, encouraging him to persevere and reminding him why he started this journey.

And Darwin delivered – both on and off the court. Over four years, he earned his Bachelor's degree in Finance, then went further to complete a Master's in Business. On the court, he became a steady contributor to the team – not a superstar, but the kind of reliable player every coach loves: low turnovers, solid defence, and a calming presence in tight games. In his final season, he hit a game-winning shot in a conference playoff – Coach English emailed me that night with a two-word message: "He delivers." I don't think I've ever felt a warmer glow of vindication. Darwin had justified the trust.

Yet, the true measure of this story is not the points he scored or the degrees he earned – it's what Darwin did with them. Today, Malvo "Darwin" Joseph lives in New York City, working in finance. But if you ask him his real passion, he'll talk about giving back. He hasn't forgotten Soufriere or St. Lucia. He started an annual book drive for the schools in his hometown, sending boxes of textbooks and novels to the local library and youth groups. He mentors young St. Lucian students and athletes via Zoom on weekends, guiding them on college applications and training regimens. He sponsors a local under-16 basketball tournament – providing jerseys and modest scholarships to standout players. In essence, Darwin became exactly the kind of community-focused individual I knew he was. He's extending the chain of mentorship onward. That, to me, is the sweetest victory.

Reflecting on that journey, I realize how much I personally gained from it. It taught me what it means to lead without a title. There was no blueprint or obligation for what I did. It was an act of conviction. And it opened my eyes to how many others like Darwin existed – young people with talent and heart, just needing someone to remove a barrier or two. It's what I later conceptualized as the economics of trust and opportunity. You invest time and belief into someone, and the returns ripple outward in ways you can't always predict but can definitely feel. Darwin's success echoed in Soufriere; kids there now talk about him as an example: "If Darwin made it to college, maybe I can too." One small drive up a highway helped light a spark in distant minds.

During that drive, I also confronted my own past of rivalries and reconciliations. The prompt of being alone with my thoughts brought up memories of Coach Kerry Dickerson – my college rival turned friend. Kerry and I had been on opposite sides of the fierce Emporia vs. Washburn university rivalry. We practically hated each other on the court, fuelled by school pride and personal competitiveness. But after college, life threw us together – we played on the same summer team, and later, when he was coaching, I reached out to him about recruiting St. Lucian players. Breaking the ice with Kerry was initially as awkward as an ill-timed jump shot. Here was the guy whose teams tried to run us off the court, now sitting in my mother's living room in Castries because I convinced him to visit and see our talent firsthand. (Yes, I famously promised him a "nice hotel" and then put him up at my mom's house – a story we laugh about now.) The old rivalry melted away over homemade fish broth and dominoes with my uncles. We realized we wanted the same thing: to help young players grow.

Together, we built a pathway for dozens of Saint Lucian and Caribbean athletes to attend Kansas colleges. Kerry's network and my initiative created a pipeline: those Caribbean Nights at Kansas schools where they'd celebrate the new students we sent, the equipment donations like the pro-grade hoops Washburn University gifted to our island.

Why do I bring up Kerry here? Because driving to Park University for Darwin's sake was part of the same continuum of turning rivalry into partnership, competition into community. Kerry taught me that sometimes your opponent today can be your ally tomorrow if you find common cause. Darwin taught me that the kid trying to steal the ball from you might one day hand you the ball to take the last shot for him – in other words, trust and roles evolve. I often think: what if I had held grudges? What if I had been too proud to befriend Kerry, or too insecure to help Darwin (thinking maybe he'd overshadow my legacy or something silly like that)? I would have missed out on some of the most meaningful work of my life. It's a lesson I carry now into politics – in Castries North, I'm running as an independent, which means I don't have a big party machine. Some might call me a rival or spoiler to the established parties. But I see potential allies everywhere, even among those who once opposed me on something. If the cause is right – like providing opportunities for youth – I'll work with anyone, red, yellow, or blue. I've learned to measure people not by the label of rival or friend in the moment, but by the openness of their heart and the alignment of their values with serving others.

The drive to Park University also gave me a metaphor I return to in my mind: leadership as a journey, not a destination. Literally, I was on a journey to try and help someone. Philosophically, it's the idea that we move, we act, we steer – and along the way we reflect and adjust. I recall crossing the Missouri River on a wide bridge during that trip, the water below glinting. It struck me that the river didn't care who I was or what I intended; it flowed regardless. In life, there's a current of events that will go on with or without our input. Leadership is deciding to paddle, to navigate that current, maybe even to redirect a small part of it for the benefit of others. That day I wasn't content to sit on the riverbank and wish Darwin good luck; I jumped in to help swim him across. President Obama often spoke about the audacity of hope – not hope as naive optimism, but hope as action against the odds. Driving hours to advocate for an unknown kid from a dot-on-the-map island to a U.S. coach – that was an audacious hope in motion. And it paid off because it was backed by genuine intention and preparation.

In the years since, I've made many other trips and calls on behalf of young people – sometimes for sports, other times for academics or jobs. Not all have panned out as dramatically as Darwin's story. There were disappointments: the player who got homesick and came back early, the student who didn't gel with the foreign culture and transferred elsewhere. Each time I asked myself, Was it worth it? And the answer has always been yes. Because doing nothing would guarantee zero progress. Trying at least gives a chance. And amazingly, even the attempts that "failed" bore fruit in other ways – one young man who dropped out of a U.S. college later told me that just getting there, if only for a semester, expanded his sense of what he could do. He returned to St. Lucia and started a small tech business, which he said he'd never have had the courage to do if he hadn't tried life abroad for that short stint. Effort echoes.

Mentorship, duty, independent action, loyalty, trust – these were the themes swirling in my mind throughout that journey and in writing about it now. They are the quiet pillars of leadership that don't always get headlines. They don't come with titles or ceremonies. But they build up communities in profound ways. Darwin's success wasn't in a manifesto or a five-point plan; it was in an unplanned act of mentorship that became a catalyst. This has shaped how I envision serving Castries North. I see an entire constituency full of "Darwins" in various forms – talented, overlooked people who could soar if someone cleared the runway for them. They might not all be athletes; they could be aspiring coders, nurses, entrepreneurs, or mechanics. My question is, can we as a community take those drives, those leaps of faith, for each other more often? I intend to. As an MP (should I earn that honour), I won't wait for perfect schemes from on high to help someone; I'll use initiative. If a kid in Bisee gets a partial scholarship to study in Canada but can't afford the flight, why shouldn't we crowdfund or find a donor right then and there? If a single mother in Sunny Acres has a job opportunity but no one to watch her kids after school, why can't we organize a neighbourhood rotation? Independent action, guided by duty to our neighbours – that is the ethos I want to ingrain.

Near the end of Darwin's journey, a moment stands out. After graduating, he came back to Saint Lucia for a visit. We drove down to Soufriere together. This time we weren't in a rush; we meandered, stopped by a viewpoint to gaze at the Pitons looming over his hometown. Darwin turned to me and said, "Coach" – he still called me Coach – "Coach, you know you kinda changed my life, right?" I responded, "No, brother, you changed your life. I just drove part of the way." He laughed. We sat there in silence for a bit, listening to the breeze in the trees. Then he said, "I'm going to make sure some other Lucians gets to do this too." I believed him.

That drive to Park University, what a simple thing it was. Just a man, a car, and a mission. Yet it encapsulated so much: the breaking of barriers between rivals, the act of faith in another's potential, the preparation of a leader (me) in the most unorthodox classroom – the open road. It prepared me to serve a wider community because it taught me scale; if I could help one person like this, why not dozens or hundreds with a bit more authority and resources? It taught me humility; I couldn't play the game for Darwin, only he could, just as as a representative I can't live people's lives for them, I can only open doors. And it taught me the value of saying "yes, I'll do it" when others might say "not my responsibility."

In many ways, I consider that journey to Park University a kind of personal checkpoint. When times get tough or cynics ask why I bother with this independent candidacy, I think back to that feeling of purpose on the highway, and the outcome that vindicated it. It reminds me that doing the right thing often means traveling alone for a stretch, risking looking foolish, but that's okay. Not every drive will end in a celebration; but every drive changes you, hones you.

I returned from Missouri that day not just with a tentative nod from a coach, but with a renewed understanding of who I am. I am someone who will drive through dawn to fight for another's chance. That's the kind of representative I aspire to be for Castries North. One who hops on the proverbial bus and takes the journey alongside you, or ahead of you to clear the way, rather than sitting back expecting you to fend for yourself. One who turns former adversaries into teammates for the common good, who mentors without keeping score, and who trusts the people enough to invest in them.

A few years ago, I wrote in a social post about Darwin, summing up what his story meant. I said: "That's the power of sports. That's the power of trust. Darwin's story grew straight out of our soil. It started with a step so small you could miss it – a guard deciding not to bite on a head fake – and ended with a man carrying his community in his heart to New York." It was a poetic way of connecting the dots: the small discipline on court reflecting a larger discipline in life, the mirror of competition reflecting one's true character.

Today, Darwin's story is one I share often, not to boast about what I did, but to illustrate what any of us can do. You don't need a title to lead; you need a heart that cares and the courage to act. Mentorship can be as simple as a drive and a conversation. Loyalty to community sometimes means breaking the rules of rivalry or bureaucracy to do what's right. And trust – trust is the currency that can buy someone's future. I trusted Darwin, he trusted me, Coach trusted us, and now a whole community benefits.

In the wider picture, as I prepare to serve Castries North, I carry this lesson: Government initiatives and policies are important, yes, but change also rides on those quiet drives – the unheralded efforts, the one-on-one interventions. Scaling that ethos up is my dream. If every capable person in our constituency took one other under their wing, imagine the chain reaction of upliftment. I intend to use the platform of leadership to encourage exactly that kind of culture. Because I know it works – I've lived it on a small scale.

So here's to the drives, the journeys undertaken for others. Here's to Darwin for vindicating a rival's faith. Here's to Coach English for hearing out a stranger's plea. Here's to Coach Kerry for coming to an island he had no connection to, just on another rival's word, and discovering friends and purpose. Here's to all those who will read this and perhaps be inspired to take their own "drive" – literal or figurative – to extend an opportunity to someone in need.

The chapter of that single journey ends with success: Darwin got his opportunity, made the most of it, and the ripples continue. But the story's moral is ongoing. In many ways, A Drive to Park University isn't really about a drive or a university; it's about the road of service. It's about how one trip changed two lives – his and mine – and how it set the stage for many more.

As I finish writing this, I have before me a photo: it's Darwin and me, standing in front of Park University's gym on the day he graduated, both of us beaming in cap and gown (I insisted on wearing one of his spare graduation caps for the picture). That image captures what I believe leadership in public life should produce: tangible human outcomes. Not just policies, but people empowered, trajectories altered for the better. In the next chapter, I will pivot from the personal to the political – delivering a "report card" on how Castries North has been managed and how it could be. But even in that analysis, you'll see the imprint of these stories. Because to me, every grade on that report card ultimately ties back to individuals like Darwin, like you, like me. Did our leaders create more chances or stifle them? Did they trust and invest in people, or did they hoard power? Keep Darwin's journey in mind as we examine those questions. It's a compass for what is possible when leadership is personal, daring, and caring.

4

The Report Card

It's report card day in Castries North. Not for our students – for our leadership. After years of the same representative holding the seat, it's time to grade the performance honestly. As a former teacher and coach, I know the value of a fair assessment. A report card isn't about attacking or praising for the sake of politics; it's about measuring outcomes against our potential. And in Castries North, the contrast between what is and what could be is stark.

In this chapter, I will lay out a structured evaluation of key areas – Infrastructure, Education, Youth & Sports, Health, and Representation – and then paint the picture of what each could look like under new leadership. Consider this the midterm grade and the final project plan all in one. The tone will be frank (we have to face some uncomfortable truths), but also hopeful (because there are clear, practical ways to turn things around). We owe it to ourselves as a community to be honest but not bitter – to call out neglect where it exists, but also to channel any disappointment into determination for change.

Each section will start by summarizing the current state – essentially the "grade" our constituency has earned in that area under the current administration. Then, I'll outline the alternative: what an "A+ scenario" could be with proactive, community-centred leadership (and specifically what I plan to do differently). All of this is grounded in real information – not just my opinions, but data, observations from residents, and even statements and actions (or inactions) of our current rep documented over time. You will see references to prior documents, interviews, and constituency data, because I believe in backing up words with evidence. By the end of this report card, I hope you'll see that Castries North has been held back not by lack of talent or ideas among its people, but by a poverty of performance in representation. And more importantly, you'll see that with the right approach, we can go from failing grades to top of the class.

So, pencils ready. Let's mark this report card.

INFRASTRUCTURE: CRUMBLING FOUNDATIONS VS. CONSTRUCTIVE FUTURE

Current State (Grade: D): Castries North's infrastructure is, in a word, crumbling. This isn't hyperbole – take a drive (if you dare) through our side roads and you'll feel it. Potholes have potholes. Drains are often clogged or broken, leading to water pooling and mosquito breeding grounds. The main thoroughfares – e.g., the Corinth-La Clery road, the Vide Bouteille road – have seen some maintenance, but mostly superficial. In many of our neighbourhoods, residents say things haven't improved in 10, 15, even 20 years. Stephenson King, our current MP, has been in power here for over two decades in various capacities, and yet it seems Castries North has been left exactly the same. If infrastructure were the only metric, one could argue things have actually gotten worse relative to our needs and population growth.

Let's break down the core infrastructure issues:

- **Roads:** We have a mix of major roads under national government purview (like the John Compton Highway along our west coast and the Choc Highway) and secondary roads under local/community purview. The highways, to be fair, are maintained decently in terms of surface (because they serve national traffic), but even they suffer from congestion design flaws, lack of pedestrian crossings, and flooding at low points. The secondary roads in Castries North are often narrow, lack sidewalks, and are peppered with breaks. The road up Morne Du Don, for example, is a climb through cracked asphalt and encroaching bushes. People living there have told me no significant roadworks have occurred in over a decade beyond filling a pothole here or there. The internal roads in Sunny Acres, Vide Bouteille, Entrepot, etc., have been largely ignored unless a VIP happens to live there. It's not just an aesthetic issue; it's safety and cost. Bad roads mean more vehicle damage (an extra burden on families) and in some cases delayed emergency response (ambulances and fire trucks navigating carefully).

- **Drainage & Flood Control:** Mention "rain" to a Castries North resident and you often get a worried look. Why? Because we've normalized the idea that a heavy rain will flood yards or transform certain streets into rivers. The drains in La Clery overflow; the channels in Vide Bouteille can't handle runoff from the hills. The sad reality is, some flooding occurs simply because no one clears the drains until after disaster strikes. I've seen drains so choked with silt and plastic bottles that grass is growing out of them – a clear sign of long-term neglect. We also lack proper retaining walls in spots where erosion risks are evident (e.g., parts of Union, Morne Du Don). The Ministry of Infrastructure often responds to these issues after something collapses, rather than proactively. Our current MP, being a former Prime Minister and Infrastructure Minister himself, certainly has (or had) the clout to get ahead of these issues. Yet, the performance is lacking. It's telling that since I launched my campaign, suddenly we saw a flurry of hurried infrastructure tidying – grass cut, community courts painted, cleanup campaigns popping up – as if all it took was a bit of political competition to wake up the machinery. I can't give a passing grade to an approach that only fixes roads or drains when an election looms.

• **Utilities (Water, Electricity, Streetlights):** While water supply is largely stable in Castries North (thanks to system upgrades, not thanks to our MP per se), street lighting is a glaring failure. Whole community lights have been out for over 10 years. For instance, the La Clery playing field lights, as mentioned, remain dark for a decade – a symbolic and literal dark spot. Various residential areas report streetlights reported as faulty years ago still not addressed. It creates security risks and just an atmosphere of abandonment at night. The electricity grid and water lines themselves are maintained by LUCELEC and WASCO respectively – but an active MP would liaise constantly to ensure our area's issues are prioritized. That hasn't been happening in any systematic way.

In summary, our infrastructure under the current leadership gets a "D" because it's dangerously close to failure in many parts and desperately behind where it should be. I won't say "F" because yes, some things still function (we do have roads and drains, just not good ones), but the trajectory has been downward or flat when it should have been upward.

What Could Be (Vision – Grade: A- or better): Under proactive leadership, Castries North's infrastructure can transform from a liability into a launchpad of community pride. Here's how:

• **Comprehensive Road Rehab:** We will initiate a Castries North Roads Programme that maps every single road and footpath in the constituency, rates its condition, and schedules repairs/upgrades over a 5-year timeline. This is where national funds (like the CDP – Constituency Development Programme) will be lobbied for vigorously. I'm talking about basic paving, not gold-plating. A drive that normally takes 15 minutes shouldn't take 30 because you're zigzagging around craters. We have engineers in the diaspora and locally (some retired) – I'd form a small advisory group of them to ensure we use modern, cost-effective methods (for example, exploring permeable pavers in some areas to also help with drainage, or cold mix asphalt for quick patches that last through rain). With better roads, not only do we reduce daily wear-and-tear costs for citizens, we also open up our community – businesses are more likely to invest in a place with decent access, and overall quality of life goes up.

• **Drainage and Flood Mitigation Masterplan:** Rather than piecemeal fixes, Castries North needs a mini "masterplan" for drainage. We know the flash flood zones: near the La Clery river, the Vide Bouteille junction, parts of Choc. I envision partnering with the Ministry of Infrastructure and external aid (maybe CDB or World Bank small grants that exist for climate resilience) to build a few key projects: enlarge the primary drains (e.g., widen and deepen the La Clery canal), install backflow prevention where drains meet the sea (so high tide or storm surge doesn't send water back up into the streets), and implement community flood alert and response systems. On a simpler note, routine maintenance must be scheduled and budgeted. I would ensure that our Castries Constituency Council (which our MP can influence by attending and advocating) sets a calendar for drain clearing before the wet season each year. It's not rocket science; it's political will. I recall a resident wryly telling me, "We only see drain cleaners when some minister is coming for a tour." In my tenure, drain cleaners will be a regular sight – unsung heroes who prevent health crises and property damage. We'll celebrate them, not just deploy them for show.

• **Lights and Utilities Overhaul:** If given the chance to serve, I will treat every faulty streetlight as an urgent safety issue. Immediately, a full audit of all streetlights and community lighting in Castries North will be conducted (in collaboration with LUCELEC). Then fix them in batches, area by area. The technology today favours LED lights – they last longer and consume less power – so we might as well upgrade as we replace. The goal would be that no child should have to walk home from a lesson or game in the dark wondering if someone lurks in the shadows. An A-grade infrastructure means lights that work, water that flows, power that's reliable. We have that capacity. Saint Lucia is not at war, we're not under sanctions – there is no excuse for us to have people living as if in the 1970s candlelight era in some zones. I'll also push for solar lighting in public spaces (like along Vigie Beach or some back roads) – this is cost-effective long-term and many international partners fund such green initiatives.

• **Public Spaces and Maintenance Culture:** Infrastructure isn't just utility lines and concrete; it's also public spaces – parks, sidewalks, community buildings. Right now, many of those are unkempt (e.g., the little park in Summersdale was left to overgrow until residents trimmed it themselves). Under my leadership, we'd implement a "Adopt-a-Spot" program inviting businesses and civic groups to help maintain specific parks or spots, with clear signage crediting them. It's a model used globally – people take pride in keeping an area clean/painted when their name is associated with it. Also, small infrastructure like benches, bus shelters, and signage can greatly improve daily life. We'd inventory needs (for instance, how many bus stops lack shelters? quite a few in Castries North) and systematically address them, using a combination of government funds and sponsorship.

An "A" in infrastructure doesn't mean everything new and shiny – it means functional, reliable, and serving the people's needs. I firmly believe in showing results you can step on. As I've pledged elsewhere: I will show you projects when they are done, with proof you can step on or drive on. Imagine walking down your street not having to sidestep muddy puddles or broken glass from an always-dumped garbage heap, because now there's proper drainage and regular garbage collection. Imagine the main roads so smooth and ordinary that they "barely earn a nod" because we're so used to them being well-kept. That's the ordinary excellence we should strive for.

EDUCATION: WASTED POTENTIAL VS. WORLD-CLASS OPPORTUNITIES

Current State (Grade: C-): Education in Castries North is an interesting mix of assets and underutilization. We are home to several top schools by reputation including – St. Mary's College (SMC) for boys in Vigie, there's the legendary St. Joseph's Convent for girls, Castries Comprehensive Secondary (CCSS), Vide Bouteille Secondary School, and a number of primary schools just outside or on our borders. On paper, one might think we're well-covered. However, having schools physically present is not the same as providing our constituents with educational empowerment. The quality of support and breadth of opportunities are where we're lagging.

WHAT'S LACKING?

- **After-School Programs and Academic Support:** Many students in our constituency attend school, then head home to environments that might not be conducive to further learning – perhaps cramped conditions, or parents working late, or simply no culture of homework because no one's there to supervise. There is virtually no structured after-school program widely accessible in Castries North right now. We had community centres, but as noted, places like VBCC have not been operating at capacity. The current MP has not initiated any known constituency-wide education program. If a child struggles with reading in primary school, the intervention they rely on is luck – maybe a good teacher, maybe a parent who can afford a private lesson. That's not a system; that's chance. We can't give more than a C grade when so much is left to chance.

- **Tertiary and Scholarship Guidance:** I've spoken to bright young people in Bisee and La Clery who finished secondary school and were sort of left dangling, unsure how to apply for university or even local college. The Ministry of Education has some programs, but it's impersonal and many slip through the cracks. The current rep could have a Constituency Education Council or something – a team of volunteer educators and professionals – but there's none that anyone knows of. The only efforts I've seen are either from NGOs or one-off charity from private entities. For instance, a local pastor might gather some youths for homework help – but that's not funded or encouraged by our leadership, it's just a generous individual action. Meanwhile, the idea of linking our schools with outside opportunities has been notably absent. In a small country, networking matters. Who opens doors for our kids? Right now, few. We do hear of scholarships, but many go unclaimed or unknown to the masses.

- **Infrastructure of Schools:** While the schools fall under the Ministry, as MP I'd still take interest in their state. SMC has historic buildings that periodically need repair; CCSS had some labs that were outdated the last time I checked. I give a C- and not a lower grade because the schools are functioning and producing good students despite everything (testament to our teachers and students' grit). But they could do so much better with strategic support.
- **Early Childhood and Adult Education:** These are two ends of the spectrum often overlooked. Early childhood (daycares, pre-K) in our area is mostly private or community-run, not systematically supported. Adult education – for those who maybe dropped out or need a second chance – virtually nonexistent in Castries North. I don't know of any continuing education or skills training centre in our constituency (people have to go to Castries City or beyond). That's a gap affecting youth who aren't in the academic stream as well as older folks who want to up-skill.

Given these, our education component scrapes by with a C- because literacy rates are decent and schools open daily, but we're far from unlocking the full potential of our human capital.

What Could Be (Vision – Grade: A): Education is the great equalizer – I'm living proof of that, as are many who left humble backgrounds to thrive because of schooling and scholarships. My vision is to make Castries North a powerhouse of educational opportunity, not just for those naturally gifted or lucky, but for every willing learner. Here's how we get an A:

- **Castries North Connect & SAT Education Plan:** I have already articulated a program I call Castries North Connect, which will link every school in our constituency to a major university or college overseas. This isn't just symbolic twinning; it means establishing relationships where our schools can benefit from exchange programs, visiting lecturers, pen-pal programs, and crucially, scholarship pipelines. For example, we connect SJC with a community college in the U.S. that is open to taking a couple of our students each year on reduced tuition. We connect SMC (although national, many CN boys go there) with maybe a Jesuit college network given its Catholic heritage – to tap into existing networks. Alongside that, I intend to launch an SAT and College Prep initiative. We will offer free SAT training classes in the constituency (maybe on weekends at a school computer lab) so that our students aiming for U.S. colleges have support. Also, workshops on how to apply for financial aid, etc. This kind of hands-on guidance can produce the next Darwin or Frank who goes abroad not just on athletic ability but academic prowess. I imagine having "College Nights" where alumni (we have many CN folks who studied abroad) come back and mentor current students on navigating that path.

• **After-School and Homework Centres:** We have to fill the 3pm-6pm void for our children. I propose using existing spaces – e.g., the La Clery Resource Centre, VBCC, even church halls – to host supervised after-school programs. We can recruit volunteer tutors (we have many capable retirees and even secondary school top students can help primary kids) and also see about modest stipends for coordinators through government youth employment schemes. A key part of my plan is to incorporate a digital learning component: set up a few computers or tablets (solicited via corporate donations or diaspora) so kids can do research or educational games after school rather than roam aimlessly. I'd also integrate life skills sessions, maybe once a week – let's teach typing, let's teach how to budget money, etc., in those centres. These programs keep kids safe, improve their performance (studies show structured after-school time boosts grades), and ease the burden on working parents.

- **Mentorship and Career Exposure:** We've talked about sports mentorship, but academically and career-wise, we also need mentors. I plan to establish a Castries North Mentorship Registry, potentially as part of a "Diaspora Skills Bank". Suppose a girl in Sunny Acres wants to be a doctor – I want to link her with a doctor originally from our area who can guide her. A boy in La Clery interested in coding – pair him with an IT pro from our community. These are usually informal connections, but I want an organized approach: sign-up drives, mentorship mixers, etc.

- **School Infrastructure and Support:** Even though school facilities are a government thing, an MP can rally support for specific improvements. For instance, if CCSS needs a new science lab, I can coordinate a fundraising drive involving alumni and businesses (and yes, sometimes naming rights or credit on a plaque goes a long way in motivating donations). For primary schools, maybe our constituency can sponsor a "mobile library" that circulates among them, or ensure each has a functioning computer lab by partnering with NGOs. Also, internet access is part of education infrastructure; pushing for free Wi-Fi hotspots at community centres or around schools can help those who can't afford big data plans to still get online for learning.

- **Adult and Continuing Education:** I strongly believe in "no one left behind." I would work to bring programs like CARE (Centre for Adolescent Renewal) or NSDC (skills training) to have satellite courses in Castries North. Whether it's a GED equivalent for someone who dropped out, or a skills course like plumbing, electrical, or hospitality, offering it within the community (perhaps using a school after hours) means more people can attend. This not only upgrades our workforce, it also fights social issues – busy, hopeful people are less likely to fall into crime or depression.

What does an "A" look like in everyday life? It's a constituency where every student knows that if they want to learn or achieve something, there is a path and support for them. Where parents don't have to worry about their child falling behind just because they can't afford a private tutor – because the community has their back. Where our schools become models of innovation – imagine SMC and CCSS students collaborating on a science fair that gets national attention, or a Castries North Reading Challenge that significantly raises literacy in primary kids.

I often say we must focus on "opportunity, access, and transformation". Education is exactly that. With targeted efforts like the SAT Plan for Castries North (to prepare students for global scholarships) and linking with universities, we transform the narrative. Castries North could be known as the place that produces not just sports stars but Rhodes Scholars, tech entrepreneurs, and civic leaders – because the community cultivated them. I'm bold enough to aim for that because I've seen the raw talent here, and I know the only difference between a kid from here and one from a fancier place is exposure and support.

YOUTH & SPORTS: NEGLECT AND NATURAL TALENT VS. NURTURING EVERY YOUNG PERSON

Current State (Grade: C): If there's one thing Castries North is rich in, it's youth potential. Our communities brim with young people who are talented – whether in sports, arts, academics, or just raw leadership ability. But potential means little if left untapped. Currently, support for youth outside of formal schooling is limited and inconsistent. I give it a "C" because some positives exist (mostly driven by individuals, not systemic support), but for the most part our youth are underserved.

Observations:

• **Sports Facilities Ignored:** We have multiple sports facilities in Castries North: the Vigie multi-purpose sports complex (though that's more national), community courts at Vide Bouteille (VBCC), La Clery playing field, a small court in Morne Du Don, school courts, etc. Many of these have been in a state of disrepair or lack of improvement for ages. Our sports facilities have literally been ignored according to my earlier statements, and it's true – e.g., the La Clery field has had no major upgrade in decades, the VBCC court was locked and not maintained due to internal issues, etc. The current MP, despite being Minister of Sports at one time in his career, has not left a mark here. It's volunteers – the youth football coaches, the netball enthusiasts – who keep things going on sheer will. The lack of lights and equipment at these venues screams neglect.

• **Youth Programs Lacking:** Beyond sports, what structured youth programs are there? Not many. We don't have, for instance, a Castries North Youth Council actively supported by the MP's office. There's a National Youth Council branch but I rarely hear of it doing constituency-specific work. Job attachment or summer internship programs for youth in Castries North? If any exist, they're low-key. The current approach to youth seems to have been "keep them quiet with a little summer party or a one-off donation to a team" rather than strategic empowerment.

• **At-Risk Youth Outreach:** We do face issues with some youth being involved in crime or idling. The root often is they feel there's nowhere to channel their energy positively. I know some who hang by the block not because they want trouble but because nothing else is engaging them. Our leadership's response often has been policing rather than preemptive outreach.

- **Cultural and Creative Opportunities:** Youth isn't just sports. We have artistic youths, musically talented ones. There's hardly any platform for them. Other constituencies have maybe small cultural festivals or talent shows – we could, but we haven't, at least not in any sustained way.

The reason I don't grade this lower than C is because despite the neglect, our youth and a few local heroes have achieved commendable things – be it individual sports scholarships obtained, community volunteer projects, etc. That's to their credit, often with little thanks to official support.

What Could Be (Vision – Grade: A): I see the youth of Castries North as our greatest asset. Investing in them yields returns for decades. My plan here aligns with what I might call a Youth Empowerment Revolution at the constituency level.

KEY INITIATIVES

- **Upgrade Sports and Recreation Facilities:** First order: fix what we have. That means refurbishing the La Clery playing field (proper pitch maintenance, new goal posts, seating, lights reinstalled), unlocking and renovating the VBCC court (resurface the court, new hoops, lights). Also, identify any other pockets: e.g., the "rundown court next to the Ministry of Transportation" which I have envisioned turning into a Castries North Pickleball Centre. Yes, pickleball – a sport trending worldwide that all ages can play. That idea I floated is more than a quirky notion; it's a case study in converting neglect into vibrancy. Transforming that derelict court by the Ministry (which is in our constituency) into a pickleball centre hits several benefits we listed: revitalizes space, gives workers exercise options, brings community together, improves safety, can attract tournaments, and stimulates local economy. With minimal investment, we can make that happen and use it as a model for other micro-projects.

- **Organize Structured Leagues and Camps:** If we have facilities, we must use them. I will spearhead regular community sports leagues – football, basketball, netball, cricket tape-ball – across Castries North. Not just one-off "fun days," but proper leagues with schedules, referees (even volunteer refs can be trained), and small prizes or trophies. This keeps youth (and even older folks) engaged consistently. We also will host skill camps: I have connections through sports – imagine an annual basketball camp where I bring in international coaches or former players (like Kerry or others who'd love to visit) to train 50 of our kids intensively for a week. The same with football or track. These camps not only build skill, they build discipline and dreams. Chapter 5 of this book (sneak peek from its title at least) seems to go into camps – and indeed I'm passionate about them because a camp changed my life.

- **Youth Leadership and Civic Engagement:** We're not going to treat youth only as players on a field. They are future leaders. So, let's start a Castries North Youth Council that actually has teeth. Give them a small budget and let them plan a project each year (with guidance). It could be a charity drive, a community mural, anything. Let them feel the weight and reward of civic action early. Also, establish a Youth Mentorship Pairing (in overlap with the education idea) so each vulnerable youth has someone looking out for them. I think of it as "adopt one youth" campaign: encouraging adults to not in a formal adoption, but in a neighbourly guiding way, take interest in at least one young person's progress. Show up to their games, ask about their homework, encourage them. If every stable adult did that for one kid who might lack support, nobody falls through the cracks.

- **Creative Arts and Culture:** Why can't Castries North host an annual talent showcase or mini-festival? We have Vigie beach for example – a great venue for an evening youth arts festival. Or use the SMC auditorium or any venue to let our singers, poets, dancers have a stage. I will support creation of youth clubs – drama club, debate club (maybe revive the legacy of VBCC debates), music groups. Possibly partner with the Cultural Development Foundation for resources. We might even incorporate cultural exchange: those university links could extend to exchange students visiting us, bringing say a jazz workshop or theatre improv workshop to our youth.

- **Employment and Entrepreneurship:** Not to forget, youth need economic pathways. I will fight to bring programs like the Youth Economy (something government is touting at national level) right into Castries North with training sessions on entrepreneurship, small grants for youth start-ups in the constituency (imagine a youth who wants to start a graphics design business – we could help find him a used computer and initial capital). And for more immediate jobs, coordinate with local businesses for a Castries North Internship Program where every summer a set number of youths can intern at a business or government office arranged through the MP's office.

An "A" for youth and sports would mean no young person says "there's nothing to do." Instead they'd say "I have practice" or "I'm going to that workshop" or "I'm volunteering at the community event." It means the energy of youth is flowing in positive channels. Also, a notable effect: crime and antisocial behaviour usually drop when youth are busy with positive pursuits. It's not just my assumption – it's evidenced by many communities worldwide. We already saw how one spark – for example, a Legends Football event where past players were honoured – brought out community spirit. I was part of such an event and even my political opponent joined in celebrating; sports and youth engagement can unify beyond politics. Let's make that the norm, not the exception.

In sum, under my watch Castries North will become known as the Youth Constituency – the place where if you're a young person with an idea or a talent, you will find support, facilities, and an audience. No more dark fields and closed doors. We'll turn the lights on (literally and figuratively) for our youth.

HEALTH: AILING SERVICES VS. HOLISTIC COMMUNITY WELLNESS

Current State (Grade: C-): Health is wealth, they say, and by that measure Castries North has been impoverished. We have one official health centre in our constituency – the Babonneau Health Centre La Clery extension, commonly just referred to as the La Clery Health Centre. It's a small clinic meant to serve basic healthcare needs (maternal and child health, chronic disease check-ups, minor ailments). The reality: it's understaffed and under-equipped, and notably closed on weekends. In a population of over ten thousand, we rely on a tiny clinic that doesn't even operate full time.

Points of concern:

• **Limited Health Centre Hours and Staff:** As mentioned, weekends it's closed, which means if you fall ill on a Saturday you either wait or go to Victoria Hospital (well, OKEU Hospital now, which is outside our constituency). Even weekdays, the hours are like 8am-4pm. Working people can rarely use it unless they take time off. Staffing has been an issue: often just one nurse or part-time doctor. If that nurse is on leave, services are curtailed. It's not the staff's fault – they do their best – but the system has not prioritized expansion here.

• **Services Offered:** There's no pharmacy at the health centre, no lab. So even if you see the nurse or doctor, you likely have to go elsewhere to fill a prescription or do a blood test. That reduces the utility of having a community clinic. People might say "why bother, I'll just go to town." The result: many skip preventative care altogether until an emergency hits.

- **Emergency Preparedness:** No ambulance station in Castries North; the nearest is the Fire Service in Castries or Gros Islet. The response time can be slow if those are busy. There have been cases of medical emergencies in our area where neighbours had to rush someone to hospital in a car because waiting wasn't an option.

- **Public Health and Environment:** Our current situation with infrastructure (flooding, poor garbage disposal in some spots) also poses health risks (dengue fever from mosquitoes, water-borne diseases). Yet I haven't seen a concerted public health education or vector control campaign championed by our rep specific to these issues in our area. Again, any efforts are general from the ministry, not tailored local initiatives.

- **Mental Health & Social Support:** Almost entirely neglected at the constituency level. Youth facing depression, elderly dealing with loneliness, etc. – these aren't on the radar.

I give a C- because baseline healthcare just about exists (not an F, we do have a building and some staff), but it's so insufficient that outcomes are suboptimal. I recall residents complaining that the health centre is "just for baby vaccines and blood pressure" – anything more serious you cannot rely on it.

What Could Be (Vision – Grade: B+ aiming for A): Healthcare is one area where an MP has to work closely with central government, but there is still a lot of room to innovate at the community level. My goal would be to make Castries North a model of community wellness. We might not have a big hospital, but we can ensure primary healthcare and wellness services are accessible and modern.

Key improvements:

• **Upgrade and Extend Clinic Services:** I will lobby the Ministry of Health to upgrade the La Clery Health Centre to a Polyclinic status gradually. This would mean longer hours (including possibly a rotation for some evening or weekend clinics), more staff (nurse practitioners who can handle most common issues, a doctor more regularly on duty), and additional services like a dispensing pharmacy window and basic lab tests (blood sugar, etc.). If budget is a constraint, we can start small: maybe open on Saturday mornings, or have a late clinic on Wednesdays. Perhaps partner with NGOs – St. John's Ambulance, Red Cross – to use the facility on off-hours for community health fairs. I'm aware the healthcare system is national, but an MP who pushes and provides creative solutions can get pilot programs done. We could propose that Castries North's clinic be a pilot for extended hours primary care (taking pressure off the A&E at OKEU Hospital). Closed on weekends is a phrase I want to eliminate from our clinic's description.

• **Mobile Health Outreach:** If the people can't come to the clinic, sometimes the clinic must go to the people. I envision periodic mobile health drives – set up a tent at Sunny Acres one Saturday for screenings (blood pressure, diabetes, vision). Do the same in Vigie or Bisee on other days. We have many medical professionals originally from our community who visit or would volunteer for a day. Let's tap into that diaspora skills bank again: a visiting nurse from New York on holiday might be thrilled to spend one morning doing a hypertension lecture and checks at our community centre. Organize it and they will come.

• **Health Education and Preventive Programs:** Prevention is better (and cheaper) than cure. I'd initiate programs like Community Exercise Groups – for example, a morning seniors' walk in Vigie or aerobics in La Clery field with a volunteer instructor. Our role is to facilitate – provide maybe some basic equipment or just the encouragement. Tie this with public education: monthly health talks at the community hall (topics like managing diabetes, stress relief, etc., possibly led by local doctors or even via a video link with experts). One idea: A "Know Your Numbers" campaign – we challenge everyone in the constituency to know their blood pressure, sugar, cholesterol by providing free screenings and tracking. It gets people proactive about health.

- **Mental Health and Counselling:** This is often neglected, but so needed. I'd work to create a volunteer counsellor network – perhaps leveraging church counsellors, retired social workers, or even a partnership with the psychology unit at SALCC (local college) for interns. We could have a weekly session offered somewhere private where youth or others can drop in to talk or get counsel for issues like depression, family problems, etc. Also consider dedicating some resources to tackle drug abuse if present – link with existing NGOs for outreach in the community.

- **Environmental Health:** Work on those drains and garbage collection is part of preventing disease. I'd liaise with the city council to ensure garbage is collected regularly and indiscriminate dumping (which can breed vermin) is policed. Encourage cleanup campaigns (the one I planned for La Clery river, and others) not just as one-offs, but regular community service days. We saw how once our campaign started pushing, the incumbent's people suddenly did cleanups; well, I don't need an opponent to motivate me, the community's health motivates me. Clean surroundings mean fewer rats, mosquitoes, and a healthier population.

- **Leveraging Technology:** Why not set up telemedicine for our clinic? Perhaps the clinic doesn't have a specialist, but you could have a computer where, say, once a week a specialist abroad or in the capital does consultations with patients via video call. I know doctors in the diaspora who might volunteer an hour or two virtually. For example, a cardiologist could advise difficult cases remotely, saving someone a trip. This is a bit aspirational, but with Starlink and other internet improvements, it's doable on small scale.

An "A" in health for us would be when residents feel confident that common health needs are met right here. That a sick child on a Saturday isn't a crisis because our community has some provision. That chronic patients (diabetics, hypertensives) are being monitored and guided so they don't end up in hospital with complications. And beyond treating sickness, that our community is actively promoting wellness – from healthy eating programs (imagine linking farmers to have a veggie market day and nutrition advice) to exercise groups.

Let's get more pickleball as a chill sport and as a health initiative, especially for seniors. It's a low-impact exercise ideal for older folks or those who want to start getting fit. We highlighted its benefits: improving cardiovascular health, balance, mental well-being. When we transform that abandoned court into a Pickleball Centre, it's as much about public health as sport. Government often doesn't think that way, but we will.

I'd downgrade ourselves from an "A" maybe if we can't have a full hospital or every specialist on site – that's okay, realistically we might be a B+ because major emergencies will still go to the main hospital. But the community will be healthy in the holistic sense: physically active, cared for at the primary level, educated on health, and environment conducive to good health. That's my target.

REPRESENTATION: FACELESS STATUS QUO VS. FAITHFUL, ACTIVE SERVICE

Current State (Grade: F): This is where the current leadership utterly fails the people of Castries North, in my frank assessment. Representation isn't just showing up in Parliament to vote; it's about being the voice and champion of your constituency's needs, about being present and accountable. Our current MP – and I say this with all due respect to the office he holds – has given us what I termed "faceless, faithless, and non-performing" representation.

Why such a harsh grade?

• **Lack of Visibility and Engagement:** Many constituents joke (with truth behind it) that they only see our MP when it's election season or when a top government official is visiting. Community meetings? Rare. Platforms to hear people's issues? Nonexistent, or done as formality. He's been described as a "ghost" by some residents because you wouldn't know who represents us from activity on the ground. A good MP should have a presence – through clinics, community walk-throughs, responding to letters etc. For years, people felt they had "no real representation", that their concerns were not being voiced or addressed.

• **Transactional Politics:** There's an undercurrent that our MP maintained his seat through what we call "transactional politics" – doing favours for a select few or patronage around election time, rather than performing consistently for all. As I quoted elsewhere, some dodge honest grading of him by blaming parties, but those honest know where responsibility lies. For instance, every Wednesday, folks line up at constituency offices across the island for personal assistance (like school fee help, a voucher, etc.). A sarcastic comment from the interview I read: "We don't have to be beggars every Wednesday going to a constituency office." But that's what it's become under him – people reduced to pleading for little scraps, because there's no empowering system in place. That is a failure of representation in my book: if your constituents feel like beggars, you have failed them.

- **No Advocacy on Bigger Issues:** Where was our MP's voice on national issues affecting Castries North? For example, when the St. Jude Hospital fiasco dragged on (a national disgrace with local resonance), or when there were controversial land deals possibly affecting our area's heritage, did he speak up? From what I've seen, "Castries North deserves a rep who speaks up when our history and culture are under threat – not one who stays silent." But we got silence or compliance. He switched parties (left UWP to run independent in 2021) not out of some fiery stand for Castries North's needs, but seemingly for personal positioning. That move did nothing to improve Castries North's fortunes. If anything, it gave him another election win but then he just cozied up to the new Labour government without officially joining (hence no one even knows what exactly he stands for aside from staying in power). "Why hasn't he formally joined the Labour Party?" I once rhetorically asked – implying perhaps that he wants the best of both worlds: in government side but not bound to their accountability. That kind of opportunism doesn't serve us; it serves him.

- **Performance Metrics:** Look at tangible outcomes after his decades. Infrastructure – worse. Youth – neglected. All things we covered. He's held power "through every government change but left Castries North exactly the same". If nothing changed in 10 years, why expect change in the next 5 with him? That was my message. In any job, if you underperform, you'd be replaced or reprimanded. In politics, he's been rewarded with re-election partly due to inertia and party politics. But that doesn't erase the F grade for actual service delivered. The fact that my independent campaign spurred sudden action (grass cut, courts painted, etc., as earlier noted) is evidence that he could have done those things anytime, but didn't until challenged. That is essentially an admission of neglect.

• **Constituency Office and Council:** Yes, we have a constituency council by law and an office. But the synergy between MP and Council hasn't produced much. An engaged MP would empower the local council to prioritize community projects and ensure government funds reach there. We see patchy results at best. And the office – how many feel comfortable going there to voice an issue? It's more seen as a place to seek minor financial help than to engage in development discussions.

Thus, representation gets a glaring F for failing to truly represent and uplift the constituency. Too often kings are distant, expecting loyalty but not earning it with performance. And I openly say: We are not beggars; I am not a king. The era of bowing to a politician and begging must end in Castries North.

What Could Be (Vision – Grade: A): Accountable, Transparent, Active Representation – that's the trifecta I aim to deliver. What does that mean practically?

• **Regular Communication and Accessibility:** As MP, I would hold quarterly town hall meetings in different parts of the constituency – Vigie, La Clery, etc. – to report on what I've done and hear directly what's working or not. Also, maintain a strong online presence for those who use social media, to update on projects (I already do a lot of that campaigning, and it'll continue in office). Importantly, an open-door (or at least open-phone) policy: dedicate, say, every Friday morning for walk-ins at the constituency office. If I can't personally meet everyone, my team will, and serious issues will get my follow-up. People should know their rep by name and face and feel comfortable approaching.

• **Transparency in Plans and Spending:** I have pledged something radical for politics here: I will publish what I plan to do, every week; tell you who is doing it, with what money, by when; show when it's done, and if I fail, say so and fix it. Essentially, a running log of constituency work. This could be a bulletin board at the office or a Facebook page where on Monday I post "This week: repairing streetlights at X, meeting with Min. of Infrastructure about Y, community cleanup at Z on Saturday" and then next week, report outcomes. And any community funds I control (like CDP projects) will be publicly listed: e.g., "$50k allocated for road fixing on Pine Drive – contractor: ___, expected finish date ___." That level of transparency is rare, but it's how you build trust and keep yourself honest. I invite constituents to hold me to deadlines – circle dates in red and call me out if I slip.

• **Active Championing in Parliament:** I will show up and speak up. Whether I'm in government or opposition benches, I'll use every opportunity in Parliament to push Castries North issues – from asking questions about delayed projects to contributing to debates on national matters that affect us (crime, cost of living). And unlike the current rep, I won't shy from taking a principled stand if a policy harms my people, even if it means disagreeing with a PM of whichever party. Being independent actually frees me to vote and talk purely in the interest of Castries North without toeing a party line – a freedom I intend to use vigorously.

• **Inclusive, Non-Partisan Approach Locally:** I will work with anyone who is willing to help Castries North – regardless of their political stripe. This means collaborating with government agencies even if I'm not part of the ruling party, and also encouraging community groups of all kinds (church, sports, youth, business) to have a say in plans. The constituency development plan I drafted came from listening to many voices. I want to institutionalize that by perhaps forming Advisory Committees for major sectors. For instance, a small Infrastructure Advisory Team of community members to help prioritize projects (who better than residents to know which road is worst?), a Youth Council as discussed for youth ideas, etc. This devolves some voice to the people regularly, not just at election time.

• **Ending the Beggar Mentality:** Instead of encouraging dependency, I'd flip it to empowerment. If someone comes every week for a "handout," I'd rather find them a job or get their kid in a scholarship – something sustainable. I'd emphasize work programs over welfare (except for truly vulnerable groups like the disabled or elderly who need assistance). The interview snippet where I said "we have things in our constituency that we can do, we don't have to be beggars" – that will be my mantra turned into action. We'll create opportunities such that people earn and contribute, keeping dignity intact. When support is given, it might be through something like a community service exchange (you get help with house repairs, you volunteer in a cleanup next time, etc.). We want pride, not pity.

An "A" in representation means the people feel represented. They feel their voice is heard in decisions. They see their representative often and not just in ceremonial ribbon-cuttings but sweating with them in cleanups, cheering with them at games, mourning with them at funerals. They trust that if an issue arises, their rep will go fight for it, not hide or blame someone else.

One thing I will absolutely ensure: I will not allow Castries North to be taken for granted in any administration. Sometimes MPs in safe seats coast; I refuse. If government tries to ignore our needs because I'm not from their party, I will make noise publicly – use media, use parliamentary questions – until we get our fair share. Conversely, if I align with a government, I won't do so meekly – my support will hinge on delivering tangible things to Castries North, not just giving them a vote in House.

In short, my representation will be bold, insightful, and community-centred (to use the user's words). Bold in standing up to powers for our sake, insightful in coming up with creative solutions and not the same old tricks, and community-centred in that every decision asks "how does this benefit the people living here?" instead of "how does it benefit me or my party?"

Now, having gone through this "report card," let's recap the contrast:

- In Infrastructure, we move from crumbling roads and dark streets (D grade) to smooth commutes and bright neighbourhoods (A grade achievable) with systematic repairs and maintenance.

- In Education, from chance-based progression (C-) to guided, world-class opportunity (A) through after-school programs, international linkages, and support at every level.

- In Youth & Sports, from a state of neglect (C) to being the beacon for youth development (A) with facilities restored, constant programs, and youth leading alongside.

- In Health, from limited care (C-) to community wellness (A or at least a strong B+) via an upgraded clinic, outreach, and preventive health culture.

- In Representation, from faceless and failing (F) to dynamic and accountable (A) with transparent, engaged leadership.

These aren't pie-in-the-sky dreams. I deliberately kept solutions practical, because I fully intend to implement them, not just campaign on them. Many are already underway in planning stages – for instance, I've drafted a detailed Castries North Constituency Plan which includes much of the above; it's not about promises on a platform but about "practical action". I shared glimpses of it, talking about sports economics, after-school programs, and more. I also talk about harnessing our diaspora and building partnerships as means to these ends.

I want to emphasize the philosophical underpinning: dignity and ownership. Throughout this chapter, the thread is giving people back their dignity (no begging, no stagnation) and ownership of their community. As I said elsewhere: "I want a constituency that acts like owners. Owners don't wait for kings." We, the people of Castries North, must see ourselves as the owners of this community – the MP is just the chief steward or servant, not a monarch. In the future I envision, when someone asks "Who is your representative, really?" I want you to be able to say, "A worker. One of us." And you'll have evidence: you'll point to a fixed crossing, a flowing drain, a clinic line that moves because service is efficient, a child with a scholarship – and say that is the proof of representation.

No more crowns on politicians' heads – our crown will be on our streets: meaning the visible improvements, the ordinary dignity of a community that no longer has to bow or beg, but stands upright. That is the ultimate goal of this report card exercise – to show that we can get there, and to invite everyone to join in making it happen. As I often write as my signature rallying cry: Castries North deserves more. We deserve investment, opportunity, respect – not calculated neglect. The current state of affairs was the result of calculated neglect, placated by handouts. The future state will be the result of calculated effort and genuine care, yielding empowerment.

Let this chapter stand as both an indictment of the past management and a promise of the future management. I have essentially graded the incumbent's tenure – mostly failing – and laid out the syllabus for my own. You, the people, will be the ultimate examiners of whether I meet those high standards I've set. And I welcome that. I've played and coached enough games to know that when the final whistle blows, you own your score. I intend to own every outcome – good or bad – under my watch and keep striving for the "A" until the very end.

The report card for Castries North can and will improve – because we will improve it together. No heroes on white horses, just neighbours rolling up sleeves. No kings decreeing from on high, just public servants doing the work on the ground. It's time to discard the old report card of excuses and poor marks. We're writing a new one, and we'll make this one count – for every community, every family, every individual in Castries North. The bell has rung; class is in session; it's time to learn from the past and ace the future.

Part II – #SportsEconomics: From Courts to Campus

5

Camps, Coaches, and a Doorway

The church bell in La Clery rings before the sun gets ideas. By the time the first light rinses the hill, sneakers are already skidding on a damp slab of concrete, a plastic whistle is on the lanyard around my neck, and somebody's mother is walking up with a carrier bag of bakes because she knows hungry stomachs foul up good drills. We line the boys and girls in rows – little ones in the first rank, long-footed teenagers towering in the last – and we start with the quiet work that nobody claps for: ankles warm, hips open, shoulders loose, lungs awake. Ten minutes in, you can feel it: the court is a classroom. Chalk is sweat. The exam is tomorrow.

I did not come to this by theory. I came to it by camp. Years ago, a summer program at the old La Pansee school put a whistle in my life the way a lighthouse puts light in the sea. An American coach named Ron Freeman stood in a circle of children calling for jumping jacks and names; I was a restless boy who couldn't sit still, and for the first time that energy had a home. He invited me to the States. I grew six inches one summer, learned to run lanes, learned to compete with the best high-schoolers in New Jersey, learned the discipline behind talent. That camp is the hinge my life swung on. Camps can do that. They tilt a life toward a doorway.

So when people ask me why I've spent so much of my life organizing summer camps, I tell them: because a camp saved me. Because the island is full of boys and girls with the same voltage in their bones. Because sometimes the most powerful thing a representative can do is to make a place where the right work happens again and again.

HOW A CAMP BECOMES A DOOR

A good camp is not bacchanal. It's a factory floor – tight shift, clean lines, reliable output. We keep it simple:

• Mornings: skill blocks that stack – footwork → finishing → spacing → reads. If you don't respect the alphabet, don't expect to write poetry.

• Midday: classroom time – SAT vocab, free-writing prompts, budgeting basics, a talk from a nurse on sleep and simple nutrition.

• Afternoon: controlled scrimmages with an error quota – stop when the turnovers hit the limit, reset the concept, then play it right.

We use a learning rhythm I borrowed from my own years of teaching and the discipline of precision practice: short rituals to open and close sessions, immediate feedback channels (coach, video, or a simple objective rep-count), and one clear skill target per block. Camps that run on detail produce athletes who can run their lives on detail.

The drills get us ready for the floor. The talks get us ready for the world. It might sound like a lot for a "basketball camp," but the "economics" in #SportsEconomics isn't a slogan – it's a design. Sports are the hook. Education is the ladder. Every day ends with a quiet sheet: what did you learn, who did you help, where did you fail, what is the fix? Over time, those answers become a habit. Habits become a future.

THE MORNING WE BROKE A RIVALRY

Back when I was in Kansas, the fiercest line on my schedule was the Turnpike Tussle – Emporia State versus Washburn. I wore the hate for Washburn like a warm-up jacket. After university, life did what it does: took two competitors, put us on the same summer circuit (Team Kansas), and taught us that rivalry is a child of distance. Kerry Dickerson wore Washburn blue. I wore Emporia gold. We became friends. Years later, when I was back home teaching in Saint Lucia and lining up scholarships for our players, Kerry was recruiting. I reached out. I told him we had young men who could help his program and help themselves. I told him to come.

When he landed, I had promised a hotel. He slept at my mother's house. We laughed about it then and we still laugh. But that visit did more than embarrass me: it opened lanes. From that start we built pathways for dozens of Caribbean athletes to Kansas; the connection grew so visible that schools began hosting Caribbean Night to celebrate it. Not just basketball – track and field, volleyball, academics too. A rivalry turned into a bridge. That's sports economics: what begins as competition, if you have the patience and the pride under control, becomes opportunity.

A few years after those first visits, Kerry was still in our gym, still shaking hands in our neighbourhoods. One camp ended with a scholarship for a young man we called Snake – Sherman Barthelmy – one of the smoothest wings the island has produced. He trained with a discipline that tells you who raised him: 5 a.m. sessions at Saint Mary's College with Ewan, work before work. His talent carried him to Drury University and later to a master's in logistics. The kid who cut through the lane like he owned the air became a professional with a passport and a plan.

You can put a number on a court rental or a box of cones. You can't put a number on what it does to a young person to have a stranger from Missouri tap his shoulder and say, "You belong." That is the quiet arithmetic of these camps: one visitor, many doors.

TURNING THE COURT INTO A CLASSROOM

Here's the rule for the morning block: no lazy feet. We begin with base – stance, steps, pivots – until the movement looks like a language. Then we introduce one constraint at a time: keep the dribble alive after contact; finish off two feet under pressure; find the lift spot when the ball drives. If a group hits the mistake limit, we stop. Not to scold, but to learn. It's not punishment; it's pedagogy. The tighter we draw the box, the smarter the decisions inside it.

After lunch we switch classrooms. We pull out notebooks. We map a scholarship pipeline on the whiteboard: Talent ID → SAT prep & CSEC reinforcement → coach introductions → campus visits &

showcase film → scholarship packaging → the accountability loop (grades, strength & conditioning logs, and community service hours) → degree → job. Then we put names on each rung. You'll be surprised how fast a teenager stands up straighter when the box next to his name says "3.0 GPA target by Term 2 – tutor: Shanna." This is what I mean when I say a court can teach you to run your life. It's not the crossover. It's the calendar.

I tell them my own story because it matters that they see failure and repair are part of the path. I had to go to summer school four years straight to keep the academic side honest. It could have gone left, like it goes left for too many boys who fall through the cracks. Sports built me the structure; the classroom made it real.

THE AFTERNOON WE LAID A PIPELINE

I'm often asked how we make the camps count beyond a week in July. The answer is we braid our small rope into a bigger one.

First strand: we invite coaches and recruiters into the island, yes; but we also cultivate alumni who return as mentors, donors, and connectors. You see that in the way Ewan helped broker equipment for the National Sports Complex and later became part of a wider bridge into Kansas programs. You see it in how our network of coaches, athletic directors, and school leaders abroad says yes to a WhatsApp message when they know the name comes with homework already done.

Second strand: we stitch sports and academics tight. Camps run SAT sessions built for our students – mock tests, vocab games, reading fluency drills – because the scholarship pipeline is not a dunk contest; it's an application process. When a camp produces a player who can attack a closeout and write a clean personal statement, coaches stop seeing risk and start seeing return.

Third strand: we formalize the ladder. That's why I've been working on the Castries North Connect idea – linking every school to a partner university and publishing the terms clearly so families can plan. We've already proved the concept with an agreement that allows Saint Lucian students to pay in-state tuition rates at Washburn University, and we are extending the model with Emporia State. That means a mother in Vide Bouteille can dream in numbers, not just wishes.

WHAT CAMPS MEASURE THAT SCORES DON'T

A camp is a place to teach the part the box score can't see: how to be coached; how to lose and move; how to carry the team water and then take the shot; how to apologize; how to finish reps when nobody is watching. That's why our alumni are more than stat lines.

Jimmie Inglis grew up on Gros Islet sand, worked the beach with us, prepared for SATs, and took the long step to Rutgers in the Big Ten. His footwork was textbook; his mind for improvement, better than that. He earned his degree, took a master's, built a life in business. If you're looking for a tidy definition of sports economics, that's it: disciplined practice turning into degrees and durable opportunity.

Jonathan – "Big Joe" – from La Clery, shook the Complex in the 1990s, raised the ceiling on what high school basketball could feel like in Saint Lucia. He raised the standard, then crossed the water, took his chance at Queens College, and now manages at Mercedes-Benz in Charlotte. The crowd's noise fades; the competence remains. That is also the arithmetic of a camp.

Mervin Leo started late – almost seventeen before he got serious – but he turned a steep climb into a record-breaking career at Queens College and then turned that into a bachelor's, an MBA, and a new generation of athletes guided by his hand. System produces scholar; scholar extends system. That is scaffolding, not luck.

Frank Baptiste is one more proof. An SMC boy from Castries North, he earned a basketball scholarship to Park University and finished with a finance degree. If you ever doubt that a morning at SMC or Vide Bouteille can be the start of a global life, read that line again.

And then there's Jeremiah Vitalis of Marchand – quiet, humble, two-foot jumper with more lift than sense would predict. He trained under Augi Jones, came up to the States, ground his way through junior college to a scholarship, then built a career in construction project management while coaching AAU and giving back. Camps don't just make players. Camps make citizens.

BRINGING COACHES DOWN, LIFTING ATHLETES UP

We brought coaches and recruiters because the island's talent deserves a live look. Kerry Dickerson came, saw, and believed – because belief is easier when a drill runs on time and a kid meets your eyes with a firm "Yes, Coach." The image I keep from those weeks isn't the highlight dunk; it's the huddle at day's end, everyone on one knee, sweat on the floor like chalk dust, the future standing politely in the doorway waiting for us to open it.

We also brought ideas down – playbooks from coaches I studied and admired. Ron Slaymaker's insistence on footwork and spacing, the simple beauty of motion that looks like five people thinking the same thought; the old-school demand for game shots from game spots at game speed. We studied systems from the Midwest and translated them into drills that fit Saint Lucian rhythm and space. I'm careful to say this plainly: not every coach we learned from slept on a spare mattress in my mother's house. But every coach who shaped my camps taught me the same lesson – attention is love, and love looks like organization.

When you mix that attention with island generosity, you get moments that would make a cynic blink. Like the day a camp photo with Kerry turned into a full scholarship for Sherman "Snake" Barthelmy. Like the morning we set out cones at 4:50 a.m., and Ewan and Snake were already waiting, laughing, having beaten the sun by a full ten minutes. One camp; one connection; a degree; then a master's; then a career. The cynic still blinking.

WHY CAMPS ARE ECONOMICS, NOT JUST ENTERTAINMENT

The word "economics" is not a costume we put on sports to sound serious. It's what happens when a camp ripples.

Consider the path: a week of organized training turns into a conversation with a coach; that conversation becomes an invitation; the invitation becomes a scholarship; the scholarship becomes a degree; the degree becomes a job; the job becomes money that pays rent, then a mortgage, then a child's school fees; the network becomes a book drive, a mentorship, a business partnership, a skills transfer back home. The circle gets bold.

That's why I talk so much about diaspora skills, about using our camps as a front door for engineers, nurses, coders, and teachers from abroad to come home and teach – even just for a week – then keep the mentorship going online. It's why I push for formal ladders like CN-Connect and practical agreements like the Washburn and Emporia tuition pathways. Sports lures attention. Structure turns attention into outcomes.

THE CAMP DAY (A PLAYBOOK)

0600–0730: Foundation

Lines on the floor. Ball-handling ladders. Finishing on contact. For the older group we add a decision tree: drive-kick-lift, or paint touch → spray → swing. If the turnover count crosses five in a ten-minute block, we blow the whistle, reset, and teach the error. The scoreboard is a teacher too.

0730–0815: Mobility & Breakfast

Bananas, water, bakes. Stretch and laugh. The joke is part of the glue.

0815–0945: Position Schools

Guards: pace and pressure release. Wings: second cuts, foot-in-the-ground. Bigs: pocket passes, seal angles, short roll reads. Everybody: free throws with breath work (count your exhale; own your tempo).

0945–1030: Classroom A

Reading aloud, vocabulary games, a ten-minute writing sprint: "The hardest thing I did this week." The quiet kids bloom when you let them finish a thought.

1030–1130: Classroom B

Scholarship pipeline 101. We pull up a list of alumni by community and track where they are now. We read two sample personal statements: one clumsy, one clear. Then they write a paragraph and we workshop three. The camp learns to give and take feedback without collapsing into foolishness.

1130–1245: Matchups

Controlled scrimmage. Two coaches with clipboards in the corners. "Shot selection" and "help communication" scored separately from points. The best talkers change games.

1245–1300: Close Ritual

Reflect, log, reset. One outcome. One fix. Then home to rest, because the next day asks for more.

WHAT THE CAMPS GAVE BACK

The beautiful thing about running camps year on year is the return you can't predict. A boy comes back as a man, with a degree and a laugh the island knows. A girl who kept stats and ran the water table becomes a physiotherapist who volunteers to lead mobility blocks. A parent who organized the snack table starts a neighbourhood walking club that meets at the same court, three evenings a week, laughing off the weight of their day. The camp becomes a habit; the habit becomes a culture.

When people ask me for evidence, I give names, not adjectives.

• Jimmie Inglis: beach drills, Rutgers, Big Ten, degree, master's, business. A young man who took a move and made a mindset.

• Jonathan "Big Joe": shook the Complex, raised the standard, Queens College, a family built on competence and gratitude.

• Mervin Leo: late start, records, bachelor's, MBA, and then he turns and builds a ladder for the next set.

• Frank Baptist: SMC to Park University to Finance – one more Castries North son who turned a basketball into a bridge.

• Jeremiah Vitalis: lift, humility, scholarship, project manager, youth coach. A two-foot jumper and a two-handed life.

- Sherman "Snake" Barthelmy: 5 a.m. reps, Drury degree, master's in logistics – proof that discipline is a superpower in any industry.
- Malvo "Darwin" Joseph: Park University, finance and business degrees, now a mentor running book drives for Soufriere's youth.
- Ed from Soufriere: Emporia State, degree, business career in Kansas – and yes, the shot-blocking record survived his four-year assault.

These are not trophies on my shelf. They are proof of what disciplined community effort does.

THE HARD PARTS (AND HOW WE HANDLE THEM)

It is not all smooth cones and scholarship letters. Some afternoons the rain comes sideways and we sprint to pull tarps. Some mornings a child arrives with eyes that say he didn't sleep or eat well; the camp becomes a kitchen first. There are weeks when transcripts are late or passports take too long or a coach sends a soft "no" and I have to look a young man in his ribs and tell him the truth: we need another year; higher grades; better film; real conditioning. Real love does not lie.

We also wrestle with the old island disease: the idea that unless there's a banner and a ribbon-cutting, nothing counts. A camp is the opposite of that. It is a thousand small quiet acts that move a life an inch a day. When we do our job, nobody notices in the moment. They notice years later when a scholarship turns into a specialist turns into a good father or mother turns into a neighbourhood that refuses nonsense.

WHAT WE ASK OF THE VILLAGE

We ask for space: a court in workable shape; a classroom with a whiteboard; a storeroom for balls and cones. We ask for volunteers who can keep time and take attendance, who can pour water and pour encouragement – same rhythm. We ask for parents to trust the process and for veterans to return as teachers. We ask for the diaspora to bring skills, not just gear, and to keep the mentorship going when the plane lifts off. We ask for the state to do the basics – lights, drains, small works – and then get out of the way and let the village be a village.

When we get those pieces right, the results are not abstract. They are as real as a memorandum of understanding that knocks international tuition down to in-state rates for our children, signed and spoken aloud. They are as immediate as a phone call to Emporia to mirror that model. They are as human as a camp huddle done properly – everyone on one knee, eyes up, hands steady, ready to shout "family" not as a slogan but as a description.

THE PROMISE

I've joked that I went to summer school four years in a row and came out with humility as my major. It's not really a joke. The work taught me to respect the plain truth: talent without schedule is noise; dreams without a ladder are tricks. Camps gave me a ladder. Camps let me spend the back nine of my life holding that ladder steady for the next person up.

When I say we're building a constituency where sports feed education and education feeds opportunity, I'm not selling a poster. I'm describing a camp morning writ large across a map – from Vigie to Vide Bouteille to Sunny Acres to Bisee – where courts, classrooms, and clinics act like one machine. The output is not medals. It's competence.

The output is not likes. It's letters of offer and first paychecks and engineers who still answer messages from home.

I close this chapter where I started: with a whistle on a damp morning and a bell that rings too early for most but just right for those who want it. What looks like a drill is a lesson in attention. What sounds like sneakers on concrete is a country teaching itself to move. What feels like a small island is a big classroom.

We are not beggars; we are builders. And every camp is a doorway to excellence – open, lit, and waiting on the next name.

6

Case Study: Malvo "Darwin" Joseph (Soufriere)

The first time Darwin challenged me on a full court, I laughed. Not because he couldn't guard me, but because he wouldn't stop. Step for step, shoulder for shoulder. Give me some space. He was trailing me like rent was due. When I came home in the summers, we'd lace shoes up for national-team runs that felt like war: mismatched pinnies, a clipped whistle, a gym that turned hot as coals. Darwin's assignment was always the same – stay in front of Bax. He took it personal, and I respected that. A man who takes a job personally will build a life out of it.

Those sessions were not polite basketball. You learned who would duck a screen and who would blow it up. You learned who loved the noise and who could find quiet inside it. And you learned, if you had eyes for it, that Darwin's game was changing. The feet told the truth first. Less reach, more slide. Less lunging, more angles. He started playing defence like a good mason lays block – solid base, clean lines, no wasted motion – then he began to add layers: first step into space, counter-foot spin, a mid-post patience that didn't belong to a young man in a hurry. The body kept the evidence, but the mind had shifted too. He was seeing the floor a beat earlier than the rest of us. That's when I thought: this one is ready for a doorway.

Camps and good coaching tilt a life toward a door. In Chapter 5, I told you how bringing coaches onto the island – people like Kerry Dickerson – and running camps with structure turned our courts into classrooms and our rivalries into bridges. Darwin's story grew straight out of that soil. He and I had spent years elbow to elbow, but it was one graduate-school summer when I really saw it – the sturdier base, the calmer head, the patience to let a play breathe. I didn't wait for proof on paper. I drove to Park University, sat in Coach Claude English's office, and asked him to take a chance on a Saint Lucian he hadn't met yet. The rest is history. Darwin seized the opportunity. He earned a degree in finance, then a master's in business. Today, he lives in New York and still reaches back – book drives, mentorship, hands outstretched to the youth of Soufriere. That is the road, and it starts with a step so small you could miss it: a guard deciding not to bite on a head fake.

THE MIRROR AND THE MEASURE

You want to know who you are as a player? Watch the feet. You want to know who you are as a person? Watch what you do when nothing is working. Darwin taught me both.

He guarded me like a mirror – if my hips lied, his angle told the truth. When he reached, I set the trap; when he slid, I had to earn every inch. Over time, the mirror sharpened. He traded chases for cut-offs, gambles for geometry. His stance got honest, and with it, his reads improved. Those are small things to a spectator and everything to a recruiter. A coach watching film wants to see a player who makes the easy thing look easy under pressure. It sounds modest, but it's management in disguise – risk control, decision hygiene, an eye for the highest-percentage action.

The older I get, the more I see how footwork and patience rhyme. Footwork is your promise to the future – every rep is a small deposit. Patience is the discipline not to spend it all on the first flashy opportunity. Darwin banked his reps and spent them wisely. That's why, when I walked into Coach English's office, I wasn't selling a highlight dunk. I was describing reliability, growth, and a man who had learned to carry responsibility on the court without losing his head. That's a scholarship in any language.

SOUFRIERE MORNINGS

Every community gives an athlete a rhythm. Soufriere gave Darwin balance – mountain and sea, heat and wind, work and worship. You feel that in his game: a composure that isn't learned in a day. Plenty of young men can jump; fewer can wait. Waiting is its own skill, especially when the crowd wants noise. Darwin could put the ball on his hip, shift the defender with a half-look, and still choose the third best option because it was the right one for the moment. That's a grown man's decision inside a young man's body.

I remember a morning at the Soufriere court when the lines were faded to memory and the rim had a mean lean to the left. We chalked makeshift lines, swept the dust with an old coconut broom, and ran a footwork circuit: stance ladder, two-foot stop series, shoulder-to-chest finishes with light contact, then close-outs into wall-sits to remind the legs about truth. Darwin ran that circuit like he had something to prove to himself. He didn't skip the boring parts. That's always the tell.

Later that week he guarded me in a scrimmage and forced me into the seam I least wanted – toward help, not away from it. I barked, because old dogs bark when the young ones nip properly. He just smiled, reset his feet, and lived in my chest another possession. There's a kind of courage in staying exactly where the hard thing is. That's patience. That's also how a young man becomes the kind of student who will sit for a finance exam, scan a jittery question, and calmly work the method.

TRUST AND PARK

There are decisions that look dramatic, and then there are decisions that are simply necessary. Driving to Park University felt like the latter. I didn't carry a file, a highlight reel, or a fancy pitch deck. I carried trust. Trust is heavy when you're placing it on a coach's desk. You have to mean it. I told Claude English what I had seen: a defender who knew how to be late in the right way and early in the right places; a guard whose feet could carry him through a bad shooting night; a student who would treat a syllabus like a set play and run it till it passed. Coach English said yes to a person he hadn't met because he believed the messenger and the message. That's another piece of sports economics: credibility is a currency, and you spend it on the next young man.

We've made a habit of talking about scholarships as if they fall from the sky. They don't. They come from a sequence:

1. A body of work that tells the truth without applause.
2. A witness – a coach, a mentor, a rival – willing to say, "I vouch."
3. A gatekeeper who still believes in judgement more than flash.
4. A student prepared to grind through the paperwork and the patience.

Darwin had the work. I became the witness. Coach English was the gatekeeper. The student never flinched.

FOOTWORK, THE QUIET TEACHER

Let me be specific about footwork. There are some keys:

- **Base before burst.** We drilled stance until quad burn; inside edge of the shoe, knees over toes, shoulders stacked, eyes soft. From that base, the first step got honest.
- **Angles over reach.** We punished reach-ins – two push-ups for the hand that stabs; reward the slide that cuts the lane. It rewired instincts.
- **Two-foot truth.** Finish off two feet in traffic until you can feel your hips under you; teach the gather as a breath, not a panic. The and-ones come later.
- **Decision ladders.** Drive-kick-lift and its cousins. We counted turnovers like a teacher counts the "ums." Blow the whistle at five; reset the concept; do it right.

Darwin took to that structure like a man takes to a map. He wasn't the loudest in a huddle, but when he spoke, heads tilted. Some players spray their energy like a hose on the wrong setting. Darwin turned his to a steady stream. You can run a season on that.

PATIENCE

Sometimes we give patience a bad name. Sometimes we just want instant results, actions, lots of heat. But patience is not delay; patience is control. A patient guard is a dangerous one: he can slow a possession until a defence shows its weakest seam. Darwin would reject an early three just to see if the corner would sleep on the lift. He'd turn down a drive to test the help. That wasn't fear. That was information-gathering. The same habit shows up later in a classroom, then in a career. A man who can wait one more beat on a ball screen can read one more line in a term sheet.

I could feel that impatience in myself when I was young – the need to prove, to break a record, to be the loudest achievement in the room. It took me years (and, truth be told, four summers of swallowing my pride in summer school) to learn that the quiet wins last longer. Darwin was learning it earlier. That's why I bet on him.

THE ECONOMICS BEHIND THE SCHOLARSHIP

People sometimes ask why I put sports and economics in the same sentence. Because the pathway is economic, start to finish. A camp introduces a coach to a player. A coach's eye becomes an invitation. An invitation becomes a scholarship. A scholarship becomes a degree. A degree becomes a job. A job becomes a mortgage payment and school fees and stability. And when that person remembers where he came from, he sends something back – not just money, but know-how. Darwin's story is textbook: Park University opportunity, finance degree, business master's, New York grind, and then the return flow – book drives and mentorship for Soufriere's youth. That's a closed loop, island to world and world to island.

In public we celebrate the signing day photo. Privately, the work is mail and meetings: FAFSA forms, transcripts, visa appointments, housing deposits, strength plans, study halls, the occasional tough call home when homesickness shows up like a late-night wave. The difference between a story that finishes and a story that fades is usually a system. In Chapter 5 I described the "ladder": Talent ID → SAT prep and CSEC reinforcement → coach introductions → scholarship packaging → accountability loop (grades, conditioning logs, service hours) → degree → job. Darwin climbed every rung.

A SCHOLAR IN SNEAKERS

The thing about a finance degree is it doesn't care how many points you scored last night. It cares whether you can sit with a spreadsheet and make sense of it; whether you can see a cash flow as clearly as you see a fast break; whether you understand that risk has a cost and time has a value. Darwin put down the ball when class demanded, picked it back up when practice called, and learned to let the two disciplines inform each other. A sound stance looks a lot like a balanced ledger: nothing leaning too far, nothing fancy for the sake of it.

When he took the next step – graduate business school – he was choosing to add another gear to the transmission. Plenty of good players never make that choice. That's not an indictment; it's an invitation. If you can survive a pre-season, you can survive a semester of managerial accounting. The rigour lives in both places. Darwin proved it.

NEW YORK, AND THE RETURN FLOW

A Saint Lucian in New York multiplies. That city will either eat you or teach you. Darwin chose to learn. He worked, he built network, and he kept his compass pointed home. I measure success by return flow: what comes back? In his case, it came back as books in the hands of Soufriere kids, as guidance delivered gently to a teenager who thinks his dream is too far away, as a message that says "I did it, and so can you – here's how." That "here's how" is everything. A letter of encouragement is sweet; a checklist is power. He gave both.

I've watched many of our athletes move abroad and felt the distance open like a tide. With Darwin, the tide never carried him out of sight. He turned citizenship into a verb – an action repeated. You see it in small decisions: answering a WhatsApp from a coach back home; buying extra copies when a bookstore runs a sale; booking a flight at Carnival not just to jump but to sit with a group of Form 5 boys and talk honestly about recruitment, discipline, and the danger of believing your own poster.

LESSONS FROM A GUARD WHO WAITED

If you're a young player reading this, here's what Darwin's path teaches in the language of drills:

1. **Win the boring reps.** Stance. Slides. Two-foot finishes. These are not punishments; they are the parts of your future that people can trust.

2. **Film your patience.** Don't just cut highlights; cut a reel of correct decisions. Send a coach the possession where you didn't shoot because the better shot was one pass away.

3. **Get a witness.** Play hard enough, long enough, that someone credible will drive to a coach's office and put their name on your name.

4. **Treat school like strength training.** Class is not a break from basketball; it is the reason coaches recruit you without fear.

5. **Build a return plan.** Decide before you leave how you will give back – mentorship hours, a book drive, a skills clinic. Write it down now so success doesn't make you forget.

If you're a parent: ask to see the plan, not just the passion. Ask your child to show you the ladder we talk about. Ask the coach to show you how this week's drills link to next year's scholarship.

If you're a coach: measure the right things. We don't count just points; we count "help calls," "second cuts," "error-limit resets," and the number of times a player helps another player set their feet. That's the camp; that's the classroom.

RIVALRY, FRIENDSHIP, AND THE BRIDGE WE BUILT

I'm obliged to say this plainly: none of this happens without bridges. Years before Darwin's opportunity at Park, my own rivalry in Kansas (Emporia State vs. Washburn) became a friendship with Kerry Dickerson that grew into a pipeline for Caribbean athletes – basketball first, then track, volleyball, and academics. That pipeline taught me how to talk to coaches, how to package a player, and how to ask boldly but cleanly. It's how I knew I could sit in Coach English's office with an empty hand and a full conviction. The camps, the visitors sleeping in my mother's guest room, the scholarships at the end of a whistle – they all add up to a simple sentence: the island can trust the outside world when we build the right systems and send the right people across. We proved it, over and over.

THE DOOR IN

When a young person from Soufriere steps onto a campus in the Midwest, the island walks in with them – accent, manners, stubbornness, generosity. A scholarship is not an escape; it's an exchange. The campus gets our talent and our grit. We get their labs, their libraries, their alumni lists. Then we bring the knowledge home.

Darwin's book drives are more than charity. They are a signal to the next generation that the island doesn't end at the coast. His mentorship calls are not pep talks; they are a syllabus: practise schedules, sleep targets, study habits, the code of conduct that keeps you trustworthy in a dorm full of strangers. The camp ethic turned into a life.

It's easy to list degrees – finance, then business – and say "done." But listen for the unsaid numbers. The cost of a false step in a pre-calculus class. The price of one roommate who thinks the party never ends. The interest rate on a missed curfew when your coach stops trusting you. The currency of reputation. Darwin survived all that because he had built a habit of paying attention. The feet that stayed quiet in a press learned to stay quiet when the room got loud. That's why I called it patience earlier, but it's more than that. It's stewardship – of your minutes, your knees, your promises.

AN OPEN LETTER TO A FUTURE DARWIN

Young man,

I see you at the back of the gym with the ball you borrowed because your own is peeling. I see you staying after to fix the push-shot that crept in when you got tired. I see you watch the older boys and copy the wrong things first – the chest bump, the noise – before you learn to copy the right ones – the stance, the eye contact, the apology. Here's the truth: you don't need to be the loudest to be the best. You need feet that tell the truth and a mind that can wait.

What we will ask of you is simple, not easy: show up early, leave last, take notes, drink water, learn names, shake hands, say thank you, write your own schedule, follow it, then fix it. On days when the rim leans and the lines are ghosts, we will chalk them back. On days when you want to believe the lie that you are stuck, we will show you a ladder.

And when the day comes that someone sits in a coach's office with your name in their mouth, let it be because you made small promises and kept them – on the court, in the classroom, and in the spaces between. When the letter arrives, take it. Then write back home.

– Bax

FOR THE RECORD

Because I know there will always be questions, here is the public record we can point to: Darwin and I were national-team sparring partners for years; he guarded me each summer when I flew back from the States. Seeing his growth during my graduate-school years – especially his footwork and composure – moved me to drive to Park University and vouch for him directly to Coach Claude English. He was offered the opportunity, earned his finance degree, then a master's in business, and today he lives in New York, where he continues to give back – book drives, mentorship, community work centred on Soufriere's youth. That is not campaign myth; those are facts stamped into our island's memory.

WHAT THE COMMUNITY CAN COPY TOMORROW

If there's a headline lesson for Castries North – and for Soufriere, for Marchand, for La Clery – it's that we can reproduce this story on purpose. You don't need a miracle; you need a method.

- **Method 1: Court to Classroom Circuit.** Every camp day includes 90 minutes of footwork and 60 of academic prep. Make it law.
- **Method 2: Witness Network.** Keep a living list of coaches and alumni who will pick up the phone. Don't wait for scouting to be random.
- **Method 3: Pipeline Calendar.** Publish the scholarship milestones – SAT dates, transcript deadlines, showcase windows – on the school wall and in WhatsApp groups.
- **Method 4: Accountability Loop.** For every athlete, maintain a simple dashboard with grades, practice logs, and service hours. Review it weekly.
- **Method 5: Return Flow Pledge.** Every scholarship recipient signs a one-page pledge to give back 20 hours a year – mentoring calls, a book drive, a clinic – nothing fancy, just faithful.

We've already begun codifying parts of this method under CN-Connect and our diaspora skills push, using exactly the kind of relationships and credibility that opened doors for Darwin. I keep repeating this because it matters: when a community organizes itself around clear ladders and honest feedback, young people climb.

Years from now, when someone in Soufriere mentions Darwin's name, I hope they remember the book in a child's hand more than the box score. I hope they remember the way a defender can make a scorer better, the way a rival becomes a reference, the way a single car ride across a state can be the hinge on which a family's future swings. We don't have to inflate this with fairy dust. The dignity is enough: footwork done properly, patience chosen repeatedly, a scholarship earned honestly, a degree hung modestly, and a life spent lifting the next person up.

There is a photograph in my mind that no camera took: a summer gym, late, the floor shining with the effort of a day, the whistle at rest, and a young guard tying his shoe for one more rep he doesn't owe anyone. That rep becomes a habit. The habit becomes a call I can make to a coach. The call becomes a letter. The letter becomes a degree. The degree becomes a man standing in a school in Soufriere with boxes of books and a laugh that says he remembers where the key to the gym was kept.

If you take nothing else from this chapter, here's this: the doorway to a higher level is built from small choices that start at your feet. Darwin made those choices. And so can you.

7

Case Study: Joel Polius (PDJSS)

The morning light over Vide Bouteille doesn't flood the court; it creeps. The net, if there is one, hangs tired and honest. Chalk dust from yesterday's lesson still ghosting the baseline. By the time the first ball thuds, the place is awake in that Castries way – soft laughter by the gate, someone's little sister in slippers, a teacher passing with a nod that says make it count today.

I remember the first time Joel rose in that space. Not a showy rise, not a cocky one. Just a clean, two-foot lift that seemed to right every crooked thing in the gym. He didn't float; he drove air like a stake.

Landed square. Reset. No fuss. Some boys jump like they are escaping. Joel jumped like he was arriving.

If you've followed my work, you know the thread by now: camps with a clock and a purpose; coaches who came down because we built trust; a court turned into a classroom with an error quota and a ladder that climbs from footwork to scholarships to degrees to jobs. Joel's story lives inside that thread. He came up through PDJSS (PDJSS) – Vide Bouteille Secondary School – one of those campuses that has raised more quiet warriors than it gets credit for. And yes, there's a thing about PDJSS boys and vertical leap: a spring in the legs, especially off two feet, that makes coaches stop their clipboards mid-scribble. Joel had that spring, in thick measure. The first truth I'll put on paper is simple: he wasn't initially awarded a basketball scholarship. The second truth is sweeter: he earned it, and he carried that discipline all the way to an NAIA conference championship push at Nelson University.

"Discipline that travels" is what happens when a boy learns habits on a Castries court and those habits pay rent for him in a faraway gym, then again in a classroom, and then again in a boardroom. Joel's career is that phrase turned into a life. The vertical leap got us watching; the discipline kept us watching. PDJSS (PDJSS) will always be proud of that two-foot explosion – any coach who ever saw him load the hips and rise will know what I mean – but the thing that made me want to write this chapter is not flight. It's the way he learned to land: on time, on task, and on the next responsibility.

There's a moment in every young athlete's life when the hard thing asks its plain question: Are you going to be talented, or are you going to be reliable? Talent will walk you to the door. Reliability opens it.

At PDJSS (PDJSS), we built days that quietly test this. Morning blocks: stance ladders, angle slides, two-foot finishes through touch

– no whistles for flair, only for truth. Midday: reading and writing sprints, scholarship paperwork checklists, SAT vocab that sneaks up as games. Afternoon: decision ladders – drive, kick, lift; paint-touch, spray, swing – with a turnover cap that resets the drill the instant the count is hit. You'd be surprised how quickly a teenager comes to worship the beauty of "do it right" when the consequence is not scolding but repetition.

Joel took to those days like a craftsman to a bench. He didn't need music, and he didn't need an audience. He needed the next rep. That's when I knew: his leap was going to take him somewhere, but his habits would make him stay there.

The first news wasn't pretty. No scholarship. Not then. I've seen boys shrink under that verdict. It's a bruise if you let it be. He didn't. He went back to the base – stance, slides, two-foot truth, shot diet, sleep discipline – and he gave us permission to be honest: the shot must simplify; the turnover rate must come down; the personal statement must read like the person writing it. When the next window opened, the answer matched the work. He earned the scholarship he had been behaving toward. That envelope did not fall from the sky; it arrived because his days were moving in its direction. In pursuit of worthy goals, we must understand that "Not yet" doesn't mean "no".

I like to say that a scholarship is just a receipt – proof that you've been investing all along. Joel's receipt had line items: early mornings; cut sugar; shin splints iced without complaint; injury-prevention work nobody sees; notes from film sessions penned in his own hand; a calendar that actually ruled his days. Discipline is public eventually, but it always starts private.

WHY PDJSS MAKES JUMPERS – AND NEIGHBOURS

People ask me why so many PDJSS athletes jump the way they do. I'll give you my unscientific answer. Part of it is simple exposure: PDJSS has been a crossroads for hungry coaches and hungry kids. You repeat the right mechanics enough times in one place and a signature emerges. But the deeper reason is cultural: Vide Bouteille holds its boys close while telling them the truth. You can feel the village in the way players carry each other through drills, the way a lunchtime laugh resets the morning's frustration, the way a teacher will pull you aside and talk about an English essay without ever making you feel small. That mix – pressure and care – trains legs and character. Joel is cut from that fabric: explosive, yes; generous, more importantly.

NAIA NIGHTS AND THE CALM INSIDE NOISE

When Joel stepped onto the floor at Nelson University, he carried the island in his shoes. That's not poetry; it's physics. Two-foot jumpers who learn balance in small gyms move through contact like accountants count money – deliberate, patient, exact. In NAIA conference play, that kind of base doesn't just win highlights; it wins possessions. One more rotation, one more rebound in traffic because your hips stayed under you, one more contested finish because you didn't jump out of your own shot. The league is full of brave athletes. The ones who keep showing up deep in March are the ones whose feet tell the truth.

When Nelson played its way into conference championship contention, that truth was visible from the first horn: tempo controlled by guards who could change pace without changing standards; wings who didn't foul when tired; bigs who boxed like they'd get paid by the angle. Joel's contribution lived in the connective tissue of those moments: the second cut that cracks a zone; the middle-third seal that buys a guard a driving lane; the weak-side board snatched clean because you loaded before you leapt. If you were watching for only posters, you might have missed how much he got right. If you watch basketball like a teacher, you'd have smiled all game.

THE SCIENCE OF TWO-FOOT TRUTH

I won't leave you with slogans. Let's talk about how we train the thing you saw every time Joel lifted.

- **Load:** knees not caved in, hips behind heels like you're sitting into a promise, sternum proud but not flared.
- **Link:** ankles, knees, hips fire in sequence – not a panic jump; a rhythm jump. Count one-two-rise under your breath until the nervous system knows the hymn.
- **Land:** absorb with the same honesty you lifted with – soft elbows, quiet spine, eyes that don't lie about dizziness.

We built his vertical on a foundation of low-tech discipline: tempo squats, depth drops into strict holds, pogo hops that teach honest stiffness, and a diet of sleep we guarded like a team statistic. But the secret sauce wasn't in a snazzy drill. It was in the way he treated the slow reps with the same reverence as the fast ones. *If you want a leap that lives in March, you have to respect December.*

"DISCIPLINE THAT TRAVELS" IN THE CLASSROOM

A good jump doesn't pass an exam. What does is the same habits, translated. You can feel the PDJSS (PDJSS) influence here too: the child who keeps his notebook straight tends to keep his life straight. Nelson University isn't a poetry name in this book; it's a place with real labs, real lectures, real deadlines. Joel learned to walk from the weight room to a workstation without changing his standards. It's one of the reasons I push #SportsEconomics as more than a T-shirt – because the discipline of sport, when harnessed intentionally, transfers into the discipline of study and then into the discipline of work.

To the parents who read these pages, wondering if all these early mornings are worth it: a scholarship is not a medal; it's a timetable. It requires the same trust and stubbornness you'll need when a homesick call arrives at 1 a.m. from a winter campus your son has never seen in his dreams. The reason Joel held steady in those months is that he had practiced steadiness. The footwork of attention. The core strength of patience. The breath control of choosing a better shot over an easy one.

HOW A PIPELINE – BORN IN RIVALRY – HELD THE LADDER STEADY

A bitter Kansas rivalry softened into a bridge that has carried Caribbean kids where their talent could meet the right eyes. Kerry Dickerson wore Washburn blue when I wore Emporia gold, and it should have ended there – in trash talk and a box score – but we chose to build something more useful: a network of coaches and administrators who trust our word, our camps, and our kids. That network didn't just help the Shermans and the Jimmies; it helped make calls on behalf of quieter stories, the ones without a viral dunk. It's the kind of credibility that lets you ring a coach, speak a name like Joel's, and be heard as more than a salesman. That's what I mean when I call sports an economy – relationships compounding into opportunity, year after year.

People sometimes hear "pipeline" and think of luck. Luck is a spark. A pipeline is plumbing. It's flights arranged, gym doors opened, scholarships packaged, host families briefed, and a WhatsApp that never sleeps when a boy needs a word. It's also reciprocity: coaches who fly down sleep in a spare room in La Clery, and later the island raises a banner at a "Caribbean Night" because the exchange went both ways. The same bridge that helped a Marchand wing at 5 a.m. and a Soufriere guard in a coach's office kept the ladder steady when Joel's window opened.

THE NIGHT THE GYM CHANGED SHAPE

I keep a private film room in my head where all the best possessions live. One of Joel's came late in a tight conference game. Nelson was behind one, two minutes to play, the gym breathing heavy. The defence had decided to be brave; they pinched the paint and dared us to blink. Joel caught on the slot, jabbed, retreated, then did nothing for one beat. It was the most dangerous thing he could do. The defence panicked first – help wobbled toward the ball, the weak-side tag floated. He didn't attack the wrong gap; he passed to the open one. Two passes later, the ball returned to his hands like a favour being called in. Now he went – two feet under him, a shoulder through a shoulder, a finish that didn't care for the foul. And because he landed ready, he led the press break on the next possession, finding a cutter for a lay-in that sealed it. Score it how you like; I scored it this way: patience earned, patience spent, points banked.

That sequence is why I preach boring things with a lover's zeal – error caps, stance ladders, breath on free throws. The spectacular is just the faithful in fast forward.

A WORD ABOUT "MOST EXPLOSIVE"

Careful readers will note that I am sparing with superlatives. I'm not afraid of them; I just know they retire badly. Still, I'll put this on the record: in a school that has produced its share of leapers, Joel belongs near the top of the two-foot charts. I'd say one of the most explosive to come out of PDJSS. Call it the kind of rise that made the backboard blink. I've watched a lot of island ball. He is in that room. And if you want me to prove it, I'll point you to the way he could create vertical with tight space – no run-up, no drama, just ready hips and a core that didn't lie.

WHAT "INSPIRE" LOOKS LIKE ON A TUESDAY

Sometimes we talk about inspiration like it happens on podiums with microphones. More often, it looks like a WhatsApp voice note sent on a Tuesday night in November to a 16-year-old who just got cut and thinks the world is over. It looks like showing up at PDJSS with a bag of training bands and saying "Do this three times a week for six weeks, then call me back." It looks like sitting in a school office explaining to a mother that the scholarship letter is a promise of work, not an escape clause. Since graduating, Joel has been that kind of presence – pointing young men and women toward the best version of themselves without ever pretending the road is a straight line. That's the afterlife of a good athletic career: the quiet multiplication of competence.

The seven habits Joel carried from PDJSS to Nelson to the rest of his life

1. Start low, stay tall. Stance before swagger. The way you set your feet tells your future.

2. Respect the second beat. The first opening is not always the best one; a patient guard makes defenders confess.

3. Cut your errors, not your corners. If the turnover count hits the cap in practice, stop and fix the concept. Do it right or don't do it again.

4. Write like you hoop. Clear sentences, clean footwork. Your personal statement is a film session in prose.

5. Sleep on purpose. Recovery is not a luxury; it's part of the workout.

6. Serve the village that made you. The return flow – mentorship, materials, attention – is not charity. It's rent.

7. Treat discipline as a passport. If your habits are strong, they will cross oceans and still spend.

These are not aphorisms for walls. They are the private rules of people who keep showing up when the noise fades.

A CORRIDOR OF NAMES THAT MAKE THIS CHAPTER POSSIBLE

Nobody climbs alone. I'd be a liar if I didn't draw the corridor of names that held the door open for a generation – coaches and administrators who picked up calls, rivals turned allies, camps that ran like clockwork, families who pushed the car to make sure a boy reached the gym before 6 a.m. The Kansas corridor that began as the Turnpike Tussle and matured into a pipeline is one of those public miracles we don't memorialize enough. It gave wash to kids from Marchand and Vide Bouteille and Soufriere alike. If you ever see a photo of our camp where a visiting coach stands with a grin too wide for his face, know that the smile is paid in scholarships. Know too that these bridges helped a boy like Joel become more than a leaper; they helped him become a standard.

THE SPREADSHEET UNDER THE STAT LINE

I have an unromantic streak that keeps books. A scholarship is money saved; a degree is earning power multiplied; a disciplined life is risk reduced. When Joel carried his two-foot truth into NAIA conference play, people saw points and rebounds. I saw a ledger: travel stipends spent properly; class attendance at 98%; fines avoided because curfew wasn't a debate; maintenance lifts performed as prescribed; video watched without a coach begging. It's not that I don't love a windmill dunk – I'm not dead. It's that I love the way competence becomes repeatable wealth. That's the core of #SportsEconomics. We can tell these stories with confetti, or we can tell them with receipts that show how a community becomes richer in people you can depend on.

TO THE NEXT PDJSS (PDJSS) GUARD

Young brother,

If you are reading this on a phone that's telling you to scroll instead of to plan, put it down for ten minutes. Stand up. Set your feet as if a coach who loves you is watching. Get your hips under you. Count one-two-rise, softly, five times. Now sit and write: three habits you will keep before January, three people you will thank before Sunday, three drills you will master before the next tournament.

Do not be intimidated by the word "scholarship." It's not a fancy noun; it's a list of verbs. Show up. Study. Sleep. Send the email you are afraid to send. If a "not yet" arrives, read it as instructions, not an obituary. Remember that PDJSS produced boys whose leaps made crowds gasp, and remember that the island respects most the ones who land well and return to teach.

When the letter arrives – because letters do come to people who move like letters – accept it with humility. Then answer this island back with service.

– Bax

8

Case Study: Jimmie Inglis (SMC/ Gros Islet)

The sea at Gros Islet wakes up before the town does. On training mornings the wind moves first, then the gulls, then the water lifting itself in thin, regular breaths. Jimmie and I would meet there with a ball that didn't care for sand and a plan that did. You learn balance on that shoreline – ankles talking to calves, calves talking to hips, breath talking to brain. We worked footwork patterns chalked into the damp packed sand, ran resisted sprints where the tide turns soft to heavy in a step, and finished with a cool-down that looked more like prayer than sport. After drills we'd sit with salt on our lips and talk through the other side of the work: SAT words, application essays, the honest costs of leaving home. That was the classroom before the classroom, the long game hiding in a morning ritual.

To most people Jimmie was the tall boy from SMC who could move like a guard and jump like the sea had loaned him springs. To me, even back then, he was something rarer – a young man who could take correction without breaking stride. Plenty of athletes can perform; fewer can adapt. Jimmie had that adaptable mind that turns drills into decisions and decisions into durable outcomes. He grew up in Gros Islet, came through the VBCC youth program, played senior ball, then did what almost nobody from an island of 180,000 expects to do: he crossed into the Big Ten at Rutgers, competed at that level, and kept going – degree earned, master's completed, and then the pivot that matters most to me: athlete to businessman. That is what "sports economics" looks like without the slogan – discipline that pays off long after the crowd goes home.

THE BEACH AS A TEACHER

The sand forgives nothing and teaches everything. When you load your hips wrong, it slides you into confession. When you land lazily, it steals your next step. So we kept our progress honest: stance ladders scratched with a shell; angle slides that punish reachy hands; two foot truth on finishes because the sea hates panic jumps. We'd layer in decision ladders – drive kick lift and paint touch spray swing – until the body could do them without a coach on the shoulder. We capped errors the way I cap turnovers in a camp: hit the number and you stop, reset the concept, and do it right. The beach is fair. It gives you whatever you give it – with interest.

But those mornings weren't only sweat. After cooldown we opened notebooks. I would quiz him on vocabulary, ask him to rewrite a paragraph of his personal statement, or talk through a mild but real fear: leaving a small island for a huge campus, learning to be a stranger and still be yourself. One of the measures I came to trust in Jimmie was how gently he faced that fear. He didn't banter it away. He put it on the table and worked it like a drill. That is a grown skill in a teenager. It foreshadowed everything.

FROM SMC AND VBCC TO THE WORLD

People in Castries know what SMC does to boys who pay attention: it insists. Pair that with the VBCC spirit – community first, youth built brick by brick – and you get a reliable pipeline of young men who treat a court as a training ground for life. Jimmie is part of that genealogy. If you draw the path on a map it looks simple: Gros Islet sand → SMC discipline → VBCC crucible → Rutgers. If you walk it, the path feels like a thousand quiet choices you make when nobody is clapping. That's why I keep saying "discipline that travels." When your habits are real, they get stamped like a passport. You can spend them in a Big Ten gym, in a lecture hall, and later in a boardroom without changing currency.

At Rutgers, Jimmie became proof that a Saint Lucian can go toe to toe in one of the toughest conferences in U.S. college basketball. That's not romantic inflation; that's a fact with weight. Kids in the States dream of that stage; an island boy stood there and did the work. The part that filled me with the most pride wasn't any single play. It was the way he used the court to structure his life. He treated deadlines like defensive assignments, time management like a press break, and respect like spacing – you plan it, you protect it, and you don't crash into your teammate's lane.

"PRECISION PRACTICE" – THE WAY WE BUILT THE ENGINE

I don't believe in busywork. We built Jimmie's engine with a four week rhythm I call precision practice: one keystone skill, one sub component, drilled at the edge of current ability with tight feedback. We kept each bout short and sharp – timed sessions, clear targets, and stop rules to prevent practicing mistakes. Then we reviewed the tape, logged the reps, and set the next micro goal. In other words, we practiced like engineers. The beach drills made his feet honest; the practice design made his improvement inevitable. Four honest weeks of that is worth four boastful months.

That approach mattered later when the coursework stacked up. An athlete who has learned to isolate a sub skill can isolate a sub topic in accounting or finance and train it the same way – bounded task, repeatable drill, measurable target, focused bouts. Confidence doesn't come from hype; it comes from a stack of receipts you can point to and say: I did the work, and here is how. That's the same ledger I ask our young people to keep – on court, in class, and in life.

WHY "BUSINESSMAN" IS A SOLID PUNCHLINE

One day the last official game arrives. The jersey folds, the whistle stops, and you're left with the person the game built. In Jimmie's case, that person stood up well. He finished his degree, completed a master's, and stepped into the business world with the same footwork he used to split a trap – patient, efficient, eyes up. It's the quiet after the noise that tells you whether a program works. For me, the best one line summary of his story is "athlete to businessman," not because money is the measure, but because competence is. He turned speed and structure into judgment and judgment into value. That is a Saint Lucian export the whole island should brag about.

HOW THE BRIDGE GOT BUILT (AGAIN)

A rivalry in Kansas grew into a pipeline that's still paying people. When I wore Emporia gold and Kerry Dickerson wore Washburn blue, we were set up to dislike each other. Then we grew up, played together on Team Kansas, and started building bridges. That friendship became a professional corridor: coaches visiting Saint Lucia, camps that ran on time, scholarships arranged with care, yes – but also volleyball, track, and academic opportunities that followed the same path. That pipeline didn't deliver only Jimmie; it helped certify the whole idea that Saint Lucian talent is real and reliable when packaged with structure.

I tell that story here not to pat backs but to show infrastructure. In a small country, mentorship and logistics are our highways. One person's credibility can carry many names. The hoops at the National Sports Complex, the guest room at my mom's house, the coaches who kept coming back – these are the beams under the road. The next part of that road, for a player like Jimmie, was Rutgers and a degree. The beginning was Gros Islet sand and a notebook. The middle was a hundred acts of trust you'd miss if you weren't looking.

WHAT THE BIG TEN CHANGED, AND WHAT IT DIDN'T

The arena size changed. The geography changed. The pressure changed. What didn't change was the logic of the game. A closeout in a small gym obeys the same physics as a closeout in front of ten thousand.

Your feet are either right or wrong; the ball either moves on time or it doesn't. I loved watching Jimmie apply island habits to American noise. He didn't invent a new self to survive it; he used the self he had built. When a conference is testing your nerve, a man falls to the level of his practice, not the height of his hope. He had practiced well.

And when the arena went dark and class went on, he still had a schedule that ran without applause. That's the quiet secret to these stories – their centre is never a dunk; it is a calendar. Every day you keep the calendar, you accumulate a kind of compound interest in trust. Coaches trust you, professors trust you, employers trust you – and then communities do, too. That's how a single athlete turns into a multi year example the next boy or girl can point at and say, "I know what right looks like."

SMC MANNERS, VBCC MUSCLE, GROS ISLET STEEL

Let me pause to give SMC and VBCC their props. Saint Mary's College still shapes posture – how to carry yourself in rooms where nobody knows you. VBCC still insists that your gifts belong to Lucia first and the world later. Gros Islet still teaches steel – the willingness to work before the sun has its say. Jimmie was raised by that triangle, and it shows. He could out jump you, yes, but he could also out listen you. He could sprint, and he could also study. That compound profile is why he travelled well – country to campus, campus to company – without getting rid of the parts of himself that made him solid to begin with.

THE "ECONOMICS" IN SPORTS ECONOMICS – COUNT IT PROPERLY

I keep using the phrase because I want us to count what matters. Jimmie's story is not a poster; it is a ledger. Line items include volunteer hours at youth sessions when he's home; the degree and the master's tucked into a CV; the business career that pays tax and school fees and maybe, one day, payroll; the intangible but real confidence he gifts to a 15 year old who hears "Rutgers" and realizes that Saint Lucian accents don't disqualify excellence. When people ask me to justify investing time and small money in beach cones and SAT prep books, I point to that ledger. It's a return in people – the only return a small country should spend its best energy chasing.

THE DRILLS BEHIND THE STORY

Footwork block (beach edition):

• Stance circuit: ten steps each direction with knees tracking, no drift; pause into isometric holds.

• Angle slides: defender's hips toward the ball, hands quiet, chest squared; whistle on reach.

• Two foot gathers: three finishes – through contact, over length, around angle – count your breath into each lift.

• Decision ladder: drive kick lift; cap at five errors; reset immediately; run it right.

Study block (notebook edition):

• Vocab sprints: 12 words, 6 minutes, two sentence usage tied to a personal story.

• Essay micro revisions: one paragraph, one clarity goal, rewrite in 10 minutes.

• Admin checklist: passport date, transcript request, test registration, reference letter ask – one box ticked daily.

We repeated those until they became muscle memory. When Jimmie reached Rutgers, the drills translated cleanly. The best training travels because it is built on principles, not gimmicks.

THE CONVERSATION THAT REPEATS

After beach work we often had the same talk in different clothes. He'd ask what leaving would feel like. I'd tell him the truth: the first winter is a thief; the first week of classes a new language; the first quiet weekend a mirror. Then we'd turn the fear into a plan: find the Caribbean students office; book weekly calls home; schedule tutoring before you need it; join a church or a club so your weekends have faces; build a sleep rhythm and guard it like a lead. He took those notes like he took coaching – without drama, with intent. That's how I knew his next chapters would read well.

WHAT "ONE OF THE FIRST IN THE BIG TEN" MEANS

Sometimes we read lines without feeling their weight. This one deserves a pause: one of the first players from Saint Lucia to compete in the Big Ten. In pure sporting terms, that's a severe jump in levels. In cultural terms, it's a rewrite of what a Saint Lucian boy thinks is possible when he laces his shoes. The size of our population is a dare: if even one does it, then others can, because the method is teachable. Jimmie's ascent widened the lane for everyone behind him. You can measure that in belief. Belief has a GDP.

THE RETURN FLOW

Success that doesn't flow home is just tourism. Jimmie's move has never been to disappear into a foreign zip code. He returns – in person when he can, by message when he can't. He speaks to kids with the same tone he used to listen on the beach: clear, kind, no nonsense. He doesn't sell miracles; he sells method. Here's the lift pattern; here's the study rhythm; here's the travel checklist; here's the conduct that keeps doors open once you walk through them. That is community wealth – the kind that survives recessions and election cycles.

THE CORRIDOR THAT CARRIED MANY

Let me widen the frame again, because the corridor matters. The Kansas bridge – born from a rivalry and matured by friendship – delivered more than one name. It brought coaches to our courts, hoops to our Complex, scholarships to Marchand and Soufriere and Vide Bouteille, and a reputation that made calls easier across the Midwest. It also gave us case studies we could point to when we asked ministries and private partners to co invest in camps, SAT prep, and small works that keep facilities usable. A pipeline isn't a myth; it's logistics and love with a schedule taped to it.

SEVEN PORTABLE RULES JIMMIE EXEMPLIFIED

1. **Start with feet.** The game sits on them; so will the rest of your life.

2. **Practice like an engineer.** One skill, one sub skill, one month – tight feedback, clear targets.

3. **Ask for the work nobody sees.** Film note taking, sleep tracking, admin chores – these are scholarships in disguise.

4. **Choose mentors who correct you.** If they can't tell you "no," they can't carry your name to a coach.

5. **Treat class as conditioning.** It hurts different, but the lungs it builds will carry you long after sport.

6. **Make the first return before the first cheque.** Give advice, give presence, give an example.

7. **Finish the drill.** In sand, in study, in career – finish.

Those rules sound simple because they are. Complexity is where we hide when we don't want to try.

A LETTER TO A GROS ISLET TEENAGER WITH A WET BALL

Young sister or brother,

If you find yourself this week on the same shoreline with a ball that slips in your hands because it carries the sea, count that as a gift. Set your stance. Feel your ankles speak. Slide until the pattern is clean. When you feel silly, keep going. Then go home and read two pages you didn't plan to read, and write a paragraph you didn't owe. Repeat that for a month.

Don't be fooled by the word "scholarship." It is not a lottery ticket. It is an invoice with a balance you can pay in daily currency: wake ups, reps, notes, and choices. When someone says you can't from a place like Saint Lucia, remember that a boy from Gros Islet stood in the Big Ten and then stood taller as a businessman.

When it's your turn, travel well. Then return flow.

– Bax

THE BUSINESS OF BEING DEPENDABLE

Every time I look back at an athlete to business story that worked, I find a common denominator: dependability. Coaches trust you, professors trust you, colleagues trust you, clients trust you. Dependable people are an economy's quiet engine. Jimmie joined that engine. Look at the habits again – early mornings that nobody demanded, essays rewritten after soreness, calendars kept, calls returned. That is what employers pay for; that is what communities rise on. I want Castries North full of this habit set. That's why our constituency platform keeps saying publish the schedule, finish the job. It's not just a works program; it's a culture program.

Some readers will ask: why include Jimmie Inglis in a book about Castries North? Two reasons. First, because SMC sits on our map and our boys and girls look up at those gates daily. Second, because method scales better than anecdotes. If a camp on an island can help produce a Big Ten student athlete who becomes a competent professional, then a constituency can use the same method to produce nurses, coders, welders, and teachers. We've already begun formalizing that with CN Connect and a Diaspora Skills Bank that turns goodwill into a timetable. A good pipeline doesn't care what you pour into it – basketball today, biomedical tech tomorrow. The operations are the same.

WHAT WE WILL COPY TOMORROW MORNING

We're not writing to admire ourselves. We're writing to copy ourselves. Here's the executable checklist Jimmie's chapter gives us for the next generation:

• **Beach circuits at scale:** weekly coastal footwork sessions for youth 12–18, paired with a reading sprint under a tent – ball work first hour, books next 30 minutes.

• **Error quota scrimmages:** every school team adopts a turnover cap in practice; hit the number, stop and reset; publish the trend weekly.

• **Notebook audits:** random spot checks of personal statements and study notes; celebrate clean pages like game winning steals.

• **Mentor bench:** alumni like Jimmie commit to monthly micro sessions on WhatsApp with named students; attendance tracked, topics pre set.

• **Pipeline calendar:** SAT dates, transcript deadlines, visa windows printed and posted at SMC, VBCC, and secondary schools; WhatsApp broadcast reminders three weeks, one week, and one day out.

- **Return flow pledge:** every scholarship athlete signs a one page agreement to give 20 hours a year back – clinic, call, classroom talk.

None of this needs a new ministry. It needs a schedule, a spreadsheet, and a culture that treats boring excellence as a love language.

THE PLAY I KEEP REPLAYING

I keep one Rutgers possession in my private film room the way a musician keeps a favourite bar from a concert. It wasn't a poster. It was a possession that refused panic – a pause that made the defence confess, a pass that honoured the spacing, a finish that used two feet and a steady chest, and a retreat into defensive shape as if the last two points didn't entitle him to celebration. That's the moment I knew the beach had travelled inside him. The ocean's patience, the island's steel, the school's manners – they all showed up in a single sequence and then went back to work. That is the person you want in your business, your classroom, your government, your home.

CLOSING THE LOOP: FROM GROS ISLET TO ANY ISLAND CHILD READING

What the sea taught us, the world paid for. A Saint Lucian boy trained where the tide argues with the shore, carried that argument into a giant conference, and then into a career that still respects mornings and notebooks. His story is not unique because he is magic; it is replicable because he is disciplined. That is the good news hidden in the salt: we can do this again, and again, and again – if we keep our promises small and our habits large.

The chapter belongs beside Darwin's (footwork, patience, scholarship) and Joel's (vertical leap, NAIA contention) for a reason.

Together they describe a ladder: camps that run on time, coaches who cross water, students who keep schedules, communities that return flow, and pipelines that turn rivals into allies. They also describe a kind of citizen I want Castries North to mass produce – humble, prepared, and useful. Jimmie is that kind. His beach is still teaching us. Our job now is to keep sending students to class – on the court, in their books, and then into the world.

9

Case Study: Sherman "Snake" Barthelmy (Marchand/SMC)

The morning we first set cones for Snake at Saint Mary's College, the world had not fully made up its mind to be bright. A faint line of pink sat on the ridge behind Marchand, the kind of light that turns dew into a quiet warning: move carefully. Ewan was already leaning on the fence, the way early men do, and Snake – Sherman Barthelmy – walked in with that springy calm I came to recognize as his signature. He said good morning softly, as if he didn't want to wake the day too rough, then laced and went to work. We started with base: stance, slides, two-foot gathers through touch. No music, no noise – just the sound of a young man deciding to live inside discipline. It stayed like that for months, then years. At 5 a.m., before shifts, before school, before excuses, two Marchand sons and a whistle turned a court into a life plan.

On the court, Snake was current. Not showy current – the kind that burns out and leaves a smell of melted plastic – but clean electricity, routed properly. He moved as if each step had a schematic. A last-second plant, both feet under him; a first step that didn't waste; a jumper with a release that kept promises. The nickname fit: he slipped into seams, shed contact, struck when the backside blinked. Off the court he was the opposite of an exclamation point – soft-spoken, steady, the sort of student you ask to lock up after practice because you know he'll make sure the lights are out and the gate is clasped. That contrast – current on the floor, quiet off it – prepared him for everything that came next. He was a Saint Mary's College boy who wore humility like a uniform, even when the gym wanted noise.

ONE CAMP, ONE MENTOR, ONE DOOR

By now you know how we built our ladders: precision camps that run on time; decision drills with error caps; classrooms tucked into midday; coaches who fly in because we keep our word; a pipeline maintained not by magic but by calendars. Snake's doorway sits right inside that architecture. There's a photograph from one of those camps – the one that brought Coach Kerry Dickerson down. In the picture, everything looks simple: a coach smiling under a hot Saint Lucian sun, a row of children holding balls that are too big for their hands, a court that's seen more rain than paint. The simple thing you can't see is this:

at the end of that camp, Sherman "Snake Man" Barthelmy earned a full scholarship to the United States. The door opened because the work had been moving toward it, silently, for a long time.

People often mistake the scholarship letter for the story. It's only the receipt. The story was the morning schedule he kept when no one was clapping; the way he would nod when corrected and then do the rep again without rolling his eyes; the way he carried Marchand with him – not as a swagger, but as a responsibility. Snake's gains were compound interest on small choices: finish off two in traffic; take the next right shot; trust the rotation; lock the gate; answer the message; show up again. And when the letter did come, it fit him like a well-made suit: no flex, all function.

THE MARCHAND–SMC APPRENTICESHIP

I am honest enough to admit I have favourites among drills. The uptake step into a two-foot finish is one of them: small drop, gather, rise through contact, eyes quiet on the square. Snake treated that sequence like a promise he meant to keep. It's not the kind of clip that goes viral, but it's the kind of habit that lets a player survive in February when legs feel like cement. Plenty of boys love the fast twitch. Snake loved the reliable lift.

Marchand gave him the ethic and the edge. SMC gave him the manners – the gentlemanly precision that lets you walk into rooms and be trusted beyond your first impression. Ewan supplied the persistence. "See you tomorrow?" he would say, a question shaped like a challenge. Tomorrow always came at five. That rhythm baked a seriousness into Snake's game that travelled well beyond our island.

I've told before how Washburn and Emporia rivalry matured into a recruitment corridor, how Ewan helped line up the expensive hoops at the National Sports Complex from Washburn's generosity, how one favour led to another until what we had wasn't luck but infrastructure. Snake benefitted from that road work. We had coaches who took our calls, administrators who trusted our packaging, and a camp culture that made visitors nod. The pipeline was ready; Sherman had earned his place in it.

ELECTRICITY, DIAGRAMMED

If you want to understand why Snake was "electric," stand under the basket when he drives middle. He doesn't bounce off you; he goes through the gap you give him. The electricity is not a sprint; it's a series of honest angles that happen faster than your brain is used to processing. Here's the sketch of what made it work, with elements we are now familiar with:

- **Base before burst.** He sat into a stance that kept his hips under him. The lift was a clean transfer, not a panic.

- **Angles, not reach.** His hands were patient; his feet did the defending. When he attacked, he picked the seam, not the shoulder.

- **Two-foot truth.** In traffic, two feet, window, square. Off either foot when space allowed, yes – but against contact, he respected the platform.

- **Decision ladders.** Our camps used error quotas – turnovers capped; hit the number, reset the concept. Snake learned to value do it right over do it again.

The result was a player who looked inevitable. And inevitability is a recruiter's favourite adjective, even if they don't say it that way.

THE SCHOLARSHIP – AND EVERYTHING AROUND IT

That camp with Kerry wasn't a spectacle; it was a system doing what it was designed to do. We hosted; we kept time; we showed improvement; we did classroom; we behaved. Out of a week like that, a coach gets to see more than hops. He sees how a kid listens. He sees how a kid recovers from a mistake. He sees how a kid lifts a teammate. That's how a scholarship offer should happen – not because of charm, but because of proof. For Sherman, the offer was the natural continuation of mornings with Ewan and reps with purpose. He left with a ticket to the United States and a timetable disguised as a dream.

I tell our younger players this often: a scholarship is not an escape; it is an appointment. It comes with a schedule. Pack your calendar before you pack your suitcase. Snake didn't need the lecture. He had been keeping appointments with himself at five, for years. The transition to U.S. college life wasn't easy – the cold, the distance, the accent that makes some people hear you wrong – but he had prehabbed for all of it. He carried quiet with him like a tool.

CHARACTER OFF THE COURT

The most consistent feedback I got about Sherman from teachers and coaches was some version of this: he is reliable. That word doesn't get enough confetti. A reliable person is an economy's quiet engine. Reliable people open the gym and close it right. Reliable people keep their transcripts clean. Reliable people become the reason a coach picks up the next call from Saint Lucia. On a small island, that matters more than we say. One person's dependability buys credit for the whole village. Snake paid on time.

I remember once, in the run-up to a camp, we discovered the equipment closet in a state I will politely call "tourism." Balls half-inflated. Cones hiding. Tape looking like it had a bad night. I arrived at dawn ready to lecture. Snake, not yet a star, had already sorted it: balls pumped, cones stacked, floor swept. He didn't post about it. He didn't wait for thanks. He got the tool ready so the work could happen. That's who he was in rooms without cameras.

THE DEGREE, AND THE MASTER'S AFTER IT

From the story of a scholarship, let me move to the part I love saying aloud: Sherman earned his degree at Drury University. Then he went further and completed a master's degree in logistics. Logistics is a discipline with no time for drama – inventory, routes, constraints, deadlines. In other words: a grown man's version of running an offense. I smiled when I heard his choice because the fit was perfect. The same instincts that make a wing find space and deliver on time make a professional manage systems that must behave under pressure.

Sports economics is not about turning athletes into stock tickers. It's about tracking the return on discipline across decades. A degree is personal credibility in paper form. A logistics master's is a promise to the marketplace: this person understands flow, waste, and time. Saint Lucia needs exactly that in every sector – people who can look at a broken chain and fix it. Sherman turned his craft into that competence.

THE KERRY CONNECTION – THE RIPPLE THAT KEEPS MOVING

You've heard me say that the Turnpike Tussle rivalry between Emporia and Washburn became a bridge. Bridges only matter if they carry people. Kerry Dickerson is one of the engineers of that bridge. Back when Snake's story was taking shape, Kerry was recruiting for Central Missouri. He wasn't hunting for miracles; he was looking for reliable upside. Our camps, our courts, our early-morning discipline made Saint Lucia a known quantity in his notebook. People don't say it this way, but it's true: the island had a brand. That brand helped the offer land and stick. Kerry's own career blossomed – assistant roles in the Midwest, and now the athletic director's desk at Missouri State University. He still visits Saint Lucia. He keeps the connection personal, not transactional. That is how a pipeline avoids rust.

When I talk to ministries or private partners about co-funding camps, SAT prep, or even the small works that keep a facility usable, this is what I mean by "ripple." One camp leads to one scholarship that builds one degree that returns as one mentor or one administrator or one donor who will pick up the phone the next time we need a door opened. That is economics – not a theory, a flow.

ON HUMILITY AND HEAT

It's a pleasure to write about a player who never made me manage his ego. Some talents arrive with an entourage of opinions. Snake arrived with a notebook. It freed us to coach. It created space to be specific. Turn your toe in slightly. He would. Show your hands before the catch. He would. Two feet when the bodies are heavy. He would. That's what humility looks like in a gym – not self-hate, not shrinking, but the professional willingness to adjust in public. If you want to find tomorrow's leaders, look for that trait.

There's a story the old men in Marchand will tell: a stubborn boy is a blessing until he doesn't bend. Snake's stubbornness bent toward improvement. That's why the heat of the game didn't cook him. He could carry that heat without spilling it on teammates or teachers. When the noise rose, he got clearer. That quality wins in basketball.

It wins in classrooms. It wins in warehouses and offices. It wins in marriages. It is the habit of attention under load.

DRILL BOOK: HOW THE MORNING MADE THE MAN

For the coaches, parents, and kids who ask for the how, not just the hallelujah, here's the portion of our drill book that made the most difference in Snake's development:

Foundation (20 minutes)

• Stance ladder: 6×30-second holds, knees tracking, sternum quiet, breath counted.

• Angle slides: 4×10-yard sets, hands behind back to kill reach habit; whistle on drift.

• Two-foot gathers: 3×8 reps through light contact pads, finish in the window; immediate reset on drift.

Decision tree (15 minutes)

• Drive–kick–lift: target = 0 turnovers per 10-possession block; hit 3 turnovers, stop and repair.

• Paint–spray–swing vs shell defenders; clipboards in corners to track "correct but failed" vs "incorrect but scored."

Capacity (10 minutes)

• Pogo series; depth drops into strict holds; ankle stiffness taught like grammar.

Close (5 minutes)

• Reflection: one thing learned, one thing to fix; log it; build tomorrow's rep plan from today's honesty.

This looks small on paper. It is large over years. It is how you build electricity that doesn't blow fuses.

THE UNSEEN CURRICULUM

Because sports can seduce us into thinking all improvement is physical, I stress the unseen curriculum – what we taught under the trees, over bakes, after the sweat:

- **Admin competence:** meet deadlines; check passports; organize transcripts; ask teachers early; copy documents twice.
- **Communication:** shake hands; send thank-you notes; write the personal statement like you want a responsible adult to say yes.
- **Sleep & food:** protect a bedtime; eat for tomorrow's legs, not tonight's cravings.
- **Community:** help set up; help tear down; talk to the shy child; share the drill you just learned.

Snake learned these as part of his day. That is why the next parts of his life kept working.

PROOF, NOT MYTH

Saint Lucia is a storytelling island. We deserve stories that don't turn people into perfect idols. Sherman's proof points are plain: scholarship earned at the end of a camp with Coach Kerry in our gym; Saint Mary's and Marchand roots; 5 a.m. training sessions with Ewan; degree earned at Drury University; master's in logistics completed; character that made coaches trust the next phone call; a visiting coach whose career rose to an athletic director post and who still comes back to the island. Each of those claims rests on documents, photographs, and memories shared by many, not just me. That is how we should tell these stories – as evidence that a method works.

THE RIPPLE IN REAL TIME

Let me draw a line right here, in the present, between one camp and a constituency plan. Snake's arc strengthens the case for the Castries North Connect program – formal school-to-university linkages, clear tuition arrangements, named mentors, and public timelines. The same disciplined ladder that helped a Marchand wing climb into a degree and a career can serve a choir director headed to a music program, a coder headed to a Midwest lab, a nurse headed to clinicals. The core transfer is the same: show up → do it right → package your work → keep your word. The bridge Kerry helped us build for athletes becomes a highway for scholarship across disciplines. That is the development model I will keep explaining until the cynics grow tired of me: take what already works in sports and apply it to everything else.

And if you want a reminder that bridges are human, not abstract, it's this: the same man who evaluated our boys as a recruiter now sits at a desk that can authorize entire programs. He still steps off a plane in George F. L. Charles with a smile. That's not sentimentality; that's a network kept alive by respect and results.

A LETTER TO THE BOY WITH A NICKNAME HE DIDN'T ASK FOR

Young man from Marchand,

You don't have to live up to a nickname. Make it live up to you. If they call you "Snake" because you move well, then learn to move well through every part of your day – classroom, home, street. Set a watch for 4:40, not 5:00. Arrive early enough to hear your own thoughts. When a coach tells you something that hurts your pride, write it down and turn it into a drill. Do not rehearse hurt; rehearse fixes.

Promise me three things: you will keep your transcript tidy; you will lift off two in traffic; you will return what you learn to somebody younger without waiting to be asked.

A letter will come if you act like a person who deserves one. Open it. Pack a notebook. Thank the people who ironed your shirt. And when you land far from home and the air is wrong and your stomach doubts you, remember that there is a fence at SMC where early men lean and wait – and that you are one of them now.

– Bax

THE AFTER-STORY

What I want for our children – and for their parents reading this – is to know that a chapter like this isn't an exception you admire and then move past. It is a pattern you copy. We can reproduce Snake's arc across Castries North if we honour the same inputs. In Chapter 5 we laid out the camp ladder. In Chapter 6 we showed how footwork and patience turned into a scholarship when a guard named Darwin kept his head. In Chapter 7 we watched a vertical leap at PDJSS become NAIA contention and a habit that travelled. Here, in Chapter 9, Snake gives you the link between electricity and ethics – speed that stays useful because character carries it.

So let's say it again: publish the schedule; finish the job. If you are a coach, write the turnover caps on the wall and enforce them without apology. If you are a parent, post the SAT dates on your fridge and practice your child's personal statement aloud with them until it sounds like a person you would hire. If you are a student, set your alarm and keep your feet honest. If you are in the diaspora, come home for a week and teach a drill you've learned in your field – logistics, nursing, code, carpentry, marketing. The island's pipeline strengthens every time we exchange more than affection.

GRATITUDE, NAMED

I've seen a lot of gyms. Very few generate the kind of mornings that make a man. Marchand did. SMC did. Ewan did. Kerry did. Snake did. My mother did, when a promised hotel turned into a guest room, because sometimes that's how bridges begin – on a couch you didn't plan to use but a story needed. The photo from that camp isn't just a memory; it's a map. It shows a path from a fence at dawn to a desk with an American diploma on it, to a schedule stuck on a fridge in Castries North, to a new generation learning to carry themselves in rooms where nobody knows their names yet. That is a map worth printing twice.

WHAT WE WILL COPY TOMORROW MORNING

• **5 a.m. standard:** one community court in Castries North designated for early-session access; rotating mentors; attendance logged; simple drills; everybody welcome.

• **Camp + classroom pairing:** every holiday camp includes a minimum of 60 minutes of study skill and scholarship packaging per day – no exceptions.

• **Error-cap practices:** school teams track turnovers and "incorrect-but-scored" decisions; publish weekly trend to athletes and parents.

• **Mentor assignment:** each athlete matched with a named adult (local or diaspora) to answer three practical questions a month – academics, training, logistics.

• **Return-flow pledge:** every scholarship student signs a plain one-page agreement to deliver 20 hours of mentorship or service to island youth each year – fulfilled, tracked, and celebrated.

That's not rhetoric. That's logistics – Snake's kind of language, turned into policy.

When I see Snake now, I don't see a highlight; I see a habit. I see a man who can be trusted to carry weight without dropping it. I see Marchand and SMC and Ewan and a door that opened because a camp ran on time. If you are looking for a poster boy, you missed the point. If you are looking for proof that a small island can build reliable ladders and climb them with grace, you found it. He remains, to me, what he was at five in the morning: a quiet force moving correctly through space. Electricity on the floor. Character off it. And a ripple that still reaches the shore.

10

Case Study: Jeremiah Vitalis (PDJSS/PDJSS)

The light over Marchand arrives in small squares – first through shutters, then across the lane, then finally onto the hard court that sits there like a stubborn promise. Before the sun commits, a few early walkers pass, and you hear the first echo of rubber on concrete. That was usually Jeremiah. Not loud. Not late. Not asking for applause. Just there – soft spoken, steady, ready to work. If you didn't know better, you might miss him in a crowd. If you watched five minutes of footwork, you would not forget him for years. I've said this before and I will say it again: in all my years I've rarely seen anyone jump off two feet with more clean, honest power – maybe only Yardi from VF belongs in that argument. But even that freakish two foot lift wasn't the headline for me. The headline was his humility and the way he submitted to the work.

He is a Marchand son who graduated from Vide Bouteille Secondary School in 1998 – PDJSS (PDJSS) doing what PDJSS does: shaping habits that travel. He trained relentlessly with local coaches, especially under the firm, thoughtful hand of Augi Jones. Those sessions laid the foundation that carried him across the water. My role was simple: I watched that foundation harden and then I drove him – literally – up and down U.S. highways to several campuses until a door opened and a scholarship fit the way his work had been pointing all along.

That is the plot you will find running through this book: the camps that start at dawn, the classrooms built into midday, the discipline that shows up when it's raining, and then the car ride to the next opportunity because a young man's name has to be carried from one office to another with a credible witness. Jeremiah is a proof of concept chapter for the whole plan.

MARCHAND MORNINGS, PDJSS (PDJSS) MANNERS

If you're trying to understand where his steadiness came from, start with location: Marchand is a teacher if you show up on time. The neighbourhood presses you to decide what kind of man you want to be. It does not beg; it expects. That expectation met PDJSS's brand of instruction – quiet order, a respect for simple excellence. By the time you saw Jeremiah perform a two foot gather in traffic, you were seeing years of small rules: shoulders quiet; eyes up; land ready. Those are Marchand rules, dressed in PDJSS uniform.

Augi's drills were not circus tricks. Angle slides, stance ladders, two foot truth – reps that make a nervous system honest. When a teenager will do that work without a camera, you have a chance to build a life on it. Jeremiah did it for hours, days, months. That's the only miracle we're selling here: time multiplied by attention.

TWO FOOT TRUTH – AND EVERYTHING IT HIDES

People love the highlight. What the island saw was the lift: a short gather, hips under him, then that clean rise that makes the rim look too low for once. I'll diagram the real trick because it matters:

- Base before burst: knees tracking the toes, inside edges loaded; no knee cave; core calm.
- Sequence: ankles → knees → hips – no panic, just rhythm: one two rise.
- Land like you mean to play defence: don't "celebrate land"; arrive in balance; see the floor.

That habit did not just create posters; it created possessions you could depend on in February when legs bargain with you. He embraced that boring excellence – the kind that travels well from PDJSS to the States and then further still into offices where deadlines hit like double teams.

THE DRIVE, THE OFFICES, THE YES

He came up to the States while I was in graduate school. By the time he landed, he'd done the grunt work with Augi and others at home. My job then was chauffeur and witness. I drove him to multiple universities, sat in offices, and told coaches what I'd seen: not just the bounce, but the reliability; not just an athlete, a student; not just a mood, a method.

That is how scholarships really happen – someone with credibility vouches, and the young person's preparation makes the yes sensible. Eventually, a yes came. It wasn't a miracle; it was a receipt.

The American chapter didn't pretend to be fairy tale. It came with the usual weather, the accent jokes, the administrative grind, and the test of whether your schedule runs without your mother watching. He made it run.

THE JUNIOR COLLEGE STEP AND THE BUSINESS OF LEARNING

He did a smart thing many overlook: used junior college as a bridge year and then upgraded. New Junior College in 2003; Globe Tech in 2004; a major built across business and sports management. Some will read that like a dry CV. I read it like good tactics: build capacity, then transfer; learn to be a student of markets and teams in the same breath; say yes to the classroom with the same seriousness you give to the weight room.

If you want to understand why I keep saying #SportsEconomics, look at the stack: training → scholarship → degree path → work. That's the return on discipline. It shows up first in a transcript, then in a pay stub, then in who you mentor when you have a free Saturday. That's economics in a small country – competence compounding.

ORLANDO: PROJECT MANAGER BY DAY, COACH BY WEEKEND

After college, Jeremiah built a career in construction project management in Orlando. Think about that choice. Logistics. Budgets. Timelines. People who must show up and leave a site safer than they found it. The same traits we asked for on the court – footwork, patience, decisions with a cost – now drive a workflow. That's what I mean by discipline that travels. And when the work week ends, he coaches AAU and mentors the next set – voice notes, drill plans, straight talk that tells a boy how to carry himself on a campus he's never seen. That's the loop I want to normalize: success that returns home as instruction, not just nostalgia.

If you want the simple proof, here it is: the record on him reads "soft spoken, humble, willing to do whatever it takes," then it reads "scholarship," then it reads "construction project manager," and alongside it reads "AAU coach and mentor." That is the island's economy in a paragraph – steady people sending back more than they took.

CHARACTER OVER NOISE

I've seen talented kids burn theaters down with their noise. Jeremiah wasn't built that way. The camp days that shaped him had an error quota, not a hype quota. Blow the turnover limit, stop, correct, repeat. The "repeat" is where character grows. He didn't sulk; he treated correction like fuel. One of the reasons I will carry his name into rooms is that I can trust what happens after the clap. Take the applause out of the day and his schedule still runs. That's the kind of person a coach wants to put a scholarship on and a foreman wants to put a site on.

I keep returning to humility because it keeps paying. He didn't demand the last shot in a huddle; he demanded the next right one. He didn't "want it" more than other teenagers. He respected it more than other teenagers. There's a difference.

THE SYSTEM THAT MADE THE YES POSSIBLE

If you've read the earlier chapters, you've seen the operating system: structured summer camps (court in the morning, classroom at midday), coaches who come down because our word is good, a packaging process that makes a young player legible to a university, and a witness willing to spend credibility. That corridor exists because we built it, one season at a time. It's the same corridor that carried Sherman "Snake" Barthelmy to a scholarship at the end of a camp, and that keeps our calls to Midwest programs worth answering. Jeremiah walked that corridor too – differently, quietly, but on the same beams.

HABITS THAT CROSS OCEANS

Here's a set of simple, portable rules I watched him live:

1. Win the boring reps – stance, slides, two foot gathers. It is the plumbing under your highlight.

2. Ask for correction, don't hide from it – the fastest way to a scholarship is to fix what makes a coach hesitate.

3. Make school a second sport – if you can manage pace and space on a court, you can manage time and load in a semester.

4. Keep a clean admin desk – passports, transcripts, references: competence on paper matters more than a poster dunk.

5. Return flow early – don't wait for the perfect job to give back; coach, mentor, send materials, make the call.

That's a recipe a constituency can scale.

THE DRILLBOOK THAT BUILT A CITIZEN

For the coaches and parents who want the how, not just the hallelujah, this was the scaffolding we leaned on with Jeremiah and his group:

Foundation (25 minutes)

- Stance ladder: 6×30 second holds, breath counted; coach scans knees/hips/spine for truth.
- Angle slides: 4×10 yard sets, hands behind back to kill reach habit; whistle on drift.
- Two foot gathers: 3×8 reps through light contact; finish on the window; no "lean away" allowed.

Decision tree (15 minutes)

- Drive kick lift with error quota (max 3 turnovers / 10 possessions); when we hit the quota, stop, fix the concept, reset.
- Paint spray swing versus shell defenders; clipboards in corners to log "right decision, wrong outcome" versus "wrong decision, points." We treat process over luck.

Capacity (10 minutes)

- Pogo series; depth drops into strict holds; ankle stiffness and hip sequencing taught like grammar you can speak under fatigue.

Close (10 minutes)

- Reflection sheet: one win, one fix, tomorrow's rep plan. Short, honest, executable.

Boring? Beautiful. The same approach later became a study plan – two blocks a day with a start ritual and a close ritual, one keystone topic per week, and a visible scoreboard of streaks so that consistency becomes the pride, not just peaks. Our kids deserve methods that transfer. Jeremiah is evidence that they do.

THE JUCO LESSON MOST PEOPLE MISS

The jump from a Saint Lucian schoolyard to the U.S. college system can be too wide if you pretend it isn't. Junior college is one way to build a bridge and learn America – class rhythm, weight rooms, compliance, tutors – without being swallowed by the size of a Division I or II campus on day one. There's pride in being strategic. Jeremiah's path through New Junior College (2003) and Globe Tech (2004), majoring in business and sports management, is a blueprint I insist we teach loudly to parents who only hear "D One or die." The goal is not a label; the goal is a ladder that holds your weight.

"RARELY SEEN A TWO FOOTER LIKE THAT"

I've put this sentence on paper more than once because it's still the truest thing I can say about him athletically: for two foot jumpers from our island, he is among the best I have seen in real time. But watch the order in that claim: I say it after I talk about his character. On a small island we cannot afford to teach children that their gifts outrun their obligations. Jeremiah's gift was elite; his obligations were always paid first – show up; take correction; honour the next right task.

GIVING BACK WITHOUT A TRUMPET

You know mentorship is honest when it doesn't look like a brand. His AAU coaching is that kind – weekend gyms, water in a cooler, a drill plan that makes sense, a text on results to a parent who is doing their best. He mentors like he used to train: consistently and without fuss. The payoff isn't only the next scholarship a boy earns; it's the tone set in a room when a Saint Lucian tells a teenager, "Here is exactly what worked for me, and here's what to avoid." That's clarity – the currency our children are starving for.

WHAT THIS MEANS FOR CASTRIES NORTH

Why put this story in a book for the people of Castries North? Because it's implementable. We have everything we need to mass produce this arc:

- Camps that behave like classrooms (drills in the morning; study, SAT, and scholarship packaging at midday).
- Named witness network – a living bench of coaches and alumni willing to pick up the phone and vouch.
- Pipeline calendar – deadlines posted on the school wall and blasted in WhatsApp: SATs, transcript windows, visa appointments.
- Accountability loop – simple dashboards for grades, practice logs, and service hours reviewed weekly.
- Return flow pledge – 20 hours a year from every scholarship recipient: mentoring calls, a clinic, a book drive.

This is CN Connect in plain language – knitting schools to universities with schedules and names, not just hopes – so a PDJSS child knows what month to take which step, and a Marchand parent knows who to call when a document is late. The same network that carried Jeremiah can carry a nurse, a coder, or a welder. The operating system doesn't care which app you run.

LETTERS WE ACTUALLY SEND

To the Form 5 student at PDJSS who thinks a "not yet" is a "no":

The first answer is often a map, not a verdict. Go back to the base – stance, slides, two foot gathers; grammar before poetry. Fix the small things the next coach will notice: a cleaner shot diet, a tighter personal statement, a transcript with fewer excuses. Find a mentor. Ask them to point to three holes. Fill them. If you are humble and relentless, a door opens. It always does – maybe not where you expected, but often exactly where you fit.

To the parent who wants the truth without sugar:

Junior college is not a demotion; it's an on ramp that has saved many young lives from drowning. Ask schools about academic support, strength programs, and placement histories. Ask your child for a written weekly plan. Make sure the plan has mornings in it.

To the coach who wants to help but is tired:

Run your practice with an error quota. Publish the trend. Your kids will rise to the standard you measure. Keep the classroom hour in your camp even if the budget is thin. It's the hour that changes the rest.

THE LONG GAME, COUNTED PROPERLY

We like the splashy announcement. But the economics here is quieter:

- A boy from Marchand learns to work without a crowd.
- He graduates from PDJSS (1998).
- He trains under trusted local coaches (Augi, others).
- We drive him to find a fit; he earns a scholarship.
- He leverages junior college (2003), then Globe Tech (2004), majoring in business and sports management.
- He becomes a construction project manager in Orlando.
- He returns flow through AAU coaching and mentorship.

Each line has a cash value (scholarship dollars saved, wages earned) and a civic value (trust accrued, methods taught). Our island should measure both with the same seriousness.

Darwin's chapter (footwork, patience, a scholarship earned), Joel's chapter (vertical leap welded to discipline, NAIA contention), Jimmie's chapter (beach drills to Big Ten to business), and now Jeremiah's (work ethic to scholarships to coaching) are not separate songs; they are one rhythm: show up → do it right → package the work → cross the water → come back with more than a story. If a constituency can make that rhythm public – dates on walls, mentors on lists, drills in place – then we can build a culture where our kids default to competence.

Jeremiah's quiet yeses fit perfectly into that rhythm.

DRILL APPENDIX – "THE VITALIS CIRCUIT"

- 5 minute wake: five wall sits (20 seconds on / 20 off); focus the mind.
- 10 minute base: stance ladder (eyes on the horizon), angle slides (hands behind back), drop to gather to two foot finish.
- 8 minute decisions: drive kick lift; error cap active; track "help calls" as a metric.
- 7 minute capacity: pogo hops, depth drops, push up to plank holds (teach bracing).
- 5 minute close: write one sentence on process (what made today better), one sentence on logistics (what admin step to do today – passport, transcript, email).

Run it daily for 21 school days. Pair it with a 15 minute reading/writing block that ends with a draft scholarship paragraph once a week. It's not "advanced," it's repeatable. It builds young people who can be trusted.

A NOTE ON NAMES AND GRATITUDE

This arc belongs to more than one person. It belongs to a mother who kept a uniform clean. It belongs to Augi, who demanded the boring reps and protected a boy's belief. It belongs to the teachers at PDJSS who never reduced a student to a stat line. It belongs to every coach who opened a door when a Saint Lucian walked in with an accent and a transcript. It belongs to every small donor who bought plane tickets or SAT prep books because they wanted to be useful. And, yes, it belongs to the witness who will keep driving the long miles when he believes a young man's name should be heard in a campus office. That is the work I know how to do.

THE LAST SCENE, THE FIRST NEXT STEP

When I think of Jeremiah now, I don't see a dunk. I see a man finishing a site meeting, answering a text from a teenage guard in Saint Lucia with a voice note about footwork and patience, and then getting in his car to make weekend practice count for a team that needs an adult. That is the picture of "sports economics" I'm asking us to fund with our attention and small money – because the return is exponential, but only if we make it normal.

PDJSS gave us the manners. Marchand gave us the steel. The camps gave us the method. The car rides gave us the yes. The job gave us the proof. The coaching gives the island a chance to multiply it. That is Jeremiah's chapter – quietly written, loudly useful.

11

Case Study: Jonathan "Big Joe" (La Clery)

The first night I saw the island turn on its hinge, the Complex itself seemed to breathe. The crowd pressed close, the boards trembled, and the noise rolled like surf in a storm. It wasn't just a schoolboy game; it was a standard being raised in real time. At the centre of it – long, calm, and unbothered by the swell – stood Jonathan from La Clery, the one we called "Big Joe." He did not pound his chest. He did not ask for a crown. He simply performed at a level that forced the rest of us to grow or get out of the way. That is how ecosystems change:

one competitor lifts the ceiling, and everyone else either learns to jump or learns to watch.

THE MEASURE OF A YOUNG MAN

Before the roar, before the shaking rafters, there were quiet mornings. I pushed Jonathan harder than any player I've ever worked with. He didn't complain – not to me. He did the work, again and again, until his lungs and legs learned a new language. That resilience wasn't theatrics; it was character – an inner decision that the bar would not be set by yesterday's effort.

In training, he was a note held steady. You could set a drill to his rhythm: footwork, balance, gather, finish. When he missed, he reset like a metronome. When he made, he did not celebrate; he simply jogged back to the line. Young players watched that and learned the quiet arithmetic of excellence: repetitions multiplied by years equals gravity-defying ease. Coaches watched too – and changed their lesson plans. A single competitor can make an entire coaching staff rewrite what "good" means.

WHEN ONE PLAYER MOVES THE MARKET

Sport is culture, yes – but it is also economy. The night the Complex shook, a handful of vendors sold out early. A taxi man made two extra trips. A boy who had never cared for basketball asked for a ball the next day. Teachers who thought sport was noise noticed their students wide-eyed in class Monday, still talking about the game. Principals counted ticket stubs and did the math a second time. The word spread beyond La Clery: something was happening on court that felt worth dressing for. That energy, that community spend, that relief from the week – that is sports economics in the flesh. We did not bottle it. As a country, we did not build on that momentum. And so we learned a hard lesson: the cost of neglect is not just athletic; it's economic and cultural.

But for a stretch of the 1990s, Jonathan's dominance lifted high-school basketball to a place we had not seen. He reset the island's expectations for what a teenager could do under bright lights. Once a single player shows that level here, it is no longer a fantasy; it's a template.

WHAT THE "BIG JOE EFFECT" LOOKS LIKE (ON THE GROUND)

1) Coaches get braver.

They lean into structure – proper conditioning cycles, core strength and balance early, tactical spacing late. They demand film sessions, not just laps. They teach with intent because they finally have a living example of where intent leads.

2) Training partners level up.

Every practice is a scholarship interview. The teammate guarding Jonathan today wants to be the reason he takes a tougher shot tomorrow. That hunger raises technique across the roster – closeouts cleaner, footwork sharper, voices louder.

3) Administrators invest.

When the gym fills and stays full, principals find money for rims that don't rattle, lights that don't flicker, and a bus that doesn't break down before a road game. They hire security to make families feel safe at night matches. They care, because caring now has revenue and reputation attached.

4) Communities rediscover themselves.

Parents who never met nod at each other under the same roof. A vendor at the gate becomes a sponsor for practice bibs. A quiet kid drifts toward the after-school room because the team captain told him to come. Rival schools plan better, and better planning turns into better seasons.

5) Officiating and governance catch up.

Referees feel the pressure to improve; leagues start clinics, then certifications; schedules run tighter because the public expects professionalism once they've tasted it.

This is the multiplier power of one competitor rightly placed: the presence of excellence compresses timelines. People make in six months the changes they delayed for six years, simply because the bar is now visible to the naked eye.

THE ARC AFTER THE ROAR

There's a second half to Jonathan's story, the one that begins when the crowd goes home. After his high-school run, he left the island to play at Queens College in the U.S. – proof that our courts can be bridges, not islands. Later, he built a life in Charlotte, North Carolina, managing at Mercedes-Benz. He built a family too, and that seed bore fruit: his daughter grew into one of the top goalkeepers in the SEC, standing tall in a conference where standards are ruthless. If you want a picture of intergenerational uplift, there it is – skill to opportunity to legacy.

I think often about that arc because it highlights two truths. First: sport is a credible pathway to degrees and dignified work. Second: when the pathway works once, younger players stop asking whether it's real and start asking, "What's my timetable?" That question is oxygen for a community program.

THE PART WE GOT WRONG – AND HOW TO FIX IT NOW

We failed to capture the "Big Joe effect." We let the wave break and roll back. What should have happened was simple: codify the standards he embodied into a repeatable system – league structure, coaching clinics, talent ID, academic support, and a pipeline from court to campus.

We can correct that. In Castries North, we are writing the playbook so one special athlete doesn't become an exception but a spark.

THE BIG JOE STANDARD – FIVE NON-NEGOTIABLES

1. Structure before spectacle.

Leagues must have home-and-away fixtures, certified officiating, and posted schedules parents can trust. Start with fewer games played well; expand only when standards hold.

2. Academic guardrails.

No athlete steps on court for a competitive match unless their after-school hours are accounted for – homework first, tutoring second, drills third. We publish study hall attendance the same way we publish points and rebounds.

3. Coaching clinics with receipts.

Every school coach completes a module each term (fundamentals, injury prevention, athlete psychology). Certificates are not wallpaper; they are conditions to sit on the bench.

4. Talent documentation.

If you can dunk, you can scan. We train managers to capture game clips, compile stat sheets, and maintain a cloud folder for each prospect – transcripts, references, passport, vaccinations, highlights. The "paperwork cliff" is where too many dreams fall.

5. A living pipeline.

We maintain relationships with college coaches and admissions staff the same way we maintain our courts – with care and consistency. When a player is ready, we do not start from scratch; we update a file and make a call to someone who knows our seriousness.

THE LA CLERY SOIL THAT GREW HIM

La Clery is not a factory. It is a hillside, a field, and a web of families. In recent years, that field got the lights it deserved – one sign that the community's sporting heart still beats. We will keep that inventory tight: fields, lights, fences, benches, safe access routes; we'll publish their status and their maintenance cycles so no facility slips back into twilight.

A place feeds its players. The straighter the footpaths, the safer the crossings, the steadier the training slots, the more a raw talent can choose work over wandering. The "Big Joe effect" did not come from nowhere; it came from a community that held him upright while he learned to stand taller.

RIVALS AS BUILDERS, NOT ENEMIES

I've learned to love rivals properly. Rivalry done right is a construction site, not a war. I saw it in Kansas – the way an old grudge (Emporia State vs. Washburn) turned into a bridge for Saint Lucian athletes once we decided to use competition to open doors, not close them. That's the lesson I carry into Castries North: build rivalries that build people. (And yes, the very hoops our National Sports Complex enjoyed came from those relationships – another small reminder that smart rivalry can pay dividends off the court.)

When a player like Jonathan appears, other schools should not sulk; they should scheme – quietly and productively. "How do we prepare our kids to meet that standard?" If you prepare well enough, the crowd will one day shake for you too. That's the ecosystem rising collectively.

FROM A SINGLE COMPETITOR TO A SCHOLARSHIP CULTURE

What lifts a whole island is not one young man leaving; it is ten leaving with degrees and five returning with skills and networks. We've already seen versions of this: Joel Polius exploding off two legs at PDJSS (PDJSS) before earning his way to NAIA contention; Jimmie Inglis taking Saint Lucian grit all the way to the Big Ten, then flipping that discipline into business. These are proof points that the pathway is real when the structure is there.

Jonathan's story belongs in that line of flight. He shows the first part: how excellence at home raises the island's bar. The others show the second part: how excellence abroad becomes degrees, professions, and mentoring back into the system. The loop closes when yesterday's athletes become today's patrons – coaching, funding SAT fees, reviewing applications, Zoom-mentoring after school. That is how you turn a moment into a movement.

THE PRACTICE THAT MADE THE MOMENT

For coaches and young players who want the recipe, here's the truth: there isn't one. There are only practices, repeated until they become standards. But if I had to write the outline of the sessions that forged the "Big Joe effect," it would look like this:

- Footwork before flair.

Ladders and lines. Hips and ankles. Two-footed takes. Ten minutes daily. No excuses.

- Finishing in traffic.

Pads and bumpers; finish after contact; finish off glass; finish with either hand. Count makes, not attempts.

- Balance under fatigue.

Closeouts after sprints; defensive slides that end in a controlled gather; no wild hands; nothing heroic – just clean.

- Shot diet.

Teach what a good shot looks like for each player in each situation, then hold them to it. Make the math honest; desire will follow.

- Situational scrimmage.

Start possessions at 62–60 with 1:27 on the clock; then at 48–50 with 0:38; then down three with no timeouts. Teach poise.

- Classroom film.

Ten minutes twice a week. No sound. Watch feet. Stop the video on the load, not the leap. Ask: "What did your hips say?"

You can run those sessions under an almond tree if you have to. Standards don't require marble; they require discipline.

ONE LIFE, THREE LENSES

When I speak of Jonathan, I see him in three frames.

Frame one: the competitor who forced our island to admit we could play at a higher level right here at home. The Complex remembered his nights and raised ours accordingly.

Frame two: the pathway – a young man stepping onto a plane not just to play but to study, then to work with honour, then to parent with example. Queens College to Charlotte to Mercedes-Benz is not a fantasy line; it is a stepwise plan realized.

Frame three: the reverb

His daughter in goal in the SEC, throwing herself into shots in a conference that does not forgive half-measures. That's an island echo – the sound of La Clery's work ethic bouncing off an American stadium's far wall.

WHAT OUR CONSTITUENCY CAN DO – RIGHT NOW

If the "Big Joe effect" teaches anything, it's that a representative's office can be a switchboard for standards. Here is what we'll wire in Castries North:

1. A tight school league calendar with public fixtures, real officials, and posted scorelines. Not perfect, but punctual.

2. A Coach's Benchbook – short, living guides that fit in a pocket: practice templates, warm-up protocols, concussion basics, workload charts for multi-sport teens.

3. An Athlete Files safe at the constituency office – locked, backed up, and maintained: transcripts, IDs, video links, recommendation letters. Parents can breathe; coaches can coach.

4. Quarterly clinics (conditioning, skill, officiating) with island and diaspora instructors – measured not by selfies but by drills replicated in schools the following week.

5. Scholarship packaging sprints every May and November – two weekends where we sit with families and finish what paperwork fear started.

6. Facility maintenance cycles posted and honoured – courts lined, lights tested, rails tightened, benches painted. If a bolt loosens, someone owns a wrench and a date.

7. A "Rivalry Week" that builds, not breaks – joint community service before the game; security and transport planned; a shared code of conduct; then we play like we mean it.

If we do those seven, the next Jonathan – boy or girl – won't have to lift the island alone. The system will have shoulders ready.

WHEN A SINGLE STANDARD LIFTS ALL BOATS

I'll say this plainly: the best thing that can happen to a 17-year-old team in Saint Lucia is to run into a player who exposes their weaknesses with kindness. Jonathan did that to us. His game said, "Here is what your footwork is not. Here is what your conditioning is not. Here is what your belief is not." You can resent that mirror or you can fix what it reveals.

We choose the fix. In doing so, we also choose the spillover benefits that come with a healthier sports ecosystem: better time-keeping (and thus better school-night rest), safer facilities, a stronger link between classrooms and courts, and a pipeline that treats scholarship as a community project instead of a family miracle.

A NOTE ON GRATITUDE

We talk about stars as if they leap from cliffs. They don't. They take stairs others hold steady. Jonathan climbed stairs poured by teachers who stayed late, friends who rebounded after practice, a mother who ironed a uniform, and coaches who believed repetition is love in a useful form. My role was simple: to push, to demand, and to insist that the standards he set for himself become the standards our island expects from itself.

He met that push with grace. He never gave me the satisfaction of a complaint. He gave me the privilege of watching an ecosystem rise around a boy from La Clery who turned pressure into poise and poise into precedent.

THE LAST WORD (FOR NOW)

If you want to be inspired by Jonathan's story, do not build a statue. Build schedules, rails, and routines. Light the La Clery field and keep it lit. Put tutors at tables and put names on files. Teach the next boy, the next girl, that a standard set on Friday can be met on Monday if you carry it home and do the quiet work. Then watch: the Complex will shake again – not because we found another miracle, but because we finally learned how to multiply one competitor's courage into a culture that lasts. And with that culture, we won't lose the momentum again; we will name it, fund it, and track it – until excellence is not an event but our everyday habit.

12

Case Study: Mervin Leo

There are records that fall with fireworks, and there are records that fall the quiet way – one drill, one exam, one stubborn morning at a time. Mervin Leo did it the quiet way. He didn't arrive in form-five with a gym bag full of trophies; he arrived almost late to the sport itself – nearly seventeen before he picked up basketball seriously – and then proceeded to rewrite what "late" can mean in a young Saint Lucian's life. He rose from Leon Hess Comprehensive, earned a scholarship to Queens College, broke nearly every basketball record on that campus, and left with the thing that keeps paying long after applause fades: degrees – first in Computer Information Systems, then an MBA. All the while, he pulled others behind him, designing a pathway that helped our boys and girls collect scholarships of their own. That is the pattern worth copying: performance, paper, and a hand extended back.

I knew Mervin before the headlines. Before Queens. Before "MBA." Long before that, there were those pre-dawn sessions in La Clery and Derek Walcott Square – run with Ali Coco, then meet in the Gardens, then race to make it to class at Hess for 9:30. That was our daily covenant: work first, uniform next. If you'd passed us most mornings you'd have seen nothing glamorous – two skinny boys and a ball, a little sweat on the asphalt, and a clock we refused to lose to. We were classmates; we were competitors; we were proof that discipline is not a speech – it's footsteps.

"LATE" IS NOT TOO LATE

Saint Lucia is hard on late bloomers. We like prodigies and prodigious behaviour; we're not always patient with children who find their lane near the bend. That's why Mervin's start matters. He didn't organize his teenage years around youth leagues from age ten. He caught the sport at almost seventeen – and then trained like time was a debt he intended to pay in full. Within a few years he drove through the door that so many only knock on: a scholarship to Queens College in the NCAA. There, he didn't just star – he set the standard, shattering nearly every basketball record the programme had on the books. And while scoreboards celebrated, he did something essential and unfashionable: he finished his classes, took his CIS degree, then stayed long enough to earn an MBA. That's a Saint Lucian playbook in three lines – start where you stand, squeeze what you have, leave with paper.

When people ask, "How do we scale #SportsEconomics so it isn't luck?" I point to that paragraph. It's not just that he won; it's how he won. His wins ran on rails – habits, files, deadlines, and a refusal to let a bad week become a bad path.

THE SYSTEM BUILDER

You know a model is real when it produces results for other people. Mervin didn't treat his own departure as a finish line. He turned around and built paths. The system that produced one of our island's great shot-blockers and a Division I standout, Arnold Henry, was designed by Mervin – a former national player and scholarship recipient who understood that a programme beats a pep talk every time. That's not a slogan; that's a fact written in other people's opportunities.

He organized, he documented, he mentored, he argued with the calendar and won. He packaged young talent with the one thing coaches trust more than highlights: proof – transcripts, SAT scores, references that told the truth, and clips that showed growth, not only flair. He did the unglamorous middle: visa forms, medicals, immunization cards, the checklist that kills more dreams than any defender ever did. And because he had walked the road himself, he could call a boy out when the gym was full but the homework file was thin.

This is the kind of model we must scale. If one man in Saint Lucia can turn personal excellence into a repeatable assembly line of scholarships and degrees, imagine what a constituency office can do when it treats that as a public project instead of a personal hobby.

FROM RUN-AND-GUN TO RAILS-AND-RULES

Let me tell you plainly what Mervin's method looked like under the hood – because we're going to institutionalize this in Castries North.

1) Start with the late bloomers

Don't only scout the wunderkinds. Put eyes on the sixteen-year-old who just discovered his lungs and discipline. Build a Late Bloomer Track: three sessions a week heavy on footwork, core strength, and balance; monthly check-ins on maths and English. Make "late" a lane, not a label. Mervin is living proof that a late start is not a life sentence.

2) Paper beats talk

Create a locked "Athlete File" for each prospect. It contains: birth certificate, passport scan, transcripts, test dates, two honest references, contact sheet for parents/guardian, and a link to a highlights folder that gets updated with clips labelled by date and drill. If a coach calls, you can click, not scramble. That's how Mervin multiplied outcomes – he turned stories into folders that travelled. (Our constituency office will host and maintain these files; more on that below.)

3) Academics are weight training for the mind

No one gets packaged without minimums: class attendance tracked, homework club sign-ins, and a SAT timetable posted on a wall bigger than the league fixture. Mervin didn't leave with only a handshake; he left with CIS and then an MBA. That was not an accident; it was a priority.

4) References that tell the truth

Coaches smell flattery. A Mervin-style reference reads like a coach's notebook: "Two-foot take-off strong; right hand finish softer under contact; must add left-hand wrap on baseline; grades improved from C to B in last term; never late to practice – ever." That mix of praise and precision opens doors.

5) Mentorship that doesn't expire

The worst mistake we make is thinking "placement" equals "success." The file should stay alive through the first year abroad: monthly check-ins on coursework, minutes played, and homesickness; one call from a former Saint Lucian athlete who survived winter and cafeteria pizza; a second call before exams.

That's the Mervin method, the way I saw it – tight, honest, and relentless until the student becomes the mentor.

ONE COMPETITOR AT A TIME, ONE COHORT AT A TIME

We've seen what a single competitor can do for an ecosystem (ask the Complex rafters about "Big Joe"). Mervin's impact is the complementary lesson: what a single system can do for a generation. He engineered wins that didn't depend on his presence. He helped create opportunities that outlasted his playing days. When a boy like Arnold Henry rose into a Division I force, that wasn't chance; that was design.

And the seeds for this work were planted right here at home: the morning circuits, the community courts, the relentless routine. We didn't stumble into the Americans' office by guessing – we showed up with files and film that looked like we respected their time, because we respected our own. On air, I've said it out loud: for years I've been helping young Saint Lucians get scholarships – with no ministry middleman – by organizing camps, bringing coaches to the island, and building the bridge from court to campus. Mervin was part of that first wave – my classmate, my competitor, my co-architect for standards.

This constituency needs more than sport. It needs ladders: structured after-school spaces, a clear SAT plan, visible mentors, and a paperwork machine that ordinary families can trust. Mervin's story gives us the blueprint because he did all three parts: perform, study, and build a path for others.

Here's how we convert that blueprint into public service:

THE CN-SCHOLAR PIPELINE

- Intake & ID (Month 0–1)

School coaches nominate; parents sign release forms; our office opens Athlete Files; baseline assessments in maths, English, and physical metrics (vertical, 20-metre dash, push-ups with form).

- Study Before Shine (Month 1–12)

Two weekday study hall slots at PDJSS and one weekend slot at a partner church hall. Tutors paid small stipends. Attendance is non-negotiable. We pin the SAT calendar beside the league fixtures.

- Skill Blocks (Month 1–12)

Three 60-minute blocks weekly: footwork/balance, situational finishing, decision-making. Ten minutes of film twice a week – mute the sound, watch the feet.

- Coach Introductions (Month 3–12)

Monthly email packets to a curated list of coaches: updated clips, grades, and references. No spam. Three targets per athlete. We protect our reputation by sending ready players only.

- Packaging & Placement (Month 10–12)

We sit with families to finish the money-killing details: immunizations, financial affidavits, I-20 forms, and embassy appointments. We budget for two fee waivers and one emergency top-up per cohort.

- Year-One Retention (Month 13–24)

A diaspora mentor is assigned to each placed student. Our office keeps a "red flag" dashboard: GPA dips, playing time frustrations, or mental health strain. We intervene early.

The budget is modest; the payoff is massive. The model is proven because Mervin already piloted it – quietly, effectively, and repeatedly.

THE NUMBERS BEHIND THE FEELING

Castries North lives in the shadow of rising youth unemployment and strained household budgets. That's not theory; that's daily life. When a pipeline converts one talented student into a scholarship, the family's balance sheet changes, the school's pride grows, and the younger cousins suddenly believe their own homework matters. Mervin's story is not just an inspirational poster; it is an economic instrument that moves real outcomes in a constituency like ours. (Our data dossier tracks that youth joblessness and NEET risks remain stubborn; the cheapest counter is structured after-school and credible routes to tertiary education.)

WHAT "RECORDS" REALLY MEAN

We love to say "records shattered," and it's true in Mervin's case at Queens. But I want our boys and girls to hear the other truth: the better record is the paper – CIS degree, MBA – because paper feeds you when the jumper stops falling. Mervin's brilliance was insisting on the double haul: trophies for the shelf and transcripts for the desk. That double is the whole game.

So in our CN-Scholar Pipeline, the dashboard will always show two columns – Wins and Credits. If the left grows and the right stalls, we pause sport until the books catch up. That's not punishment; that's promise-keeping. Ask Mervin what kept him afloat in winter in the States; it wasn't applause – it was assignments done and exams passed.

MERVIN'S RULES (AS I LEARNED THEM)

- Show up even when the court is wet or the printer jammed.
- Finish drills clean – no wild hands, no hero shots.
- Tell the truth on tape – post the miss and the make.
- Paper first – there's no scholarship without a file.
- Teach as you climb – take one junior to every tough session.

Those rules scale because they're cheap and repeatable. They don't depend on a new pavilion; they depend on a new attitude.

RIVALS INTO BRIDGES

I've told the story of how rivalry became a bridge – Emporia versus Washburn turning into coaches on a plane, hoops for our Complex, and doors opened for Caribbean athletes. Mervin fits that same logic. Your fiercest competitor today becomes the co-engineer of tomorrow's programme if you care more about your community than your ego. He and I – and others – learned to treat competition as a builder, not a wrecking ball.

SCALING THE MODEL – STEP BY STEP

Step 1: Appoint a Pipeline Manager

A named person – reachable, accountable – owns the calendar, the files, the SAT list, the coach contacts. If it's everyone's job, it's nobody's job.

Step 2: Build the Diaspora Bench

We pair each cohort with three mentors abroad: one academic (for study habits and course selection), one athletic (for training load and film review), and one "navigator" (for life logistics – bank account, winter coat, campus map).

Step 3: Standardize the Tools

Templates for references, a shared highlights format, and a checklist that any parent can follow. We'll print the checklist in big letters; we won't hide the hard parts behind jargon.

Step 4: Publish a Scoreboard

Placements, degrees in progress, degrees finished. Not to boast, but to prove the path works. When proof is public, belief multiplies.

Step 5: Reinvest the Returns

Ask every placed student for one thing during December break: two afternoons at the hub to speak and to help package the next cohort. Success must pay tax – in service.

Step 6: Protect the Brand

We will not oversell any prospect. If grades dip or effort slips, we say "not yet." That honesty is our currency with coaches; once you spend it, it's gone.

Step 7: Bring Government in last, not first

This pipeline runs on community, school, and diaspora partnership. When ministries want to help, great – slot them in to fund what is already working rather than to rename it.

THE EVIDENCE IN LIVES

Arnold Henry's path – system designed by Mervin. Darwin "Malvo" Joseph's finance degree and master's after a door opened through Park. Joel Polius's NAIA run born of that PDJSS explosiveness and a structure that wouldn't let him drift. These aren't isolated miracles; they are chapters in the same manual.

And the manual itself? It was drafted by runners who became readers – children who learned to hold a ball in one hand and a binder in the other.

WHAT WE'LL MEASURE IN CASTRIES NORTH

To prove the model, we'll track six numbers and publish them monthly:

1. Files opened (with all baseline documents present).
2. Study hall attendance (as % of sessions per athlete).
3. SAT/ACT completion (and score distributions).
4. Coach conversations (three per athlete minimum, with notes).
5. Placements (offers, acceptances, enrolments).
6. Retention (GPA ≥ 2.5 and staying enrolled year-to-year).

If a number dips, we say why and fix it publicly. That's how we scale trust alongside outcomes.

WHAT ABOUT COST?

A pipeline like this costs less than you think because the most expensive ingredient – belief – comes free from people who remember their own break. Our spend goes to tutors, test fees, a part-time manager, and a travel pot for a coach to see us (or for a prospect's final campus visit where necessary). We'll stand up a CN-Scholar Fund – transparent, audited, donation-friendly – so diaspora and businesses can sponsor specific line items (e.g., "five SAT fee waivers" or "one month of tutoring"). Every dollar gets a receipt and a story.

THE HOME COURT STILL MATTERS

We owe our youths safe, lighted places to train and study. That means court lights that click on every evening, a rail where steps are steep, and sidewalks that don't trip prams or seniors. Facilities are not the story, but they are the stage; if the stage is broken, the actors bleed.

(We're already keeping an inventory of fields and facilities – including La Clery's lights – so the stage matches the standard of the play.)

A WORD TO THE LATE STARTERS

If you're fifteen or sixteen and just getting the itch, you're not late – you're hungry. You are exactly who Mervin was when he decided that a boy from La Clery could live in a book and a gym and be good at both. You'll need to learn fast, listen tightly, and fall in love with repetition. Bring a notebook to practice. Ask your coach what three things you must fix before term's end. Show your teacher your study plan. And when the highlight clip looks more like footwork than fireworks, smile – you're building a game that travels.

A WORD TO PARENTS

Your child's talent doesn't eliminate the paperwork; it multiplies it. Don't be shy about the forms. We will help you. Bring every document you have to the hub; we'll scan and file. Ask us the "silly" questions; there are no silly questions when a visa appointment is involved. Please keep one promise to your child: bedtime. Sleep is a scholarship aid; late nights are a tax.

A WORD TO COACHES

Protect the brand. If you send a coach a clip, make sure the clip shows effort and the classroom is in order. If you vouch for a boy or girl today, you're vouching for the next ten who will come through your hands. Call me when you need me to be the bad cop. I will say "not yet" when "not yet" is the honest answer.

THE LINE THAT MATTERS MOST

Mervin Leo in my opinion is one of the finest student-athletes to come out of Leon Hess Comprehensive – second only to Julien Alfred. I already wrote that, and I stand by it. You could argue about who else is number two; you cannot argue with the pattern: start, surge, study, serve. That is the model. That is the scale.

THE LAST 60 SECONDS OF A CLOSE GAME

Imagine the clock at 1:00. Down one. Ball in Mervin's hands. Here's what he'd say if we turned the timeout into a town hall:

- Execute: run the set we practiced – don't invent a new one in crisis.
- Secure the rebound: if the first attempt misses, the second is ours.
- Look up: hit the open man – no heroes, just habits.
- Foul wisely: don't lose your head when the whistle blows.
- Finish: the drill is not over until the net snaps or the buzzer sounds.

Now replace "possession" with "pipeline." Replace "shot" with "scholarship." Replace "rebound" with "retention." That's the game we're playing in Castries North. We will execute. We will secure. We will look up. We will finish.

And when the buzzer sounds – when another child boards a plane with a backpack and a binder, when another degree arrives by post, when another parent cries in a parking lot because the thing they dreamed aloud has a date and a dorm room – we'll have a quiet moment, the way Mervin taught us. No fireworks. Just a tick in the Completed column, a new name on the mentorship list, and the humble work of starting the next possession.

Because that is how records truly fall in a small island that refuses to be small-minded: one disciplined life at a time, multiplied by a system that belongs to all of us. Mervin proved it. Now let's scale it.

13

Case Study: Walter "Ninja" (Park University)

The first time I spoke Walter's name to a coach in the States, my voice carried equal parts warning and respect. "There's a guy on the island who can jump higher than me and he's got a better jump shot." When you hear a competitor admit that out loud, understand: a standard just moved, and pride learned some manners. The man was Walter – "Ninja" to most – and his story is the clearest window I have into how a jump shot becomes a job, how sweat becomes software, how a court opens the door to a career where your main uniform is a laptop and a notebook.

We weren't friends at first. We were opposites across a painted line, the kind of rivals who sharpen each other with heat – shoulder to shoulder, mouth guard between teeth, no conversation until the buzzer. I respected him because I had to. He respected me because I made him. Good rivalry is a mirror; it tells the truth you can't dodge.

Years later, that same rivalry turned into a lane out. When I began bringing coaches to Saint Lucia and connecting our best youths to colleges, the first scholarship I helped secure was for Walter Eubain. We brought him up, placed him in junior college to get his feet under him, and he pushed through – degree in hand, life moving forward. That was my proof of concept: a door we could open for kids who didn't want charity; they wanted a chance.

And then came the part we should print on the wall. Through basketball, Walter earned a bachelor's in Computer Science from Park University in Missouri and became a software engineer. Sport didn't end; it evolved – discipline and pattern-recognition carrying from the paint to the codebase. That single sentence is why I keep insisting that #SportsEconomics isn't just flights and uniforms; it's degrees, professions, and whole families lifted because the pipeline held steady.

WHAT THE BRIDGE LOOKS LIKE (UP CLOSE)

Standing at the sideline you see layups; standing at the laptop you see logic. But the movements rhyme.

- **Shot mechanics → debugging.** On court you break a miss into shoulders, hips, foot placement, release. In code you break a failure into inputs, function, side effects, test. In both crafts, you learn to stop blaming "luck" and start tracing causes.

- **Film session → code review.** We used to freeze a possession at the gather and ask, "What did your feet say?" In engineering, peer review freezes a diff and asks, "What did your assumptions say?" Same humility, different artifacts.
- **Playbook → version control.** The way a team agrees on sets and counters is the same way a team agrees on branching and merges. Sloppy playbooks and sloppy repos both waste time and goodwill.
- **Conditioning cycle → sprint cadence.** You periodize training; you structure sprints. Weeks have a tempo. Discipline makes talent useful, again and again.

Walter's path proves that a youth who learns to think in sequences, accept feedback, and return the next day can survive the transition from hardwood to hardware. But transition doesn't happen by magic. It happens because a system sits under the story.

THE FACTS THAT MATTER

Let's anchor the headline before we build the lesson.

- Walter "Ninja": fierce competitor at home; the first athlete I helped secure a scholarship for after returning to the island to organize camps and connections. We placed him at a JUCO, he stayed the course, earned his degree.
- Through basketball, he earned a BSc in Computer Science from Park University (Missouri) and is now a software engineer – textbook sport-to-STEM.
- The Park pipeline is real. Frank Baptiste from Castries North went to Park University too, graduating in Finance (elsewhere noted as an Accounting & Finance double major) – one more track showing sport as an engine for degrees that employers respect.

The counsel I gave my coach back then – "this guy jumps higher than me" – wasn't hype; it was a heads-up that Saint Lucia had athletes with ceilings higher than most people imagined. What we needed was a bridge, not a brochure.

FROM RIVAL TO REFERENCE: THE "NINJA" ARC

Rivalry made us sharper; structure made us successful. I didn't just "spot" Walter; I did the boring middle: calls to coaches, exams scheduled, visas prepped, a timeline that treated deadlines like rim height – no negotiation. Those early years taught me what later became our playbook: get the athlete seen, get the academics handled, and keep the file tight.

The first placement taught the second. The second taught us capacity. And as our network deepened, the doors multiplied – Washburn here, Emporia there, coaches comparing notes, the same way Emporia-Washburn rivalry turned into a bridge that later brought hoops for our National Complex and opened pathways for Caribbean athletes. On a small island, even rivalries can become infrastructure if you treat pride as a resource instead of a religion.

Walter's leap from JUCO to Park and into Computer Science wasn't a brand change; it was a method change. Think of it like switching defensive schemes: same fundamentals, new angles. He traded box-outs for "big-O," set plays for design patterns, and learned to love a green test suite the way he once loved a green light in transition. That is the bridge: take habit from one arena and cash it in another.

SPORT ⟶ STEM (HOW CASTRIES NORTH WILL DO IT)

Walter's story is where my constituency plan meets the ground. If we want ten more "Ninjas," we can't rely on chance; we must bake the bridge into everyday life.

1) The CN After-School "Code & Court" Lab

Two rooms under one roof: tables and whiteboards for homework, laptops for coding drills, cones and bands for conditioning. We alternate rhythm – books first, drills next – so the day has both focus and release. "Code & Court" sends a message: we value your mind and your body; we'll build both. (This complements our SAT plan already on deck.)

2) The Diaspora Skills Bank – Tech Bench

Our diaspora list must include software engineers and IT pros who can Zoom in monthly to review student projects, grade GitHub repos, and give practical feedback on internships, bootcamps, and course choices. When the lesson is by a Saint Lucian in tech, youths lean in.

3) Athlete Files that include Code

Every scholarship-minded athlete gets a digital folder with transcripts, SAT dates, coach references and a link to a basic coding portfolio (Python notebooks, JavaScript exercises). Why? Because a coach who can tell an admissions officer, "This kid also builds small apps," is a coach whose email gets read.

4) Park & Friends Network

Park University is proof; we don't need to reinvent credibility. We will maintain relationships with admissions and coaches (not just in basketball). We'll add two to three partner schools with strong CS programs open to Caribbean students. We won't spam; we'll send quality.

5) A Laptop & Data Bank

Talent can write code with pencil and paper, but the world compiles in silicon. We'll pool refurbished laptops, load a starter dev environment, and partner with ISPs for education data bundles.

6) Quarterly "Ninja Sprints" (6-week cycles)

Borrowing from Walter's conversion, each sprint pairs a sports micro-goal (e.g., 1,000 quality finishes) with a STEM micro-goal (e.g., build-and-ship a small web tool). The end is public: scrimmage then show-and-tell. Winning teams are those who shipped and passed, not just scored.

7) Placement & Retention

It's not enough to place our youths; we must keep them through year one. That means diaspora mentors, check-ins on GPA, and soft-landings when the first winter bites or the first bug resists. We'll run retention like we run endgame: calm, deliberate, with options.

THE PLAYBOOK INSIDE THE PLAYBOOK: WALTER'S FIVE

For a youth reading this, here's the short version of the long story – Walter's rules, in my words:

1. Compete clean. Respect the craft enough to refuse shortcuts. Hard things done honestly become your backbone later.

2. Study like you dribble – every day. The tape doesn't lie and neither do transcripts. Keep both tidy.

3. Learn one language of the future. For Walter, it was Computer Science. For you: Python, JavaScript, or SQL – something that forces you to think in sequences and responsibility.

4. Carry a file, not a fantasy. Birth certificate, passport, transcripts, references, test dates, clips, code links. If opportunity calls, reply with a link – not a promise.

5. Transplant discipline. The same focus that made you a better defender will make you a reliable developer. Don't leave discipline in your sneakers.

WHAT COACHES AND SCHOOLS MUST DO (IF WE'RE SERIOUS)

• **Coach honesty = reputation.** If we oversell one athlete, ten behind him pay the price. Send truth in your references – effort, attitude, academic trendline.

• **School partnership** = predictability. Set aside the room for "Code & Court." Post hours. Keep them. A youth can only build a habit if you keep a door open when you said you would.

• **League standards** = leverage. Games start on time, officials trained, scores recorded. That discipline bleeds into exams and applications because the same adults are modeling seriousness.

• **Metrics = learning.** We'll publish numbers: files opened, study-hall attendance, SAT completions, offers, acceptances, first-year retention. When something dips, we fix it out loud.

"BUT NOT EVERYBODY IS NINJA"

True. And that's the point. We're not building a pipeline for one prodigy; we're building a ladder for many. Walter shows how one fierce competitor can turn sport into a STEM life. Frank shows how another can use sport to go study Finance at Park and come home with skills for the balance sheet. Between those two, a spectrum opens: accounting, engineering, data, design. Our job in public service is to make sure that spectrum isn't reserved for the loudest or the luckiest.

A WEEK IN THE LIFE OF THE BRIDGE

Monday

7:00 a.m. Clinic opens early. Parents refill meds, then drop kids at school. (Health first; everything else stands on it.)

3:30 p.m. Code & Court opens; a volunteer engineer dials in to review beginner Python exercises.

5:00 p.m. Conditioning circuit; same youths learning loops in code are now learning to keep a defensive stance without losing breath.

Tuesday

Lunch hour: guidance counsellor scans three transcripts into new Athlete Files.

After school: mock SAT. Two students nail the reading passage they struggled with last week.

Wednesday

Coach shoots film in practice, labels clips by drill for later learning.

Dev mentor shows how to debug a failing test. The room feels familiar: pause, rewind, correct. Film session in another tongue.

Thursday

Parents' hour. Fifteen minutes per family. We explain Park's entry requirements, visas, fees, and how the Diaspora Skills Bank can help with mentorship.

Friday

Scrimmage. Then sprint demo: a team shows the small budgeting web app they built to help track travel costs for away games. Not fancy – useful.

That cadence looks simple. It is. The magic is in keeping it – weeks into months into culture.

WHAT WE LEARNED THE HARD WAY

In the 1990s, Saint Lucia saw what a single competitor could do when "Big Joe" shook the Complex. We failed to build on that energy island-wide; the moment moved on. With Walter, we learned a different lesson: build files and rails beneath the talent. When we did, a jump shot funded a Computer Science degree. Structure kept the story from becoming folklore. Our constituency plan is a second chance at institutional memory – so the lift becomes habit, not a headline.

TEN PRACTICAL "NINJA" DRILLS FOR THE BRIDGE (SPORT + STEM)

1. Two makes, one miss (film & fix): record three finishes; critique the miss; re-run until the fix appears.

Code twin: write three unit tests – two passing, one failing – then refactor to green.

2. Footwork ladders, quiet hands: ten minutes of feet without the ball.

Code twin: ten minutes of typing without mouse – learn keybindings, stay in flow.

3. Shot diet chart: track good attempts vs. hero shots.

Code twin: track pull requests merged vs. rewritten – learn to choose clarity over clever.

4. Conditioning box: 30–30–30 (slides, sprints, stillness).

Code twin: 30–30–30 (read, write, review).

5. Zone break with eyes up: find the seam; don't force.

Code twin: when blocked, read docs or ask for a hint; don't hack blindly.

6. Free throws under breath control: count your beats; own your pace.

Code twin: timed katas – simple problems with calm focus.

7. Mirror rep: copy the exact foot placement of the best mover on your team.

Code twin: rewrite a teammate's solution in your style; compare.

8. Film no-sound: watch feet, not lyrics.

Code twin: read diffs without comments; narrate logic yourself.

9. Teach-back: explain a drill to a younger player.

Code twin: whiteboard your function to a non-coder – own the idea.

10. Endgame: 0:58 on clock, down one – play it smart.

Code twin: 30 minutes left in sprint, feature half-built – ship a thin slice that works.

This is how you braid two disciplines until they pull the same direction.

THE COMMUNITY'S PART (AND PAYOFF)

Parents: keep bedtime sacred, keep documents in one folder, keep questions coming. We'll scan everything and keep backups in your child's Athlete File. If you can spare two Saturdays a term, come help proctor a mock SAT or watch a crossing during Code & Court hours.

Businesses: sponsor a sprint prize that's useful (data plans, a refurbished laptop), mentor a project (POS app for your shop?), host an intern – sport kid or not.

Diaspora: give us hours, not just dollars. The hour you spend explaining arrays or resumes on Zoom is the hour a future engineer stops guessing and starts building.

Schools: keep the room open on time. Publish the timetable beside the sports fixtures and clinic hours. Predictability is dignity.

The payoff is visible. A bus stop that actually shelters, a court that lights at dusk, a room where SAT scores rise and the first Python app blinks "hello" at a child who didn't think they were "that kind of student." This is constituency work: not speeches, but hinges – small, oiled, and strong.

WALTER'S REVERB

I want to finish the way Walter finished his layups – quiet, efficient, net barely moving.

He was a rival who turned into a reference point. He was the first placement I helped shepherd, the "proof-of-bridge" that told me we could build an assembly line of opportunity from our little island. He leapt into the air and then into an industry. He showed that the same mind that reads a defender's hips can read a compiler's error. He showed that a Saint Lucian boy can walk into Park University a student-athlete and walk out employed in a field that grows while you sleep.

His journey is a message to every youth in Castries North who thinks they started too late, who thinks they're "just a baller," who thinks code is for somebody else SALCC. The bridge is real. The lane is open. We built the first posts with rivalry; we'll finish the span with routine. So here's the charge:

- **lace your shoes,**
- **open your notebook,**
- **fix one weakness this week – on court and on keyboard,**
- **bring your documents to the hub, and**
- **let's package your talent like we mean it.**

The day you ship your first app and hit your first free throw under pressure, you'll feel the same thing Walter felt the day Park became home: the island can be small, but your life doesn't have to be. And when your first paycheck arrives with your degree on the wall, do what he and Frank did – turn around and pull the next child over.

That's the economy I'm here to build: not just money earned, but ladders installed. One jump shot. One scholarship. One semester. One repo. One job. Then back to the court to teach. Then back to the hub to mentor. That circle is our real victory lap.

And if, along the way, some coach in America hears me say again, "There's a kid on the island who can jump higher than me and has a better jumper," smile. It means the bridge is holding – and the future is already walking across.

14

The Pipeline We're Building

It is clear that #SportsEconomics is not just theory or a slogan – it's a real chain of events that can carry a young Lucian from a neighbourhood court to a college campus and onward to a career. Consider how the ripple works: "a week of organized training turns into a conversation with a coach; that conversation becomes an invitation; the invitation becomes a scholarship; the scholarship becomes a degree; the degree becomes a job; the job becomes money that pays rent, then a mortgage, then a child's school fees; the network becomes a book drive, a mentorship, a business partnership, a skills transfer back home". We've seen it happen. Malvo "Darwin" Joseph went from the Soufriere court to Park University and earned business degrees; Joel Polius leapt from Vide Bouteille Secondary to an NAIA championship run; Jimmie Inglis took Saint Lucian grit to the Big Ten at Rutgers and flipped that discipline into a business career. These are not isolated miracles or lucky breaks – "they are proof points that the pathway is real when the structure is there". In other words, when we build a pipeline, talent stops being a lottery and starts being a system.

I've been both a product and an architect of this kind of pipeline. As a teenager I got a basketball scholarship that changed my life's trajectory. Years later, after my playing days, I found myself back home doing for others what my mentors had done for me – organizing youth camps, bringing international coaches to the island, and opening doors from court to campus. I wasn't sent by any ministry or driven by politics; I did it for "the love of basketball and the love of community". The results were real: "within that four-year period at St. Mary's College, I was sending people to university every year... just working". Those early efforts taught me a truth I carry into public service today: luck might spark a career, but a pipeline is built – "flights arranged, gym doors opened, scholarships packaged, host families briefed, and a WhatsApp that never sleeps when a boy needs a word". In short, a pipeline is logistics and love with a schedule taped to it, not magic.

Now, as the parliamentary Representative for Castries North (and an unapologetic basketball lover), I'm working to scale this pipeline for all our promising youth. This chapter lays out a clear vision and strategy – the rungs of the ladder we must climb – to use sport as a vehicle for social mobility and community development in Castries North and across Saint Lucia. In Chapter 5, I introduced this ladder; here we break down each rung and outline what families, schools, and my office must do to make the system work. The rungs are straightforward: Talent ID → SAT Prep → Coach Introductions →

Scholarship Packaging → Degree → Job. Each stage demands a team effort and a commitment to the values we've celebrated in these stories: grit, mental toughness, and conscientiousness (the discipline to do the unglamorous work). As you'll see, the themes from Darwin's patience to Joel's discipline to Jimmie's long-game mindset are woven into every step. Our goal is to turn exceptional personal stories into an ordinary, replicable pathway – a pipeline that any hardworking boy or girl can follow with the support of a determined community. Let's look at each step of that pipeline and the roles we all must play.

TALENT ID

The first rung of the ladder is Talent Identification – finding young people with the raw ability and the drive to pursue opportunities beyond our shores. In truth, Saint Lucia doesn't lack talent; it lacks organized ways to spot it early and develop it deliberately. Talent ID starts on the ground: a PE teacher who notices a lanky Form 2 student with good footwork, a community coach who sees a kid draining jumpers at the Vigie court at dusk, an older player who drags a younger one to 5:00 a.m. workouts. I've seen how one standout can lift those around them – when a player like Jonathan "Big Joe" from La Clery came along and "forced our island to admit we could play at a higher level right here at home," other schools had a choice: sulk or step up. The smart ones quietly asked, "How do we prepare our kids to meet that standard?" That question is the heart of Talent ID: it's about creating an ecosystem that doesn't resent excellence, but replicates it.

Identifying talent isn't just eyeballing who can score or run fast. It means spotting the traits that make for long-term success: coachability, work ethic, resilience. At our summer camps, I learned to watch not only who made the most baskets, but who was first to arrive and last to leave. I'll never forget the morning we set out cones in the pre-dawn dark at 4:50 a.m. and found two teenagers already waiting – laughing and stretching, having beaten the sun by ten minutes. One of them was Sherman "Snake" Barthelmy from Marchand. That kind of dedication at dawn told me more about his future than any highlight reel. Sure enough, one camp's chance connection (a photo with visiting coach Kerry Dickerson) turned into a full scholarship for Sherman. He went on to earn his degree and a master's in logistics – "proof that discipline is a superpower in any industry". The lesson: raw talent shines brighter when paired with grit and discipline. Our job is to find those sparks early and fan them.

How do we formalize Talent ID in Castries North? It starts with the schools and community clubs. I've launched a plan for a tight school league calendar – regular inter-school games with real officials and posted scorelines. Organized competition gives every promising player a stage to be seen consistently, not just at one annual sports meet. It also sets a standard: you can't hide in a structured league; if you have potential (or weaknesses), we will see it and address it. But beyond formal games, Talent ID is year-round. That's why our camps and clinics cast a wide net, welcoming kids of all skill levels to come learn. You never know who might show up a bit unpolished but hungry to improve. We pay special attention to late bloomers. If you're 15 or 16 and only just "getting serious," we have a message for you: "you're not late – you're hungry... Bring a notebook to practice... when the highlight clip looks more like footwork than fireworks, smile – you're building a game that travels." In other words, we see you, and we'll invest in you if you invest in yourself.

To make Talent ID systematic, we've introduced an intake process at the constituency level. It works like this:

- **Schools:** Each secondary school coach or PE teacher nominates promising student-athletes at the start of the program. We're talking about the kids who show potential on the court or field and the attitude to grow. This isn't just about raw points per game; coaches are looking for those who hustle in drills, listen to feedback, and bounce back after losses. Once identified, these students undergo some baseline assessments – not only in vertical jump or sprint speed, but also in academics (a quick check of math and English fundamentals). The idea is to gauge both their athletic and academic starting points.

- **Families:** Parents and guardians need to buy in early. When a coach flags your child as a prospect, we'll ask you to sign a simple release form and information sheet so we can start officially tracking and helping your kid. We'll create an "Athlete File" for them (more on that in a moment). Your role at this stage is to support their participation – make sure they get to practices and training on time, encourage their dreams but also their studies, and communicate with us about any challenges. If a kid needs bus money to attend an extra training or struggles with time because of chores, let's talk and solve it together. From day one, we want families to be our partners in this journey. Show up to the games when you can; your applause or even just your presence matters more than you know to a 14-year-old finding their confidence.

- **Representative's Office:** My office functions as the hub for this whole talent identification program. We open an Athlete File for each nominated student – a secure digital and physical folder where we keep copies of transcripts, IDs, medical forms, and eventually game stats and videos. Think of it as a pre-scholarship dossier that will travel with the student through the pipeline. By starting this file early, we avoid the "paperwork panic" later. If you can dunk, you can scan – meaning if a kid can perform on the court, we can certainly make sure the paperwork off the court is in order. My team also coordinates the baseline testing days (with volunteer trainers and teachers) to measure things like vertical jump, 20-meter dash, GPA, etc., as mentioned. We're essentially establishing a starting line. Finally – and critically – our office commits to being the Pipeline Manager at this stage. We have a designated officer whose job is to know the name of every kid in the program, track their progress, and ensure none "fall through the cracks" in these early months.

I often say this pipeline runs on community, not bureaucracy. At Talent ID stage, that means everyone has a job. The neighbourhood coach running a Saturday clinic at Vigie has as much to do with spotting the next star as the fancy scouting combine. A parent making sure a kid's shoes are patched up for practice is part of talent ID. A school that keeps an eye on a kid's behaviour and grades is doing talent ID – because attitude and academics are as vital as athleticism. And my office keeping a detailed spreadsheet of prospects is talent ID too, because what gets measured gets mentored.

We ask the community to help in simple ways. For example, we've enlisted local youth clubs and church groups to alert us if they see a youth with promise. We maintain a WhatsApp hotline for tips – "Hey, Bax, there's a tall girl in Form 3 at Gros Islet who rebounds like crazy, someone should check her out." We will check her out. If she's the real deal, we'll get her into the pipeline. We refuse to let even one worthy talent slip by just because they weren't at the "right" school or known to the "right" coach.

Talent ID is the foundation of everything that follows. It's the most inclusive step – cast the net wide, err on the side of giving a kid a chance. Because the truth is, you can't predict perfectly at 14 who will make it big. Some stars burn out; some late-comers surge ahead. So our philosophy is: identify many, invest in those who commit, and watch who rises. And remember, talent isn't just physical. A sharp mind, a strong character, a team-first attitude – those qualities make a coach say "I want that kid in my program" just as much as a 40-inch vertical. We've seen it: a player who "meets your eyes with a firm 'Yes, Coach'" will often go further than one who merely dazzles and drifts. So we teach our scouts (formal and informal) to look for grit and coachability. A boy who loses a game but stays after to put up extra shots, or a girl who claps for her teammates even on the bench – that's talent, too.

Finally, talent identification is not a one-time event; it's continuous. Every school term, every summer camp, every neighbourhood 3-on-3 tournament is another chance to find the next prospect. We keep the door open. And to every young athlete out there dreaming of an opportunity: help us find you. Work on your game, yes, but also work on your attitude and your grades so that when we come looking, we see the complete package in-the-making. I often advise young players: "Get a witness. Play hard enough, long enough, that someone credible will drive to a coach's office and put their name on your name." If you do that, believe me, we will notice – and we'll get to work on the next rung of the pipeline.

SAT PREP

If talent is the engine, academics are the fuel. No matter how high you can jump or how sweetly you shoot, a college scholarship will evaporate if you can't qualify academically. The second rung of our pipeline – SAT Prep (and academic reinforcement broadly) – is about making sure our students are scholarship-ready in the classroom. This is where grit meets the grind of books and exams. It's also where many dreams have faltered in the past. We're here to change that, systematically.

Let's start with an uncomfortable truth: for years, plenty of Saint Lucian athletes with college-level talent didn't make it to campus because of grades or test scores. I nearly fell into that trap myself. As a young man, I had to attend summer school four years in a row to keep my GPA up while playing ball. I've joked that I majored in humility in those summers, but it's not really a joke – it taught me that "talent without schedule is noise; dreams without a ladder are tricks". The ladder for a sports scholarship has academic rungs at every step. We won't let our kids skip them.

The plan is straightforward: as soon as a student is identified as a prospect, we throw academic weight behind them. In practice, this means structured study time, tutoring resources, and a focus on standardized tests like the SAT (and CSEC/O-Levels where relevant). At Castries North we are establishing the CN SAT Academy, a program that gives our student-athletes the tools to compete academically with peers from anywhere. We schedule "two weekday study hall slots at Vide Bouteille Secondary and one weekend slot at a partner church hall" for the cohort. These are supervised sessions where homework gets done and extra drills in math and English take place. We pay small stipends to qualified tutors to be there – investing a few dollars to make sure no one is falling behind in algebra or essay writing. Attendance is non-negotiable: if you're in the pipeline, you will show up to study hall, just as surely as you show up to practice. We literally "pin the SAT calendar beside the league fixtures" on the notice board. That symbol matters – it shows that test dates are just as important as game dates.

It's crucial that everyone – families, schools, and my office – treats academic prep not as a box to check but as the make-or-break factor of the pipeline. We have a saying: "The scholarship pipeline is not a dunk contest; it's an application process." A kid who can windmill dunk but can't write a coherent personal statement is not going to get very far. Conversely, a kid who has decent skills and can also nail a respectable SAT score and write a thoughtful essay will find doors opening. One coach told me plainly, "Class is not a break from basketball; it is the reason coaches recruit you without fear." Coaches need to trust that if they give a Saint Lucian kid a scholarship, he or she will survive the college coursework. We intend to give them that confidence in every one of our students.

Here's how we break down responsibilities in the SAT Prep stage:

- **Families:** Your role is to set the right environment and expectations for academics at home. In practice, it means simple things with big impact. Enforce a regular study routine – even on days without formal study hall, your child should have quiet time to read or revise. Limit distractions, especially on weeknights; if there's one less party or community "lime" your teen attends because they're preparing for an exam, that's a worthwhile trade. Also, please keep one sacred promise: bedtime. I tell parents bluntly, "Sleep is a scholarship aid; late nights are a tax." If your son or daughter is up at midnight on TikTok, they are robbing their own SAT score. So help them develop disciplined sleep and study habits. Another ask: engage with their academics actively. Ask about homework. Show up at PTA meetings if you can. Even if you never took the SAT yourself, show interest in the prep books or the vocabulary they're learning. Your moral support can steady them when the pressure mounts. And don't be intimidated by the process – "Your child's talent doesn't eliminate the paperwork; it multiplies it. Don't be shy about the forms. We will help you... Ask us the 'silly' questions; there are no silly questions when a visa appointment is involved." In short, be present and proactive. We, as a community team, have your back on the technical stuff, but we need you to stay in the loop and ensure your child doesn't slack off or panic in the academic arena.

• **Schools:** The schools in Castries North are the academic training ground for our athletes. We're working with principals and teachers to integrate our pipeline students' needs into the school system. For example, Vide Bouteille Secondary has agreed to host the weekday study halls on campus, making it easy for students to transition from classes to extra study. Schools will also help us by providing progress reports – if a pipeline student's grades in a subject start slipping, we want to know immediately so we can intervene with tutoring or mentoring. I've also proposed an idea of publishing "study hall attendance the same way we publish points and rebounds". Imagine a bulletin that not only shows the top scorer of the week, but also which students have perfect study attendance. It sends a clear message: academics and athletics live together. Schools are embracing this because it ultimately makes their academic outcomes better too. Additionally, schools can align their curriculum or extra classes towards test readiness – for instance, organizing an SAT math review session open to all Form 5 students. We aim to synchronize the school calendar with the pipeline calendar: if SAT is in March, the term before is heavy on prep. And crucially, no student in the pipeline should miss their exam registration – school admins will coordinate with us to ensure every eligible athlete registers for the SAT/ACT on time (and we'll cover fees if needed). Lastly, I'm asking schools to enforce a rule: no play without schoolwork. If a kid is cutting class or failing, they don't step on the court until it's fixed. This "academic guardrails" approach (homework first, drills second) sets a firm expectation that the "student" in student-athlete comes first.

• **Representative's Office:** My office will coordinate the CN SAT Academy logistics and resources. We budget for test prep materials, from books to online programs, and even simple things like extra notebooks and pencils for our study halls. We also cover SAT fees or CXC fees for families that can't afford them – money will not be the reason a kid skips the SAT. We recruit and pay the tutors (some are local teachers making a little extra, some are diaspora volunteers doing video sessions). We set score targets for each student based on the requirements of the scholarships we might pursue. For instance, if Emporia State needs a 1050 on the SAT for admission, we'll make sure the student and their support team know that number and aim for it. My office also maintains the calendar of all key academic dates – exam registrations, result release dates, application deadlines – and, as part of what we call the "pipeline calendar," we blast reminders in WhatsApp groups and community boards. One method we use is the Pipeline Calendar Method: publish every important date on the school wall and WhatsApp – "SATs, transcript windows, visa appointments" – and send reminders 3 weeks, 1 week, 1 day out. That way, no one can say "I didn't know" when a deadline passes. Additionally, the rep's office coordinates CSEC reinforcement. Many of our prospects still need to get good CSEC passes (O-Levels). We arrange extra lessons for critical subjects like Math and English if needed, because a scholarship might hinge on those grades too. Finally, we make the academic progress visible to all stakeholders: we track scores and improvement. If a boy's SAT practice test jumps from 900 to 1050, we celebrate that like a game victory, because it is. And if anyone's scores stagnate, we bring in help or new tactics – maybe a one-on-one tutoring for reading comprehension or a peer study group pairing a strong student with a weaker one. In summary, my office treats the academic side with at least the same seriousness as the sports side – probably more. As I often remind everyone: a degree is the true trophy we're after, and the road to it is paved with textbooks, not just basketballs.

The beauty of focusing on academics is that it creates options. Not every talented athlete will go pro in sports, but every one of them can earn a diploma or degree that opens professional doors beyond the court. When I tell the story of Jimmie or Mervin or Joel, the crescendo isn't that they scored points in college – it's that they earned degrees and launched careers. Jimmie's "long game" led him to a master's and a business career. Mervin Leo started serious training late but still broke records at college and came home with an MBA to complement his athletics accolades. They made it because, alongside every wind sprint and jump shot, they hit the books. This is why I say a disciplined practice can turn into durable opportunity – because the discipline an athlete learns (early mornings, repeated drills, attention to detail) is the same discipline that aces exams and nails job interviews. In one of our case studies I put it plainly: "the discipline of sport, when harnessed intentionally, transfers into the discipline of study and then into the discipline of work." SAT Prep is where that transfer begins in earnest. We're teaching our youth that grit is as much about grinding through algebra problems as it is about going to the limit on the court. Mental toughness means facing down a tough exam the way you'd face a tough opponent – with focus, practice, and confidence. And conscientiousness? It's turning in every assignment, keeping a planner of study tasks, and yes, treating "sleep as part of the workout" so your brain is sharp.

By the time our pipeline athletes reach the actual SAT exam day, they will have taken multiple practice tests, reviewed their weak spots, and walked into the exam hall knowing that an entire community has their back. We even plan to have a little ritual: the night before the SAT, our office will host a pizza and pep talk session for the cohort – feed them, ease their nerves, remind them of breathing techniques, and enforce that early bedtime. And on test day, they'll find a small motivational note in their pencil case (prepared by us with their parents' help) saying something like, "You've got this – your hard work will pay off."

The result we're aiming for is not that every kid gets a perfect score; it's that every kid gets a good enough score to qualify for opportunities and that none of them are surprised by the test. We demystify it, drill it, and execute it. Just as in basketball we practice a play until it's second nature, we want our students to handle an exam like it's just another drill they've mastered. When we do this right, here's what happens: A coach sees a player's highlight tape and is interested; the first question is often, "Can he handle the academics?" – and we will be ready to answer with transcripts, test scores, and a confident yes. That leads us to the next stage of the pipeline: making those all-important introductions to the coaches and programs that could be our students' ticket to a degree.

COACH INTRODUCTIONS

If we've done the first two rungs right – identified real talent and fortified it with academic readiness – we earn the chance to stand at the door of opportunity and knock. Coach Introductions is the third rung of the pipeline, where we connect our athletes with college coaches and recruiters. It's the step that turns local potential into international opportunity. But it's also a step that must be handled with great care, professionalism, and credibility. We're not just showcasing a player; we're putting our reputation as a community on the line each time we recommend a Saint Lucian athlete to a college program.

I learned how crucial credibility is back in my Kansas days. A bitter rivalry between my college (Emporia State) and another (Washburn) unexpectedly blossomed into a bridge for Saint Lucian athletes. My friend-turned-ally Coach Kerry Dickerson (the former rival) became one of our biggest pipeline supporters. Why? Because over time he saw that when Marcellus St. Rose (or "Bax") calls about a kid, that kid is prepared. "We chose to build something useful: a network of coaches and administrators who trust our word, our camps, and our kids," I wrote earlier. That trust is gold. It "lets you ring a coach, speak a name like Joel's, and be heard as more than a salesman." We have that now – a Kansas corridor of coaches, and an expanding network beyond, who will take our call. But we must earn it again and again with every introduction.

In practical terms, Coach Introductions involves packaging and presenting our athletes to the programs that fit them well. It's not a one-size free-for-all or a spam-a-thon of highlight reels. It's targeted and relationship-based. Here's how we operate:

• **Representative's Office:** My office acts as the switchboard and curator for coach outreach. We maintain what I call a "living pipeline" of contacts. That means we keep in touch with college coaches, admissions officers, and athletic directors at various institutions – some in the U.S., some in Canada, even a few in other regions open to international students. We update them periodically on what's happening in Saint Lucia. They know that if they get an email or WhatsApp from us, it's worth a look. As one section of our plan states, "We maintain relationships with college coaches and admissions staff the same way we maintain our courts – with care and consistency. When a player is ready, we do not start from scratch; we update a file and make a call to someone who knows our seriousness." This sums it up. Because we've been preparing that Athlete File since Talent ID, when it's time to introduce a player, we have all the materials ready: game clips, stats, academic records, personal statement, references – even a scanned copy of their passport if needed. We typically prepare an email packet each month for each rising prospect: a short intro, a link to a highlights video (compiled and updated with their latest games), a one-page profile with grades and test scores, and perhaps a quote from a coach or teacher attesting to the kid's character. We never mass-send these. Instead, we identify maybe three target schools per athlete to approach (often based on academic fit, level of competition, and scholarship availability). Our office basically plays talent agent and admissions counsellor in one – but as a public service, not for commission.

- **Schools/Coaches (Local):** The local school coaches and club coaches remain very much involved here. They help my office identify which programs might suit a particular student. For example, a PDJSS coach might say, "This boy is good, but he's probably better suited for NAIA or junior college first than NCAA Division I," and we'll tailor our outreach accordingly. The schools also provide references – a principal's letter about the student's leadership, or a teacher's note about their academic commitment can carry weight in the recruiting process. One thing we insist on is honest filming and stat-keeping. At this stage, every game the student plays is essentially an audition. So we train team managers or younger assistants to capture game film and compile stats for each prospect. There's a saying in our program: "If you can dunk, you can scan," meaning we won't accept that a kid has great highlights but no academic or personal info on file. We ensure everything is documented. Schools make sure to promptly fulfil transcript requests and certify things like class rank or upcoming graduation dates, because when a coach is interested, they often immediately ask for official documents. Additionally, if a coach wants to speak to the current coach, our local coaches step up. It's not unusual for, say, Coach Tony from SISSS to be on a call with a college coach from Kansas, answering questions about a player's attitude or coachability. We prep our local coaches for those calls – reminding them to be candid about both strengths and weaknesses. Credibility is key: if a student struggles to go left or has a temper issue that they're working on, we'd rather the coach hear "he's improving his left hand and learning to channel his emotions" than to pretend the kid is flawless.

- **Families:** For the family, this stage can be both exciting and stressful. Your son or daughter might suddenly be emailing daily with a coach from abroad, or entertaining several options. We guide families on how to communicate and what to expect. Number one: keep your child grounded and truthful. No embellishing their stats or making promises. We've taught the students that as well – "tell the truth on tape – post the miss and the make" is one of Mervin's rules. That honesty extends to conversations. If a coach asks a player, "What are your grades like?" we've coached them to answer honestly and positively: e.g., "I'm a B student in math, working with a tutor to make it A; I got 1100 on the SAT and aiming higher next try." We ask families to reinforce this honesty. Also, be responsive: check your email and WhatsApp frequently. Opportunities can move fast. If a coach plans a trip to St. Lucia or wants your child on a Zoom call, try to accommodate it. We know it's a lot – suddenly discussing travel, and college, and money – but lean on us for help. We will sit with you to draft emails, prepare for interviews, even tidy up the living room if a coach is visiting your home! The main ask is: trust the process and keep communication open. If you have concerns (like safety at a particular school, or the area of study your kid will pursue), voice them. We have likely encountered these questions and can provide perspective. Lastly, families can help by being hospitable: when coaches visit the island to scout, we often ask families to join for a friendly meal or gathering. It helps the coach see the support system behind the player. It humanizes the whole process – this isn't just a recruit, it's someone's beloved child and a product of a caring community.

A key part of Coach Introductions is "protecting our brand." Over the years, Saint Lucia's reputation in some coaching circles has become that of a place to find hidden gems who, once properly prepared, turn out to be excellent student-athletes. We want that reputation to grow. So we never oversell a player just to get them off the island. If an athlete isn't quite ready – be it athletically or academically – we will say "not yet" and hold off on pushing them to colleges. I've told local coaches: "If you send a coach a clip, make sure the clip shows effort and the classroom is in order. If you vouch for a boy or girl today, you're vouching for the next ten who will come through your hands." That is a serious responsibility. If we hype up an unprepared kid and he washes out, the door might shut for others behind him. So we adhere to the rule: honesty is our currency with coaches. We'd rather delay a student's recruitment by a year than send them off half-baked and burn a bridge. This sometimes means having tough conversations. I've had to look a talented teenager in the eye – one who was sure he was U.S.-bound next month – and say: "We need another year; higher grades; better film; real conditioning. Real love does not lie." Those moments are hard, but they are part of pipeline maintenance. The kids usually take it to heart and come back exponentially stronger, academically and athletically, because they know we're right. And when we do make the introduction, it lands.

To give you a picture of what success looks like at this stage, let me recall two quick stories:

• In Darwin's story where I sat in Coach Claude English's office to pitch him. That was pure relationship capital at work – Coach English knew my word was solid. One conversation changed a life because the introduction was backed by trust and truth.

• Second, a kid from Soufriere we'll call Ed. We spotted Ed at a community game – tall, skinny, raw but eager. We took him under our wing, and by the next year we thought he could make it. Instead of sending video only, we funded a campus visit trip: brought Ed up to the States, visited five colleges, let him meet coaches face-to-face. He ended up with multiple offers, chose Emporia State, and got his degree (he even tried for my shot-blocking record there). This was a more resource-intensive approach, but it shows we'll go the extra mile – literally – when a personal touch is needed to secure a scholarship. My office is budgeting modestly for things like "a travel pot for a coach to see us, or for a prospect's final campus visit where necessary." Not every recruitment will justify it, but knowing it's an option can seal a deal in borderline cases.

Now, on the structural side, I want to mention one of our innovations: the Athlete Files safe at the constituency office. We touched on it in Talent ID – we open a file for each prospect – but by the Coach Introduction stage that file is fat and vital. It contains everything: transcripts, certificates, a copy of their passport, immunization records, SAT scores, the works. We treat those files like gold. They are locked, backed up digitally, and maintained with updates as students progress. This means when a coach says "I'm interested in Jane Doe, send me what you have," we can reply immediately with a tidy package. It spares the parents from desperately searching for documents in the attic or the school admin from rushing a transcript. As I like to say, "Parents can breathe; coaches can coach." We handle the admin so the focus stays on opportunity.

Coach Introductions is also where we leverage the diaspora and alumni networks. Many of our past scholarship students – once they're in the collegiate system – become informal scouts or at least connectors. They alert us: "Coach, our team needs a forward next season, any Lucians coming up?" or they help host a visiting youngster. It's beautiful reciprocity: those who benefited reach back to pull others through. Even coaches who have come to love our island contribute. We've had visiting coaches from the U.S. come run clinics (like Kerry, Ron Slaymaker, Stan Kesler in the past). When they return home, they often put in a good word about Saint Lucian players to their colleagues. There's an anecdote I cherish: our island's pipeline success got so visible in Kansas that some colleges started hosting a "Caribbean Night" at games to celebrate the connection. Imagine that – what began as a couple of rivals doing a favour turned into an established corridor sending multiple athletes abroad.

At this stage, mental toughness and character start to play an even bigger role. We prep our kids that when they talk to coaches or visit campuses, they are under a microscope. This is where all those lessons about comportment, eye contact, and speaking confidently pay off. I remind them: "the highlight dunk isn't what gets you there; it's the huddle at day's end, everyone on one knee, sweat on the floor like chalk dust, the future standing politely in the doorway waiting for us to open it". In other words, coaches notice the little things – did the kid shake hands and say "thank you" after the workout? Does she listen when corrected? Does he seem arrogant or team-oriented? We emphasize these soft skills relentlessly in our camps so that by the time an introduction happens, our athletes naturally present themselves as humble, hungry, and disciplined young men and women.

By the end of this Coach Introduction phase, our goal is to have one or more solid offers or ongoing recruitments for each student in the pipeline. The ideal scenario is having a choice – maybe two scholarship offers to compare. That's not always in our control, but we aim for it. At minimum, we strive that every student who has stuck with the program and met the academic requirements gets at least one placement, whether it's a full athletic scholarship, a partial scholarship combined with financial aid, or even placement at a school that offers in-state tuition through an agreement (like the one we secured with Washburn University). We've negotiated pathways such as allowing Saint Lucian students to pay local tuition rates abroad, which is a huge financial break. All these levers – relationships, reputations, agreements – come into play to create opportunities.

With a foot in the door thanks to a coach's interest, we move to the next critical stage: turning interest into an actual scholarship and enrolment. That's where the paperwork and persistence of Scholarship Packaging come in.

SCHOLARSHIP PACKAGING

This is the nitty-gritty, nuts-and-bolts stage that often goes unsung: Scholarship Packaging and Placement. It's not as flashy as hitting the game-winning shot, but without this work, the game never even happens. This is where we gather every piece of paper, navigate every bureaucratic hoop, and do everything humanly possible to turn a verbal "you're on our radar" from a coach into a tangible acceptance letter and scholarship award. In many ways, Scholarship Packaging is the most administrative rung of the ladder, but it's also where a lot of good initiatives fall apart for lack of follow-through. Not on our watch. If we've guided a student this far, we will shepherd them (and their family) through the final maze of forms, fees, and formalities.

I often describe this stage as converting a great story into a contract. We celebrate a "Signing Day" photo when a student commits to a college – but what led to that moment? As I wrote earlier, "In public we celebrate the signing day photo. Privately, the work is mail and meetings: FAFSA forms, transcripts, visa appointments, housing deposits...". It's hours of painstaking form-filling, phone calls to admissions offices, checking and re-checking that nothing is missing. The difference between a story that finishes (with a degree) and one that fades away is usually this system of support at the Scholarship Packaging stage. We are building that system so no one is left to "figure it out" alone. Here's what happens during Scholarship Packaging, broken down by stakeholder:

- **Representative's Office:** We coordinate a comprehensive, step-by-step checklist for each student's placement. Think of it as a personalized project plan that starts the moment a student gets a positive signal from a college. It includes everything: application form submission, scholarship application (if separate), financial aid forms (like FAFSA for U.S. schools), exam score submissions, transcript sending, passport renewal if needed, student visa process, booking flights – everything. My office team essentially becomes a temporary administrative assistant for the family. We hold what we call "scholarship packaging sprints" twice a year (typically May and November, aligning with when most admissions are happening). These are weekends where we invite all pipeline families who are in the application stage to come to a central location (our office or a school computer lab). We figuratively and literally roll up our sleeves and sit with families to finish the paperwork that fear might have started but not completed. Lines like passport forms or visa appointments can be intimidating; we fill them out together. If a mother is shy about an online form, our staff will type while she provides the info. We double-check every document: birth certificates, exam certificates, medical records for immunizations (some schools require proof of shots), bank statements for visa proofs of finance – we make a list and ensure there's a checkmark next to each. Part of our budget includes covering specific costs at this stage: "two fee waivers and one emergency top-up per cohort". That means if a student needs an application fee paid or a test score fee sent, we handle it. The "emergency top-up" is maybe a last-minute $200 needed for a housing deposit or an extra suitcase – basically a small fund for unexpected needs. We also help families navigate any scholarship packaging from the school's side: often a coach will arrange an athletic scholarship letter, but maybe the student needs to sign and return it by a deadline; we ensure that happens. If there are external scholarships or government scholarships available, we help fill those too. Our guiding mantra here is that no deserving Castries North student will miss out on an opportunity due to paperwork or logistics. If I have to personally drive a parent to the embassy for a visa interview at 6am, I will (and I have done similar in the past).

- **Families:** For families, this stage can feel like drowning in forms. It's stressful – you're thrilled your child got an offer, but then comes the avalanche: university acceptance packets, immigration requirements, medical check-ups, endless signatures. We urge families: do not panic; we are in this together. Your main job is to gather and provide information. Find those documents (birth paper, exam results, etc.) and bring them to us. "Bring every document you have to the hub; we'll scan and file," I tell parents. That's right – we digitize everything for them so it can't go missing. Also, families must be honest and thorough. Don't hide or sugar-coat anything on forms; if your income is low, that might actually qualify the student for more aid. If a question confuses you, ask – as I said, there are no silly questions in this process. We also ask families to be vigilant about deadlines – which we, in turn, are reminding them of. For instance, student visa appointments: the U.S. Embassy might have limited slots, so once you have your I-20 form (a document from the school for visa), you need to act fast. We encourage parents to apply for the passport early on (during Talent ID stage we actually flagged whose passports are expiring, etc.). Another piece: financial planning. Even on a full scholarship, a student might need some initial money for airfare or dorm supplies. We sit with families to budget for this, but we ask them too: try to save something, rally family support if possible, start a little fund for your child's departure. We've seen communities hold a BBQ fundraiser to buy a plane ticket for a student – that's the spirit we love. If your child's scholarship is partial and requires some family contribution, be upfront about what you can or cannot do; we will look for gap funding, but we need clarity. Lastly, once all the formalities are done, families should focus on the practical send-off: luggage, clothing for cold weather (for those headed to winter climates!), etc. And importantly, talk to your child about independence. No form covers things like doing laundry or cooking simple meals, but those are life skills they'll need abroad. We have some orientation for that, but family advice and reassurance goes a long way. In short, at this stage your support turns into project management of sorts – checking off tasks, making sure your child is prepared for Day 1 in a new land. It's hectic, but joyous hectic.

• **Schools:** The student's current school plays a behind-the-scenes but critical role here. They must swiftly provide certified documents – final transcripts, proof of graduation, recommendation letters on official letterhead, etc. We've had instances in the past of transcripts being delayed and nearly costing a visa date. So we have arrangements: the Ministry of Education and school principals know that any pipeline student's document requests are priority. We often hand-carry sealed envelopes from a school to the DHL office to send to a foreign university. Schools also often have to fill out portions of student-athlete forms, like confirming the student's status or that they aren't on academic probation, etc. We ensure the schools are aware and they do it promptly. Moreover, many schools hold send-off ceremonies or recognition for students who earn scholarships –

that's a nice morale boost and encourages younger ones. Schools can also store any belongings if needed, or help coordinate with alumni networks (some schools have past students abroad who can look out for the newcomer). One forward-thinking measure we use: We ask schools to post a list of all required documents and deadlines on their bulletin board for any child aiming for college. This transparency holds everyone accountable. Essentially, the school is the springboard and it must ensure the student jumps with all the necessary velocity (documents and preparation) into the next phase.

A crucial aspect of Scholarship Packaging is the student's involvement. Up to now, we and the adults have done a lot for them. But I believe in doing things with them, especially at this age. So we require the students to attend those packaging sprint sessions too. They need to understand the process – after all, this is their life. We have them fill out their portions of forms (with guidance), write their own personal statements or application essays (with feedback from us, but it must be their voice). This does two things: it builds their sense of responsibility and it teaches them skills. When they need to apply for internships or jobs later, they'll know how to navigate paperwork because they've done this. It's also a test of their conscientiousness: will they show up with the documents, will they follow through on tasks? Most do, because by this stage they're highly motivated – they see the finish line ahead.

Let me highlight the story of Mervin Leo's cohort as a model of this stage. Mervin, whose journey we chronicled, was part of a generation of players who "engineered wins that didn't depend on his presence… opportunities that outlasted his playing days". He and I and others built a system where, for example, when Arnold Henry (another talented player) got a scholarship offer, we all rallied to handle the paperwork by design, not by guesswork. We marched into the Ministry for transcripts together, we filled forms together. As a result, Arnold made it to a Division I college. Nothing was left to chance. Design beats guesswork every time in this process. Mervin's influence was so strong we dubbed our formal plan the "CN-Scholar Pipeline (built in Mervin's image)". That blueprint explicitly calls for exactly the actions we're discussing: intake, study support, coach emails, packaging, and then monitoring. It's not theory – we pulled it from real life examples that worked.

One more unseen hurdle at this stage is mental and emotional preparation. Getting the paperwork done is one thing; preparing a young person to actually leave home and thrive is another. We therefore include in our pipeline a sort of orientation. In those last weeks, we cover topics like "Living in a Dorm 101" or "Dealing with Culture Shock." We assign each outgoing student a diaspora mentor – typically a St. Lucian living near their college or at least in the same country – to be a phone call away if they run into trouble or just loneliness. As part of "Year-One Retention" planning, "a diaspora mentor is assigned to each placed student. Our office keeps a 'red flag' dashboard: GPA dips, playing time frustrations, or mental health strain – we intervene early.". This actually bridges into the next section (Degree completion), but it starts here: before the student even leaves, we line up that safety net. I often personally brief the mentors on each student – "Hey, this is a quiet kid, check on him if he doesn't call" or "She might need help buying winter clothes, can you assist?" – and they do, gladly. The Saint Lucian diaspora is one of our greatest assets. We have former students turned coaches, professionals, etc., abroad who are eager to guide the next wave. In packaging, we make those handoffs.

By the end of the Scholarship Packaging stage, if all goes to plan, the student has: an admission letter, a scholarship letter detailing the financials, a student visa in their passport, a plane ticket, and a clear idea of what happens on arrival (who's picking them up, where they will stay, etc.). We essentially consider the pipeline a success only when that student is physically on campus, registered for classes. There's a lot that can go wrong in the final stretch – I've seen flights get cancelled or a family emergency flare up – but we stay vigilant until the handoff is complete.

It's a community victory every time a scholarship gets "packaged" and a kid boards that plane. I've seen parents cry tears of joy and relief in the airport parking lot after sending off their child, because what was once a distant dream is now real. Those moments are powerful. But as I often remind my team, that departure is not the end of the story – it's the end of a chapter. The next challenge is ensuring that scholarship turns into the diploma and the opportunities we promised. That brings us to the next rung: Degree – finishing what we started.

DEGREE

When one of our students lands on a college campus, it can feel like they've made it. In a sense, they have overcome enormous odds to get there. But in another sense, they are like a freshman athlete at the bottom of a new ladder. The scholarship is not the finish line; the degree is. Our pipeline's ultimate success metric isn't the number of kids we send to college – it's the number of kids who graduate and walk off that stage with a diploma in hand, ready for the next phase of life. This rung, "Degree," is about supporting our young people through college to completion. It's about retention, perseverance, and making sure the investment pays off for them and for all of us.

College life will test everything we've instiled: their grit (to push through tough semesters), their mental toughness (to handle homesickness or the shock of more demanding competition), and their conscientiousness (to juggle class, practice, and personal life responsibly). We cannot assume that just because we got them there, the work is done. Part of our pipeline strategy is to extend our support through the college years – especially that critical first year when the adjustment is hardest.

Here's how we address the Degree stage:

- **Representative's Office:** My office remains a sort of "home base" for our students even after they depart Saint Lucia. We implement what we call the Accountability Loop or Year-One Retention Plan. Concretely, we keep a simple dashboard (a spreadsheet) of each student's key indicators: GPA each semester, credits earned, any notes like injuries or major personal events, and their athletic progress (did they redshirt? did they start playing? etc.). We don't do this to micromanage them, but to spot red flags. If a student's GPA drops below, say, 2.5 (the usual threshold to stay eligible for sports), an alarm goes off on our end. We will reach out – first to the student: "Hey, everything okay? Need help in any class? Let's find a tutor" – and if necessary to the college's academic advisor or even our diaspora mentor on site to get them help. Similarly, if we hear a student is not getting playing time and is discouraged, we talk them through it or have a former athlete chat with them about patience and work ethic. This is the beauty of having a pipeline: we don't forget about you when you fly off. We treat you almost like you're still part of a team back home – because you are. The office also facilitates a support network among the students themselves. We connect all our Saint Lucian scholars via group chat so they can lean on each other (a student at a Kansas school might share advice with one in Texas about coping with winter, for example). We also encourage them to join Caribbean student associations if their campus has one. From an administrative standpoint, we help with any transfers (if a school is not working out and the student needs to switch, we advise) and we keep their original files updated with any new documents (like if they declare a major or earn academic awards). And when graduation nears, we assist with applications to graduate school or other opportunities just as vigorously.

- **Families:** For the family, having your child abroad in college is a proud moment, but it can also be an anxious time. We counsel families on how to best support their college student. Staying in touch is key – schedule regular calls or video chats, send care packages if you can (even a letter or local snacks mean the world to a homesick student). But also, give them a bit of space to grow. College is where they learn adult responsibilities, so while you should check on them, resist the urge to solve every problem for them – let them try first, and just assure them you're there. One specific request we make to families is to not put undue financial pressure on the student. In some cases, when a kid goes abroad, relatives think the child will start working and sending money home. We strongly discourage this during the undergrad years. We want them focused on studies and sport, not working extra shifts to send money back (unless truly necessary). The real payback will come after graduation, when they can get a good job. So we educate families: the best way your child can help you now is by succeeding in school. Another thing: keep them rooted. Remind them of home values and stay interested in their experiences. If they struggle, encourage them. If they succeed, celebrate them and remind them to stay humble and hungry. Some parents, frankly, might feel a bit out of their depth discussing college stuff – that's okay. Just listening to your child talk about their classes or their new friends is enough. And if you sense something off (like they sound depressed or extremely stressed), please alert us or their mentor. We'd rather check in unnecessarily than miss a cry for help. On a practical note, families should handle any administrative tasks back home that could affect the student – for example, if a scholarship requires a document from Saint Lucia or a signature, the family can liaise with my office to get it done so the student doesn't have to worry.

- **Schools (Saint Lucia):** The role of the original school shifts here into legacy and continuity. One of the most powerful motivators for a student abroad is knowing their achievements matter to people back home. We encourage the schools to stay in contact with their alumni. Vide Bouteille Secondary might have a teacher shoot an email saying "Congrats on your Dean's List!" or St. Mary's College might invite a holiday-returning student to speak to current students about college life. These gestures remind our scholars that they carry the pride of their school and country. It fuels them to persist when times get tough. Also, schools benefit from these connections. When our graduates come back on break, they often visit their old schools – some run a clinic or give a talk. That inspires the next cohort and creates a culture where going abroad for university is not an exception but an expectation. Furthermore, schools can help by providing any documents or recommendations needed for scholarships to continue (some scholarships ask for yearly progress reports signed by someone). They also keep an ear out for opportunities – sometimes colleges ask schools for more prospects (for younger classes) if the current one is doing well. So the pipeline loops: a successful college student makes the school eager to send more, and the college eager to take more from that school.

A big part of ensuring the degree gets completed is keeping the student integrated and balanced in their new environment. The structure we gave them at home – early mornings, study halls, etc. – suddenly isn't imposed; they have to impose it on themselves. I like to say "discipline is public eventually, but it always starts private". Now they are in that private realm of personal choice, often without anyone looking. We trust that the habits ingrained in them will hold. Many times, they do. For example, Joel Polius carried his relentless practice habits into college, and I recall saying "people saw points and rebounds; I saw a ledger: travel stipends spent properly; class attendance at 98%; fines avoided because curfew wasn't a debate; workouts done as prescribed". In short, he treated his scholarship like a job and a mission, not a free ride. That "ledger" mindset – where a "scholarship is money saved; a degree is earning power multiplied; a disciplined life is risk reduced" – is what we want all our students to adopt. It's literally a financial outlook: blowing off class or partying too much isn't just youthful folly, it's burning money and chances. We emphasize this pragmatically, and they get it.

Our diaspora mentors are extremely helpful in reinforcing these values on-site. If a student starts slipping, sometimes an older Lucian in the area can take them for a weekend, give them a home-cooked meal and a pep talk, maybe a little island-style reality check ("You didn't go all the way there to waste time, did you?" in our dialect can be very effective coming from an auntie-figure!). We have mentors focusing on three aspects: academic guidance, athletic guidance, and life logistics. For example, an academic mentor might advise on course selection or study tips for a challenging class. An athletic mentor (maybe an alumnus who played college sports) might help them analyse game film or adjust to the higher level of competition. A navigator mentor helps with life skills – opening a bank account, finding the cheapest way to call home, or dealing with winter gear. This three-pronged support ensures that for most issues that arise, the student has someone to call besides just their coach or the overwhelmed international student office.

It's important to remember that not everything will be smooth. Some students will struggle with grades, some might get injured and lose playing time, some might even lose a scholarship if the coach who recruited them leaves the school (that happens). We prepare our students for adversity: "control what you can control, and communicate the rest." If something beyond their control happens, they must let us know quickly. We've had cases where a student-athlete decided to transfer schools (for more playing time or a program change); we jumped back into recruitment mode to find them a new home. The pipeline doesn't stop at departure; it flexes and continues.

Another element we track: graduation rate. We tell every student: your goal is graduation on time if possible (4 years for a bachelor's), or at most with one extra semester or year if you redshirted or did a tougher major. We celebrate degrees publicly. I plan to have a section in our constituency newsletter or website listing each person who graduates and what they earned – e.g., "Jane Doe, B.Sc. in Nursing, University of X (2027)". When a degree arrives by post to the family back home, trust me, we are often there taking a photo and clapping. Because that paper is gold. As I wrote, "we love to say 'records shattered'… but the better record is the paper – because paper feeds you when the jumper stops falling". We drive that home constantly. If a student is slacking because maybe they think they'll go pro and "don't need a degree," we remind them with examples – how many have that dream vs. how many actually make a living at sports, and how even those who go pro have short careers and need to work after. 100% of our pipeline kids will need a life after sports, and the degree is the bridge to that life.

Often, by senior year, our students truly get it. They start mentoring younger ones themselves, embodying what they learned. Take Jimmie, for instance: after graduating and starting his career, he would come home and talk honestly to form five boys about "the danger of believing your own poster" – telling them not to get caught up in hype and to focus on the substance. Or Darwin, who in grad school would fly down at Carnival time not just to have fun but to "sit with a group of boys and talk about recruitment, discipline". When our scholars display that maturity, we know they're on track to finish strong.

To make sure they reach that finish line, we also plan to publicly track and celebrate the numbers that matter. Earlier in the chapter, I listed six numbers we'll publish monthly: files opened, study hall attendance, SAT completion, coach conversations, placements, retention (staying enrolled with GPA ≥ 2.5). That last one – retention – is a key indicator of whether our kids are staying on the degree path. If retention dips, we say why and fix it. This transparency keeps us accountable: if a student drops out or fails out, we won't sweep it aside; we'll analyse it: Was it preventable? Did we miss a sign? And we'll adjust our support for others accordingly. Perhaps we needed more math prep, or maybe a stronger pre-departure orientation on mental health. The pipeline is a living program, and we learn and improve continuously, what we call "learning loops" in governance – measure, adjust, and get better.

When a student finally completes their degree, the whole village should feel proud – and usually does. It's not just a thrill for the student; it's a new professional, a new leader, a new mentor being minted for our community.

That segues into the final rung, which is where the pipeline ultimately aims: turning those degrees into gainful jobs and a cycle of reinvestment into the community. The promise of #SportsEconomics isn't fulfilled until that graduate is in the workforce, contributing to society, and ideally helping the next kid up the ladder. So let's talk about the endgame: jobs and the cycle of success.

JOB

Every degree is a means to an end – and that end is a good job and a stable career. When I say "sports is economics," I mean that a single athletic opportunity can ripple out to create financial stability and community uplift that lasts decades. The final rung of our pipeline is about securing that outcome: turning a young graduate into a employed, empowered adult. And even beyond that – encouraging them to become a link in the chain for others. This is where the pipeline becomes a loop, feeding back into new talent ID, new opportunities, and community growth. It's the big-picture vision we're striving for in Castries North and Saint Lucia at large.

Let's break down the significance: When one of our pipeline students lands a job after college, several things happen. Personally, they achieve independence – they can earn, start a family, build a life. Family-wise, often their income helps lift their household out of hardship (they might pay for a sibling's schooling or secure a mortgage for their parents). And community-wise, we suddenly have a role model and potentially a resource in a new industry. Think of it this way: a kid leaves on a sports scholarship and comes back a few years later as, say, a software engineer – now our island has one more tech expert, one more mentor, one more taxpayer even. That's social mobility and community development in action.

I'll revisit a few examples to illustrate: Jimmie Inglis, once a boy doing beach workouts on Gros Islet, ended up with a master's degree and a career in business. He's now part of the "genealogy" of our program – someone who can hire others, advise others, maybe start a business here someday. Jonathan "Big Joe" went from electrifying local courts to earning his chance at Queens College in New York, then landed a management role at Mercedes-Benz in Charlotte. The "crowd's noise fades; the competence remains" – meaning no one in

Charlotte cares he was a high school star, but they sure care that he's good at his job. And he is, because the same excellence he showed on court became excellence at work. Walter "Ninja" used his athletic springboard to jump into the tech world; his "sweat became software" – he's literally writing code now, maybe even some day writing a program that could benefit St. Lucia's government or businesses. These are transformations that sport set in motion, but education and opportunity carried through.

So how do we, as a pipeline community, help at the Job stage? After all, you might think it's out of our hands once they graduate. But there's plenty we can do:

• **Representative's Office and Broader Community:** We are setting up what's called the Castries North Connect (CNConnect) program to link our secondary schools, our scholarship pipeline, and now employers. We are basically creating a ladder that doesn't end at graduation but extends to internships and job placements. For instance, we are compiling a Diaspora Skills Bank – a roster of St. Lucians abroad who are in various industries (engineering, nursing, IT, teaching, you name it). These folks can offer mentorship, yes, but also maybe job referrals or partnerships. If a Saint Lucian in London hears of a job opening that fits one of our new grads, they can alert us or the person directly. We also encourage our new graduates to consider returning home, and we plan to work with local businesses to recruit them. Nothing would be better than a brain gain – an accomplished young person bringing their skills back to the island. But even if they don't return immediately, they are part of our extended network. Our office keeps in touch with alumni of the pipeline. We celebrate their career milestones on our social media or newsletters – not as fluff, but as real indicators of success. For example, if Darwin Joseph gets promoted at his New York firm, we mention that as a proud update: one of our own thriving abroad and still giving back (since Darwin indeed mentors and does book drives for kids at home). And speaking of giving back: I have a principle called "Reinvest the Returns." I ask every graduate: give at least one thing back in that first year after you graduate. It could be time – like helping the next cohort with their scholarship paperwork in December when you're home. It could be mentorship – like doing Zoom calls with kids. It could be a donation – maybe you sponsor an SAT textbook or a basketball net for a school. It's not about money, it's about mindset: success must pay tax in service. This way, the new professional stays connected and the pipeline becomes self-sustaining, fuelled by gratitude and duty.

• **Families:** When your child becomes a working adult, the dynamic changes. The best thing families can do at this stage is to encourage their independence and growth. If they choose to stay abroad for work, support that decision without guilt – the exposure and experience are valuable. If they choose to come home, celebrate that and help them reintegrate. Some families might expect the new graduate to now "repay" all their sacrifice. I gently advise: give the young person space to find their footing. Yes, they will help – many do start helping siblings or parents financially – but remember they are possibly carrying student loan debt or need to save for their own future too. It's a balance. Families should continue to be emotional support. Transitioning from college to work life is its own challenge. I've seen some of our alumni struggle with that first job or living alone for the first time. A grounded home base (even virtually through calls) keeps them steady. Also, celebrate them! A degree and a job – these are huge achievements for the whole lineage. Throw a little gathering when they return home first time, invite the neighbours, make them feel like the hero they are. That pride fuels their confidence at work.

• **Schools (and younger students):** Here's a beautiful thing: when one pipeline student secures a good job, we use that story to educate and inspire the next generation. Schools invite the alum to speak or at least send a message that we share during assembly. We point and say, "See, that could be you in a few years – a civil engineer or an accountant or a physical therapist – because you stuck with basketball (or netball or track) and your studies." These stories change mindsets. Instead of seeing sports as a dead-end or just entertainment, our community starts seeing it as a legitimate pathway to success in life. The phrase I often use is we're turning a "family miracle into a community project". No longer is a kid making it out something rare and magical; it's becoming normal enough that everyone works together systematically to make it happen, over and over. When this sinks in, parents of the next crop of kids are more willing to let them train hard, or to prioritize a practice because they see it can lead somewhere tangible. Schools too begin to allocate resources differently – maybe investing in better coaching or facilities because it's not just play, it's part of students' career development.

I want to highlight the economic ripple effects that often go unnoticed. When a young person from Castries North goes abroad, gets a degree, and lands a job, "the circle gets bold". That was my way of saying the impact widens in that earlier quote. The job means income not just for that person but often flowing back home – money that pays rent, then a mortgage, then a child's school fees. In some cases, it's literal: one graduate might send money to build a family house or fund a sibling's college. In other cases, it's more indirect but still significant: that family now has one less dependent, maybe they can invest in a small business or improve their living conditions. Over a generation, these shifts can change the economic landscape of a community. Imagine 10 students every year achieving this. In ten years, that's 100 young professionals. Even if half return home and half stay abroad but stay connected, you have dozens of families in Castries North lifted to middle-class stability, and dozens of diaspora allies in various industries. That's huge for an island our size.

And then there's the network effect. One graduate in a company might pull the next one in. We already see this in micro form: coaches who took one Lucian athlete are eager to take the next because the first did well. Similarly, a company that hires one of our people might say, "These Saint Lucians are hardworking, let's get more." This has happened with our nurses overseas, and it can happen with our pipeline scholars too. It's also reciprocity, the same bridge that helped a Marchand wing at 5 a.m. and a Soufriere guard in a coach's office kept the ladder steady when Joel's window opened. In job terms, the same bridge that helped Joel get an internship might later help a younger Saint Lucian get hired at Joel's company, because Joel vouches for them. We aim to cultivate a fraternity/sorority of pipeline alumni who lookout for each other and for their juniors.

Now, let's not forget the community development aspect explicitly. When these individuals return (temporarily or permanently), they seed change. Darwin in New York didn't just enjoy his salary – he started book drives for Soufriere's youth. He's transferring knowledge and resources back home. Jimmie mentors youth in his quarter. Jeremiah Vitalis, who got a construction management career, coaches kids in his spare time. We see scholars becoming benefactors: "yesterday's athletes become today's patrons – coaching, funding SAT fees, reviewing applications, Zoom-mentoring after school". This is the virtuous cycle I dream of. One success creates another. When I talk about making it count, this is it – making each success count for more than just itself.

From the perspective of my office, once someone reaches the Job stage successfully, they have "graduated" the pipeline, but they are also now a stakeholder in it. I half-jokingly tell them at their graduation: "You're an investor in this pipeline now – whether you like it or not!" We invite them formally to join our CN Pipeline Alumni Council (that's a thing we are forming). Not a heavy responsibility, but a platform where they can give input or volunteer in small ways, and certainly a network among themselves. This council might meet once a year over the holidays when many are home. They share experiences and advise us on how to improve the pipeline. It's like having our own panel of experts who have lived it.

Finally, at the society level, the more we do this, the more we chip away at cynicism and despair. Saint Lucia has long had a brain drain issue – our bright kids leave and many don't come back. Some see that as an absolute loss. I see it differently: if even those who leave stay connected, and if enough come back with skills, we can turn brain drain into brain circulation. A pipeline doesn't only send water out; it can also bring water back in. Some of our best and brightest may one day return to start new industries here, or at least to share knowledge. And even those who stay abroad can be bridges for trade, investment, etc. One day, perhaps one of our sports scholars-turned-business executives helps set up a branch of their company in Saint Lucia, creating dozens of local jobs. Why not? The possibilities grow as the network grows.

Let me close this with a vision: I imagine a photo, maybe a decade from now. It's a reunion of pipeline alumni at Vigie beach. In that photo there's a doctor, an engineer, a teacher, a banker, an entrepreneur – all from different graduating classes, all from Castries North or nearby, all once kids at our summer camp or school league. They're laughing, playing a pick-up game in the sand for old times' sake. Around them are current kids watching, thinking, "wow, these guys and gals were just like us." And one of the alumni is saying to the kids, "You want to be in this circle? Here's what you do…" – and they spell out the same pipeline: work hard, study, listen, seize the opportunity. That image to me is the culmination: a self-perpetuating pipeline, a culture of expectation that sports can carry you to college and beyond, and that success is normal and meant to be shared.

In the words I've already written and believe in: "one disciplined life at a time, multiplied by a system that belongs to all of us", we change what's possible in a small island. Each life is a proof of concept; together, they are a proof of community. We started Part II with the hashtag #SportsEconomics, and now we see fully what it means: the conversion of effort and talent into tangible returns – degrees, jobs, better lives – and then reinvesting those returns to keep the cycle going.

The pipeline we're building is in fact already under construction, rung by rung, through the stories and strategies we've shared. It's our job now to scale it up. As I move to Part III, which dives into education and skills more broadly, I carry this momentum with me: Sports was our pilot project. It showed that with structure and heart, we can crack open the world for our youth. Next, we'll apply the same approach to academics, vocational training, and more. But we will never abandon what we've built here in Part II – we'll only reinforce and expand it. Because it's working. On to the next possession. The play is set, the team is strong, and we intend to execute and finish, again and again, making it count for every child who dares to dream.

Part III – Schools & Skills That Pay

15

Castries North Connect (CN Connect)

Castries North Connect is a simple ladder linking Castries North secondary schools to universities and employers – mentors, mock interviews, and reference letters that land. Let me return to the Darwin story. I took a chance drove to Park University and sat down with Coach Claude English, a veteran coach I trusted. I told him, "Coach, there's a player in St. Lucia who looks like me, plays like me, and deserves a shot. I don't have a tape, but trust me – give him a chance." I had no highlight reel in hand, just my word and conviction.

Coach English listened. Because of that one conversation, Darwin got an opportunity he had only dreamed of. He earned his degree in finance, then a master's in business, and launched a professional life in New York. Most importantly, he never forgot home – he's running book drives and mentoring young people in his hometown even now.

That is the power of a single connection. It's not just about one scholarship or one job – it's about opportunity, about lifting entire communities, about changing lives. But here's the thing: it shouldn't take a lucky meeting or a personal favour from "Bax" to link a talented kid in Castries North to the wider world. We have to stop leaving our youths' futures to chance encounters. We need to build a simple, reliable ladder that any student with ambition can climb – from our secondary schools in Castries North straight to universities, training programs, and employers at home and abroad.

CN Connect is that ladder. This chapter lays out how we will create Castries North Connect (CN Connect) – a structured pipeline that links our two major secondary schools in the constituency with real opportunities beyond graduation. Whether a student's goal is university, a technical career, or landing a decent job right out of school, CN Connect will provide the rungs they need: adult mentors who guide them, mock interviews to build confidence, reference letters that carry weight, and job shadowing experiences that open their eyes.

FROM CLASSROOM TO CAREER: BRIDGING THE GAP

Castries North is blessed with some of Saint Lucia's finest secondary schools: St. Mary's College (SMC) at Vigie, St. Joseph's Convent (SJC) at Cedars Road, Castries Comprehensive Secondary School (CCSS) at Vide Bouteille, Patricia D. James Secondary School (PDJSS)—formerly Vide Bouteille Secondary—at La Clery, Sir Ira Simmons Secondary

School (SISSS) at Choc, and the Saint Lucia Seventh-day Adventist Academy (SDA Academy) at Sunny Acres.

Year after year, these institutions shape bright, capable students—young men and women with talent, grit, and ambition. Yet too often, after the final exam and the graduation handshake, those dreams stall. Some students don't know how to apply for an overseas scholarship or even where to look. Others walk into a job interview and freeze, never having been taught how to speak confidently about their strengths. Some wait for mentors who never appear—no one to vouch for them, to guide them, or to open that first crucial door.

The result is painful but familiar: potential left on the table. A promising girl from SJC or PDJSS ends up unemployed. A gifted boy from SMC or CCSS drifts between odd jobs. A quiet achiever from SISSS or SDA Academy gets overlooked simply because she doesn't have a network. The bridge between education and opportunity remains unfinished, and our country loses more talent than it can afford.

I've seen that gap up close. In my own youth, I nearly fell through it—not for lack of ability, but because there was no system to catch a late bloomer like me. I was fortunate: basketball became my passport, turning a court in Vide Bouteille into a campus overseas. But not every young person will be saved by a jump shot. We need something deliberate—a living bridge between classroom and career—so that no student with promise, from any of these schools, ever slips between the boards.

CN Connect is about bridging that school-to-opportunity gap with a proactive, hands-on approach. It will start in the classroom – working with our Form 4 and Form 5 students (the last two years of secondary school) – and extend to the campus and the workplace. Think of it as a local-to-global highway for Castries North youth. On one end, you have a teenager in Bisee or Vigie polishing up their résumé, and on the other end you have a university admissions officer in Barbados or New York, or a hotel manager in Gros Islet, ready to take them on. CN Connect will be the sturdy bridge between them.

What does this bridge look like in practice? It's built on four main programs: mentorship, employability training (like mock interviews and résumé building), a community-based reference letter system, and job exposure opportunities. Each of these addresses a specific weak link that currently holds our youth back.

MENTORSHIP THAT MAKES A DIFFERENCE

Every young person benefits from a guide – someone a little further down the road of life who can show them the way. Many of us were lucky to find mentors informally. I think of my mother, a community pillar who instilled in me the value of service, or coaches like Ron Freeman who spotted my hyperactive energy and redirected it into sport. But not every child finds that mentor. CN Connect will guarantee it.

Under CN Connect, every Form 5 student in Castries North who opts in will be paired with a mentor for their entire final school year (and ideally continuing into that critical first year after graduation). We will draw mentors from all walks of life – a mix of local professionals, entrepreneurs, retired educators, and even Saint Lucian diaspora volunteers connected through our forthcoming Skills Bank (more on that in Chapter 17). The key is to match each student with someone in their field of interest: if a student thinks she might want to be an engineer, we'll pair her with a young civil engineer from the community or abroad. If another loves the idea of starting a business, we connect him with a local business owner who knows the hustle.

Mentors will meet with their students at least twice a month – sometimes in person, sometimes via Zoom or a phone call. The sessions can be informal chats about goals and life, or very structured check-ins on progress (for example, "Have you finished that college application essay? Let's review it together."). We will provide basic training to mentors on how to coach and motivate effectively, because not every great professional automatically knows how to mentor a teenager. But many will; in fact, I've already heard from Saint Lucians overseas who are eager to help if we just create the mechanism for it.

One of the first tasks of mentors will simply be exposure – widening the lens for these students. A mentor can open a student's eyes by sharing their own journey: "Here's how I got into accounting, here were my struggles, here's what a typical day at my job looks like." They can introduce practical knowledge that schools might not teach explicitly – how to network politely, how to budget for living on your own, how to cope with setbacks. This kind of wisdom transfer is priceless, and it's something our community has in abundance if we tap into it.

We will formalize the mentorship matches early in the school year (let's say each September). The MP's office, working with the school guidance counsellors, will host a "CN Connect Launch" workshop where mentors and mentees meet, possibly signing a sort of mentorship agreement outlining how often they'll communicate and what goals they're aiming for. This sets expectations clearly on both sides. As an actionable step, I want the first cohort of mentors ready by September of the first year in office – even if it starts with a modest 20 mentors and 20 students. Over five years, we can grow that until every willing student in Castries North has a mentor.

FROM MOCK INTERVIEWS TO REAL CONFIDENCE

If mentorship is the first rung of the ladder, skills training is the second. Our students need to walk into any interview room or networking situation ready – not intimidated, not clueless, but confident and prepared. Under CN Connect we'll run a series of practical workshops and mock interview sessions to build those soft skills.

We'll start with something simple: communication and presentation workshops. These might be weekend bootcamps or after-school sessions where professionals volunteer to teach students how to introduce themselves properly, shake hands firmly, make eye contact, and articulate their thoughts. It sounds basic, but these small things are often the difference between a great first impression and a missed opportunity. For example, I envision a Saturday morning session in the CCSS auditorium where a human resources manager from a local company comes in and says, "Okay, pretend I'm a potential employer or a scholarship committee – sell yourself to me in 60 seconds." The students will stumble, laugh, learn, and improve together.

Then, as they near graduation, each student in the program will go through at least two full mock interviews. These will be one-on-one, scenario-based interviews tailored to the student's goal – a job interview simulation for those heading straight to work, and a university admissions or scholarship interview for those applying to college. We'll rope in volunteers who have hiring experience or who have sat on scholarship panels. After each mock interview, the student gets direct feedback: "Here's where you did well, here's where you need work." We'll cover common questions, teach them how to highlight their strengths through personal stories (no need to be shy – blow your own trumpet, as we say), and even how to handle curveball questions. By the time a real interview comes around, our Castries North youth will have essentially done it already in practice.

To support this, we'll create a small library of resource materials – simple guides like "Top 10 Interview Questions and How to Approach Them" or "Dress Code 101 for Interviews," possibly included in Part VII of this book as templates and checklists. I don't expect every family to have the know-how or resources to guide their teenager on these things; that's where community must step in.

Hand-in-hand with interview prep is résumé and application prep. Starting in Form 4, we will hold resume-writing workshops. The goal is that by the time they finish Form 5, each student has a polished one-page resume listing their academics, any sports or clubs, community service, skills, and a clear objective. We'll show them examples of good resumes. We might even utilize teachers from the English department or folks from the business community to review each student's draft. The same goes for college application essays – our mentors or a volunteer team can help critique personal statements to really make them shine.

Now, I can already hear a few skeptics: "Isn't this too much hand-holding? When we were kids, nobody taught us these things." Perhaps not. But times have changed. The competition out there is fiercer than ever – whether it's for a scholarship in the U.S. or a job at a bank in Castries, our students aren't just competing with each other, they're effectively up against a global pool of talent. Giving them these skills isn't coddling them, it's equipping them to compete and excel. And frankly, many privileged kids naturally get this grooming – their parents might work at an office and show them the ropes, or they might attend schools that emphasize these skills. I'm making sure every kid in Castries North, not just the well-connected, gets the same fighting chance.

REFERENCE LETTERS THAT ACTUALLY OPEN DOORS

If you've ever applied for a job or a university spot, you know how crucial a good reference letter can be. It's that outside voice vouching for you: "I've seen this young woman overcome challenges and she's got what it takes", or "I supervised this young man during an internship and I can attest to his work ethic." The sad reality, though, is that many of our brightest students struggle to get strong reference letters. Perhaps their teachers are overworked and write a bland, generic note. Or maybe they don't know any professionals personally to ask for a recommendation. Some youths simply don't ask at all, because they're shy or unsure whom to approach.

CN Connect will set up a Reference Letter System to fix this gap. Here's how it will work: We'll maintain a roster of reputable community members – think retired principals, respected coaches, business owners, church leaders, even diaspora professionals – who are willing to be on call as reference letter writers for our young people. This doesn't mean handing out fake praise to just anyone. It means that as students participate in our CN Connect activities (the workshops, the mentoring, community service projects), these community referees get to know them and can honestly endorse their character and achievements.

For example, say a student, Alisha, regularly attends our Saturday leadership sessions and volunteers at a local community clean-up I organized. She's shown up on time, demonstrated leadership among her peers, and I've gotten to interact with her through these programs. When it's time for Alisha to apply for an overseas scholarship or a job at a local bank, she can request a reference letter from the CN Connect roster. Someone like me (as MP) or another well-known mentor who has worked with her will write a letter highlighting her qualities: her discipline, initiative, community spirit, academic effort, whatever fits. Because that reference is coming from an established figure and contains concrete examples, it will carry weight.

To avoid any hint of favouritism or impropriety, we will put some structure around this. Students will fill out a short reference request form where they list what they need the letter for, the deadline, and whom among the roster they think knows them best to write it. The chosen referee can only speak to what they know – if I only interacted briefly with Alisha, perhaps it's better her sports coach who trained with her for two years writes the letter. The point is, nobody in Castries North with talent and work ethic should miss an opportunity just because "nobody who matters knows me." We will know them. Our community will know them. And we will stand by them on paper.

As MP, I intend to personally sign as many of these reference letters as needed once I have sufficient basis to vouch for someone. I recall how one letter of introduction or phone call can tip the scales – much like my visit to Coach English for Darwin. Through CN Connect, those in positions of influence will use that influence to lift others, not as a favour or nepotism, but as an earned recommendation. If a student has put in the work, shown dedication (say, attending all our prep sessions, improving their grades, helping out in community events), then by all means I will write to the principal of Sir Arthur Lewis Community College or the HR manager at Sandals or the admissions office at Monroe College on their behalf. That's what representation can and should do – not just build footpaths and drains, but build bridges for people.

We'll also train students on how to request a reference properly – because that in itself is a life skill. They'll learn to ask respectfully and early (not last-minute panics), provide their resume or a draft letter to help the referee, and to always follow up with thanks. These courtesies go a long way and set them up for professional life.

TRY OUT THE FUTURE: JOB SHADOWING AND INTERNSHIPS

Textbook learning has its limits. Sometimes a teenager needs to step for a moment into the real world of work to ignite their ambition or clarify their goals. That's why the final component of CN Connect is a job shadowing and internship pipeline. We want our students to get a taste of various professions while still in school – to spend a day or a week seeing what it's like to be a nurse at Victoria Hospital, an engineer at C.O. Williams, a chef at a Rodney Bay restaurant, or an IT technician at Digicel.

We will partner with at least a dozen businesses and institutions, both within Castries North and in the wider Castries area, to host student shadowing opportunities. Fortunately, Castries North and its environs are home to many prime workplaces – from the airport at Vigie to the broadcasting studios, banks, government offices, and retail centres around Choc. Our strategy is to start by leveraging personal networks (and yes, likely calling in a few favours!). For example, I will ask a friend at a local engineering firm: "Can you take two students for three afternoons to show them what your work involves?" Or we might coordinate with the Ministry of Tourism to let a couple of interested youths shadow an officer during preparations for an event.

The commitment from businesses will be kept reasonable. We're not asking them to run a whole summer program (though down the line, internships could extend into summer jobs). We're asking for short, focused exposure stints. Ideally each Form 5 student in CN Connect will get at least one half-day site visit to a workplace of interest, and one longer work attachment (say, a week during Easter break or after exams) if the company is willing. We'll take care of the logistics: transportation for students if needed (we can use the constituency van or partner with parents for carpooling), and matching students to sites.

To illustrate, imagine a student from Sunny Acres who thinks he might want to become a pilot or work in aviation. Through CN Connect, we arrange for him to spend a day at George F. L. Charles Airport in Vigie, shadowing ground staff, air traffic controllers, and airline personnel. He might come away thinking "Wow, I love this environment," or even "Actually, this isn't what I thought, maybe I prefer engineering." Either outcome is valuable – it's better to learn these things early. Or take a student interested in medicine: we could have them shadow a nurse or lab technician for a few days at a local clinic, or even at the La Clery Health Centre which I hope to expand as a multi-use facility (though that's a topic for healthcare in Part IV).

For those inclined toward business, we might coordinate with a large supermarket at Choc or a store in Gablewoods Mall – these are significant commercial nodes right in our constituency. They could observe retail operations, marketing, customer service. One afternoon watching the store manager handle inventory and customer complaints could teach lessons no textbook can.

We won't forget the public sector either. Many youths might consider a career as a teacher, police officer, or civil servant. Through the Ministry of Education or local police station, we can set up an "Explorer Day" for them too. In Castries North, for instance, we have a police station not far away and government offices – a student could sit in on a class with a teacher at a primary school or see the day-to-day at a government department.

Crucially, these experiences should be more than passive observation. We will prepare both the host and the student to engage actively. Students will go in with a list of questions they've prepared (mentors can help with this): "What do you enjoy about your job? What qualifications did you need? What challenges do you face?" And hosts will be encouraged to let the student try a hand at something safe but real – maybe it's helping to greet customers, or assisting a lab tech with filing results, or observing a team meeting. When the day or week is over, we'll debrief with the students – get them to share what they learned, maybe write a reflection. This not only reinforces the learning, it also helps others hear about different fields from their peers.

Finally, as CN Connect matures, I aim to convert some of these relationships into actual internships or traineeships for our youth. The immediate goal is exposure, but the ultimate goal is employment. If a business spots a bright young person during a shadowing stint, they might say, "We'd like to bring you on as a summer intern – maybe even offer a job after graduation if you pursue this field." We will actively broker those introductions. It's a win-win: companies get eager, trainable talent; our young people get a foot in the door. In fact, I will lobby for a formal MoU (Memorandum of Understanding) with the Chamber of Commerce or Employers' Federation to each year take on a certain number of interns from Castries North schools. Government can set an example too: perhaps each Ministry could take two or three recent graduates for a 6-month internship program. As MP, I can't dictate private hiring, but I can certainly influence and facilitate – that's part of the job, using the convening power of the office to create opportunities.

LOCAL-TO-GLOBAL: THE BROADER STRATEGY

CN Connect is not an isolated initiative; it's one piece of a broader vision to create local-to-global opportunity pipelines for our youth. In Part II of this book, I talked about "#SportsEconomics" – using sports as a springboard to education and careers. We saw how a structured approach turned athletic talent into degrees and jobs. For instance, we saw that a pipeline from a neighbourhood court through SAT prep to a college scholarship can transform lives. But not every young person is an athlete or will follow that exact path. Part III (this section) is about broadening that pipeline to academics, skills training, and youth empowerment at large.

CN Connect fits into this like the foundation of a house. It catches everyone at the end of secondary school, regardless of whether they dribbled a basketball or led the science club. It says: "Okay, you've got your school diploma (or even if you don't quite have it yet), now here are the next steps to turn it into something tangible – a college acceptance, a trade certificate, a job."

Think of the stories we highlighted earlier: Darwin from Soufriere got his chance because someone connected him; Joel Polius made it from Vide Bouteille Secondary to a U.S. college team and proved the impact structured programs can have. Those were individual cases. CN Connect aims to make that the norm rather than the exception. When we succeed, it will no longer be newsworthy that a kid from Castries North got into a top university or launched a career at 19 – it will be expected.

This program also complements the next chapters in very direct ways. Our CN SAT Academy (Chapter 16) will work in tandem with CN Connect – as students prepare academically for scholarships, CN Connect prepares them in soft skills and links them to mentors. The Diaspora Skills Bank (Chapter 17) will feed into CN Connect by providing a pool of diaspora Saint Lucians to serve as mentors, guest speakers, and even recruiters for opportunities abroad. And the AfterSchool programs (Chapter 18) will ensure kids have safe, constructive places to be long before they reach Form 5 – seeding the discipline and broad interests that CN Connect then takes to the finish line.

Let me be clear: CN Connect is ambitious, but it is also very practical. Much of it doesn't require huge new government spending or bureaucracy. It requires coordination, communication, and a representative willing to knock on doors and make phone calls on behalf of his constituents' children. It's about leveraging goodwill: and believe me, our community and our diaspora have plenty of that once you activate it. Instead of each family struggling alone to figure out how to get little John or Jane "through the system," we create a community support system that nudges them along, step by step.

IMPLEMENTATION TIMELINE & PARTNERS

This won't happen overnight, but we can start laying the groundwork from day one of taking office. Here's a rough timeline of how I envision rolling out CN Connect:

- **First 100 Days:** Meet with principals of CN secondary schools to discuss the CN Connect framework and get buy-in. Begin compiling a list of potential mentors (through alumni networks, community organizations, and that diaspora database). Reach out to a few key businesses to gauge interest in hosting interns or shadowing students. Form a small CN Connect Task Force – maybe 4-5 individuals including school guidance counsellors and one or two youth leaders – to refine the program details.

- **By Month 6:** Pilot some workshops at the schools. For example, run one mock interview afternoon with a small group of students to test the concept. Host a "career talk" event where we invite a couple of professionals to speak at an assembly about their careers and the skills required – this doubles as a way to introduce the idea of mentorship to students and get them excited. Start pairing a first batch of mentors and mentees on a trial basis (even if informal).

- **Year 1 (Academic Year kick-off):** Officially launch CN Connect at the start of the school year (likely September). This includes a formal mentorship kickoff event at the school auditorium, distributing our CN Connect Guidebook (with tips on interviews, resumes, etc.), and scheduling the year's upcoming workshops (e.g., one per month). At this stage, maybe we have, say, 30 students signed up and 30 mentors – a manageable pilot group. Also by end of Year 1, secure formal agreements with at least 5 companies or institutions for job shadowing slots in Year 2.

- **Years 2-3:** Expand the cohort. By year 2, aim for 60–80 students (which could include Form 4s as well, starting early). Incorporate feedback from year 1 – maybe students wanted more practice interviews or found the resume workshops really helpful and want more depth. Start an annual "Opportunity Fair" – instead of the old-style career fair where people just hand out brochures, this would be a fair where local businesses, government agencies, and scholarship programs come to actively connect with our CN Connect students. They might conduct on-the-spot mini-interviews or accept CVs. In year 3, goal could be 100+ students involved (including possibly some youths from the community who already graduated but are NEET – not in education, employment, or training – we won't exclude them if they want to join the workshops to improve their chances).

- **Years 4-5:** Institutionalize it. By this time, CN Connect should be a known and expected part of the Castries North education landscape. We'll work with the Ministry of Education to see if parts of it can be integrated or supported at the national level (perhaps as an official extracurricular program or via the guidance counseling units). We'll also seek sustainable funding or sponsorship – maybe a local bank sees the value and wants to sponsor the printing of materials or provide stipends for interns. In these later years, I'd love to see earlier graduates of CN Connect coming back as mentors for the next generation – the ultimate measure of success is when the system becomes self-perpetuating.

Throughout, key partners will include the schools (principals, teachers, guidance counsellors), who are critical gatekeepers; the Ministry of Education, for alignment with national youth development goals; the private sector (via Chamber of Commerce or sector associations); and of course the community and diaspora members who volunteer as mentors and referees. Non-profits and youth organizations can slot in too – for instance, local NGOs like the Sacred Sports Foundation or volunteer groups could help run life-skills workshops.

We will track outcomes meticulously. Each year, we'll ask: How many students participated? How many got into tertiary education programs? How many found jobs or internships? How did they rate the program's helpfulness? This data will be shared openly, as part of the Castries North "scorecard" I intend to publish, so we can learn and adjust. If we see, for instance, that 15 students got overseas scholarships in a year and 10 of them were part of CN Connect, that's a big signal that the program is working and should be strengthened.

A COMMUNITY THAT STANDS BEHIND ITS YOUTH

As we come to the close of this chapter, picture this: a Form 5 student at St. Mary's College walking out of his graduation ceremony. He's the first in his family to finish secondary school. In the past, that might be where the story ends – he might drift, uncertain what to do next. But with CN Connect in place, he's not walking out alone and unsure. He already has a mentor who's helping him navigate an application to an auto-mechanics apprenticeship. He has attended workshops that taught him how to present himself and he's done a couple of mock interviews.

He shadowed a team at a local garage for a week, so he knows he likes the work. He even has a reference letter from a respected community engineer ready in his folder. That young man is empowered to take his next step.

Multiply that story by dozens of students each year, and you begin to see the transformative power. We often talk about brain drain in Saint Lucia – our best and brightest leaving. Well, I'm not afraid of our youth going abroad to study or work; I want them to gain experience and success, whether at home or overseas. What I don't want is talent drain through the cracks – young people whose potential drains away unused because no one extended a hand.

Castries North Connect is our way of extending that hand early, steadily, and sincerely. It says to every student: You have a ladder in front of you. Climb as high as you can – we're right behind you to hold it steady. With this in place, the old mentality of patronage politics – where a representative might swoop in to "help" one favoured student as a one-off act – will be replaced by a culture of systematic, fair support for all. This is what representation in the 21st century should look like. Not a king dispensing favours, but a community building ladders.

In the next chapter, we'll dive deeper into one particular rung of that ladder that I've mentioned in passing here: preparing our students academically to seize those scholarships and spots in universities. It's one thing to have mentors and mock interviews; but if the exam scores and readiness aren't there, the opportunities can still slip by. That's where our CN SAT Academy comes in – a plan to boost test scores, study habits, and academic confidence so that Castries North kids are not just eligible for opportunities, but competitive for the best of them. Let's make sure they're ready to climb.

16

The CN SAT Academy

Not long ago, I was chatting with a group of teens at Vigie and I asked them about their plans after secondary school. A couple wanted to go to university abroad, one talked about community college, another shrugged and said, "Maybe find a job, not sure." I posed a simple follow-up: "What's your SAT score?" Blank stares. None of them had taken the Scholastic Aptitude Test – the SAT – which is often a ticket to U.S. colleges (and the scholarships that come with them). In fact, most hadn't even thought about it, or assumed it was only for the brainiacs or those going to fancy private schools. This is a problem. If we want our youth to seize global opportunities, we have to aggressively prepare them to meet global standards – and that includes standardized tests like the SAT, solid grades (GPA), and a strong academic foundation.

I'll confess something personal: when I first left Saint Lucia for university in the States on a basketball scholarship, I was not academically ready. I could run circles on the court, but in the classroom I was behind. The first year was a rude awakening – I struggled with reading assignments and basic study skills that my American peers had mastered in high school. I used to have to go take classes to slow my brain down so I can learn to read properly. I didn't get that training until I got to university. Can you imagine? I had graduated secondary school and even completed A-Levels, yet I had never properly been taught how to learn in the way I needed for college. I basically had to re-train myself at age 19. And I did – with a lot of extra work. Every summer for four years straight during university, instead of coming home to relax, I went to summer school to catch up. I joke that I went to summer school four years in a row – most people who do that end up with three degrees. In my case it was remedial work, not additional degrees. It paid off eventually – I improved my reading, earned my Bachelors and Masters, and even made the Dean's List by the end. But it was a tough, humbling road.

I don't want the next generation of Castries North youth to struggle like I did or to miss out because their academic foundation was shaky. They shouldn't have to pray that a U.S. college coach will "hide" them academically for a year while they catch up. Instead, let's prepare them ahead of time to excel both on the field and in the classroom. That's where the CN SAT Academy comes in.

The CN SAT Academy will be a focused academic readiness program aimed at boosting our students' performance in three key areas: standardized test scores (especially SAT), core subject mastery (especially math and English), and overall study discipline (GPA maintenance). It's "academy" in the sense of a structured supplemental school – think of it as evening classes or Saturday bootcamps that complement regular schooling, run right here in the community. If CN Connect (from the last chapter) is about hooking our youth up to opportunities, CN SAT Academy is about making sure they have the academic muscle to grab those opportunities and hold on.

THE ACADEMIC REALITY CHECK

First, let's face the facts of where we stand. Saint Lucian students are bright and capable, but our exam results show some glaring weaknesses. For instance, in the most recent CSEC (Caribbean Secondary Education Certificate) exams, English A had about an 85% pass rate, but Mathematics lagged at roughly 42%. That means more than half of our students are failing math by the regional standard. The situation is improving slowly (that 42% was up from 38% the year before), but it's nowhere near good enough. These numbers matter because math and English are the twin pillars of almost every higher education opportunity. Whether you want to do engineering or business or even art, foreign universities and scholarship boards will scrutinize your math and English skills – often through exams like the SAT or ACT, or through your CSEC/CAPE grades.

Moreover, many of our student athletes – the ones who might get a sports scholarship – meet the athletic criteria but fall short academically. I've seen talented players miss out on U.S. college offers because of low SAT scores or because their grades didn't meet the NCAA eligibility minimum. That is a preventable tragedy. If a youth has the talent and the drive, a test score shouldn't be the thing that stops them at the gate. Right now, too many don't even attempt the

SAT due to lack of preparation or confidence. Nationally, we have no sustained culture of SAT prep in our public schools – a gap that countries like Barbados have started to fill with government-backed programs for student athletes. In fact, Barbados' Ministry of Youth and Sports launched a dedicated SAT programme and already nearly 150 young Barbadian athletes have benefited, getting themselves ready for U.S. college requirements. If they can do it, so can we, and we should not limit it to athletes alone.

The CN SAT Academy will target Form 4 and Form 5 students (and recent graduates where feasible) in Castries North, especially those who aspire to attend university or snag scholarships either at home or overseas. It will also welcome those who simply want to improve their academic standing – maybe a Form 5 student who isn't sure of plans yet but wants to keep doors open by getting good grades and test scores. We'll coordinate closely with the schools, but this program will largely be run outside regular school hours, to give it the flexibility and intensity we need.

DRILLS, TIMETABLES, AND TARGETS: HOW IT WORKS

What does the SAT Academy actually do? In a word: practice. Supervised, structured, relentless practice – the kind that turns weaknesses into strengths. We will run the academy in cycles aligned with the school terms and the international testing calendar. A typical cycle might look like this:

• **Baseline Test:** At the very start, we give every participant a diagnostic SAT test (or a diagnostic CSEC math/English test for Form 4s not yet ready for SAT). This baseline isn't for bragging rights or shame – it's to identify where each student is starting. Maybe John scores 480 on the Math section and 520 on Evidence-Based Reading

& Writing, for a total of 1000 (just an example). Maybe Sarah scores higher on English, lower on math, etc. We map out the common trouble spots – algebra, geometry, reading comprehension, grammar.

• **Personalized Study Timetable:** Each student, with our tutors, creates a study timetable. For example, John's plan might be: Monday/Wednesday evenings 5–7pm is Math practice time, Tuesday/Thursday 5–7pm is Reading & Writing practice, plus a half-day session on Saturday for full-length practice tests every two weeks. We essentially build an "SAT season" the way you'd have a training season for sports. During school holidays (Christmas break, Easter), we might ramp up with mini-camps – say a 3-day intensive where they do a lot of drills.

• **Drills and Skills Workshops:** On a weekly basis, the Academy will hold after-school or evening classes. These are not tedious lectures, but interactive sessions tackling specific skill areas. One week the focus might be math problem-solving techniques: tackling tricky algebra word problems or geometry questions. Another week, a session on critical reading: how to quickly analyse a passage and answer questions accurately. We'll teach test-taking strategies too – eliminating wrong answers, time management (e.g., don't spend 5 minutes on one tough question when you could get 5 easier ones done in that time). The idea is to demystify the test. The SAT has a certain style; once students recognize the patterns, they perform much better.

• **Practice, Practice, Practice:** Every two to three weeks, as I mentioned, we simulate exam conditions for practice. Saturday morning 9am, all Academy students gather at a classroom (maybe at CCSS or a community centre) and sit a timed practice SAT exam. We score it, return results, and track everyone's progress. This does two things: (1) it steadily reduces test anxiety (by exam day, they've done this so many times it feels familiar), and (2) it lets us adjust our teaching. If we see, for example, that 80% of students keep missing questions on data analysis, then we know to double down on that topic in the next drills.

• **Target Setting and Monitoring:** At the start, each student will set a target score (with guidance). If John got 1000 on the baseline, maybe he aims for 1150 by the real test – ambitious but doable with work. We also set sub-targets, like "improve Math by 100 points" or "get at least 10 out of 15 questions right in the Reading section next time" depending on the area. We keep these targets in focus, almost like a game. I'd like to put up a scoreboard (maybe virtually via a group chat or an online portal) – not public shaming, but something where students see their own improvement chart. Nothing motivates like seeing your practice score jump from, say, 1000 to 1100 over a month. It creates a hunger to hit that next milestone.

The Academy will have a small team of tutors/coaches. These could be teachers from our schools who we compensate for extra hours, recent college grads who did well in these exams, or even volunteer/ exchange tutors (perhaps Peace Corps volunteers or Fulbright scholars – we'll explore all options). We'll also incorporate online resources heavily. Khan Academy, for instance, offers excellent free SAT prep modules integrated with the College Board's system. Every student with a smartphone or computer access can use those for extra practice, and we can track their progress online. Part of our job is just to introduce them to these tools and make sure they use them.

A critical aspect is we won't neglect the regular school curriculum either. In fact, improving fundamentals for SAT goes hand-in-hand with improving CSEC/CAPE results. If we teach a student how to tackle complex reading passages for SAT, that skill helps them in, say, History or Biology class when they have to read dense material. If we drill algebra and basic trigonometry for SAT, that directly helps their CSEC Math where often the pass rates are dismal. So the Academy will also function as a supplemental class for core subjects. If a student is struggling to pass Maths in Form 5, you bet we'll be giving them extra help in the Academy sessions, because getting that CSEC Math credit is just as crucial as any SAT score for their future. We might even open up some sessions just for general tutoring – not strictly SAT, but any Form 5 who needs help with a tough topic in math or English, come in and we'll work through it.

BALANCING BOOKS AND BALLS: INTEGRATING ACADEMICS WITH SPORTS

One thing I want to emphasize is that CN SAT Academy is for everyone – not only the stereotypical top-of-class student. In particular, I want our student-athletes deeply involved. Historically, there's been this notion that if you're pushing sports, academics will lag, and vice versa. We are going to obliterate that false choice. Castries North will be the place where being a top athlete and a top student are two sides of the same coin.

How do we integrate the two practically? One way is scheduling. We will coordinate the Academy sessions with sports training schedules so they don't clash disastrously. For example, if the basketball team practices every weekday at 4pm, we might hold SAT Academy classes at 6pm on certain days – giving the players time to shower, grab a snack, then hit the books. Or we utilize the naturally lighter training days (if Friday is an off-day for practice, we do a study session then). In some cases, we might incorporate study sessions into sports programs – I've run basketball camps where kids do shooting drills, then immediately after, we circle up for 30 minutes of vocabulary drills or math quizzes. It sounds funny, but trust me, it works. I remember training with a young man, Jimmie Inglis, who went on to play Division I ball. We'd be out on the beach at 5:00 AM sprinting on the sand, and after that workout, we'd sit down on the same beach and go through SAT flashcards while catching our breath. That was our routine – sweat, then study. Jimmie had the discipline to do it, and he ended up not only excelling in sports but also earning his degrees. This kind of dual mentality – that an athlete is also a scholar – is what we will actively cultivate.

We'll also enlist coaches as allies. Any coach who works with our youth in Castries North, whether it's football, netball, cricket, you name it, will be briefed: academics are non-negotiable. I envision a policy where, for example, if a student-athlete consistently skips SAT Academy or lets their grades slide, the coach has a word and maybe even benches them until they shape up. Conversely, we celebrate the ones who are killing it in the classroom too – make them role models. Maybe at a school assembly we hand out special recognition to the "Scholar-Athlete of the Month" who improved his math grade or aced a practice test while also leading the team. Culture is powerful; if we make studiousness a cool trait among our youth, peer pressure will do a lot of good.

What about the students who are not into sports? They are equally important, obviously. The "Academy" branding might sound sporty but it's just to convey structure and intensity. For the science whiz or the aspiring artist, we will tailor the program too. Perhaps a student aiming for a university music scholarship needs to focus on portfolio and auditions – we'll still encourage them to do SAT Academy for the academic side, but also give them flexibility to pursue their craft. The key is personalized support. That's why maintaining a healthy tutor-to-student ratio is important – we don't want 1 teacher to 50 kids. We'd rather break into smaller groups where needed (e.g., a special math remedial small group for those starting very low; an advanced group for those aiming 1400+ scores to challenge them further).

I'd also love to integrate some tech and gamification. We could, for instance, have an online leaderboard (opt-in) for practice quiz performance, or organize friendly competitions: maybe SMC vs CCSS in a "SAT Prep Quiz Bowl" or something. Imagine a Jeopardy-style contest where teams from each school compete on math problems and vocabulary. It brings some of the competitive fun of sports into academics.

KEEPING SCORE: GPA AND SCHOLARSHIP OUTCOMES

Raising SAT scores is one goal, but it's not the only marker of success. GPA stabilization is a phrase I use to mean ensuring students keep their school grades up, especially during the critical final year. It's common that by Form 5, some students take their foot off the gas or get overwhelmed and their grades slip. We want to intervene before that happens. The Academy tutors, in coordination with school teachers, can identify students whose term grades are sliding and provide mentoring or extra tutoring. For athletes, we might start a mandatory "study hall" one afternoon a week – come to the library and do your homework under supervision – as is common in U.S. high schools and colleges for teams.

We'll set a tangible target such as: No CN Academy student will fail a core subject in Form 5, and aim for, say, 90% of Academy participants to graduate with at least a "B" average (or whatever equivalent, since different schools use different scales). Ambitious, yes – but if we don't aim high, we won't achieve high. We'll measure things like: how many improved their class rank or how many passed CSEC who were previously failing. Every success story becomes motivation for the younger ones coming up.

And then there's the holy grail: scholarship competitiveness. We want to see more Castries North youth winning scholarships, whether it's government of Saint Lucia scholarships, UWI Open Campus bursaries, U.S. college athletic scholarships, or international merit scholarships from abroad. Let's put a number on it: suppose currently 5 students from our constituency each year might get substantial scholarships (just an illustration). I would aim to double that in 3 years, and double again in 5. So maybe in five years' time, 20+ students from Castries North are getting significant scholarships annually. These can include sports scholarships, yes, but also academic ones. There are opportunities out there – sometimes underutilized – for Caribbean students. A well-prepared student will stand out in all those pools. Through CN Connect we'll help them apply, but through the SAT Academy we'll ensure they meet the criteria.

Let's also commit to transparency and accountability for this program. We will track median SAT scores for our cohort and (without naming names) share the improvement data. If the average score was 900 and it rises to 1050 after a year of Academy, that's concrete progress we can celebrate and then work to improve further. We'll also tally how many scholarships or university admissions each graduating class attains, as one metric of our success in academic prep. Nothing speaks louder than results. When parents see that "hey, kids from our community are suddenly getting into University of the West Indies or Monroe College or winning the Government Island Scholarship because their grades and scores shot up," buy-in will only grow.

RESOURCE NEEDS AND PARTNERS

To execute this plan, we will need resources – but not an astronomical amount. We need space for classes (which our schools can provide after hours – their classrooms or computer labs sit empty in evenings and weekends). We need teaching materials (SAT prep books, past papers, etc. – which we can acquire; some can be downloaded or donated). We likely need to cover stipends for those tutors/teachers who lead the sessions – that's worth budgeting for, and can possibly be covered by reallocating some existing education funds or seeking corporate sponsorship (a local business might sponsor the Academy in exchange for some community goodwill and branding).

The Ministry of Education should be a key partner – not to run it (sometimes waiting on a ministry means waiting forever), but to endorse it and perhaps assign a liaison or provide content support. The US Embassy and other international partners are also useful allies. The U.S. Embassy in Barbados supported a workshop for those Bajan student-athletes; our local U.S. Embassy or even organizations like the Peace Corps could help by providing expertise or volunteers. I will certainly knock on those doors. Imagine if we could get a handful of Peace Corps volunteers whose sole job is to help with literacy and math tutoring in our district – it's not far-fetched; they have programs like that worldwide.

The diaspora will also have a role to play here. I know former students from Castries North who aced the SAT or who went to colleges abroad and even taught test prep as side jobs. Through our Diaspora Skills Bank (next chapter), we can tap into that brainpower. Picture a Zoom session where an experienced St. Lucian tutor now living in New York conducts a virtual SAT math workshop for our Academy students back home. Or diaspora folks donating the latest edition prep books. It's all part of leveraging every advantage for our kids.

I also see potential to involve our university alumni network at home. For instance, Sir Arthur Lewis Community College (SALCC) has faculty and top students who could mentor or tutor the secondary students in their subjects. Maybe some of the SALCC students preparing to go off on scholarships themselves come and tutor the younger ones – creating a near-peer mentorship loop.

In terms of funding, beyond small local contributions, we could explore grants. There are international grants for education quality improvement, and NGOs focused on youth development that might fund such initiatives. As MP, I won't hesitate to write those proposals and make the case that a dollar invested in St. Lucian youth education yields massive returns for development.

THE PAYOFF: A CULTURE OF EXCELLENCE

What will success look like? Picture this: It's a Saturday afternoon at the end of the school year, and we're holding a little ceremony at the Castries Comprehensive Secondary School hall for our CN SAT Academy graduates. They've got their official SAT score reports in hand. Nearly all of them have improved dramatically from their first diagnostic test. There are smiles, even tears of joy, as we announce where some of them are heading: "Jason earned an $80,000 scholarship to Missouri Valley College thanks to his basketball talent and a solid 1200 SAT score." "Leah scored 1300 and is accepted into the University of Toronto's engineering program." "Three of our students will be starting at University of the West Indies with government scholarships." And even those who aren't going off to school immediately stand up and say, "I never thought I'd be able to score above 1000, but I did. Now I'm confident I can handle whatever courses or training come next."

The parents in the audience realize that something new, something good is happening – a break from the old pattern where high potential too often fizzled out after secondary school. The younger students in Form 3 or 4 who are watching get inspired and maybe a bit competitive:

they want that moment for themselves in a year or two. The whole community starts believing that our kids can match any from any fancy private school or big country, given the right preparation.

And let's consider one more payoff: Improved education outcomes aren't just for individual benefit; they uplift the whole society. Better educated youth means a more skilled local workforce, less unemployment, and even less crime long-term (since opportunities displace desperation). In Part I, I talked about crime prevention needing social approaches. Well, this is crime prevention too – a kid buried in SAT books every evening is one less kid idling on the block vulnerable to negative influences.

By ingraining a culture of disciplined study and high aspirations, we also counteract the narrative of brain drain. Yes, some of our best will go abroad – and we'll celebrate them – but many will come back with degrees, or contribute from abroad, or simply raise the bar of expectation for everyone. We stop assuming that top-tier academic achievement is "for other people's children" – it's for ours, right here in Castries North.

The CN SAT Academy, combined with CN Connect, is going to produce a generation of young people who are as comfortable in the library or science lab as they are on the netball court or the cricket pitch. Well-rounded, confident, and ready. When our youth step into those foreign universities or competitive local job markets, they won't be wide-eyed and lost like I was initially – they'll be saying, "I've been trained for this, I belong here."

As we look ahead, there's another treasure we must not forget to tap into for our education and youth development agenda: our own people out in the wider world. We've mentioned them – the diaspora. Many Saint Lucians abroad are eager to give back more than just a barrel or a Christmas donation; they want to share skills, knowledge, and create opportunities. In the next chapter, we'll build on that momentum. With our students better prepared than ever academically, and armed with the soft skills and confidence from CN Connect, the Diaspora Skills Bank will be the bridge that connects them (and our schools and projects) to our global family – engineers, doctors, tech experts, teachers, all contributing to Castries North's rise. The world is about to get a lot smaller and a lot more accessible for our youth.

17

The Diaspora Skills Bank

On a quiet weekend last year, I shared on social media that a few students in Castries North were starting the term without basic school supplies. I didn't make a big fuss – just a note, as part of my usual updates. Within hours, a Saint Lucian living in New York, Daniel, reached out: he wanted to help. By the end of that very weekend, while others were enjoying a Labour Day cookout, Daniel was driving around his city collecting notebooks, pencils, and backpacks. He even skipped part of a holiday jump-up to do it. A week later, a big box arrived in Saint Lucia filled with quality supplies. Because of one diaspora son's quick action, dozens of our primary school kids had brand-new materials in hand. Daniel didn't ask for thanks or publicity – in fact, he preferred to stay anonymous. But I'll thank him here, because his story is a perfect little example of what our diaspora can do, and often wants to do, for their homeland.

Now, multiply Daniel's story by a hundred, by a thousand. Imagine all the "Daniels" out there – Saint Lucians across the globe who have skills, knowledge, ideas, and goodwill to share, not just goods or money. We have an engineer in London who's designed bridges, a registered nurse in Toronto with decades of experience, a software developer in Silicon Valley working on cutting-edge apps, a teacher in Martinique who understands bilingual education, a small business owner in Miami who knows how to hustle in a competitive market. These are our people. They may live 5,000 miles away, but their hearts are never far from home. The trouble is, we as a country (and as communities) haven't made it easy for them to plug in and contribute beyond sending the occasional barrel or money transfer. Too often, "diaspora engagement" has just meant asking folks abroad to donate cash. Don't get me wrong – remittances and donations are vital. But we're leaving an even richer resource untapped: their expertise and experience.

This is why I'm proposing the Diaspora Skills Bank. It will be a living registry – essentially a talent database – of Saint Lucians abroad who are willing and ready to share their know-how for the development of communities like Castries North. In simpler terms, it's like a matchmaking service between a need at home and a resource in the diaspora. Instead of us in Saint Lucia saying "If only we had an expert in X to help with this project," we'll have a way to quickly find one – because she might be in Brooklyn or Birmingham or Barbados, and already on our list.

I know this idea can work because I've seen hints of it in action. Recall from Chapter 15 the story of Malvo "Darwin" Joseph – he's built a life in New York, but he "never forgot home… running book drives, mentoring young people, and giving back to the youth". Or take another example: Ewan – a Saint Lucian who studied in Kansas. After graduating, Ewan organized a special program that opened doors for other Saint Lucian students to attend his alma mater, Washburn University, even arranging tuition discounts for them. One person abroad created opportunities for many back home. That's diaspora engagement at its finest. The Diaspora Skills Bank aims to make stories like Darwin's and Ewan's not just personal initiatives, but part of an organized, ongoing collaboration between our people abroad and our community here.

HOW THE SKILLS BANK WILL WORK

The concept is straightforward. We will invite Saint Lucians overseas to register in the Skills Bank through a simple online platform (and via our embassies/consulates for those less techy). When they register, they provide information like: name, origin (so we know their Saint Lucian roots or the community they care about, e.g. "from La Clery, Castries North"), current country/city, field/profession, specific skills, and importantly, how they are willing to help. Maybe one person can volunteer to be a mentor to a student interested in their field. Another might offer to give a virtual guest lecture or host a workshop when they visit Saint Lucia. Someone else might say, "I can serve as an advisor on any project related to agriculture" because that's their specialty. We'll collect all that into a database.

On the home side, we (the Rep's office, local schools, community groups, etc.) will maintain a running list of needs and opportunities. For example:

- SJC's science club needs a guest speaker in marine biology.
- The health centre is organizing a community health fair and could use a doctor or nurse to do a Q&A.
- A group of young entrepreneurs in the constituency want mentorship on writing business plans.
- The after-school program is starting a robotics class but needs guidance setting up.
- Even outside the youth sphere: maybe a local farmer co-op wants advice on irrigation technology.

For each need, we'll search the Diaspora Skills Bank. If we have a marine biologist Lucian in, say, Florida, we ask if she'd do a Zoom session with the science club. If there's a doctor in London originally from our area, we invite him to participate in the health fair virtually (or time a visit home to coincide). If there's a business consultant in New York, have her pair up with our young entrepreneurs via monthly video calls to guide their plans. You get the idea. The Skills Bank turns what used to be "I wish someone could help us with this" into "Let's call on Ms. X from the Skills Bank, she knows this area."

We will also actively encourage diaspora members to propose ideas. The communication isn't one-way (us asking, them giving); it's two-way. Perhaps a group of Saint Lucian engineers abroad wants to do an "Engineering Day" workshop for schools via webinar – great! Or a successful chef overseas wants to collaborate with our hospitality training program at Sir Arthur Lewis Community College – fantastic. The Skills Bank platform will let them see posted needs and also submit their own offers or proposals for projects.

To keep things organized and responsive, I plan to designate a Diaspora Coordinator (likely someone in my team or an enthusiastic volunteer liaison) who manages the platform and relationships. This person's job is to keep communication flowing: making sure diaspora volunteers are acknowledged and looped in, and that local requests are promptly addressed. In some cases, we'll need to vet or prioritize requests – obviously, we can't overwhelm one willing diaspora person with too many asks, and we must ensure that when we bring them in, we use their time effectively with a well-defined task.

FROM VIRTUAL MENTORSHIP TO HANDS-ON PROJECTS

What exactly will diaspora members in the Skills Bank do? There are several modes of engagement, each suited to different kinds of contributions:

1. Virtual Mentorship & Coaching: This can be one-on-one or in small groups. For instance, through CN Connect we might identify a student who's keen on a career in software development. We look in the Skills Bank, find a Lucian software engineer at Google, and match them. They set up a monthly video call or even just WhatsApp chats to guide the student – discussing what courses to take, how to build a coding portfolio, etc. Similarly, a young teacher in Castries North could be mentored by an experienced Saint Lucian educator abroad, exchanging teaching strategies. These mentorship relations can be immensely motivating. Sometimes just knowing that someone who shares your background has made it in that field, and is rooting for you, propels a young person to new heights.

2. Guest Lectures & Knowledge-Sharing Sessions: Not every engagement has to be long-term. Sometimes a single impactful session can light a spark. Picture a "Diaspora Expert Series" where, say, every month we host a Zoom webinar in Castries North open to students and the public. One month it's a Saint Lucian NASA engineer talking about careers in STEM. Next month, a renowned chef dialing in from a restaurant in London, sharing culinary science tips with our hospitality students. We set up a projector at a school hall or community centre, people gather, and our guest presents and takes questions. In some cases, if the person is visiting Saint Lucia for holidays, we grab them for an in-person talk or school visit. This kind of exposure can broaden horizons in a way textbooks can't.

3. Short-Term Workshops & Training: This goes a step further than a one-off lecture. For example, a diaspora group of nurses might vacation in Saint Lucia and spend two days conducting a first-aid workshop for teachers and students – certifying them in CPR and first response. Or an IT professional might run a week-long coding camp (perhaps virtually over evenings) to kickstart a coding club. The idea is more intensive skill transfer. We formalize these as needed. The Skills Bank coordinator would work to identify the right locals to participate, arrange venue or online setup, and ensure follow-through (e.g. materials are sent out beforehand, etc.).

4. Project Collaboration & Consulting: Sometimes we might have a specific community project that needs expert input. Say we want to design a small footbridge over a drain in a neighbourhood – a diaspora civil engineer could look at the plans and give feedback pro bono. Or a local start-up is trying to break into export markets – a diaspora marketing specialist could review their strategy or even connect them with networks abroad. These can be more ad-hoc, as-needed engagements. Essentially, our community projects won't be limited by the expertise on-island; we can draw on the global Saint Lucian brain trust. I recall how David Collymore's journey (a high-jumper from Castries North) didn't end with his immediate personal success – he used his connections abroad to get scholarships for several other young athletes to follow the same path. That's a form of project collaboration too: one person turning their individual reach into a pipeline for others. We want to replicate that logic in many domains.

5. "Return & Teach" Trips: While much can be done remotely, there's nothing like face-to-face engagement. The Skills Bank will coordinate with willing diaspora professionals to actually come to Saint Lucia for short stints focused on knowledge exchange. For example, a diaspora agronomist might come for two weeks (maybe while on vacation home) and during that time, we organize visits for them to local farms, meetings with our Agriculture Ministry folks or young agriculture students, and perhaps a public seminar. They enjoy their visit, but also leave behind practical recommendations and new techniques. We can label these as "service vacations" – diaspora folks combining a trip home with structured volunteer service. To encourage this, we could lobby for some incentives: for instance, maybe the government can offer a small tax deduction or at least public recognition for those who undertake such stints. Or simply, as the MP I coordinate to ensure their schedule is productive and appreciated (maybe a community thank-you event or media highlight).

6. Material Support with Expertise Attached: In some cases, diaspora might indeed send equipment or materials, but we'll ensure it's paired with guidance on usage. Imagine a group of alumni abroad raising funds to send laptops to our schools (that happens sometimes). Through the Skills Bank, we'd involve an IT pro in that group to help set up a maintenance plan or training for teachers on using the new tech. So the donation isn't just a drop-off; it's a package of goods + know-how, which is far more effective.

A key point is that this isn't about supplanting local professionals or cutting corners. It's about supplementing and enhancing what we have. Saint Lucia is small; we won't have every specialist on island. But somewhere in our global family, we probably do. "Castries North benefits from the best of both worlds: the talent at home and the talent abroad, working together to lift our community." That's the vision: a seamless collaboration.

MAKING IT FORMAL, MAKING IT REWARDING

For diaspora engagement to be sustained, we must nurture relationships and show genuine appreciation. Here are some ways we'll do that:

• **Recognition & Feedback:** Whenever someone from the Skills Bank contributes, we will publicly acknowledge it (with their permission, of course). If Dr. Jane Doe in Boston spends an hour mentoring a student here, we'll drop her a thank-you note, maybe highlight her and the student's progress in our community newsletter or Facebook page (again, if she's okay with it). Not for vanity, but so the diaspora volunteer feels the impact and the community sees the value. We can institute annual awards or certificates – for example, "Castries North Global Partner Award" given to a few outstanding diaspora contributors each year, perhaps presented at an independence celebration event or so. Often these folks aren't looking for praise, but a little recognition goes a long way to strengthening the emotional connection.

• **Streamlined Logistics:** One thing that frustrates diaspora who try to help is red tape or cost. We will work to remove barriers. If a diaspora member is donating equipment for a workshop at a school, I as MP will coordinate with Customs or the relevant ministry to try to get duty waivers or expedited processing (the government already sometimes does this for charitable donations – we'll leverage those channels). If a volunteer needs a venue for an event here, we'll sort it out with the local school or community centre at no cost to them. Basically, we'll roll out the red carpet for any diaspora person coming in to help. They're giving us their most precious commodity – time – so let's not make them jump through hoops. I will personally intervene if necessary to cut bureaucracy; that's part of my job.

- **Integration with National Efforts:** It turns out that nationally, Saint Lucia is moving in this direction too. The government established a Diaspora Affairs Unit and even noted that they are exploring "methods for data and skills capture" to harness diaspora talent for development. Our Castries North Skills Bank can serve as a model or pilot for how to do this on a community level. I will share our results and methods with the national Diaspora Affairs office. Conversely, if the government sets up a big online platform for diaspora skills (say a national database), we will plug into that rather than reinvent the wheel. The goal is synergy, not silo. In fact, Castries North could be the leading light that shows the rest of the country what's possible when you concretely connect diaspora expertise to local needs.

- **Maintaining the Network:** A database can go stale if not managed. We'll keep it alive. That means periodic outreach: sending a quarterly e-newsletter to everyone in the Skills Bank with updates on projects, success stories, and new opportunities to help. Creating a community among them too – perhaps a Facebook or LinkedIn group specifically for Saint Lucian diaspora who are part of the program, so they can share ideas and even collaborate with each other ("Hey, maybe we three engineers can together plan a summer tech bootcamp back home next year?"). We want them to feel like members of a meaningful movement, not just a name on a list.

- **Expanding Over Time:** Initially, our focus will be on education, youth, and community development needs in Castries North – because that's our immediate mission. But I foresee that if it works, this Skills

Bank approach can expand to serve the entire constituency's needs (e.g., small business growth, health initiatives, even infrastructure advice) and inspire other constituencies to do the same. Eventually, a national Saint Lucia Skills Bank might emerge. Castries North will have been the trailblazer. And those diaspora who joined with us from early on will have the pride of saying they helped start it at the grassroots.

TIMELINE AND TARGETS

As with other initiatives, we set goals:

• In the first 6 months of launching, I'd aim to register at least 100 diaspora members in the Skills Bank database. We'll do this by reaching out through social media, diaspora associations, our foreign missions, and personal networks. I suspect 100 is easily achievable once word spreads, because people have been looking for a structured way to contribute.

• By the end of Year 1, we should have facilitated perhaps 20+ distinct engagements (mentorships, lectures, etc.) via the Skills Bank. That might include, for example, a series of 5 guest lectures, 10 ongoing mentor pairings, and a couple of workshops or consults on community projects. We'll document each.

• In Years 2-3, grow the participation to hundreds of diaspora. Possibly partner with the national Diaspora Affairs Office for a more robust web platform. We can set up an annual "Diaspora Skills Month" where each week of that month we showcase contributions or have a flurry of activities (somewhat like how some countries have a Diaspora Day or Homecoming).

• By Year 5, I'd love to see a core group of diaspora who make it a point to regularly engage with Castries North – almost like an extended advisory and support network for the constituency's development. And we'll measure outcomes: e.g., how many students benefited (maybe 50 students mentored or taught by diaspora experts over 5 years), how many community projects improved, etc.

One specific target: If just one diaspora connection results in a new scholarship or internship for one of our youth each year, that alone is a win. But I expect far more ripple effects – new ideas implemented, new contacts made, even business or investment leads (sometimes a casual mentorship chat might inspire a diaspora investor to partner on a venture back home, who knows).

Let's also not underestimate the symbolic power here. For a long time, some abroad have felt disconnected or that their country only calls them when it needs a donation or for a Independence Day gala. Meanwhile, some folks at home sometimes harbor a false notion that those who left have "abandoned" the country. The Skills Bank initiative actively bridges that emotional gap. It says, we're one people, working together across oceans. When a teenager in Castries North can say, "My mentor is a Saint Lucian who works at Microsoft in Seattle," that is a pride and a bond that goes both ways – the teen is motivated, and the mentor feels reconnected to the island's future. It knits our global family tighter.

FROM GLOBAL TO LOCAL IMPACT

Ultimately, the Diaspora Skills Bank is about making globalization work for the smallest community. Castries North may only be a few square miles on a map, but with a diaspora network engaged, our effective "brain radius" extends worldwide. We won't hesitate to call on the "people power" of Saint Lucians abroad when tackling our local challenges. Need a solution for neighbourhood flooding? Let's see if one of our diaspora civil engineers has ideas. Want to launch a new after-school tech course? Get curriculum tips from our diaspora tech educators.

This chapter's proposals might sound ambitious – coordinating people across time zones – but technology makes it easier than ever. The pandemic taught us how much can be done remotely. Now we will leverage that comfort with Zoom and Teams for something deeply positive and productive. I have a vision of a virtual round-table, where a teacher from Castries North, a professor in New York, a curriculum expert in Castries (Ministry of Education), and a techie in Canada are all brainstorming together on how to improve, say, our STEM classes or our school safety protocols. That kind of collaboration was rare in the past; it will become normal through the Skills Bank.

By bringing our diaspora into the daily development work of the constituency, we also inspire the next generation to think globally. A student who has been mentored by someone abroad is more likely to have the confidence to venture out for opportunities – and likewise to return and contribute. We're creating virtuous cycles of knowledge transfer.

As we transition to the next chapter – which deals with something very local and immediate, our after-school programs and safe spaces – keep in mind that even in those down-to-earth initiatives, the diaspora can play a supporting role. Whether it's funding a portion of a community centre renovation or volunteering virtually to run an after-school coding class, the Skills Bank will dovetail with our on-the-ground efforts. In the final chapter of this Part, "After School Built Right," we turn to how we structure those vital hours from 3 to 6 pm for our youth. And rest assured, the lessons and resources from our diaspora will be woven into that plan as well. With local hands and global knowledge together, we can build after-school programs – and indeed any program – that truly make it count.

18

After School Built Right

Every weekday around 3:00 p.m., a familiar scene unfolds in many of our communities. The school bell rings, kids flood out of classrooms, and then… far too often, chaos or solitude. Some wander the block with nothing to do, others cram into a shop playing games on their phones, a few might head home to an empty house because their parents are still at work. Those afternoon hours, unsupervised and unstructured, are when trouble can start brewing. I've lived it and I've seen it: when "our children have no safe spaces to play or learn after school", they end up "just hanging about, and it's not safe." Idle time becomes the devil's playground, as the saying goes. In Castries North we've had our share of neighbourhood mischief and more serious incidents that trace back to teens with too much free time and too little guidance between school and dinnertime.

It doesn't have to be this way. We can turn those idle hours into growth hours – a time of day kids look forward to because it's fun, enriching, and safe, and parents breathe easier knowing their child is in good hands. After School Built Right is my plan for a structured after-school program across our constituency that provides exactly that: safe spaces in every neighbourhood, steady mentorship and coaching for the kids, engaging activities that build skills, and a firm but positive code of conduct to keep everyone on track.

Let's start with the vision: I see, for example, the auditorium at Castries Comprehensive Secondary open and buzzing with activity until early evening, or the Vide Bouteille Cultural Club (VBCC) – which I grew up around – revived as an after-school hub where 30, 40, 50 young people gather daily under adult supervision. I see the schoolyards and community courts in La Clery, Bois Patat, and Sunny Acres not empty and locked at 3:30, but alive with pickup basketball games, dance practice, art projects, homework circles – all under an organized program. I see a roster of committed mentors, teachers, and volunteers circulating, helping a younger child read a book in one corner, coaching a group of boys through a drill in another, or teaching a cluster of girls how to code a simple app in the computer lab. And I hear laughter – the good kind – and constructive chatter. Then at 6:00 or 6:30, everyone heads home, a bit more tired, a bit more learned, and a lot safer and happier.

SAFE SPACES, EVERY DAY

The foundation of After School Built Right is the safe space – both physically safe and emotionally safe. Physically safe means we hold these programs in secure, kid-friendly locations. Fortunately, Castries North has several facilities we can leverage: the secondary schools and primary schools in the area, and community centres like VBCC or the ti kawé (little community buildings) in some neighbourhoods. We will partner with the Ministry of Education and community groups to open up these venues for after-school use. If a school has security concerns, we will arrange for a key and a supervisor to be present so nothing is left unprotected. It's far better to have a classroom full of children doing activities than to have them in the street or a rum shop's porch.

Emotional safety is equally critical. The after-school space must be a place where every child feels welcome and protected from bullying or harm. We will establish a zero-tolerance policy for fighting, bullying, or abuse within the program. Clear rules will be laid out on day one: respect your peers and supervisors, keep language clean, resolve conflicts with words or get an adult – no fists. If there are long-standing turf rivalries or clique tensions (which sometimes spill over from neighbourhoods or schools), the program will actively work to defuse them. One advantage of having a structured program is you can deliberately mix kids from different areas in team-building exercises so they learn to see each other as teammates, not enemies. It's hard to keep hating the boy who was your partner in a three-legged race or your teammate in a quiz competition.

We will also involve parents and guardians in setting the tone. Upon enrollment, parents will sign a simple contract outlining the behaviour expectations and agreeing to support them (for instance, if their child misbehaves repeatedly, they'll cooperate with corrective measures). The community as a whole benefits from this, so it's fair to ask community members to contribute to the positive environment – whether it's a shopkeeper keeping an eye out as kids walk home, or a neighbour volunteering as a hall monitor once a week.

STRUCTURED PLAY AND SKILL-BUILDING, NOT BABYSITTING

A key word in this initiative is "structured." This isn't a bunch of kids just left to their own devices in a playing field. International experience and common sense tell us that just corralling youth in one place isn't enough – you have to engage them. The after-school program will have a daily schedule of activities to provide routine and variety.

A typical afternoon might look like this:

• *3:00–3:30 PM: Arrival and snack time.* (Many kids are hungry after school. We'll provide a simple healthy snack – perhaps through collaboration with the school feeding program or sponsors – so they can recharge. A banana, a cheese sandwich, something to tide them over.)

• *3:30–4:30 PM: Homework Help / Academic Hour.* This is quiet time where everyone either does homework or engages in reading or educational games. Tutors (including teachers or capable older students) circulate to help anyone stuck on an assignment. Studies show, and our own anecdotal observations confirm, that many students arrive home from school in the afternoon while their parents are still at work, so they have no one to supervise or encourage them to do their schoolwork. At our program, by the time 4:30 rolls around, a good chunk of homework is done, which relieves parents and improves academic performance. This homework hour is absolutely foundational – "education first," even in an after-school fun setting.

- *4:30–6:00 PM*: *Club Activities and Sports.* This portion is more active and varied. We'll have different clubs or stations that children can choose from, led by coaches or volunteers:

On the field/court: Sports practice (football, netball, cricket, basketball – rotating through the week). For example, Mondays and Wednesdays might be basketball clinics (tying into our #SportsEconomics pipeline), Tuesdays and Thursdays football, Friday could be a fun sport like volleyball or even introduce something novel like fencing (Soufriere's program taught fencing to great effect!).

Indoors: Arts and crafts corner, where kids can draw, paint, or do drama and music. Perhaps one day a week is a drama workshop, another day is choir or drum lessons if we find a music instructor.

Life skills workshops: We schedule weekly or biweekly sessions on topics like personal finance (simple budgeting for teens), communication and conflict resolution, health and hygiene, or career talks. These can be interactive games or discussions. The program in Soufriere (run by Sacred Sports Foundation) integrated life skills alongside sports – we'll do the same.

STEM/Tech club: Using school computer labs or donated kits, kids might learn basic coding, robotics, or do science experiments under supervision. We might partner with groups like the Science and Robotics Association or diaspora techies via Zoom to run cool experiments.

Community service projects: Occasionally, instead of regular clubs, we might have the group do something for the community – clean up the schoolyard, plant trees, visit an elder care home to perform a song. This instils values of service.

Not every site will offer every activity initially – it depends on space and staffing – but the idea is a rich menu. No one gets bored because there's always something to do, and they can discover new interests. A child who came just because he loves basketball might find out he also enjoys painting. A shy girl might blossom when given a role in a little play or dance routine.

Throughout these activities, the emphasis is on building character and skills. The fun is a vehicle for growth. One student from the pilot in Soufriere said, "this program has benefitted me in so many ways: it has taught me good sportsmanship, leadership, teamwork, and how to cooperate with others." Those are exactly the outcomes we want: children learning to lead, to collaborate, to be disciplined and respectful – all while enjoying themselves.

- *6:00 PM*: *Closing Circle and Dismissal.* We gather everyone to cool down, maybe do a short reflection or prayer or team chant, share any announcements (like "game this Saturday" or "happy birthday" shoutouts). Then the kids head home. We ensure none are left stranded – parents either pick up, or in cases where kids walk, we try to have them walk in groups if possible, or arrange a drop-off for those farthest (maybe a minibus making a couple of rounds if funding allows, or volunteers giving lifts). Safety from door to door is considered.

MENTORS AND ROLE MODELS AT THE HELM

For After School Built Right to truly succeed, it needs dedicated people to run it – the kind with patience, energy, and heart for youth. In designing the staffing, we'll use a layered approach:

Program Coordinator: At least one responsible adult overseer per site (or per program if one person can cover two small sites on alternate days). This could be a teacher willing to take on an extra role (with a stipend), a trained youth worker, or even a collaboration with a local NGO where they provide a staff member. The coordinator handles the schedule, discipline issues, and liaises with school and parents.

Mentors/Facilitators: These are the people running specific activities. Ideally, a mix of talents: a sports coach or two, an arts instructor, a tutor for homework, etc. We will draw from multiple sources:

Teachers and School Staff: Some teachers might welcome a paid extra hour or two to supervise homework or run a club for extra income, plus they know the kids academically. We'll coordinate with their unions and ministry to make sure it's agreeable and fair.

Community Volunteers: This includes retirees (imagine a retired principal helping kids read, or a former nurse teaching first aid), parents, and enthusiastic young adults. We will establish a simple vetting (basic background check and interview) because child safety is paramount – only trustworthy individuals will be placed in charge.

Youth Leaders: Older students (Sixth formers, college students, even Form 5s who are responsible) can volunteer as peer tutors or assistant coaches. In fact, part of our program can incorporate a leadership track for these older youth – they get community service hours and experience, and the younger ones get near-peer role models. Over time, we create a cycle where today's participant becomes tomorrow's mentor.

Police Youth Club Officers: The Royal St. Lucia Police Force often supports youth clubs. Inviting an off-duty officer or dedicated youth officer to occasionally be present (in plain clothes, acting as a mentor not a cop) can help with discipline and break down negative perceptions between youth and police. They might lead a session on conflict resolution or just shoot hoops with the kids while chatting about life choices. We saw earlier that heavy policing isn't the answer to youth crime – but positive engagement is.

NGO Partners: We will collaborate with any active organizations. The Sacred Sports Foundation's "Beyond the Bell" program, supported by USAID, was a model that served 570 boys and girls across St. Lucia, St. Kitts, and Nevis. If they or similar NGOs are available to assist in Castries North, we'll gladly partner rather than reinvent the wheel. They have training modules, sports equipment, and experience.

Diaspora Contributors: As discussed in Chapter 17, diaspora can plug in too. A diaspora professional might not be on-site daily, but could conduct a monthly virtual workshop or donate resources. For instance, a group of former Saint Lucian athletes abroad might sponsor uniforms or come do an annual sports clinic with our after-schoolers. Through the Diaspora Skills Bank, we can even have a rotation of "virtual mentors of the month" who join our closing circle via video to give a short pep talk or Q&A – connecting kids to the wider world.

All mentors and staff will get an orientation on the program's goals and methods – essentially a short training. We'll cover basics like managing groups of children, first aid (we'll always have a first aid kit and an adult trained to use it present), conflict de-escalation, and how to spot any signs of deeper issues (e.g., if a child shows signs of abuse or acute distress, the mentor knows to flag it confidentially to the coordinator, who can involve school counsellors or social services as needed).

Crucially, we'll maintain a low adult-to-child ratio. Research and common sense say one adult cannot effectively supervise 40 kids in a free-form setting. We'll aim for something like 1 adult per 10-15 children during activities, and even tighter during homework time (maybe 1 tutor per 5-10 kids depending on needs). That means if 50 kids attend a site, we want perhaps 1 coordinator, 3-4 adult mentors, and a handful of youth volunteers. It's an investment in manpower, yes, but the returns – safer kids, better students, less trouble in the streets – are well worth it.

HOLDING THE LINE ON BEHAVIOUR

"Built Right" implies not only offering activities but also instiling the right values and discipline. As mentioned, we'll have a code of conduct. I want to dig a bit into how we enforce it constructively.

First, consistency is key. The rules will be clearly posted and explained: treat each other with respect (no insults, no bullying), listen to the supervisors, no leaving the premises without permission (for safety reasons), maintain a positive attitude (we actually encourage them to support each other, not tease someone for trying at a new skill). We won't tolerate any drugs, alcohol, or weapons obviously – any serious infraction like that results in suspension and involvement of parents and possibly authorities.

For everyday discipline, we implement a graduated system:

• Minor issues (not listening, running off, minor horseplay): the mentor gives a verbal reminder or maybe assigns a quick timeout (sit out of game for 5 minutes to reflect).

• Repeated or moderate issues (frequent disrupting, teasing others): a meeting with the coordinator and perhaps a call to parent. We might have the child do a small "repair" action, like help clean up equipment (turning discipline into a learning moment of responsibility).

• Serious issues (fights, bullying, defying safety rules): immediate intervention by coordinator, parents called in for a conference, possibly a short suspension from the program to send a message that we mean business about safety and respect. But importantly, we invite them back with a behaviour contract – we don't want to expel kids unless absolutely necessary, because often the ones acting out are the ones who need this program most. There might be underlying issues; we'll try to address those by maybe pairing that kid with a mentor specifically.

• If a child really cannot comply after many chances, we may have to remove them for the sake of others. But we'll coordinate with school counsellors or social workers in such cases to find alternative help – we won't simply discard a troubled youth.

Positive reinforcement will be the flip side. We'll recognize "good behaviour" and effort. For instance, each week the mentors might pick a "Star of the Week" – not just the best athlete or student, but perhaps the most improved behaviour or the one who helped others the most. Their name gets cheered and maybe they get a small reward (donated books, a certificate, a feature on our social media). Group rewards too – "If we go a whole month with good attendance and behaviour, we'll have a little party or a field trip." This gives them something to work toward.

Already, many of our youth are craving structure and belonging. Often, gangs and bad company lure teens by offering what looks like structure and belonging (albeit destructive). We're providing the positive alternative: a place they belong and a structure that supports them. And let me tell you, once momentum builds, the culture can shift dramatically. In communities where robust after-school programs have been implemented, you often see a drop in juvenile incidents and an increase in school performance. Why? Because the peer norm becomes trying in school, cooperating with adults, planning for the future – versus the old norm of street toughness or apathy.

Consider the data: The USAID pilot programs reported that participating youth showed improved attitudes toward school and better social skills. And those programs specifically targeted "vulnerable youth" – often kids from difficult home situations. In one Vieux Fort program, the organizer noted, "Of the 56 children... only 11 have both parents. A lot of these young children… are doing quite poorly in school and have issues at home or social issues. In some cases, they are sexually active, drinking alcohol, and either themselves or their families have a history of crime and violence." That's a profile of kids on the brink. But she goes on to say "the transformation has been quite incredible… when the bell rings, they know it's a good program. I think a lot of the young people might not realize how much they're developing, becoming more mature and better equipped to handle challenging situations." If transformation can happen for those high-risk 11- to 16-year-olds, imagine what it can do in Castries North for our kids if we implement it right. We will catch many before they fall into those risky behaviours.

FUNDING AND SUSTAINABILITY

How will we fund all this? It's a fair question – quality programs aren't free. However, we can be creative and multi-streamed in funding:

• **Government Budget:** As MP, I will push for allocation of some existing education or youth development funds toward after-school programs. For example, the Ministry of Youth could reallocate a portion of its budget that might be under-utilized elsewhere. Even the security budget – investing in after-school is investing in crime prevention, which saves costs later on. I will make that case in Parliament. Perhaps we pilot in Castries North with central government support, then expand nationwide.

• **Community Development Programs:** There are programs like the SSDF (Social Development Fund) and donor grants targeted at youth. We will write the proposals. If USAID or UNICEF or the EU or even friendly governments have grant calls for youth initiatives, we'll be at the front of the line with our plan (which, by being detailed in this book, is essentially ready to present).

• **Private Sector Sponsors:** I intend to approach local businesses – especially ones that benefit from a safer, better-educated community (which is basically all of them). For instance, a bank might sponsor an "Academic Corner" providing supplies and perhaps a stipend for a teacher-tutor; a telecom company might donate free internet or tablets for a tech club; a supermarket or bakery could sponsor the daily snack. In return, they get goodwill and maybe some branding rights like "Massy Stores After-School Fitness Hour" (tastefully done).

• **Diaspora Contributions:** Our diaspora, through the Skills Bank, could contribute both expertise and funds. A group of alumni from SMC abroad might raise money to refurbish the school hall for after-school use or ship sports equipment. Remember Daniel and his school supplies? Multiply that by dozens of Daniels – structured diaspora giving can support program needs like uniforms, art supplies, even a stipend for a full-time coordinator's salary.

• **Volunteer Power:** By recruiting volunteers, we reduce labour costs. The more qualified volunteers we have, the less we need to pay staff, focusing funds on core coordination and materials. Castries North has many educated folks (some retired, some working shifts) who might give an hour or two a week because they care. We will rally that civic spirit.

• **Stagger and Scale:** We don't need to start with five sites at once. We can phase in. Maybe in Year 1, we launch two major sites (say one at CCSS/VBCC covering the urban part, and one at maybe a primary school in another pocket of the constituency). Show success, then scale to more communities in Year 2 and 3. Starting a bit smaller allows us to iron out kinks and demonstrate impact, which in turn helps unlock more funding for expansion.

Our aim will be to keep the program free of charge to all children. Accessibility is crucial – the ones who need this most often can't pay. We might accept or encourage a token contribution from parents who can afford it (like $20 XCD a month) to instil ownership, but it would be voluntary or on a sliding scale. No child will be turned away for money. If funding ever gets tight, we'd sooner hold a community fundraiser or cut non-essentials than start charging a fee that excludes kids.

One idea: organize an annual Community Sports and Arts Day as a fundraiser, where the kids in the program showcase what they've learned (do a little play, tournament, art exhibition) and we invite the whole community, selling refreshments, raffle tickets, etc. It becomes both a celebration of the program and a way to raise some funds and support.

Additionally, we'll measure and publicize outcomes – reduced truancy, improved grades, fewer reports of youth incidents in evenings – to make the case for continued investment. If the data shows what we expect, it will be easier to secure ongoing support from government and donors. This ties into the "scorecard" approach I have for accountability in Part VI of the book.

BUILDING A BETTER PATHWAY

After School Built Right ties together so many threads of our broader agenda. It reinforces academic success (feeding into the CN SAT Academy and better CSEC passes), it provides a talent pipeline for sports and arts (feeding into #SportsEconomics and cultural development), and it addresses social issues like crime and youth disaffection at the root. It even provides a practical outlet for those trained through CN

Connect and the Skills Bank – local youth leaders and diaspora experts can come practice their mentorship in the after-school setting.

Let's envision Castries North a few years into this program: It's a weekday evening, and you drive through Vide Bouteille or La Clery around 5:00 pm. Instead of seeing clusters of idle youths by the roadside or hearing about some school fight continuing after hours, you see the lights on at the school hall and a bunch of kids playing futsal supervised by Coach so-and-so, or a group in the library nook poring over books with Miss so-and-so. A passerby might not even realize – they'll just notice kids still at school late and think "are these children in detention?" And the answer will be, "No, they're there by choice (and some gentle nudging) bettering themselves."

One parent might tell another, "Mwen bien kontan program sala; i tenir gason mwen an plas an sekirite apré lékol, épi i ka édé'y travay pou lékól li." (I'm really happy with this program; it keeps my son in a safe place after school and helps him with his school work.) That parent has peace of mind at work knowing her child isn't roaming. Meanwhile, that boy's chances of falling prey to negative influences plummet.

And for the children, we're not just keeping them busy – we're expanding their horizons. A girl who learns to code a simple game at 13 in our after-school tech club might pursue IT in college because of that spark. A boy who discovers he loves drama might become a cultural arts teacher down the line instead of drifting into trouble. Even more immediately, these kids will carry themselves differently. They'll have more confidence, better social skills, and a sense that the community values them enough to invest time in them every single day – which, psychologically, is huge. It builds their self-worth and, by extension, their respect for others.

One participant in an after-school program noted that the kids "might not realize how much they're developing... becoming more mature and better equipped" because it feels just like fun and games to them. But the growth is happening inside. That's what we want: organic development through structured play and learning.

In closing, After School Built Right is about shaping the next generation hour by hour. It's not a flashy infrastructural project or a one-off event; it's daily, grind-it-out nation-building at the community level. It exemplifies my philosophy that representation is service, and service means being present in the everyday lives of people, especially our youth. When I say "we are not beggars and he is not a king," I also mean we should not have to beg for safe spaces for our children – it is our duty to provide them. This program is a promise that every child in Castries North will have somewhere to go after school that lifts them up.

As we end Part III of this book, let's reflect on what we've laid out: a bold, actionable agenda to empower our young people through education, skills, and support. We talked about linking schools to global opportunities (CN Connect), turbocharging academic readiness (SAT Academy), tapping the wisdom of our diaspora (Skills Bank), and now providing daily structure and safety (After School Built Right). These reforms are concrete and doable. They don't require miracles, just the will to organize and the heart to care consistently. With these in place, the kid who might have dropped out or drifted into crime can instead find a scholarship or a skilled job. The student who felt overlooked can discover a passion and a mentor. The cycle of wasted potential can be broken – one mentorship, one test score, one safe afternoon at a time.

This is how we Make It Count for our youth. Part IV will turn to another fundamental area: health and wellness in our community. But even there, you'll see the echoes of Part III – a healthy, active community often starts with habits ingrained in youth, perhaps on those same courts and fields after school. We're building, piece by piece, a Castries North where every individual – from child to senior – has the support to thrive. And it starts right here, when the school bell rings, and instead of saying "Bye, kids, you're on your own," we say "Come, let's spend these hours together and make them count."

Part IV – Health, Clinics & Active Living

19

A Clinic That Actually Works

"The best time to start was yesterday. The next best time is today."

I am fourteen years old, limping into the La Clery Health Centre with a blood-soaked rag around my toe. It's 1985. The waiting room fan creaks overhead, barely stirring the humid air. My toe is throbbing, sand still stuck to the cut from a rough football game. A nurse finally beckons me in. She cleans the wound, wraps it, tells me to "be more careful next time," and sends me off. I remember the linoleum floor and the pale green walls. I remember feeling small and nervous, but also relieved that someone patched me up. What I didn't know was that decades later, those same pale green walls and creaking fan would still be there, greeting a new generation of patients. The world moved on; our little clinic did not.

Fast forward to now. It's early morning in La Clery and I stand outside that same health centre, now called the La Clery Wellness Centre. The sun is climbing, vendors are setting up nearby, and a few elderly folks are already gathering by the clinic's door. Tuesdays are "pressure and sugar" day – the designated time for blood pressure and diabetes check-ups. By 7:30 a.m., a line of mostly seniors snakes along the ramp. Some lean on canes; some clutch tote bags with their medical cards and pill bottles. They wait patiently because they know if they miss today, they'll wait another week to be seen. I greet a few familiar faces. Miss Catherine, 72, jokes that she's "coming to get in trouble" if her blood sugar is high again. Mr. Joseph, a retired mason, shifts on his feet and quietly mentions he's almost out of his hypertension tablets. The pharmacy at the clinic has been out of stock for two weeks, and he couldn't afford all the refills at a private drugstore. His next hope is that when the doctor sees him today, the clinic might have the medication back in stock. If not, he'll leave with a prescription paper and a shrug – and not much else.

By 8:00 a.m. the clinic opens, and the small crowd files in. The La Clery Wellness Centre has two consultation rooms, a tiny pharmacy window, and a waiting area with about a dozen plastic chairs. On good days, the system works: the nurse checks vitals, the visiting doctor arrives on time, patients get their checks and meds, and everyone is out by lunch. On bad days, the doctor might be called away or supplies run out. I've seen a morning clinic stretch to 3 p.m., hungry diabetics getting jittery as they wait for care. I've also seen frustrated folks mutter that they'll just go to Victoria Hospital next time – even though that means a long trip downtown and a crowded casualty department.

Here's the truth we live with: our health centre is understaffed, closed on weekends, and unable to address the modern challenges our community faces. In the 1980s, a basic clinic might have been enough. Today, Castries North has an older population and a heavier burden of chronic disease. Roughly one in every twelve Saint Lucians has diabetes, and Castries leads the island in hypertension cases. That means hundreds of our neighbours in this constituency need regular blood pressure checks, glucose monitoring, medication refills, and advice. In the year 2025, a clinic that opens only Monday to Friday, and closes by 4 p.m., simply isn't meeting those needs. If you get a chest pain on a Saturday, too bad – come back Monday or head to the emergency room. If you work an 8-to-4 job and can't sacrifice a day's pay to attend the clinic, well, you gamble by postponing care. And if you need a basic lab test or an X-ray, prepare to commute to another facility or pay out of pocket at a private office.

The La Clery Health Centre looks the same today as it did when I burst my toe in 1985. It's practically frozen in time. No major expansion, no significant upgrade. Meanwhile, our population's needs have expanded and changed. Back then we worried about colds, cuts, maybe a baby delivery gone awry (though even then, most births were at Victoria Hospital). Today we're facing an epidemic of diabetes and high blood pressure, rising asthma in kids, mental health struggles among youth, and new threats like dengue and COVID. A clinic stuck in the past, with the same layout and mindset, cannot solve today's problems.

Let me give you a story that plays out too often: A middle-aged man from Morne Du Don, let's call him Denis, has been feeling chest tightness at night. He's the stoic type, works maintenance at a hotel, rarely complains. One Friday evening the pain gets bad. His wife urges him to go to the health centre. But it's 7 p.m. on Friday – the clinic is closed until Monday. Denis decides to wait it out. By Sunday dawn, he's in the hospital with a heart attack that could have been prevented or lessened with earlier care. Thankfully he survives, but with damage that might limit his ability to work. Now imagine if Denis had a clinic open on Saturday for a quick ECG and check-up. Or a 24-hour hotline staffed by a nurse who could advise him. These are not fantasies; they are basic services in many places. Yet here in Castries North, we don't have them. That gap between Friday and Monday can be deadly.

Beyond hours and staffing, there is the issue of quality and dignity of care. It's not just about seeing a nurse or doctor; it's about feeling respected and heard when you do. I'll be honest: my own last visit to our health centre was not pleasant. I left feeling like a bother, rushed through, and none the wiser about my issue. I've heard similar from others – a young mother in La Clery who felt judged for asking questions about her baby's nutrition; an older man who complained that every time he goes, it's a different doctor who doesn't know his history. These are not individual failings of staff (many of whom work very hard) – they are symptoms of a system that isn't set up to truly serve people. Healthcare is a whole-life issue, a dignity-centred issue. It's about a grandmother being able to manage her diabetes so she can dance at her granddaughter's wedding. It's about a teenager getting mental health support early, without stigma, so he doesn't turn to substances. It's about each of us, no matter our age or income, feeling that when we walk into that clinic we are valued and our time matters.

So, what would it look like if our clinic actually worked? Let's imagine "good" healthcare at the community level, the kind that people talk about with relief instead of frustration. First off, hours that match real life. A clinic that opens early some days or stays open later, so working families can visit without losing a day's wages. Maybe one or two evenings a week, the doors remain open until 8 p.m., specifically to serve those who can only come after work. And yes, at least a half-day on Saturdays for urgent cases or check-ups. We can rotate staff or partner with volunteer physicians to cover these extended hours – it's doable if we prioritize it. No one should have to choose between their paycheck and their health.

Next, basic meds in stock. A clinic that actually works should not constantly send people away with prescriptions for medicines that are supposed to be free or affordable on site. It's heartbreaking and infuriating when an elderly patient on a small pension is told the clinic's out of metformin or blood pressure pills, and they must find it at a private pharmacy for $50 a month. We must keep a steady supply of the common drugs that so many depend on – the metformin, the enalapril, the insulin, the asthma inhalers – and even basic pain relievers and antibiotics. This is a management issue: better inventory tracking, a little more budget priority, maybe emergency restock funds. And if the Ministry's central medical stores are having supply issues, the clinic should have authority to purchase from local distributors in the interim. A prescription that can't be filled might as well be a piece of paper. We can't pat ourselves on the back for writing "free" prescriptions if in practice the patient has to pay or go without. A working clinic closes that loop.

Just as importantly, a clinic that works has a feedback loop for fixing problems fast. What do I mean by that? I mean a culture where if something goes wrong – say patients are waiting too long, or the blood pressure cuff is broken, or the bathroom has no running water – it gets addressed quickly, not next year. In practical terms, perhaps we establish a Community Health Committee for Castries North. A small group of local residents, including maybe a retired nurse, a school teacher, a businessperson, who meet with the clinic staff every quarter. They bring community complaints and suggestions directly to the people who can solve them. And they follow up: is the issue resolved or not? For example, if we find that on diabetes clinic days the wait times are 5 hours, maybe the committee works with the nurses to implement an appointment system or a numbered ticket system so people can leave and come back instead of sitting all day. Or if mothers are complaining that the clinic's child-health days are too crowded and rushed, maybe we add an extra child clinic per month. These might seem like small tweaks, but this is how you make services human-centred. It's about listening and adapting.

Right now, it can feel like complaints about the health centre vanish into a black hole. People grumble at the bus stop or on Facebook, but nothing changes. With a proper feedback loop – whether it's a committee, a suggestion box that actually gets read, or a monthly town hall with the District Medical Officer – we create accountability. We make it normal that the community helps set the standards for their healthcare. If a nurse is regularly rude, that should come to light and be corrected. If a particular service is in demand, that should inform next year's budget to expand it. A clinic that works is one that learns and improves constantly. We won't get everything right at once, but we can get better every month.

I want to highlight one glaring area of need and opportunity: elder care and chronic disease management. Castries North, like much of Saint Lucia, is an aging community. We have more seniors now than we did 20 years ago, and they are living longer, often with long-term conditions. Ask any middle-aged person here and they'll tell you about caring for an aging parent or neighbour dealing with diabetes complications or recovering from a stroke. Yet we have very little structured support for them locally. Our health centre could be so much more for our seniors. Imagine if the clinic hosted a weekly "Senior Wellness Club." On Wednesday mornings, instead of just coming to check blood pressure, seniors could join a short exercise session in the clinic's yard or adjacent community space (a bit of gentle stretching or a walk around the block, guided by a health aide). After that, a health educator or nurse could give a 15-minute talk on a relevant topic – how to manage your medications, tips for healthy meals on a budget, or even recognizing the signs of depression and where to get help. Then maybe some social time – a cup of bush tea and a game of dominoes or quatres with peers – supervised by a community volunteer. This sounds simple, almost too ordinary to mention, right? But to an elderly person who spends most days alone at home, an event like that could become the highlight of their week. They would be moving their bodies, learning something useful, and crucially, connecting with others. Loneliness and inactivity are silent killers for our elderly. A vibrant clinic sees that and responds.

And how about preventative care at the doorstep? In years past, we had the concept of the "district nurse" who would do home visits for those who couldn't easily come to the clinic. That practice has dwindled. I'd like to bring it back in a modern way. Our constituency could have a Mobile Health Team – a nurse or health aide who, say, every Thursday afternoon makes house calls to the frail or bedridden or just the very elderly living alone. They could check blood pressure, dress a wound, ensure medications are being taken correctly, maybe even draw blood for routine tests. Family members would appreciate the guidance, and many crises could be averted by catching issues early. Funding this might mean pushing the Ministry for an extra community nurse position assigned to Castries North, or partnering with NGOs or retired medical professionals willing to volunteer a few hours a week. It's well worth exploring. Healthcare doesn't only belong in four walls – sometimes it needs to come to you.

Now, some might ask: how does an independent candidate plan to achieve all this if he's not in the ruling government or the Ministry of Health? It's a fair question. The answer is partnership and relentless advocacy backed by a clear plan. A Parliamentary Representative, even from the opposition or an independent, has influence if he comes with solutions in hand and mobilizes the community to demand them. I will knock on the Health Ministry's door with data: "Look, Castries North's clinic handles one of the largest volumes of NCD (non-communicable disease) check-ups on the island, we need more resources here." I will bring those seniors and mothers with me figuratively – their testimonies, their petitions for better hours and services. I will seek creative funding: for instance, Taiwan and the World Bank have funded health centre upgrades in Saint Lucia before. There was EC$45 million in grants for health facilities announced in the last Budget, and I will fight tooth and nail to ensure Castries North gets its fair share of that pie. No more of our clinic being left behind while others get shiny upgrades. If I have to publicly catalogue the dilapidation and the missed funding, I will. Sunshine is a great disinfectant – I will put the state of our clinic and its importance into the national spotlight until it's impossible to ignore.

But this isn't about begging central government. It's about local initiative. If given the honour to serve, I would use a portion of my constituency allowance and any discretionary project funds to start making improvements right away. For example, simple facility fixes: ensure the clinic has a generator or solar backup so that when power goes out (as it often does), vaccines don't spoil and appointments don't get cancelled. Fix that leaky roof and replace the broken waiting room benches with ones that have armrests and cushions – small touches that make a huge difference to an arthritic grandma waiting two hours. Ensure privacy curtains and working fans in exam rooms so patients feel comfortable. These are not big-ticket items; they're basic respect.

Then, structural expansion: The La Clery Wellness Centre sits on government land, and I happen to know there's some unused space to the back and side of it. Why not extend the building or add a modular annex? We could create a dedicated health education and therapy room. During clinic hours it could host group sessions – maybe a dietician doing a healthy cooking class for diabetics, or a counsellor leading a stress management workshop for young adults (did I mention we have a brewing mental health crisis among our youth? We do, and a proactive clinic would address that too). In off-hours, that room could double as a small community gym or rehabilitation space – imagine having a couple of stationary bikes, mats, and light weights available for supervised exercise sessions for cardiac rehab patients or seniors trying to improve balance. I even picture an "ice bath" or cold therapy tub in one corner, as bold as that sounds, so that our local athletes or ailing seniors can get modern physiotherapy right here without travelling to a private clinic. We have a deep sports history in this constituency – from famous cricketers to basketball stars – and many of those folks, now older, suffer the aches and pains that a bit of physio or an ice dip can relieve. Why not integrate that into a wellness centre? It would send a powerful message that health is not just treating illness, but actively restoring wellness.

In fact, let's transform the La Clery Health Centre into more than a clinic – into a true Community Wellness Hub. I have said it before and I'll repeat it here: that site can be so much more. It can be part health centre, part education space, part fitness and rehabilitation facility. During one radio interview, I laid it out plainly: "I would like that health centre to be transformed into more than a health centre – like an education centre also. That part of the constituency has a deep history in sports; we can use the clinic for elderly folks' education on diabetes, for physical fitness sessions, even an ice-bath and physical therapy area." Those weren't just words – they are now written in my plan. And I know it's achievable because we don't have to start from scratch; we just have to reimagine what's already there.

Consider the surroundings of the clinic. Adjacent to the health centre, there's open ground that's been underutilized for years. Right now it might have some scrub grass or be used for parking, but I see a small outdoor exercise park there. A few pieces of low-impact equipment – parallel bars for stretching, a walking path loop, maybe a gazebo for shade. It could be a little therapeutic garden where patients wait or recover after a session, instead of sitting on a hard bench indoors. If we plan it right, someone finishing with the nurse could step right outside and join a mild exercise class. The clinic and the park could work hand in hand – treating and preventing in one continuous loop. In public health they talk about the "social determinants of health" – the idea that health is shaped by where you live, play, work. Let's put that concept into action on the very grounds of our wellness centre.

I'm also inspired by what some of our Caribbean neighbours are doing. The government of Barbados, for example, transformed their old primary care clinics into polyclinics that are open evenings and even 24/7 in some cases for urgent care. They recognized that the capital's hospital was overwhelmed because people had nowhere else to go after hours. We have started to catch on here in Saint Lucia: the Ministry of Health recently announced plans for a Castries Urban Polyclinic at the site of the old Victoria Hospital. That's a great idea – it will offer urgent care on weekends, X-rays, even dental and eye care – and I support it fully. But Castries North is a distinct community; the polyclinic downtown won't fully substitute for a local clinic that understands our specific needs and geography. In the interim, since the Castries City Wellness Centre was closed due to disrepair, our La Clery centre has been picking up extra load – without extra resources to handle it. We've been asked to do more with the same or less. I will demand that when the fancy polyclinic opens, Castries North's wellness centre is not forgotten in its shadow. We must get concurrent investment to upgrade La Clery, to integrate it with that wider network (for instance, linking our patient records digitally so someone seen in La Clery can easily be referred to the polyclinic or the main hospital and vice versa). I will also push for the services offered at the polyclinic (like diabetic eye screening, hearing tests, etc.) to have periodic outreach days in La Clery. Maybe the polyclinic's mobile unit comes to La Clery once a month so seniors don't have to trek to town for those services. These are the kind of practical linkages an MP can lobby for if he's paying attention and fighting for his community's share.

Let me share another small but telling anecdote: Last year, a young father in Vide Bouteille told me about taking his toddler to our clinic for an immunization. The nurse was competent and kind, he said, but the environment was so drab and unwelcoming that his child cried from the moment they walked in. The posters on the wall were peeling and dated, the play corner that you see in some clinics was nonexistent – not even a single toy or colorful picture to distract a child. The little girl associated going to the clinic with fear and boredom. Her dad said, "It felt like a place you go when something's wrong with you, not a place that cares about keeping you well." That struck me. A place that cares about keeping you well – that's exactly what we need to create. So even in the seemingly superficial details, I want to change the atmosphere.

Let's involve local artists to paint a bright mural in the waiting area – something showing healthy, happy St. Lucian families, perhaps. Let's have a small bookshelf with children's books and health pamphlets. Let's pipe in some light music or educational messages rather than that deafening silence or chatter of frustration. When people walk in, let them feel a bit more at ease, like this is their space. Healing begins with feeling comfortable and respected.

Now, none of these improvements – extended hours, more staff, better supplies, new programs – will matter if the community doesn't use the clinic or trust it. So we have to rebuild trust and engagement. That's why I want to launch a "Know Your Clinic" campaign. Soon after taking office (God willing), I'd organize an open day at the health centre. Invite everyone – especially those who've given up on the clinic – to come meet the staff, tour any new improvements, and share concerns. We could offer free blood pressure checks and blood sugar tests right there as an incentive. Make it a sort of health fair with maybe a visiting doctor giving a talk or a dentist doing quick dental screenings for kids. Through transparency and openness, we signal: this is your clinic, we work for you. I'd follow that up with periodic surveys – literally going out with volunteers or health committee members, asking residents "How was your clinic experience this month? What can we do better?" and publishing those findings (with privacy of course) so everyone sees where we're hitting the mark or falling short. In a community of our size, feedback isn't hard to gather – it just takes the will to ask and listen.

Let's talk about modern challenges that our 1970s-era clinic model isn't addressing at all right now. One is mental health. The 2022 census recorded a noticeable number of depression cases in Castries, and we all know the pandemic worsened anxiety and stress for many. Our young people in particular are facing pressures around unemployment, identity, even crime and violence in society. Yet if you walk into La Clery Wellness Centre today and say you're feeling depressed or overwhelmed, what happens? There is no psychologist on staff. There's no counseling room. If you're lucky, a nurse might kindly refer you to the National Mental Wellness Centre across town, or a visiting doctor might scribble a prescription for anti-anxiety pills. More likely, you'll just be told to seek help elsewhere. We must change that. I propose that we integrate mental health into primary care here. Maybe one day a week, we have a trained counsellor or social worker available at the clinic (even if just for half a day) for walk-ins or referrals. We could partner with NGOs like the Saint Lucia Mental Wellness Association to facilitate this, or even tap into the talent of faith-based counsellors from churches in our area who have training. Also, let's train our regular clinic staff with basic skills to handle these conversations – something like Mental Health First Aid training for nurses and front-desk staff, so they know how to respond if someone comes in emotional distress. Whole-life care means caring for the mind as much as the body.

Another modern challenge: substance abuse and addiction. Our community has seen the toll of alcohol especially, and now more potent stuff like cocaine derivatives and an increase in marijuana use among youth. I know this is a heavy topic, but a truly community-oriented health service would not ignore it. We could have the clinic coordinate with the substance abuse unit at the Ministry or the nearby Turning Point rehab facility. Perhaps quarterly, they run an outreach session in Castries North – discreetly advertised as a "Wellness Check" where folks struggling with addiction can come for advice, basic screening (like liver function tests for heavy drinkers), and referral to counseling or rehab if needed. These are the proactive touches that help people before they end up in a hospital bed or in the criminal justice system.

It's about meeting people where they are. A man who would never drive himself to the formal rehab centre might just walk into his local clinic if he knows help is there and it's confidential.

I can't talk about healthcare without touching on its connection to the economy and education, because they all feed into each other. A sick community is an unproductive community. When our clinic fails, people miss work or work less effectively. Children miss school. Families spend money on taxi fares to distant facilities or on private doctors for things that should have been handled in public primary care. Those are hidden costs draining our limited incomes. By making the clinic work, we actually boost our local economy subtly – fewer sick days, less money leaking out to private health services, more peace of mind to focus on business and learning. And conversely, educating our community (through that health education aspect I mentioned) will mean healthier habits and less strain on the clinic in the long run. If a weekly clinic talk convinces five people to cut back on salty foods and exercise a bit, that's potentially five fewer stroke or dialysis cases a decade from now. That's priceless in both human and financial terms.

You know, there's a guiding principle in all this: we are not beggars in our own country, and we shouldn't be beggars for basic healthcare either. I recall the spirit of Sir George Charles – one of our nation's founding figures – who championed the dignity of the ordinary man. Dignity of work, dignity of access. What I am proposing for healthcare in Castries North is exactly that: treating every person who walks through those clinic doors with dignity, and giving the staff the tools and environment to deliver dignified care.

As I watch the last patients filter out of the La Clery Wellness Centre around midday, I imagine what this scene could be a year or two from now. I see Miss Catherine emerging not only with her blood sugar controlled, but with a pamphlet in hand about an exercise class she's excited to join. I see Mr. Joseph picking up his hypertension pills right at the clinic pharmacy, no longer worried about stock-outs. I see a young man who came in depressed leaving with a referral to a counsellor who will meet him at the clinic Thursday. I see the nurse locking up, but not for the whole weekend – because tomorrow Saturday there'll be a half-day clinic for those who can't come in weekdays. I see a building that has a fresh coat of paint, a ramp that actually isn't broken, perhaps even a new wing where a few folks are doing stretches with a physiotherapist. In short, I see a clinic that works.

This vision is not some luxury wishlist – it's the standard that our citizens deserve. It's what I will fight for, day in and day out, as part of making Castries North rise again. We fix this clinic, and we set a precedent for every other neglected corner in our community. We show that we don't accept decay; we innovate and improve.

As I lock up the gate (the last one leaving often does that in small communities), I whisper to myself the same line I often tell my kids and teammates: "We can do better. And we will." This health centre is where better begins – not in speeches, but in daily, tangible service. We owe that to our elders who built this community, and to our children who will inherit it.

Healthcare is not a favour to ask for; it is our right and our priority. I'm rolling up my sleeves to make sure the clinic at La Clery actually works for all of us. And when it does, it won't just heal ailments – it will heal a bit of our trust that positive change is possible right here at home. Enough waiting. Let's build the clinic we deserve, now.

In transforming our local clinic, we shall rediscover a simple truth: health is about respect, access, and keeping people whole. With that foundation, we can move from treating illness to cultivating wellness – in every sense of the word. Next, we'll look beyond the clinic walls, to how staying healthy also means staying active, at every age.

20

Move at Any Age (Especially After 60)

I'm standing at the Vigie beach at dawn, barefoot in the cool sand, watching a remarkable sight. There's a group of ladies and gentlemen in their sixties, seventies, even a couple over eighty, spread out in a loose circle by the water's edge. They're doing gentle stretches and arm swings in unison, faces toward the rising sun. The instructor is a retired PE teacher I know, Miss Angela – she's 64 herself and moves with the grace of someone half her age. As I join in quietly at the back, copying the slow "windmill" motion of arms, I feel a surge of optimism. The sky is turning orange, the sea breeze is waking us up, and here are elders of my community proving that movement has no age limit. One of the men, Mr. Laurent, catches my eye and grins. "Aa, Backs you finally come to exercise with us" he teases. I laugh and nod. Mr. Laurent is seventy-one and underwent knee surgery last year. A decade ago he'd have probably been home in a rocking chair at this hour. But today, thanks to this little seniors' exercise group, he's out here improving his balance and breathing, one slow squat at a time.

The truth is, for a long time in Saint Lucia there was a pervasive mindset: once you hit a certain age – maybe retirement at 65 – you earned the right to rest and basically slow down across the board. Take it easy, sit on the porch, let the "young people" do the running around. Exercise was seen as something for athletes, schoolchildren, or maybe young folks trying to "get in shape." Our elders who worked hard all their lives often embraced a sedentary lifestyle, thinking it was the natural, even the proper, thing to do. And who could blame them? We culturally revere our older folks – we don't exactly encourage Granny to go jog around the block; we expect her to be in her chair with a cup of cocoa tea. Plus, aches and pains do come with age, so many seniors feel exercise would just hurt or isn't safe.

But here's the counterintuitive truth: the older you get, the more important it is to stay active. In fact, starting exercise in your 60s or 70s can do wonders – often even more dramatic improvements than when a 20-year-old starts exercising. That's because the baseline for many of our seniors is a level of inactivity that has been slowly robbing them of strength, mobility, and independence. When they start moving, it's like water to a wilted plant. They perk up. They build muscle that prevents falls. They improve circulation, which helps memory and mood. They sleep better at night. They socialize more and feel less isolated. Motion is lotion, I've heard physiotherapists say – movement lubricates the joints, eases stiffness, and nourishes both body and spirit.

Let me share a quick story. A lady from Grande Riviere – I'll call her Auntie Marie to protect her privacy – she once told me about her turning point. She was 66 and had taken a fall in her yard. Nothing broke, thank God, but she struggled to get up and it scared her deeply. "I realized if I had broken my hip, I might never walk properly again," she said. Her doctor advised her to start some light exercise to improve her balance and leg strength. At first she scoffed: "Exercise? At my age? That's for youngsters." But the fear of another fall pushed her to try. She began by just walking to her mailbox and back, holding her grand-daughter's arm. Then down the street. Weeks later, she invested in a pair of sneakers and started going to a free aerobics-in-the-park session in town. Fast forward a year: Auntie Marie lost 15 pounds, lowered her blood pressure, and – best of all in her eyes – she can squat down to do her gardening and get back up without help. The joy and pride in her voice telling me this was unforgettable. "I feel twenty years younger, Marcellus," she said. "Should have started long time, wi." It was a revelation to her that she could actually become stronger at 67 than she was at 62. And it reinforced for me that we need to spread this revelation to many more.

So, what holds back our seniors and even middle-aged folks from exercising? Let's debunk some misconceptions. One: "I'm too old, exercise is unsafe." Certainly, not every type of exercise suits everyone, but there's almost always a safe form of movement for every age and condition. Walking is low-impact and safe. Chair exercises – yes, you can even exercise while seated – are extremely safe even for those with limited mobility. Gentle yoga or stretching can be adapted for seniors. The key is to start small and progress gradually. Another misconception: "If I didn't exercise when I was young, there's no point now." This is flat-out wrong. Research and real-world cases show even someone in their 80s who starts light strength training can improve muscle tone and bone density. The body is remarkably adaptive; it will respond to training at any age, just maybe not as rapidly as in youth, but respond it will.

And then there's the attitude of embarrassment or lack of confidence – a big one, not often said aloud. Many older people worry they'll look foolish trying to do jumping jacks or that younger folks will laugh at them using equipment at the park. We have to change that culture. We have to celebrate seniors who exercise the way we celebrate kids who win sports trophies. In my vision, if an elderly gentleman is out early doing power-walk laps around the block, the neighbours ought to smile in respect, maybe even cheer him on, rather than say "Look at the old fella, what he trying to prove." Why shouldn't the sight of older adults exercising be as normal as seeing kids playing? Frankly, I'd love to see an 80-year-old jogging in the park – it means we're doing something right as a society for someone that age to be that fit.

So how do we get there? We need a strong structural arc in our approach: identify the problem (sedentary living and its harms), make a mindset shift (exercise is medicine and it's never too late), then implement practices (concrete programs and supports to help people move).

We've identified the problem: an inactive population of seniors leading to preventable health issues. Let's talk about that a bit more with real numbers and context. Saint Lucia's life expectancy is about 74 years now, which means we are blessed to have more people living into their seventies and beyond. That also means more people living long enough to potentially develop chronic diseases or frailty. The 2022 census data hinted that about 10% of our population is over 65, and Castries North likely has even a bit higher share because it's an older community. At the same time, national surveys show high rates of diabetes and hypertension in the adult population. Many of those folks are in their 50s, 60s, 70s. What does this tell us? If we don't intervene with lifestyle changes, we're going to have an avalanche of strokes, heart attacks, amputations (from diabetic complications), and dependency due to weakness or falls. We're already seeing it. How many times have you heard of someone's grandmother "catching a stroke" and becoming bedridden, or an uncle who lost a leg to diabetes? These outcomes are devastating to families and costly to society. Yet, in many cases, a modest routine of physical activity could have delayed or prevented these tragedies. I know it's not a cure-all – but it's a powerful prevention tool we aren't using enough.

Now, shift to the solution mindset: movement as medicine; move at any age. We have to reframe exercise not as a hobby or a vain pursuit of looking slim, but as a fundamental pillar of health – as important as taking your pills, as important as brushing your teeth. Doctors worldwide now advise "physical activity" as a vital sign, right alongside blood pressure and heart rate. Our own Ministry of Health has recognized this too: they recently launched a Seniors Exercise Programme with help from international partners. In its pilot phase, they're focusing on low-impact exercises, even in elder care homes, to improve flexibility, balance, and strength. The feedback from that has been heartwarming – seniors smiling while doing simple hand and leg movements, staff noticing people are more alert and happy afterwards. This tells us the appetite is there, and once the initial inertia is overcome, seniors actually enjoy moving their bodies in gentle ways.

We need to bring that energy to Castries North at the community level, not just in care homes. So let me outline a friendly, low-cost plan for active living that especially targets those over 60, but truthfully, will benefit everyone.

1. Organized Walking Groups: This is perhaps the simplest to start. We have some natural places to walk – e.g., the Vigie stretch by the airport (fairly flat, beautiful scenery), the block around the La Clery playing field, even corridors through some of our quieter neighbourhoods in Vide Boutielle or Sunny Acres. I propose we set up "Castries North Walkers" clubs in a few pockets of the constituency. For instance, a La Clery walkers group that meets at 5:30 a.m. on weekdays for a 30-minute walk through the community (before traffic gets busy). Another could meet in the evenings, say around 5:30 p.m., for those who prefer sunset walks. We'll coordinate these with the help of community volunteers – perhaps a nurse aide or just a passionate resident like Miss Angela from Vigie beach – to lead the group, set the pace, and ensure safety. We'll hand out high-visibility vests or arm bands (safety first, as some of our roads lack sidewalks). And we'll encourage a buddy system: no one left behind. If Mr. Felix needs a breather, someone stays with him. Over time, these walks become social events as much as exercise. You chat about the news, check in on each other, maybe end with a cool-down stretch and a prayer or motivational quote. The point is to make it enjoyable so people stick with it. It's free, it's simple, and it can start immediately. All we might need to invest in are those reflective vests and maybe some printed tip sheets on walking safety and hydration.

2. Senior Exercise Classes: Not everyone will join a walking group, and walking alone doesn't cover all aspects of fitness. Some folks need more guided exercise to improve balance or target certain muscle groups. I plan to partner with the Ministry of Health's Bureau of Health Education (they're the ones doing that pilot program) to conduct regular exercise sessions in our community centres. For example, the Bishop's Gap or Monchy area might have a community hall we can use. Picture a Monday and Wednesday morning class, 9 a.m., for any resident over 60 (or even younger if they want a gentle workout). The exercises would be like what Naomi Grandison, a health educator, described in the ministry's programme: hand exercises, neck exercises, leg exercises – all slow and low-impact, focusing on keeping joints moving and muscles strong. We'd include some balance drills (like holding onto a chair and lifting one foot) because improved balance means fewer dangerous falls. We'd definitely have some light strength training: I envision handing out resistance bands – those stretchy bands – which are cheap and excellent for seniors to build a bit of muscle safely. We could do routines with cans of peas or small water bottles as makeshift weights for arm curls. Also, some deep breathing and relaxation at the end, which helps with stress and mental well-being.

The classes must be friendly and welcoming. So we'll give them a fun name, maybe "Golden Movers" or "60+ and Active" club, something that doesn't scare people off. And crucially, we make it a social circle. After class, have a little healthy snack or just lime and talk for 15 minutes. People will come back not just for the exercise, but for the camaraderie.

3. Intergenerational Activity Days: One thing I've learned is that grandparents will do amazing things when encouraged by their grandchildren. We can use that! Perhaps once a quarter, we host a Family Fitness Fun Day at the school yard or the park. We design activities where seniors and kids participate together – a simple relay race where the rule is the pair must include one over-60 and one under-15, or a dance contest mixing old-school waltz steps with trendy line dances. When grandma is out there dancing with her granddaughter to Dennery Segment music (gently, of course), she's burning calories and making memories. And the young ones see that exercise isn't just sports competition, it's play and enjoyment at all ages. Breaking the segregation of age in recreation is important to changing attitudes. It tells the community: movement is for everyone, from 5 to 95.

4. Active Aging Ambassadors: I'd like to create a small team of what I call active aging ambassadors. These would be seniors who are already active and can inspire their peers – people like Miss Angela at Vigie or Mr. Laurent who regained mobility. We feature their stories in our community newsletter or on social media (with their permission). Maybe we host a little talk where they share how being active changed their lives. When someone who "looks like me" or is my age says "I did it, and so can you," it's far more powerful than a young fitness trainer lecturing. These ambassadors can also go around with our health outreach events to demonstrate exercises or just talk one-on-one with reluctant folks. I think of it like a friendly peer pressure – the good kind.

5. Infrastructure tweaks: This overlaps with the next chapter on parks and facilities, but it's worth noting here. To encourage daily movement, the physical environment matters. If a neighbourhood has sidewalks or safe shoulders, seniors feel more comfortable walking without fear of traffic. If a playing field has a smooth perimeter path, you'll see folks using it for laps. So part of our plan to get people moving will be to invest in small infrastructure: putting a walking track around the La Clery field for instance, or installing a couple of benches along common walking routes so an older person can take a rest if needed mid-walk. Even something like better street lighting on popular routes can enable evening strolls (especially important in winter months when it gets dark early). These are small works that make a big difference in whether a person decides to step outside or stay in. I recall a lady from Morne Du Don saying she'd love to walk in the afternoons but stray dogs scare her and the road is too uneven. For stray dogs, community animal control and awareness might help; for the road, we might pave a short section. We solve the obstacles once we know them.

6. Programs for Youth and Adults: While this chapter emphasizes seniors, I want it clear that "Move at Any Age" includes younger folks too – including youth, because ironically we now have many kids and teens who are far less active than in previous generations (thanks to the lure of screens and video games). We have a paradox: some of our older folks are too inactive, and some of our children are too. So in tandem, I will also push for revitalizing school physical education and after-school sports, which thankfully I've covered in earlier chapters. But in context here, just know that when we improve parks and playgrounds (coming up in the next chapter), it helps both the 6-year-old and the 66-year-old have places to move. A senior using the park in the morning and kids playing there in the afternoon – that's an ideal scenario. And maybe sometimes they even overlap and exchange a smile or a story. That's community.

Now, I want to highlight some expert knowledge in layman terms to reinforce why all this matters. Health experts globally often say "sitting is the new smoking." In other words, a sedentary lifestyle can be just as harmful to health as smoking cigarettes – contributing to heart disease, diabetes, and even some cancers. The World Health Organization recommends older adults get at least 150 minutes of moderate exercise a week (that's like 30 minutes, five days a week), plus strength exercises twice a week focusing on major muscle groups. It's okay if this sounds technical – the point is, that's the prescription for healthy aging. And moderate exercise isn't running a marathon; it's brisk walking, cycling slowly, even vigorous gardening counts.

Another key area is balance and falls. One of the biggest threats to seniors' independence is falling. A hip fracture can literally be a life-threatening event for an elderly person – not just from the injury, but the decline that often follows. The good news: balance can be improved. There's an award-winning program called "A Matter of Balance" used in places like St. Croix, USVI, which trains seniors in simple exercises to steady themselves and also to not fear falling so much (because fear can actually make you more sedentary and thus more at risk). I'd love to implement something similar here – perhaps our active aging ambassadors can be trained in this and then teach others. Picture a class solely on balance: side-stepping, standing on one foot near a wall, practicing sitting and standing from a chair without using hands, etc. These might seem mundane, but mastering them can give an older adult huge confidence in daily life.

Let's not forget mental benefits: movement boosts mood. We have an issue of depression reported among older folks, especially those who live alone after a spouse passes or children migrate overseas. Exercise has been shown to release endorphins – natural mood lifters. I've witnessed it – a group of grannies finish a 20-minute dance session to some old calypso music and they are laughing, rosy-cheeked, maybe a little out of breath but clearly more alive than when they started. That kind of natural high is a tonic no pharmacy can bottle. It combats loneliness too – you have a reason to get out, to say hello to people, to feel part of a group.

Now, I know some seniors will say, "That's all well and good, but I have bad knees" or "I have arthritis; exercise hurts." To them I say: I hear you. Start where you are, use what you have, do what you can. If you can't walk, maybe you can do water therapy – exercises in a shallow pool (the buoyancy relieves joint pressure). If you can't stand long, do chair exercises (lift those legs, roll those shoulders right from your seat). If your hands hurt, focus on your legs. If your legs hurt, focus on your arms. The trick is to do something regularly. And actually, proper exercise often eases the very conditions that cause pain. Arthritis, for example, improves with gentle range-of-motion moves and strengthening around the joints; it hurts more when you don't move. It's like the Tin Man in Wizard of Oz – rusted solid until he got some oil. Movement is our rust-preventer.

Also, it's never too late to seek guidance. I plan for our constituency to hold periodic free fitness assessments – maybe as part of a health fair – where a physiotherapist or trained fitness instructor can briefly assess interested seniors: check their flexibility, balance, maybe their grip strength or how many sit-to-stands they can do in 30 seconds. Then give each a tailored recommendation: "Okay, Mrs. X, your balance is a bit off, I want you to practice holding onto the countertop and standing on one leg for 10 seconds each day," or "Mr. Y, your blood pressure is a little high; brisk walking will help your heart – aim for 15 minutes in the morning and 15 in evening." This kind of personalized touch can motivate them because it's like getting a prescription from a professional, but the prescription is exercise.

Let me paint a vision of Castries North if we embrace this active aging philosophy fully. I see grandmothers in La Clery meeting after church on a Sunday for a group walk in their modest sneakers and wide-brim hats, chatting and laughing as they go. I see grandfathers at Vigie playing a casual game of bocce (why not introduce that?) or even trying their hand at pickleball – that sport I'll talk more about soon – alongside middle-aged folks. I see the community centre schedule pinned up with line dancing on Tuesday, water aerobics at the YMCA pool on Thursday (we could coordinate that if transportation is an issue), and "Walk & Talk" sessions every morning in different sub-districts. I see an older couple from Monchy deciding to take an evening stroll instead of just watching TV – because the road now has lights and a sidewalk, and they feel safe. The man brings along his radio, plays a little oldie, and they reminisce as they exercise without even realizing it. I see healthier elders requiring fewer emergency hospital visits, because their blood sugar is under control and they're more robust. I see adult children less worried about their aging parents living alone, because they know three times a week Mom is out with her exercise group and someone will notice if she doesn't show up.

This isn't fantasy. I've seen glimpses of it already, like that dawn stretch class on the beach. Our Caribbean culture has always had dance and movement in it – from the kwadril to the carnival road march – so we're basically tapping into that natural rhythm we love, just in a more regular, health-directed way. We can make moving fun, not a chore.

There's also an economic angle: a community where people live healthier longer can contribute socially and economically longer. A retiree who stays fit might decide to volunteer at the library or even start a small home business for extra income, whereas if they were homebound by poor health, they couldn't. They also lighten the load on younger family members who might otherwise have to stay home to care for them. In a country like ours with a tight labour force, keeping our seniors active and independent is actually an economic boost. And consider sports tourism or activities – I think about the possibility of Saint Lucia hosting a "Masters Games" or senior sports meeting someday. Why not? Other places have seniors track events or pickleball tournaments. If Castries North became known as a haven for active seniors, that could spawn little local industries (like a smoothie stand at the park, or vendors selling coconut water and healthy snacks to walkers).

Now, to implement these ideas, I will outline clear policy support and local initiatives:

- **Lobby for Community Health Aide funding:** I will work with the Ministry of Health to allocate a community health aide whose job includes organizing exercise and wellness groups for seniors. This exists in some form in other countries – basically a health worker who splits time between checking on seniors at home and leading group activities. This person can be the backbone of sustaining all these programs. I believe external grants (like through PAHO or Taiwan ICDF, who already is involved) can support such a role if the government can't fully fund it initially.

- **Use community centres and schools after-hours:** We have physical spaces that are often idle in mornings or evenings. I will negotiate to use school halls, church yards, or the La Clery CDC court (after it's refurbished) for scheduled senior activities. Since those are off-peak times (morning after school drop-off, or early evening), it usually doesn't conflict.

- **Equipment drive:** We might organize a donation drive for exercise mats, light dumbbells, resistance bands, even old stationary bikes or treadmills that people aren't using. Many folks buy exercise equipment and it becomes a clothes rack at home. Why not put it in a community setting where others can use it? I guarantee we'd find a few willing donors. Combine that with maybe a small budget to buy basics and we equip our "fitness corners."

- **Collaboration with NGOs:** There are organizations, like Silver Shadows or HelpAge (if present here), or regional NGOs focused on elderly, that could provide training or resources. I will actively reach out to them. I've seen on regional news how islands coordinate for Caribbean Wellness Day (every September) to host big public workout sessions. I want Castries North to lead on those – like have the biggest turnout of seniors doing a group exercise on Wellness Day. A bit of friendly competition with other constituencies or islands can spark participation too.

- **Healthcare tie-in:** We will ask doctors at the clinic to "prescribe" exercise. Literally, on the prescription pad, write "30 mins walk daily" alongside any pills. There's evidence that when a doctor writes it down, patients take it more seriously. And our clinic can refer people to our programs: "Oh Mrs. Jules, your arthritis is acting up – I want you to attend the Thursday stretch class at the community centre, it will help you." The clinic and the exercise initiatives must reinforce each other.

I want to address also the especially after 60 part in the chapter title. Why highlight 60+? Because it's a pivotal time. Many in their 60s are just retiring or about to retire. It's a period of life where routines change and health often starts to show cracks. If we catch people at that moment and help them pivot into an active lifestyle as they transition out of the workforce, we can add high-quality years to their life. It's much easier to maintain good habits from 60 to 70 than to try to turn around a crisis at 75. Prevention is far better than cure. So I envision doing targeted outreach to recent retirees – say, once a year the constituency hosts a "Pre-Retirement Wellness Seminar" inviting anyone around 55-65. There we talk not just pensions but how to plan a healthy daily routine when you retire, including exercise, diet, hobbies. We could involve the National Insurance Corporation or other bodies that deal with retirees. It shows people that retirement isn't about "resting in peace" before you're dead – it's about enjoying the freedom to do things, which includes physical activities you maybe didn't have time for while working.

Let's talk nutrition for a second, because it goes hand in hand with exercise. Often when people start moving more, they also become more conscious of what they eat (and vice versa). Part of our holistic approach should involve dietary guidance for seniors. Things like eating enough protein to maintain muscle mass (many elders skimp on protein, which leads to frailty), staying hydrated, and controlling portion sizes to manage weight and blood sugar. We can incorporate mini-lectures after exercise classes: one week talk about "the benefits of local ground provisions over white bread," another week bring a dietician or knowledgeable elder to share healthy recipes (like using less saltfish and more fresh fish to cut sodium). But I'll always keep it positive and culturally relevant – no fad diets, just common-sense tweaks to our beloved foods. More dasheen and green fig, less white rice; more lean stew, less fried chicken – that kind of message. When people exercise, they often find they enjoy lighter foods anyway because heavy greasy meals make workouts harder. It's a virtuous cycle: eat well to fuel your activity, and being active makes you want to eat well.

I must mention one more often neglected group: office workers and middle-aged adults. They might be 40 or 50, not yet "seniors," but many have sedentary jobs and creeping health issues. The habits we instil now will determine the kind of seniors they become. So parallel to everything, I intend to encourage workplace wellness in our constituency. For instance, we have a lot of government offices in Castries North (the finance centre, transport ministry, etc.). I would advocate for those offices to implement "stretch breaks" or even form lunchtime walking clubs. As MP I can lead by example – literally invite the staff of a ministry next door to join me for a 15-minute walk at lunch on a given day. Some might chuckle, but some will join, and if the boss is doing it, it legitimizes the practice for others. If we normalize that, by the time those workers retire at 65, they're already used to being active.

To conclude this chapter, I want to leave you with a mental image that sums up why this matters deeply to me. It's an image of dignity and vitality in later years. I see an elderly man in Boguis – call him Mr. Emmanuel – who used to rely on his son to lift him out of a chair. Now, after months of gentle training, Mr. Emmanuel can stand up on his own and even do a little dance when his favourite song plays. The pride in his eyes is shining because he's regained a measure of independence. I see Ms. Daphne in La Clery, who used to be fearful of going outside after she had a minor fall. Now she wears her sneakers and goes on her own to buy her little groceries, walking steadily, because she's been practicing balance and leg strengthening in our classes. She tells everyone hello on her way, feeling connected again. These transformations are quiet – no one writes a news article when a 75-year-old can suddenly climb stairs without huffing – but they are profound improvements in quality of life.

And when we talk about "make it count", isn't that what we mean? Making our years count, not just counting years. What's the point of adding years to life if there's no life in those years? By promoting movement at any age, especially for our seniors, we are injecting life into years. We're saying to our elders: we still need you active and around, your wisdom walking among us, not shut inside. We're also saying to younger folks: old age can be vibrant; don't fear it, prepare for it. That is a cultural shift we sorely need – to see aging not as a slow march to the grave, but as another stage of life where growth and joy are possible.

I'll end with two punchy truths I hold dear: It's never too late to start moving. And the next best time to start is today. Whether you're 16 or 60 or 86 – if you start today, tomorrow you'll be better for it. Let's create a Castries North where that is not just a slogan, but daily reality. A community of people who might have silver in their hair but gold in their hearts, stepping lively to the beat of a healthy life.

We have talked about personal habits and community programs to get everyone moving. But to truly support an active lifestyle, we also need places to move – safe, inviting spaces to walk, play, and exercise. Our journey continues with the very concrete task of upgrading courts, parks, and even introducing new activities like pickleball, turning neglected corners into arenas of health and togetherness.

21

Courts, Parks, and Pickleball

The year is 2011. I have just moved back home to Saint Lucia after years abroad, and my heart is set on giving back through sports. I remember standing by the basketball court in La Clery early one morning. The sun was barely up. A couple of teenage boys I'd been mentoring were with me, rubbing sleep from their eyes, ready for training before school. What lay before us was a sorry sight: the once-thriving La Clery court looked like a forgotten war zone. Cracks zigzagged across the concrete like scars. The rims on the basketball hoops were bent and rusted, one missing a net and the other hanging by a thread of frayed rope. Broken glass glittered in one corner where someone's weekend bottle had met its end. The lone floodlight pole stood bare – the light had been dead for years. As we started our drills, one boy tripped where a chunk of concrete was missing. I silently cursed under my breath, then told them to take five. In that pause, with sweat already on our brows, I vowed: this has to change. That very day I went home and penned a letter to our Parliamentary Representative and the Ministry of Sports. I detailed the state of the La Clery court and the adjacent field. I talked about the potential – how dozens of youth like these boys would use it daily if it were safe and maintained. I practically begged: fix the surface, put up proper hoops, install lights so the community can use it at night.

I sent that letter. I waited. I sent another to a different official. I spoke about it on a local radio sports show, hoping to embarrass someone into action. The weeks turned to months and then years. Nothing happened. The court remained in ruins, the field patchy and often waterlogged. We improvised – brought our own nets, swept glass before practice, played by moonlight when we had to. But deep down I felt a mix of anger and sadness. Anger that our leaders didn't care enough to provide something so basic, and sadness for the kids who were denied a chance to really shine on a decent court as I had once had. That string of unanswered letters, those broken promises from various authorities, are a big part of why I decided to run for office myself. If you want something done, sometimes you have to do it yourself.

Now it's 2025, and I stand once again at that La Clery court. I run my hand over the faded sign that reads "Morne Du Don & La Clery Playing Facility" – barely legible. For a moment, I imagine it fully revived: new smooth concrete, fresh bright paint marking the keys and three-point lines, sturdy backboards with straight rims, and LED lights ready to flick on when the sun dips. I can almost hear the thump of the ball and the cheers of spectators on a cool evening. That vision is so clear I can touch it. And I'm determined to make it real. But it's not just about this one court. It's about an entire approach to community space that has been lacking and that we will set right.

Let's step back and consider the bigger picture: Castries North has faced a long neglect of its recreational facilities. Playing fields, courts, parks – the places where kids play, youth hone their skills, workers take a breather, and seniors stroll – have been allowed to deteriorate or lie unused. Remember the observation from earlier: our infrastructure is crumbling and our sports facilities have been ignored for over a decade. That's not an exaggeration. We have a major playing field in Vigie that has drainage issues and often no public restroom open. We have the La Clery/Morne Du Don field and court I described, which for years got no maintenance. The lights at the field by the Ministry of Infrastructure (by Union) were literally out for 10+ years – a decade of darkness on a facility that was once a hub for community events at night. There's a small neighbourhood park in Sunny Acres – a rarity – but its playground equipment is aging. Other areas have no pocket parks or green spaces at all, just concrete and houses, so kids end up playing in the streets or not at all.

Why does this matter? Because courts, parks, and play spaces are not luxuries; they are vital community assets. They are the open-air living rooms of a neighbourhood, where relationships form and health is built. A neglected court sends a message of hopelessness or danger, while a vibrant one radiates opportunity and safety. I often say the state of our parks is the state of our hearts – if they are abandoned, maybe so are we. We cannot let that be.

There's also a direct line from recreational spaces to social ills or successes. I've seen it: when the youth have nowhere structured to go after school – no court, no program – they wander. Idle hands find trouble. Conversely, when you refurbish a court and start a league, suddenly those same young men and women are there every evening shooting hoops or training for netball, not loitering or getting mixed up in mischief. I recall when the Marchand Grounds (just outside our constituency) were buzzing with activity in the 90s: community tournaments, weekend fun games – crime in that area dipped during those times because everyone was at the field under the lights, as participant or spectator, rather than elsewhere in the dark. It's a pattern repeated worldwide: active, well-lit public spaces discourage crime and build community. We can have that here too – in fact, we desperately need it. Our constituency has had its share of petty crime and youth violence. Reviving our sports and recreation areas is not a panacea, but it's a proven part of the prevention cocktail. It gives positive alternative paths.

Now, let's talk specific plans – the exciting stuff – of how we transform our courts, parks, and introduce a dash of something new: pickleball. Yes, pickleball – I know the name sounds funny, like something with vinegar and cucumbers – but it's actually one of the fastest-growing sports globally, and for good reason. It's fun, social, and accessible to all ages and fitness levels. More on that soon.

First, the legacy facilities: We will restore and upgrade the existing playing field and court at La Clery/Morne Du Don. That's priority one. The groundwork (no pun intended) has already started in terms of planning. I've measured the space, consulted with sports engineers about proper resurfacing techniques. The plan includes:

• **Resurfacing the basketball court to eliminate tripping hazards and provide a durable, even finish.** We'll use a high-quality outdoor sports concrete mix or asphalt topping with an all-weather seal. This isn't just about looks; a good surface prevents injuries and gives a true bounce for the ball – important for serious play.

- **New hoops and equipment:** We'll install new backboards (fiberglass or acrylic, the kind that can withstand both a monster dunk and years of sun and rain). Proper double-rims that won't bend after a few months. We'll put up fencing or netting behind the hoops if needed to keep balls from flying into neighbours' yards or the street.

- **Lighting:** This is huge. The community has been literally in the dark for too long. We will put up modern LED floodlights. They're more energy-efficient and bright. With four poles at the corners of the court, games can go on safely after sunset. But it's not just for sports – a well-lit area in the night also means folks can take a walk or families can hang out there under the stars without fear. Light chases away the elements that thrive in darkness.

- **Multi-use markings:** We will not limit to just basketball. The court can be painted with additional lines for netball (which many girls and young women play) and even smaller football (futsal) or tennis, if space allows. A versatile court gets double or triple usage. Perhaps certain evenings are netball practice, others basketball. We manage a schedule. This maximizes the investment.

- **Seating and amenities:** We'll refurbish or add a few rows of bleachers or benches along the side. People love to come watch games or just sit in the evening breeze. If possible, a simple cover over a section would be nice for shade or rain shelter for spectators. Additionally, we need a functional water tap or fountain so players can hydrate (I've seen kids use puddle water to wet their faces – we must do better). A basic restroom or at least a strategy to use existing nearby facilities is also needed for events – that may involve partnering with a nearby school or building.

- **The Field:** Right next to that court is an open playing field. Currently, it's uneven and floods in one corner after heavy rain due to poor drainage. I will allocate funds to regrade and grass that field properly. It doesn't need to be a pristine golf-course – just flat, green, and with goals at each end for football. A walking path around it would be brilliant – we can create a 200m or so loop with packed gravel or asphalt, doubling as a jogging track for adults (and seniors, as mentioned in the active living chapter). And yes, fix the drainage by digging proper side drains and maybe laying perforated pipes underground in the worst spot – not too expensive, and prevents a swamp from forming.

- **Community ownership:** We won't just rebuild and walk away – I want to establish a local Sports Facility Committee (including youths, coaches, maybe an elder or two) to oversee upkeep, organize activities, and liaise with me for any issues. When people have a hand in managing something, they protect it. We'll empower them perhaps by a small stipend or just recognition, but mostly through giving them a voice. If a lightbulb burns out, they tell us to get it fixed promptly; if someone is vandalizing, they address it.

Now, the Ministry of Infrastructure Court (a.k.a. "the court next to the Ministry of Transportation"): This is another hidden gem. It's located in the Bisee/Union area, near a cluster of government offices (Transport, Infrastructure, etc.) and also near some residential communities and the big CDC housing blocks at Union. This court in question is currently a rundown hardcourt. Weeds at the edges, cracked surface, some tired netball poles without nets. It's been sitting mostly idle except maybe by some nearby youth now and then. I see enormous potential here. This is where the Castries North Pickleball Centre comes in – a novel idea I'm championing.

Pickleball, for those unfamiliar, is like a mix of tennis, badminton, and ping-pong, played on a court about a third the size of a tennis court. You use a paddle and a plastic ball with holes. It's easy to learn, low-impact (easy on the joints), but can get fast and fun. The beauty of it is you can have a 65-year-old and a 15-year-old playing together and both having a blast. You can play doubles, making it social. It doesn't require the endurance of full-court basketball or the power of tennis, which is why it's hugely popular among older adults (but also catching on with younger folks).

Transforming that underused court by the Ministry into a Pickleball Centre hits multiple goals at once:

• **Revitalizes Public Space** – taking something neglected and turning it into a vibrant spot. Imagine painting it fresh, drawing two pickleball courts (they're smaller, so two can fit on a basketball court footprint). It goes from eyesore to attraction.

• **Supports Workplace Wellness** – all those government employees and staff in the area could pop over during lunch or after work for a quick game. Instead of sitting at a desk all day, they get activity. It's a stress reliever and team builder (maybe Inter-Ministry pickleball tournaments in the future – why not!). A healthy worker is a happier, more productive worker, as many companies know.

• **Builds Community Across Ages** – The location is accessible to youth from nearby communities, seniors, and working folks. We could schedule times: maybe lunchtime and early evening for workers, late afternoon for youth coaching or free play, weekend mornings for seniors' round-robin. A well-used facility naturally builds connections: the senior coach might start mentoring the teen, the office worker might start greeting the neighbourhood kid by name after they've played a match. Strangers become friends on a pickleball court.

- **Improves Safety** – Currently that area in off-hours is pretty dead and could attract unsavoury activity. If we turn the lights on (yes, we'll install lights there too) and have regular foot traffic of players and families, it's no longer an abandoned spot. It's self-policing in a way – people respect a place that's clearly valued and frequented. Crime and loitering don't like to hang out where there's a spotlight and a crowd.

- **Boosts Sports Tourism** – This might sound far-fetched, but pickleball is on such a rise that there are regional tournaments, travel clubs, etc. Saint Lucia could host an Eastern Caribbean pickleball open one day. People would fly in, spend in our hotels and eateries. It's niche, yes, but not impossible. And even small events – like a friendly with the expat community or visitors – bring a little extra commerce. We have to think creatively.

- **Stimulates Local Economy** – If that court is busy, guess what? Nearby vendors can sell a few extra drinks, snacks. A young entrepreneur might set up a coconut water cart or a small sports gear stall (selling balls, headbands, etc.). Activity begets commerce, even on a small scale.

- **Urban Renewal Model** – If we succeed in turning that drab space into a showcase, it's a proof of concept. We can point to it and say, "See what a small investment can do for a community's look and feel?" It can inspire similar projects in other parts of the island.

Now, how exactly will we go about this pickleball project? I've done the research on costs and layout. Very little is needed if the surface is intact. Mainly, we'll clean and resurface the court similar to the basketball one. Then paint the appropriate lines for pickleball (they're different from basketball lines – we might decide to dedicate the whole area to pickleball and not worry about other sports there, depending on community interest). We'll install proper net posts and nets (removable when not in use, to avoid vandalism). We will definitely put up fencing around, or at least at the ends, because those balls can fly out and we don't want to be chasing them into the road or bushes.

Lighting again is key – smaller area means fewer lights needed, perhaps four corner poles suffice. And we'll add a bit of seating and a shaded area if possible, since pickleball players often sit and chat between games. If funds allow, maybe even a small equipment shed that can be locked, where we store spare paddles and balls for community use (so someone who shows up without gear can borrow).

I plan to source support from the local sports associations and international bodies. There might not be a formal Saint Lucia Pickleball Association yet (it's that new here), but there is a regional presence. I've heard of a couple resorts here already building courts for tourists. I will approach them to partner – maybe they can donate a couple of starter paddles and balls, or even assist in refurbishing in exchange for some joint use or an opening exhibition event. The beauty of independent candidacy is I don't have to cut through governmental red tape to ask a private entity for help in a mutually beneficial way. If Sandals or another hotel chain is pushing pickleball for their guests, they might like the PR of helping a community court.

A crucial element is programming: a facility comes alive with organized activities. So from day one, we'll coordinate pickleball workshops – get someone knowledgeable (could be a sports officer or just someone who's played abroad) to host free clinics teaching the rules. We'll have youth vs senior fun matches. Maybe integrate it into school PE for nearby schools as a novelty. We'll certainly open it for everyone – this is not going to be an elite place; it's the opposite: come in your slippers or sneakers, we'll hand you a paddle, and you play. Easy to learn – ten minutes and most people get the hang of it, honestly. And it's addictive fun. I envision evenings where, yes, maybe even our seniors who got fitter with all that walking and class in Chapter 20 now show up to take on the "government workers" team in a light-hearted pickleball showdown. Why not? Social connection plus exercise – exactly what the doctor ordered.

Beyond pickleball, let's not forget good old parks and play areas that benefit kids especially. Castries North is largely urban/semi-urban, but we do have a few spots we can beautify as small parks. For example, the Vigie peninsular area has a nice green by the beach where families go on weekends – that could use a couple of picnic benches and maybe some play equipment. The Choc area near the National Table Tennis Centre actually has an open space which could be a mini park for the housing community there. In Sunbilt, residents have long asked for a safe play area for the little ones – perhaps a corner of an existing public property can be allocated for a swing set, etc. These aren't large capital projects. They are often about allocating land and partnering with say, the Lions Club or corporate sponsors to put in playground sets, or having a community build-day to put up a gazebo and plant some trees. I commit to identifying at least two small green spaces in the constituency that we will officially designate and develop as community parks. We might name them after local pioneers or something to instil pride.

Even sidewalks and footpaths play a role in recreation. A mother might not need a formal park if the sidewalks are good – she can push the stroller and walk safely. Part V of this book will discuss these "small works" like sidewalks, but I'll mention here: a network of walkable paths essentially creates a linear park through the community. I want to see, for instance, the entire Vide Boutielle road have a continuous sidewalk from the top by Barre St. Joseph down to the bottom by the highway – you'd see people actually taking evening walks there if it was safe from traffic.

One more component: organized sports and leagues. Upgraded facilities are a means, not an end. The end is active use. So we'll revive community sports meets – inter-block football tournaments, constituency netball competitions, three-on-three youth basketball showdowns at our new courts. You better believe I'll be out there either refereeing, coaching a team, or just cheering on. We might even start a Castries North Games – an annual mini-Olympics of sorts, where various communities compete in events (football, netball, track relays, even fun stuff like sack races for kids, and yes, pickleball championships). This not only gives purpose to the facilities; it fosters unity and local pride. Morne Du Don team vs. Monchy team in the finals – everyone comes out in their colours to support. That sense of belonging and friendly rivalry is the fabric of a strong community.

Let me touch on something subtle but important: maintenance. We've been burned before by the pattern of build–use–neglect. I won't let that happen again. Part of my policy plan is to ring-fence some funds specifically for maintenance of community assets – meaning each year, money is set aside for repainting lines, replacing bulbs, mending fences. And I want to engage youth in that as well – say, an "Adopt-a-Court" program where a local school or youth club takes pride in helping keep a facility clean and in order (maybe they do a clean-up once a month or paint over graffiti, in exchange for maybe some equipment or just recognition and pizza from the Rep's office!). Maintenance is unsexy, but it's where many good projects falter. Not on my watch. If I have to personally go tighten a bolt on a swing or sweep the court on a Saturday, I'll do it – and truth be told, I probably won't have to, because I know when people see leadership care so much, they pitch in too.

Now, the Eastern Caribbean context. We are not alone in these challenges or solutions. Barbados recently built community gyms in some of their parks. Trinidad has the famous Queen's Park Savannah – a massive public park used by all ages day and night – and they've also seen a rise of interest in new sports like parkour and skateboarding, responding by creating spaces for those. In some of the smaller OECS countries, multi-purpose courts in villages are the heartbeat of social life – St. Vincent, Grenada, they host village leagues that are the highlight of the week for citizens. I've observed those models, and one thing is common: when communities have ownership of facilities, they thrive. So a big part of my plan is not just "the government builds it," but also "the people guard and activate it." We'll perhaps set up a small "Recreation Council" across Castries North – with reps from each major area – who meet quarterly to discuss scheduling, needs, ideas for events, fundraising for extras, etc. It's local democracy in action on the playing field level.

And let's not forget, improved facilities can also feed into the sports economy and youth development pipeline we talked about in earlier chapters. That better basketball court might be where the next national team player is discovered at age 15. The lit football field could allow a talented youngster to practice into the evening and earn a college scholarship down the line. Healthy spaces breed success stories. They can also attract visitors: a properly maintained Vigie field could host regional rugby or a club cricket match; the netball court could see an inter-island friendly tournament. These are small but meaningful exchanges that put us on the map. Picture a van of youth footballers from Gros Islet coming down for a match in La Clery – they buy some snacks after, maybe tour our community a bit, friendships form. Or a team from Martinique hops over for a weekend pickleball friendly

– they'll spend in our hotels and restaurants. There's always a bigger ripple effect.

One development move I want to use here draws on a common metaphor . . . let us think of our community as a tree. The health centre we fixed in Chapter 19 is like the roots – nourishing us, keeping us well. The programs to get people moving are the trunk – giving structure and support day by day. And the courts, parks, and recreation spaces? They are the branches and leaves that reach out under the sun, vibrant and visible. They produce fruits – the joys of a Saturday league win, the laughter of children on a slide, the calm contentment of an evening walk. If any part of the tree is diseased or broken, the whole tree suffers. But if we water the roots (healthcare), strengthen the trunk (active habits), and let the leaves flourish (great facilities), the whole tree – our community – thrives. It gives shade to the weary (safe spaces to relax), fruit to the hungry (opportunities and talent development), and stands strong in storms (united and resilient in tough times). This holistic approach is what I'm after. We're not fixing one thing in isolation; we're nurturing a whole ecosystem of wellness and active living.

Let's take a look at some examples from our history. Gros Islet, our neighbouring constituency to the north, went through a transformation in the 90s. They built the Gros Islet Secondary School court and field into a quality facility and started night football in the community. I remember going to watch those Friday Night Football matches – the field wasn't even the national stadium, just a community field, but because it was lit and had a good pitch, it became a huge draw. Hundreds would come out, vendors selling food, music playing, the whole vibe was positive. That initiative kept a lot of youth engaged and actually spurred some into semi-pro careers. It also boosted small business (everyone selling BBQ and drinks made solid money on game nights). It put Gros Islet on the map for sports entertainment; even tourists staying in Rodney Bay heard the buzz and would wander to see local football under the lights. That is the power of leveraging a community facility. If it can happen there, it can happen in Castries North – in La Clery, in Monchy, in Vide Boutielle. We have talent and enthusiasm in spades, just waiting for a stage.

I also recall a counterexample right within Castries North: some years back, a private entity installed exercise equipment along the Vigie beach stretch – you know those outdoor gym stations. For a while, people used them: morning joggers would stop to do push-ups on the bars, etc. But maintenance lapsed, bolts got loose, one machine broke, and gradually they became neglected and even a bit dangerous to use. Eventually they were removed. The lesson? A great idea (outdoor exercise gear) failed because of poor upkeep and no clear ownership. I won't allow our projects to follow that path. If we put a pull-up bar or parallel bars in a park, someone is assigned to inspect it monthly. If it rusts, we repaint; if it cracks, we fix or remove before injury. It's that diligence that will set our approach apart.

Let me address some folks who might still wonder, "Why invest so much in recreation when there are other pressing needs?" Here's my answer: because recreation and community spaces are pressing needs too, just in a different way. Humans are not robots and we are not A.I. We need more than just jobs and healthcare. We need joy, we need places to exhale, especially after the stress of these past years – economic downturns, pandemic isolation, etc. Parks and courts are like public insurance for mental health and social cohesion. They keep us sane. They keep us human. I think of the parent who's had a long day's work – being able to take their child to swing at a park or kick a ball around is therapy for both. I think of the retiree who lost a spouse – joining some peers for morning paddle ball might be what keeps her going. There is immense value in these "non-essential" spaces; they are essential to quality of life. We have measured progress too long only by jobs or school scores – let's also measure by smiles at a park and laughter on a court. When Castries North's parks are busy and our courts are alive, you'll know our community's spirit is alive and well.

As I stand again at that old court, I bend down and pick a little wildflower that somehow sprouted between the cracked concrete. Resilient little thing, I think. It found a way to bloom in the harshest conditions. Our people have been like that flower – blooming despite the neglect around. But imagine if we cultivated a proper garden for them? What abundance of color and life we'd see. That's what we're about to do with our courts, parks, and recreation.

We are going to turn neglect into vibrance. We'll take that cracked court and make it the beating heart of nighttime pick-up games and weekend tournaments. We'll take that empty lot and make it a green playground echoing with children's footsteps. We'll take those rusty lights and switch them on again, signalling to everyone: Castries North is awake, active, and open for healthy business.

In a year or two, I want a drive through our constituency at dusk to reveal scenes that make you nod with pride. Over by the Ministry's pickleball court, you'll see a handful of seniors finishing up a game, waving goodbye to the office friends they played with, already planning the rematch for tomorrow. Down at La Clery field, you'll hear the whistle of a referee as two youth football teams face off under newly installed lights, a crowd gathered and the smell of someone's BBQ grill in the air. At the basketball court, you'll catch the thud of a perfect bounce pass and the collective "heeee!" as someone nails a three-pointer at the buzzer. And perhaps sweetest of all, in a little park corner, you'll witness a grandfather on a bench, happily tired after his own walk, watching his grandkids chase each other on the grass that used to be a garbage-strewn lot – now cleaned, fenced, and safe. That is the community we can build.

To close this chapter, let's set forth a challenge and a vision. The challenge is to every resident: these facilities belong to you, use them, care for them. If you see a bulb out, report it. If you see a child litter, teach them to pick it up. If you have an idea for an event, propose it – heck, organize it, I'll support you. This isn't about government providing toys – it's about all of us reclaiming our communal backyard and making it thrive. The vision is that Castries North becomes a model for urban community recreation in the Eastern Caribbean – a place where other towns say, "Go see how they did it; their community is always active and united." Why not?

We have all the ingredients: passionate people, latent talent, and now, a plan to rebuild the stage for them. Sports and recreation have always been in my blood and in our district's story (after all, look at the many national athletes who hail from here). It's time to light that fire again, not just for the athletes, but for the ordinary man, woman, boy, and girl who just want a place to play, to breathe, to connect.

Courts, parks, and yes, even pickleball – these are tools to build a healthier, safer, prouder Castries North. We're going to serve up a new reality on those courts – one where everyone, from the star point guard to the retiree picking up a paddle for the first time, has a spot and a shot. Let's make our community spaces count, because every game, every laugh, every evening stroll adds up to the kind of life we all deserve: one rich not just in years, but in living.

Rebuilding a community is not done in boardrooms alone; it's done on the ground – on clinic floors, on walking trails, on courts under the night sky. In these three chapters, we've charted a path to a healthier Castries North, in body and spirit. A clinic that cares, a culture that moves, and spaces that invite us to come together. This is my promise and my call: let's make every day, every project, every person count. The work is ours to do, and the future ours to claim, one step, one game at a time.

Part V – Small Works That Matter

22

Sidewalks, Drains, Crossings – The Short List

I set out at dawn from Vigie, walking north toward Bisee with a notepad in hand. This isn't a morning exercise route – it's a checklist of our community's everyday needs. From the salt breeze at Vigie to the busy streets of Bisee, Castries North's problems reveal themselves right under our feet. I want you to picture it: a representative walking the constituency end-to-end, noting every flooded drain, broken sidewalk, and risky crossing – because that's exactly what I did. Each stop on this journey carries a story and a purpose in our daily lives, and each is on the short list of fixes that would make daily life better.

Vigie: I start by the Vigie roundabout, where airport traffic meets community life. Here, the sidewalk suddenly disappears, forcing people to walk perilously close to speeding cars. At 7:30 a.m., I see schoolchildren from St. Mary's College walking single file on the grass because the pavement is cracked and incomplete. A grandmother pushing a stroller is forced onto the road at one point where the sidewalk ends – a heart-stopping sight with buses whizzing by. She looks at me and asks, "Why is there nowhere safe for us to walk?" It's a fair question. Nobody in La Clery or Vide Bouteille waited for a minister to fix a leaking roof in the old days; you borrowed a ladder and made a plan. Why should we wait years for a simple sidewalk repair? A continuous, safe sidewalk through Vigie is not a luxury – it's basic dignity and safety. As I promised from day one: We are not beggars; I am not a king. We shouldn't have to beg for a footpath; it's something a representative can fix with focus and a little budget.

Walking past Vigie beach, I notice the crosswalk near the park has faded to near-invisibility. Families cross here on weekends to get to the shore, and on weekdays there's a constant stream of joggers and airport staff. One resident, Mr. Emmanuel, tells me he nearly got hit last month because drivers "don't see the crossing until they're on it." A fresh coat of reflective paint and proper signage is an immediate fix – no grand project required. These little things count. A visible crossing can be the difference between an easy stroll and a dangerous gamble with traffic.

Heading further, I make my way along the L'Anse Road area behind Vigie. This part of Castries North runs along a ravine – the La Clery river – that should be a natural asset but instead strikes fear when heavy rains come. I recall vividly the November 6, 2022 flash floods;

people here haven't forgotten. Homes and vehicles were submerged in deep water as the La Clery ravine overflowed its banks. At a low bridge, I stop to talk with Ms. Celina, whose yard was ruined that day. She points out the high-water mark still staining her concrete wall. "Every time black clouds form, I start to pray," she says. The drainage is a major concern in these low-lying spots. It's not just about water – it's about anxiety. An old man cleaning debris from a culvert tells me the community had pleaded for a bigger drain here for years, "but nobody listened until the flood came." I've marked this spot as Priority #1 for drainage works. If a single storm can turn a neighbourhood into a disaster zone, then strengthening these drains isn't optional – it's urgent.

I climb the hill toward Vide Bouteille. Immediately I notice how sidewalks start and stop along the route. In front of the Camille Henry Memorial School, there's a decent sidewalk – then 100 meters on, it ends abruptly near a bend. I meet Ms. M. She's carrying groceries and walking her grandson home. Where the sidewalk breaks off, they have to step into the narrow road. It's a hairpin turn, and we both flinch as a car swings around unexpectedly close. This is exactly the kind of hazard our constituency's "short list" of fixes must eliminate. I note in my pad: "Complete sidewalk continuity on Vide Bouteille Road – critical for schoolchildren and elders." Later, I'll check maps and confirm what I suspected: we can create a continuous walkway from the top of Vide Bouteille by Barre St. Joseph down to the highway if we fill in a few missing links. That single continuous sidewalk would mean a mother in Monchy or a teacher from Sunny Acres could take an evening walk in safety, no longer forced into the road when the pavement vanishes. Small fix, huge difference.

Vide Bouteille also reveals drainage issues on the slopes. At one corner, I see where runoff has eroded the asphalt, carving a mini-ravine across a driveway. Neighbours mention that whenever it rains hard, water gushes down the hill because the drains are either too small or clogged. One gentleman shows me a spot where a small culvert is completely blocked by debris – it's basically acting as a dam. We talk about solutions: better routine clearing, maybe even a secondary channel to divert heavy flows. These ideas are straightforward; what's been lacking is follow-through. As he speaks, I'm reminded of something I've said on the platform: "Our roads and infrastructure are falling apart. The drains overflow, and no one listens to the community leaders who know the issues best." Standing here, I can see exactly what I meant. Community members like him have the diagnosis and even the cures – they just need a rep to act on them.

Pressing on, I detour briefly to Morne Du Don – a slight westward spur from my main route, but an important one. Morne Du Don sits on a steep incline overlooking the city. The retaining walls along these roads are the only things between stable soil and landslides, and many are in sorry shape. I pass one crumbling wall covered in moss, bulging outward as if ready to give way. It wouldn't take much – another torrential downpour, an undermined foundation – for that wall to collapse, possibly taking part of the road with it. Why has it been left so long? I knock on a corrugated gate nearby and chat with Mr. Denis, who has lived here 30 years. He says everyone knows why: "This part of Morne Du Don always votes the other way. So we don't get nothing fixed." His frustration is palpable. This is what happens when politics trumps service – whole communities get bypassed. I have publicly called this out: "We have an issue with our crumbling infrastructure in parts of Morne Du Don… They have supported the other party but have not got any type of representation in terms of infrastructure for years. I'm not making this up – I'm in Morne Du Don almost every week." The evidence is right in front of me. This area's absence from past "to-do" lists is precisely why it tops mine now. Priority #2 on the short list: shore up Morne Du Don's failing retaining walls and drains before the next rainy season triggers a landslide. No one in Castries North should feel punished or forgotten because of how they vote. Whether a community is deemed "loyal" or "opposition," they all pay taxes and they all deserve basic safety.

Returning to the main road, I descend toward the Choc junction, where our constituency's urban heartbeat thumps. Choc is where the John Compton Highway meets the road from Vide Bouteille, right by the supermarkets and the Gablewoods Mall. It's also where pedestrians take their lives in their hands. I arrive at mid-morning and the area is teeming: mothers with shopping bags, employees from nearby offices heading to lunch, students in uniforms waiting for buses. Yet, despite the heavy foot traffic, safe crossings are woefully few. I spot a faded zebra crossing near the Massy Stores Mega entrance, but vehicles rarely stop – it's as if drivers don't expect pedestrians on a "highway," never mind that this stretch runs through a busy commercial zone. I meet Alvin, a young man who works at the hardware store across the road. He crosses here daily and jokes that he "says a prayer at the median every time." I watch him cross: he inches out, one lane pauses (thankfully), but a car in the other lane zooms through, oblivious. We both shake our heads. This is an unsafe crossing, plain and simple. Our short list item here is clear: install proper pedestrian crossing signals or a traffic calming measure at Choc. Perhaps traffic lights, or at least a pedestrian-activated flashing light, because painted lines alone aren't cutting it. Alvin nods vigorously when I mention this plan. "We need that like yesterday," he says. Exactly – and it's doable. We have models even in our region of small crossings improved to save lives – it shouldn't take a tragedy to act.

Choc is also flanked by a swamp and drainage basin by the Caribbean Cinemas area. Locals mention that after heavy rains, the roadside near the mall entrance floods because the old canal by the mangrove fills up. This is tied to larger flood management (and I know the government has eyed projects to mitigate Castries flooding), but there are smaller interim fixes: clearing trash and vegetation from the channel, raising the sidewalk in the lowest spot, putting a couple of extra storm drains along the road. These are the kind of "small works" that yield outsized benefits – a few thousand dollars to spare dozens of drivers and pedestrians from wading through water every time we get a downpour. I've penciled it in: "Choc highway drains – clear and add inlets (Priority high during wet season)." It bears noting that after the 2022 floods, government did respond with emergency drain clearing and promised upgrades. They even started a flood mitigation project along the Corinth bypass in 2023, just north of here. We will push to ensure Castries North's Choc/Vide Bouteille flood hotspots get the same attention as part of any national resilience plan. And if those big plans stall, we'll take matters into our hands at the constituency level with the stop-gap measures I described. People should see some improvement every single rainy season – not just more sandbags.

Moving past Choc toward Sunny Acres and Bisee, I enter more residential territory again. Sunny Acres is a relatively affluent enclave – houses with tidy lawns and front patios. You might assume everything's perfect here, but even Sunny Acres has infrastructure gaps. For one, the junction where Sunny Acres Road meets the highway has no pedestrian crossing or sidewalk on one side. It's a short dash over the asphalt for joggers and residents trying to get to the beach path or bus stop. I recall meeting Mrs. Thomas, an active retiree, at her gate. She told me she likes to walk for exercise but "there's no footpath after the last house – you're basically competing with cars." Her wish was simple: a proper sidewalk or walking lane connecting Sunny Acres to the main road. After seeing it myself, I wholeheartedly agree. It's on the list. Sometimes we ignore places like Sunny Acres because they're "nice" – but every community, rich or modest, deserves safe walkways. This is about equality of dignity. As I often say, representation must be about service and real progress for the community – every part of the community.

Finally, I reach Bisee, the northern end of our journey. Bisee is bustling – it's where the city's fringe meets the countryside's start, a mix of small businesses, a major secondary school, and family homes. The Castries Comprehensive Secondary School is here, and around 3 p.m. it gets chaotic with traffic and students. One glaring need: a safer crossing or pedestrian refuge by the school gate. When school lets out, hundreds of students pour across the road to get minibuses or walk home. There's no crosswalk, no traffic officer, and cars often speed through as they head to Gros Islet or back to Castries. One teacher described it to me as "an accident waiting to happen." I stood there as dismissal approached, and it was indeed a free-for-all – kids dashing and weaving through moving cars. My heart was in my throat more than once. This, to me, is an easy call for the short list: install a proper crossing at CCSS, with signage and speed bumps to enforce slowing down. If we can coordinate with the police or traffic department to station a guard at peak times, even better. There's no excuse for leaving our children's safety to chance like this.

Bisee also has some drainage and road issues in the back streets. I walked a bit into the Blackstone area – a small offshoot community – where residents showed me a spot that floods because the main drain at the junction hasn't been desilted in years. One man pointed out the ring of water stain on his wall about a foot high: "That's Ivan's handiwork," he joked grimly, referring to some storm past. A lady next door mentioned they've asked repeatedly for the council or Ministry to clear it, and sometimes someone comes but "they never dig deep enough, so the next rain brings all the mud back." This is the kind of mundane maintenance task that should be routine – the fact it's on our short list shows how neglect can turn a simple job into a persistent community pain. So yes, we add "Blackstone main drain – full clean-out and check outlet" to the ledger. Along with it, a promise: once cleared properly, schedule it for cleaning every year before the wet season. Regular maintenance shouldn't require presidential intervention – it should be baked into how we serve.

By the time I finish my trek at the edge of Castries North, I have pages of notes. Sidewalks that vanish, drains that flood, crossings that invite disaster – every one of these is a fixable problem. More importantly, each fix matters to someone: the child walking to school, the vendor carrying her produce, the commuter catching the bus, the elder out for exercise. This chapter's title, "The Short List," is something of a misnomer only in that the list is not short in length – I've got plenty of entries. But it is short in another sense: these are typically small projects. None require millions or a new Act of Parliament. They require attention, organization, and a bit of funding. As I walked, I could practically rank them in order of priority by asking one simple question at each spot: What's the human impact? A missing sidewalk by a school – that's high impact (safety of children), so it's high priority. A cracked drain that occasionally overflows into a yard but not onto the main road – medium impact, maybe medium priority. An area where two or three issues converge (like Choc, with traffic and flooding) – that gets bumped up.

So, what's the order of attack? Safety first – anything that endangers lives (like that CCSS crossing or the Morne Du Don wall) goes to the top. Secondly, chronic pain points – the floods that ruin folks' belongings, the sidewalk gaps that daily force people into harm's way. These sap quality of life consistently and must be relieved. Third, connectivity and dignity – things that aren't about life-and-death but about allowing people to move freely and proudly in their community, like being able to walk from Vigie to Bisee on continuous sidewalks, essentially creating a "linear park" through our constituency. If we do that, an evening walk becomes not just possible but pleasant – imagine that. And lastly, cosmetic improvements – e.g. a new coat of paint on an already safe crossing, or beautifying a park space. We will get to those too (pride in our surroundings matters), but serviceable infrastructure comes first.

Crucially, this walk-through from Vigie to Bisee wasn't done in a vacuum. It reflects what you, the residents, have been telling me all along. Every stop I made, I heard echoes of past conversations at yard meetings, WhatsApp chats, and even random market encounters. Remember the community meeting in Vide Bouteille where a mother of two stood up and said, "The drain by my house overflows every time it rains – can't someone just clear it?" That drain is in my notes now, with her name next to it. Or the time in April when a group of minibus drivers cornered me at Sunny Acres and complained about the lack of a turning lane and pedestrian crossing causing confusion – I've got that down too (a road marking issue we can sort out with the transport board). This short list is your list. I've simply compiled and validated it with my own eyes and footsteps.

In doing so, I'm also building on past conversations and plans. To be fair, this constituency has seen plans before – I've dug through old council minutes and found references to some of these very issues. The difference now is that I'm publishing them, prioritizing them openly, and vowing to act. There's a saying: what gets measured gets done. Well, I've measured the length of broken sidewalk and the depth of the silt in the drains. I've mapped them. Now they will get done, one by one.

Before I end this chapter, let me highlight a small but telling example: In Ti Rocher (a little community on the fringe of Castries North), there's a footbridge that was finally built in 2022 after years of pleas. It's just a simple pedestrian bridge over a ditch – you won't find it on any front page. But for the families there, it meant not having to detour a mile to reach the main road. It was funded under the Community Development Programme, a small project that improved daily living conditions. When I visited, a resident there told me, "It's small, but it changed how we live." That stuck with me. Small works change daily life. Our walk from Vigie to Bisee has identified dozens of such opportunities – each minor in scope, but together transformative in effect.

This short list will guide my first months and years in office if I earn your trust. There are many other Castries North areas too, and those plans are forthcoming. We will tick these items off methodically. And guess what? With each one fixed, you'll be able to point to it and say, "Yes, look – that's better now." Our constituency will become a place where you can literally see progress on the ground, in daylight – not hidden in a report, not promised at some rally and forgotten. By walking this road together – figuratively and literally – we'll make Castries North a national example of visible delivery and community dignity. The journey from Vigie to Bisee will become a prideful stroll, not a tour of neglect. And that, my friends, is a walk worth taking.

23

How We'll Fund It

A plan without funding is just a speech. I've laid out the "what" – sidewalks, drains, crossings and all those small works that matter. Now let's talk about the "how." How do we pay for all this without selling our soul to some party baron or waiting forever on a minister's mercy? The good news is we have ways to fund small works in Saint Lucia that don't require political gymnastics or patronage. The even better news: I intend to use all of them, strategically and transparently, to get the job done for Castries North.

First, let's bust a dangerous myth – the idea that an opposition or independent MP can't get anything done because the government holds the purse strings. That used to be the excuse, yes. In the past, if you weren't on the Prime Minister's side, you got starved of resources. But that narrative is outdated, and I won't accept it. In 2022, Prime Minister Pierre made a point of saying he would allocate resources to all elected MPs, in all seventeen constituencies, for small projects. He even put money where his mouth is: in May 2022, Saint Lucia received a cheque of $18.5 million from the Republic of China (Taiwan) earmarked for the Constituency Development Programme (CDP). That's right – nearly 18.5 million Eastern Caribbean dollars (roughly EC$1 million per constituency on average) specifically for community-level works. And crucially, Pierre promised that this revamped CDP would be transparent, accountable, agile, and accessible to opposition Parliamentarians. In other words, no more locking out MPs who aren't in the ruling party. It's on the record, in black and white: "The revamped Constituency Development Project will be accessible to Opposition Parliamentarians". As your independent candidate (soon-to-be MP, I hope), I will hold the government to that promise and make full use of it.

So, **Funding Stream #1: CDP (Constituency Development Programme).** Think of this as our local works bank account. Traditionally, under CDP, each MP could submit a list of small projects – repaving a footpath, fixing a drain, building a footbridge, etc. The Ministry of Economic Development (or Infrastructure) would manage the execution, but the MP had a big say in identifying and prioritizing the projects. Under the previous administration, opposition MPs were frozen out; but that's changed, and I intend to make the CDP work for Castries North like never before. We have at least a million dollars of fresh CDP funds (thanks to Taiwan's grant) to draw on. I will put together our multi-year small works plan and submit it immediately. It won't be ad-hoc "freestyling" – it'll be a strategic bundle of projects.

Why bundle? Because if we package, say, five sidewalks and three drains in one contract, we get economy of scale. Mobilize one set of contractors and equipment and knock them out together. This saves money and time. Imagine instead of hiring separate crews for every little fix, we hire one to handle a batch: sidewalks in Vide Bouteille, Sunny Acres, and Bisee done in one go. We could likely stretch that EC$1 million to cover more ground by bundling sidewalks, footpaths, and drains across communities rather than doing them piecemeal. This is exactly how smart constituencies have amplified their impact. For instance, in other regions local governments have combined dozens of small road repairs into one project to get bulk pricing on asphalt. We can do the same with concrete and labour for our footpaths and drains.

Let me give you a concrete example of bundling: Suppose our short list has four priority drains to clear or rebuild – one in L'Anse Road, one in Blackstone, one in Morne Du Don, one in Choc – plus two sidewalks to extend – one in Vigie, one in Sunny Acres. Instead of six tiny procurements, we publish one "Castries North Community Works 2026" tender for all six jobs. Contractors bid on the lot. Maybe one contractor takes all, or a couple split it, but either way the overhead is lower than six separate mobilizations. This isn't just theory – packaging small works is explicitly part of my plan and frankly common sense. It's also easier to manage: I can hold one project manager accountable for the bundle rather than chasing multiple micro-projects with different people.

Now, **Funding Stream #2: BNTF (Basic Needs Trust Fund).** This is a gem that not everyone knows about, but it's been around quietly changing lives. BNTF is a program run via the Saint Lucia Social Development Fund and funded by the Caribbean Development Bank (and other donors). It specifically targets basic needs projects in communities – exactly our space. We're talking things like community access roads, footpaths, drainage, water supply, school facilities, skills training centres. Since its inception decades ago, BNTF has poured approximately US$20 million (EC$54 million) into over 100 projects in Saint Lucia. That's an average of over half a million EC dollars per project – usually grants, not loans. In the latest cycle (the 11th cycle currently commencing), they're focusing on areas like community access & drainage, water & sanitation, education, and livelihood projects – which align perfectly with what Castries North needs. In short, BNTF is money on the table for us, if we claim it with good proposals.

How do we tap BNTF? Through project submissions. Typically, the MP works with community organizations or the local council to propose a project, e.g. "Construct 500m of footpaths and drains in X community" or "Rehabilitate community resource centre in Y." These get vetted and, if they meet the criteria of serving basic needs in a poorer or vulnerable community, they get funded (mostly by grant, sometimes with a small government match). I have every intention to make Castries North a star performer in BNTF participation. If other constituencies are napping on these opportunities, we won't. For example, if Morne Du Don's retaining walls are too expensive to do fully under CDP alone, I'll package it as a climate resilience project and send it up to BNTF or even other funds. If we need a proper footpath linking a back neighbourhood in Bisee to the main road (so kids don't have to walk through mud), that's exactly the kind of "basic community access" BNTF loves to fund.

One point: BNTF cycles can be a bit bureaucratic and slow if you're not proactive. But as noted by the SSDF's leadership, they're working to reduce project gestation periods and encourage early project identification with community input. I will be on it from day one

– convening with SSDF, identifying projects early, and ensuring our proposals are shovel-ready and community-backed. By mainstreaming our discussions with relevant ministries (so we're not duplicating something already budgeted elsewhere), we increase chances of approval and avoid any embarrassment of rejected projects. Essentially, I'll run a tight ship: if a drain project is going to BNTF, I'll coordinate with Ministry of Infrastructure to ensure they aren't planning the same drain, and vice versa. This harmonization is part of using funds strategically and without waste.

Funding Stream #3: Line Ministry Budgets. Not every fix needs a special program like CDP or BNTF. The Government of Saint Lucia has ministries – Infrastructure, Education, Health, etc. – all with annual budgets that include capital works and maintenance. A savvy MP doesn't say "oh, I'll wait for CDP only"; a savvy MP advocates within the normal government budget process to channel resources to their constituency. That means building relationships with ministers and permanent secretaries, yes, but more importantly it means making a strong, data-driven case for why Castries North's needs should be addressed by national programs. I've already started on that with the Castries North Data Dossier – by identifying flood hotspots, accident-prone roads, and infrastructure gaps with evidence, I arm myself (and the relevant ministries) with justification to act. For instance, the dossier notes that Castries North has known flood risk zones like L'Anse Road/Vide Bouteille where November 2022 saw 42.5 mm of rain fall in hours and cause havoc. The Ministry of Infrastructure launched flood mitigation initiatives (like in Corinth) after that event. I will use that fact: "Look, you did X in Corinth; here's data showing we need something similar in Vide Bouteille." If they have an Urban Flood Resilience project underway (and they do, with World Bank support), I'll fight to ensure our drains and ravines are included for upgrade. If there's a national road improvement or traffic safety project, I'll insist that known trouble spots like the Choc pedestrian crossing or the Sunny Acres junction are on their list – armed with accident reports or resident petitions to back it up.

In essence, line ministry funds are our big-ticket source for things slightly above "small works" scale or for recurring maintenance. For example, major re-paving of the Vide Bouteille road or installing a full traffic light system at a highway intersection might exceed what CDP typically covers; that's where I lobby the Ministry of Infrastructure to allocate part of its national budget. And because Castries North is an urban constituency with heavy usage of its infrastructure, I'd argue investments here have high impact. I'll remind them that Castries North's roads carry not just our residents but thousands of commuters daily – fixing them isn't pork-barrel, it's national interest. And I will absolutely use Parliament's tools – questions, motions, even the Public Accounts Committee if needed – to shine a light if our area is being neglected in allocations.

Now, let's talk about keeping political strings firmly out of this equation. Historically, the ruling party would sometimes deploy or withhold small projects as political leverage – a little asphalt before elections, or "no help for you since you didn't vote for us." I reject that with every fiber of my being. As I wrote earlier in this book: Representation is not feudalism… It's a job – show up, know your people, fix problems you can reach. Nowhere in that description is there room for "only fix for friends." I have explicitly chosen to run independent because I want to serve without permission slips. That means if some party operative ever tries to tell me, "Cool down, don't push too hard for that community because they're not our base," I will do the opposite – I'll push twice as hard. And guess what, I won't be in their backroom meetings to hear such nonsense in the first place.

Let me address a scenario head-on: Suppose the government after the next election is not keen on an independent succeeding. Some cynics say, "Marcellus, if you win, they'll try to starve Castries North to make you look bad." My answer: They can try, but the system now has openings I will exploit fully. CDP is one – if they fund everyone, I'm part of that; if they suddenly don't, that's a national scandal I'll raise hell about. BNTF doesn't go through ministers – it goes through an independent process with CDB oversight; they can't just quash that quietly. Line ministries – if I'm stonewalled, I'll publish the letters, I'll ask questions in Parliament, I'll use the media. One independent voice can't topple a government, but it can sure make noise that they don't want. And I believe in the power of public scrutiny. If I go on record saying "Community X needs a drain, here's the data, I have the money lined up, but Ministry Y is delaying," that Ministry will feel the pressure, especially when citizens start talking about it. In short, sunlight and persistence will pry open any funding door that someone tries to keep closed for petty reasons.

Now, beyond government and official channels, there's **Funding Stream #4: Community, Diaspora and Private Partnerships.** This is not to replace government responsibility but to augment and expedite. We have a vibrant diaspora from Castries North – people abroad who still care deeply about their neighbourhoods. Some are already contributing quietly: I know of a group of ex-residents in New York who pooled money to repaint their community church and fix some benches in the nearby park. Why not widen that circle? For instance, we could set up a "Castries North Community Fund" – a transparent fund (managed by a reputable charity or credit union) where diaspora, local businesses, and even supportive neighbours can donate towards specific small projects. We'd use it for those little nice-to-haves that government might not prioritize immediately – say a new bus shelter by City Gate, or an extra set of playground equipment for a community park. This would be strictly voluntary and supplementary. And every dollar would be accounted for publicly (following the same rigor I demand of public funds).

Another angle is in-kind contributions. Sometimes what we need isn't cash but materials or labour. The corporate sector in St. Lucia can be a partner – for example, a paint company might donate paint if we're refreshing all the pedestrian crossings and can put their logo on our newsletter thanking them. A construction firm might lend a backhoe for a day to clear a large drain, as part of their civic duty. I'm not shy about asking, especially when it benefits the public and also gives the donor some positive exposure. Again, no kickbacks, no contracts in exchange – just straightforward "sponsor a bench, sponsor a tree-planting" type civic partnerships.

And let's not forget community labour itself – the good old kochu danme spirit (Que Kréyòl for "lend a hand"). Many of us remember when neighbourhoods organized clean-up campaigns or build together days. We can revive that, not as a substitute for government work but as a source of pride and togetherness. If we have the cement and tools (which CDP or donors can fund), I bet we can get volunteers to help pour a small concrete footpath to someone's front step who really needs it. I recall a story from Babonneau where community members built a wooden footbridge in a day to help schoolkids – only later did the authorities come and make a permanent one. That interim solution saved kids months of wading through water. So yes, if an urgent need can be met by community action safely, I will empower it – and then formalize it with proper infrastructure soon after.

Now, some might wonder: Isn't there a risk of overlapping or double-dipping funding? What if CDP, BNTF, and Ministry all accidentally aim at the same thing? My approach prevents that:

planning and communication. I will maintain a single integrated Castries North Project Matrix – basically a living document listing all identified projects and potential funding sources. If a drain can be funded by either CDP or BNTF, I mark both options but once one is secured, I update and inform the other program to avoid duplication. Regular coordination meetings with the Constituency Council (which statutorily liaises with ministries) will also help align things. This is part of being strategic – you don't just fire off requests blindly; you manage it like a program.

Let me also mention potential regional and international grants. We talked about Taiwan's involvement. There are also friendly foreign missions (like the Japanese grassroots grants, or the EU and UN small grant programs) that occasionally fund community projects – say a rainwater harvesting system for a school, or a hazard mitigation project. I will keep an eye on those opportunities as well. Being independent actually helps here: I can approach any embassy or agency without a party lens, just as a constituency looking for help. For example, Japan has a GGP (Grant Assistance for Grassroots Projects) – they've funded school improvements and community centre renovations in Saint Lucia before. If we need, say, a new retaining wall by a community centre or a small health post upgrade, I might send an application their way. It's about being creative and proactive.

Now, allow me to illustrate how these funding streams come together with a hypothetical case: the La Clery River Clean-up and Flood Prevention Project. This is a need we identified walking from Vigie (the river that runs from Cowe/Girard down to Vigie). It's heavily polluted and choked with debris, contributing to flood risk. Here's how I'd fund a solution: Use Ministry of Infrastructure routine maintenance budget to dredge and clear sections of the river (because they already budget for river desilting). Use CDP funds to build a couple of new concrete drains or collection areas in the community where runoff enters the river, to better channel the flow (small works). Tap BNTF for a complementary project: maybe creating proper footpaths and railings along the riverbank in populated sections, with community involvement – framing it as both a safety and livelihood improvement (imagine a cleaned riverbank that could even have a little green space). And engage the community for an annual river clean-up drive with support from corporate sponsors for gloves and bags, plus an education campaign about not dumping in the river (maybe funded by an environment NGO small grant). In this way, a multi-faceted problem (flooding, environmental health) is tackled with multiple funding sources working in concert – each doing what they're best at: the Ministry handles heavy duty dredging, CDP handles quick infrastructure fixes (drains), BNTF handles community infrastructure (footpaths, railings) and maybe sanitation facilities, and the community/donors handle the soft side (clean-ups, awareness).

It sounds ambitious, but it's completely achievable with coordination. And coordination is exactly what you elect an MP to do – to be the quarterback calling the plays, ensuring all the players (funding sources) move the ball downfield together. This is in stark contrast to the old style where an MP might just wait for central government largesse or, worse, only bring goodies when it's photo-op time. I refuse to operate by that playbook. I'm writing a new one – in fact, I already started writing it in Part I of this book when I talked about showing up with a plan and a scoreboard, not a slogan.

Let me share a personal conviction that drives this approach: I don't want to ever have to go begging to any Prime Minister for my constituency's survival. I want to look him or her in the eye and say, "Castries North is organized, we have our priorities straight, and we've leveraged every dollar available. We're here to partner, not beg. Meet us halfway on these bigger items, and we'll handle the rest." There's a pride in that – it's the same pride I want to instil in our community. We are done being supplicants; we'll be active participants in our own development. And money – or the lack thereof – will not be the excuse.

I often say (and I said in a recent interview): "I don't want to be a Minister, I want a budget for Castries North so we can deal with the issues. I want to be on the ground day one when I win, and put systems in place to fix those issues." That's exactly what this chapter is about. Securing the budget doesn't necessarily mean literally carving out a chunk of the national pie just for me (though something like a constituency fund could be debated in the future). It means piecing together our budget from various sources and getting it flowing quickly to needs on the ground.

Finally, let's throw in a quick look around the region for reassurance that this multi-stream approach works. In Barbados, MPs have access to a Constituency Empowerment Fund for community projects – both government and opposition MPs use it effectively for things like fixing community centres and sports facilities. In Jamaica, they have a Constituency Development Fund (not unlike our CDP) and it's actually enshrined such that each MP gets an allocation every year – opposition included – which they use for scholarships, road patching, you name it. In the OECS, countries like Dominica and Grenada leverage a lot of donor funds for village roads and footbridges – often executed by their Ministries but initiated by local parliamentary reps' advocacy. A key takeaway from these places: when systems are fair and reps are proactive, small projects get done regardless of political stripe. On the other hand, when reps are lazy or only looking for the big ribbon-cutting, constituents suffer. I refuse to let Castries North suffer from either political spite or representative inertia.

So to summarize our funding game plan: (1) Use our guaranteed piece of the CDP pie to tackle a bundled slate of high-impact projects immediately. (2) Tap BNTF for complementary and bigger community needs, making sure no opportunity is missed. (3) Aggressively lobby and collaborate with line ministries to integrate our infrastructure fixes into national programs (especially where costs or scale go beyond what CDP covers). (4) Engage the diaspora, private sector, and community volunteers for additional support on specific improvements, all in a structured, transparent way. (5) Do all of the above with zero tolerance for partisan strings – funding will be guided by need and merit, not party colours.

We will make every dollar count (yes, that's the name of this book for a reason). A sidewalk doesn't care which party paid for it, and neither do the feet walking on it. My job is to marshal the resources so that those feet have a safe path, that those homes don't flood, and that our people see tangible progress. By diversifying our funding streams and bundling our projects smartly, we can truly stretch that first EC$1 million into what feels like EC$3 million worth of improvements on the ground.

And one more thing: I will report every dollar and every project publicly. But that slides into the territory of the next chapter – where we talk about publishing schedules and finishing jobs. The short point here in the context of funding is: transparency itself is a funding strategy. Why? Because when donors and ministries see a constituency that's organized and clean with its accounting, they are more willing to funnel resources to it. If I can show that our last batch of CDP projects came in on time and on budget, maybe next year Castries North gets a bit extra love because they know it won't be wasted. Success begets success. So, let's fund these works and execute them so well that funding in the future becomes even easier to secure.

We have the means – multiple means – to get our small works done without selling out and without waiting forever. I'm going to use every single one of them. That's my promise on funding: no excuses, no delays, and no political strings attached. Just service, strategy, and delivery.

24

Publish the Schedule; Finish the Job

If there's one thing I've learned from both sports and public life, it's this: accountability is the engine of progress. You can have money, plans, and teams ready to work, but if no one is holding the clock and measuring results, things falter. In Castries North, we are done with half-finished projects and mysterious delays. The mantra for every sidewalk, drain, and crossing we tackle will be simple: publish the schedule; finish the job.

Picture this scenario in the very near future: It's Monday morning at the Castries North Constituency Office (or the "Rep's Office" as we call it). On the wall in the waiting area, there's a large whiteboard or pin-up chart titled "Small Works – Weekly Update." It lists every ongoing community project – say, "Morne Du Don retaining wall repair," "Vide Bouteille sidewalk extension by school," "Choc drainage clearing," etc. Next to each, there's a start date, a target completion date, and a one-line status. Perhaps it says "Retaining wall – Work 75% complete, finishing by Feb 20" or "Sidewalk – Delayed: awaiting materials, new finish date Mar 5." This chart isn't hidden in my drawer; it's front and centre for any constituent to see. Transparency, plain and simple. If you prefer digital, the same info is on our Facebook page or WhatsApp broadcast. But I insist on a print-friendly, minimalist design because I know Mrs. George who runs the little shop in La Clery would love to stick a copy on her counter, and the folks at the Vigie community centre can pin it on their notice board. This update won't be some glossy PR pamphlet with my smiling photo – no, it'll likely be black-and-white text, maybe our constituency logo at most. This is not about hype; it's about facts you can check at a glance.

Why go to these lengths? Because we've been burned before by what I call "progress by press release." Too often, politicians announce projects with fanfare, but then the follow-through is anyone's guess. Maybe it finishes late, maybe not at all, and usually nobody ever publicly admits if it never finished. We end up with "ground-breakings without ground-works; ribbon-cuttings without maintenance plans". Not under my watch. When we publish a schedule, we're making a promise: This will start on this date, and finish by that date. And if something changes, you'll see it updated next week on that chart – no cover-ups. Did the contractor hit a snag because of three days of rain?

Fine, new completion date, noted in red with a brief reason. Then you'll see it move the next week: hopefully to "Completed."

This level of transparency might sound radical in our political culture, but it's actually just commonsense service. Think about any good business – if you order a package, you can track it. If you hire someone to fix your roof, you expect to know when they'll start and finish. Why should community projects be any different? In fact, they should be more transparent because it's public money. I firmly believe in what I said earlier: "If we can't show you the sheet – what's scheduled, what's in procurement, what's waiting – then we're asking you to trust vibes. And vibes don't pour concrete." Well, we will show you the sheet – literally. That weekly update is the embodiment of that philosophy.

Let me delve into the format of these updates a bit, because I want you to visualize it. The design will be minimalist: a simple table or list format, easily photocopied or screenshot. Each project entry will have: Project Name, Location, Brief Description, Start Date, Target Completion, Status/Notes. If a project hasn't started yet, it might say "Pending – awaiting contractor mobilization, est. start June 1." Once it starts, we put the actual start date. If it's completed, we'll mark it COMPLETED in bold, maybe highlight it so everyone sees the wins. We won't clutter it with technical jargon; it's meant for the public. If you don't know what a project name refers to, our office staff will gladly explain (or maybe we include a tiny legend or reference like "drain near the big mango tree in X area" for clarity). The idea is anyone from an 8-year-old to an 80-year-old should be able to read it and understand what's happening.

Now, aside from the board in the office, we'll also disseminate this widely. I envision a one-page weekly or bi-weekly bulletin – call it the "Castries North Works Tracker." It can be posted on social media, emailed to community leaders, and physically posted at key spots: the council office, the health centre, perhaps the popular bus stops (City Gate, etc.), even pinned up in churches or shops if they allow. We will also send it to the local media as a matter of course – imagine the radio host saying, "Alright, let's see what Castries North is up to this week... they've completed the footpath in Blackstone, and the crossing by CCSS is 50% done." Why not? It might actually inspire other constituencies to do the same. And if it embarrasses a few others into action – hey, that's positive peer pressure for the country.

One might ask: Isn't this overkill for little projects? I say no – this is setting a standard. Small projects are what people feel directly; if we can't be transparent on those, what hope is there for larger ones? And frankly, after years of people feeling left in the dark, I want to shine light on everything. I want Ms. Catherine from Vigie to come into the office and see "Herbert Street drain – Completed Jan 10" and smile because she was the one who reported that broken drain. And maybe next to it is a before-and-after photo of the drain, printed out. Yes, I plan to use photo evidence liberally. A picture of the bad state, and a picture of it fixed. We'll keep them in a binder or on a bulletin board titled "Delivered." There is nothing like the visual satisfaction of seeing a tangible before/after. It says: We promised, we did it, here it is. I recall saying in Chapter 1 that representation is a job and "if you can't point to what you fixed on the ground, you're not representing; you're rehearsing." Well, Castries North folks will be able to point to freshly paved steps, new manhole covers, painted crosswalks – and I will literally point with you, because I'll be as proud as anyone to see these things done.

Citizen reporting will be a cornerstone of this transparent approach. It's not just me telling you – I want you to tell me and the community how we're doing. To facilitate that, we will set up easy channels. For example: a dedicated WhatsApp number or SMS line for the constituency office where you can send a message like "Streetlight out on Palm Drive, pole #14" or "Thank you, drain by my house flowing well now." And importantly, if something we marked as completed isn't actually right, I want to hear it. Maybe the contractor said he patched the pothole, but two days later the patch sunk – you snap a photo and send it with "Hey, this isn't properly fixed." That goes on the record, and we get the contractor back to finish the job properly (and we'll note it in the status – rework needed, in progress). By inviting scrutiny and feedback, we create a two-way accountability loop. No more of this one-sided "the rep speaks, you listen" dynamic. It's going to be a conversation.

In fact, I want to go a step further: community monitors. For each project, especially ones of longer duration, I'd love to have a local resident voluntarily serve as a "community monitor." If we're repairing a sidewalk in Lanse Road, perhaps the nearby neighbourhood watch or just Mr. Jones who lives there agrees to just keep an eye out and inform us if the workers stop showing up or if the materials are dumped and left, etc. Not to interfere, just to observe and report. Think of it like a neighbourhood liaison. We will finish the job – and the community will help ensure we finish strong and finish right.

Now, let's talk about what this does culturally. Restoring trust. People have heard politicians say "I'll do X, Y, Z" for decades. Often X, Y, Z remain undone or partially done. Over time, cynicism sets in. Trust erodes. I don't blame anyone in Castries North for being skeptical of any candidate's promises. That's why I'm not just asking for trust – I'm earning it through radical transparency and follow-through. When you start seeing these weekly updates and then see that the reality on the ground matches, something will shift. The first time I update a due date because something slipped, and publicly acknowledge it, you'll realize – hey, this guy owns up, he doesn't hide. The first time a completion appears and you walk by that site and indeed it's done, you'll think – alright, maybe this is for real. Trust doesn't come back overnight, but consistent honesty and delivery will nurture it.

I also believe this approach will put service over spectacle in a very literal way. How? Well, if every week we're publicly logging all projects, it becomes much harder to do the usual political spectacle of saving everything for an election year blitz. The work will be incremental and constant. You'll see in black and white that, say, 5 projects got done in Q1, another 5 in Q2, etc., rather than 20 projects magically in the months before polling. It takes the wind out of the old showmanship sails. And I'm fine with that. In fact, I want to kill the notion that development is something to parade around in rallies. Development should be daily, humble, steady. As I put it earlier: "Putting it right starts with returning the office to its owners... If you're chasing me for weeks, the system is broken." Under this regime, you won't have to chase me to know what's happening – it's on the wall and in your hand. The service (the actual works) takes centre stage, and the spectacle (political fanfare) fades away.

One might wonder: will the average person really care to read these updates? Maybe not everyone, but the ones directly impacted absolutely will. And more broadly, even if someone doesn't read each line, the very fact that it's available changes the dynamic. It's like open data – not everyone downloads the budget PDFs on a government website, but knowing it's public deters certain bad behaviour. Likewise, knowing that we're openly tracking and publishing progress means any stakeholder – media, citizens, opposition, watchdog groups – can call me out if things lag too much. It keeps us all on our toes. And that's exactly the point. The commitment to transparency is a self-imposed discipline. I'm basically saying: hold me to it, I have nowhere to hide. And I'm comfortable with that because I plan to do the work.

Let me illustrate with a hypothetical: Say we plan 10 small projects in the first 6 months. We publish them. Now, imagine by month 4, only 2 are done, 5 are in progress, and 3 haven't started. That update, sitting in public, is a huge incentive for me and my team to get moving on the remaining 3. Because otherwise every week people see "Not started" and that's embarrassing and unacceptable. It's a far cry from the usual scenario where if something is not started, the politician just doesn't mention it again and hopes you forget. No forgetting here – the list stares us in the face. It's pressure – the good kind of pressure.

To add, this transparency also extends to budgets and contacts in the long run (which Part VI of this book will dive into). But even at the project schedule level, I intend to sometimes include notes like "Funding: CDP" or "Contractor: XYZ Co." on the update. That way, people know who is doing the job and through what channel. If a contractor is slacking, trust me, folks will call them out by name – and I'll have more leverage to insist they pick up the pace or face penalties.

Let's talk about photo evidence and citizen involvement a bit more with real examples. Suppose we're fixing the La Clery/L'Anse Road drain that floods. Day 1, the crew goes out, we snap a "before" photo of the clogged, overgrown drain (maybe even use one of the flood photos from 2022 to remind us why it matters). Mid-week, we snap a couple progress photos – those might just be for our records unless someone asks. Day 5, project done, we take an "after" photo of clean, widened drains with water flowing. We post those two on our Facebook page with a brief "Before/After: La Clery Drain – Completed on time." We might print and pin those on the community centre board. Now, say two weeks later a resident messages, "It's filling with silt again after the last rain, need a trash screen upstream." That feedback goes into our plan – maybe an update: "Note: will install debris screen by July as follow-up." Then we do it and show that. This way, even once a job is "finished," it's not forgotten – we remain vigilant through citizen eyes and follow-ups.

Another example: Crosswalk repainting campaign. This is a small project but very visible. Let's say over a weekend we repaint 15 pedestrian crossings in the constituency (by schools, busy junctions, etc.) with volunteer help. We list it as a project: "Crosswalk Repainting – various locations." Start date: maybe a Saturday. End date: Sunday. Status: Completed – and we list each location done. And I guarantee you, residents will tell us if we missed one or if by Monday morning one still looks faded. They'll say "Hey, the crossing by VG Beach wasn't done!" Then I'll reply, "Thanks, we'll get that on the next round Wednesday." Then on Wednesday's update, it shows as done. See the pattern? Engagement, correction, completion.

This approach not only delivers tangible results but also educates the public on process. People will see that some things can be finished in days (like repainting lines) while others take weeks (like constructing a drain or sidewalk). They'll see what factors cause delays. Essentially, it's a civic education – you get to understand how the sausage is made, in a clean way. Over time, this can even build patience and cooperation. If folks know, for example, that materials are delayed due to a port issue (and we note that), they might be more understanding than if they were just left in the dark assuming nothing's happening. Transparency can turn potential anger into shared problem-solving.

Now, an important element of finishing the job is also ensuring quality. Transparency helps here too. By publishing that a job is "finished," I'm implicitly inviting everyone to inspect it. If it's shoddy, I expect to be called out. And I will not consider a job truly finished until it passes the "Mrs. James test" – meaning, the everyday Lucian for whom it was done agrees it's resolved. We've had enough of ceremonial completions where the real issues persist (like a "repaired" road that still floods because they forgot drainage). Finishing the job means solving the problem, not just ticking a box. So, part of our tracking will include a sort of sign-off that could involve community reps: basically verifying that what was supposed to be achieved was indeed achieved. I might do spot visits myself for each completed item (I probably will, because that's how I am). But even if I can't, someone from the office or a trusted community member will validate.

By now you might be thinking, this level of micromanagement, is it sustainable? I argue that it won't be as onerous as it sounds once it becomes routine. The first few weeks setting it up might be heavy (getting the format right, training staff to update, etc.). But once it's rolling, updating 10-15 project lines each week is not that crazy. And the benefits in efficiency and trust far outweigh the effort. Also, the constituency office will have a staff including a projects officer whose job is exactly this – tracking and liaising. The truth is, a lot of this data (start dates, etc.) exists anyway in internal paperwork; we're just making it public and digestible. It's basically converting an internal project spreadsheet into a publicly readable weekly snapshot. That is just good management.

Let me tie this back to the big picture of trust and representation. In Chapter 1, I made a pledge about a "scoreboard you can hold me against, not a slogan you can sing". Publishing a work schedule and sticking to it is part of that scoreboard. It's saying: judge me by these outcomes. I won't be able to squirm away with excuses if I fail because the record will be plain. And if I succeed, well, the record will show that too. It's laying my reputation on the line every week. That might scare some, but to me it's motivating. It keeps me aligned with my principle that representation is service, honesty, and real progress.

I also mentioned earlier in the book something I call the dignity test. For instance, Ms. Joseph coming to report a blocked drain should be treated with a process – a ticket, a schedule, a follow-up call – that affirms her dignity as a citizen. Publishing the schedule is part of that. It's an extension of treating issues as public tasks, not personal favours. When Ms. Joseph sees "Drain by VBCC – Cleared Oct 3" on the sheet, she feels valued and heard, not brushed off. When you publish what you've done, you're effectively saying to citizens: "Look, we did what you asked, because your issue matters." And when you publish what you haven't done yet, you're saying: "We haven't forgotten, it's on the list, here's when it's coming." That is respect.

Now, I won't pretend this approach will be flawless. There will be weeks something slips, or a typo in the update, or a sudden issue that bumps others (say a freak storm creates an urgent need somewhere – we'll have to re-prioritize and explain that on the chart). But the key is, you'll know about it. I recall a quote from a senior public servant: "People can forgive delays; what frustrates them is not knowing." I find that true. If you tell me "the water will be off for 3 hours," I can manage. But if it just goes and I have no idea when it's back, I get upset. Same with these works. So we will communicate, communicate, communicate.

As we steadily finish jobs and cross them off the list, something beautiful will happen: pride and trust in the community will grow. I imagine a day when a parent walking a newly repaired sidewalk with their child says, "Our community did this. We asked, and it happened. Look how nice it is now." And the child learns that civic engagement works. Or when election time comes around, instead of heated arguments, our residents simply point: "See that bridge? See that crossing? That's what was done – it's not talk." It shifts the political discourse from noise to substance.

In a sense, this approach is also a direct response to the style of governance we've endured. We've seen enough of the "rush to cut grass and patch things right before elections" routine. I noted recently that "right as we speak, there's a rush to fix the field, a rush to cut grass at the health centre" because elections are looming. That's treating people like they can't remember the neglect of the prior four years. Publishing a continuous schedule defangs that strategy. There's no need for a rush if we've been doing it all along – and if someone else tries a sudden rush, people will compare with our steady log and see through it. In short, our transparency inoculates the community against last-minute political theatrics.

To conclude this chapter, let me paint one more vivid scene of the future: It's the end of my first year in office, and we decide to host a little open house at the constituency office. We invite everyone for a "Castries North Accountability Day." On the walls we've pinned the 52 weekly update sheets from the year like a tapestry of hard work. There are red lines through completed projects, dates, names – a full chronicle. People walk along it like an exhibit: "Oh yes, I remember when they fixed that drain – here it is in April. And here by July we got the crossing painted." It's essentially our report card on display, not written by some PR person, but compiled from the real-time updates we shared all year. Now that is accountability you can literally walk through. I stand there not giving a speech about what I plan to do, but rather discussing with constituents what we did do, and taking suggestions for the next year's projects (which we'll add to a new board titled "Upcoming"). The feeling in that room is one of mutual trust and accomplishment. Not that everything is perfect – far from it, there will always be more to do – but now you believe when I say "We'll tackle that next," because you've seen a year of promises kept in real time.

This is how we restore faith in representation, one completed sidewalk and one published schedule at a time. Finish the job isn't just a slogan; it's a culture we are building. Step by step, we will prove that government can work for people in the most direct, observable ways. And once that culture takes root – once people see that service with accountability is not only possible but is actually happening in Castries North – it will be very hard for anyone in the future to take that away. The community will expect nothing less. That might be my proudest legacy if we achieve it: not just the physical fixes, but the new standard of governance we normalize.

So, let's publish the schedule and then let's finish every job on it. No excuses, total transparency, and results we can point to together. This is how we make it count – for you can count each project done, and count on each promise kept. The work is ours, the door is open. Now you can literally watch us walk through it, week by week, getting things done in plain view.

Let's finish strong, Castries North – and let's do it in the sunlight.

Part VI – The Covenant & The Scoreboard

25

The Castries North Covenant

I have spent many chapters making the case for a new kind of representation in Castries North. Now it's time to put that promise in writing – literally on the wall. I'm calling it the Castries North Covenant, a plain-language pledge any resident can read at a glance. This isn't a vague manifesto or a campaign flyer destined for the gutter. It's a working contract between me and you, the people of Castries North, with specific goals, deadlines, and responsibilities named. Consider it the one-page truth check for everything I've said in this book. If a year or two from now I'm not living up to it, you'll have it posted right there to hold me to account. As I declared from the outset: "We are not beggars; I am not a king". Representation is a job, not a coronation, and this covenant spells out how I will execute that job in service – not in status.

Why a covenant? Because too often in politics, promises evaporate or hide behind excuses. We won't play that game. This covenant will hang on the wall of the constituency office, right next to the weekly works board and community map. It will also live online, a pinned post everyone can reference. It will tie directly to the systems explained in the next chapters – our open dashboards and project trackers, our funding rules, and our learning loops – so it's not just words but a gateway to action. Think of it as the table of contents of trust: each pledge here corresponds to a program or practice you can see in motion. And it will have names. If something is to be done by a certain date, you'll know who in our team (or which partner agency) is responsible for getting it done. No orphan projects, no anonymous blame game.

Before unveiling the covenant, let me set one more expectation. This is a living pledge. By that I mean, if circumstances change or if we find a better way to solve a problem, we'll update the covenant – openly – with community input. The only thing that won't change is the ethos: service over status, public accountability, reliability in delivery. I'd rather adjust a tactic than cling to a failing promise out of pride. What I won't adjust are the values underneath. As an independent representative, I carry the pressure directly – there's no party to hide behind if something stalls. If the road is still broken or the clinic still closed, that's on me. This covenant makes that crystal clear. In fact, I invite you: circle these deadlines in red on your calendar, watch our progress like a hawk, and "call me out if I slip". That's exactly the energy I want you to bring, because it will keep me and our whole team honest.

So here it is – the Castries North Covenant – my wall-readable promise to you:

CASTRIES NORTH COVENANT (2026–2030): SERVICE. ACCOUNTABILITY. DELIVERY.

• **Open Office, Open Ears** – Goal: Constituency Office open to the public a minimum of 40 hours each week (including at least one evening and one weekend slot) with a dedicated officer on duty. Hold quarterly town hall meetings (one in each major community: e.g. Vigie, La Clery, Vide Bouteille, Babonneau Road area) to report on progress and listen to concerns. Deadline: Office hours policy published in first 30 days; first round of town halls within first 3 months, then ongoing quarterly. Responsible: Constituency Office Manager (for daily ops) and the MP (for meetings).

• **Transparent Worklog & Dashboard** – Goal: Publish a weekly bulletin every Monday listing the projects or tasks for that week (e.g. "pothole repairs on X road, meeting with Ministry of Health about clinic hours on Friday, youth sports clinic on Saturday"), along with updates on ongoing works. Maintain a public dashboard – a large wall chart and an online post – tracking key metrics: number of local works completed, after-school programs running, clinic hours kept vs. planned, and community safety fixes, as well as average response time to citizen issues. Deadline: Launch dashboard within 60 days of taking office; updates every week on Monday by 6 p.m. Responsible: MP's constituency aide for compiling updates, supervised by the MP.

• **Small Works, Big Impact (The 100-Day List)** – Goal: Complete the top 10 small infrastructure fixes identified during the campaign walk (e.g. clearing the flooded drain by Ms. Joseph's house in Vide Bouteille, patching the broken La Clery sidewalk by the playing field, installing the promised Vigie school crossing, fixing streetlights in Blackstars and Chase Gardens, etc.). These are "low-hanging fruit" that improve daily life. Deadline: 100 days from start of term for all 10 to be finished with before-and-after evidence. Responsible: Constituency Council works supervisor (for coordination) with contractors named per project. Accountability: Names of contractors and work supervisors will be listed next to each project on the works board.

• **Service Response Guarantee** – Goal: Acknowledge every public complaint or request within 48 hours and provide an initial action plan within 1 week. For common issues (blocked drains, broken standpipe, etc.), commit to a site visit or inspection within 7 days and an attempted fix within 30 days (if funding available). Track and publicly display the average response time for complaints on the dashboard. Deadline: System live from day 1 (we'll develop a simple ticket log even before office opening), first response time report after 1 month of operations. Responsible: Constituency Office caseworker (logging and follow-up), MP to review unresolved cases weekly.

• **Education & Youth First** – Goal: Establish after-school study and sports programs in at least 3 major schools or community centres within the first year – for example, a homework help and SAT prep hub at Vide Bouteille Secondary (PDJSS), a similar program rotating through the SDA Academy or Corinth area, and one at Sir Ira Simmons Secondary – with volunteer or paid tutors and coaches engaged. Facilitate at least 10 new scholarships or training opportunities for Castries North youth per year, leveraging agreements like the Washburn University in-state tuition MOU and others I've initiated. This includes academic or sports scholarships and local technical training placements. Deadline: 3 after-school programs up and running by end of Year 1; 10+ youth placements by end of each calendar year (starting 2026 if in office mid-year). Responsible: MP's Youth Development Assistant (a position I will create) to coordinate programs, with school principals and volunteer teachers; MP to handle scholarship partner outreach. Progress will be reported monthly in the Education & Youth section of the dashboard.

• **Health Access & Wellness** – Goal: Improve local health services via two key actions: (1) Extend clinic hours – pilot early opening or late closing at least one day a week at the Gros Islet Polyclinic or nearest wellness centre serving Castries North, so working folks can visit outside 8–4. Target: two extended-hour clinic days per month by mid-2026. (2) Community fitness programs – start a weekly senior exercise class or walking group in 3 communities (e.g. a "Castries North Walkers" club at Vigie or La Clery as described in the health plan) to promote active living. Target: launch within 6 months. Also commit to publishing the clinic's basic service stats (hours open vs. expected, wait times, and availability of essential medicines) on the public dashboard – shining a light on any shortfalls so we can advocate fixes. Deadline: Negotiate extended hours pilot within 6 months; initiate 3 community wellness activities within 6 months. Responsible: MP liaising with Ministry of Health for clinic hours (names of contacts will be shared); Constituency Office health liaison (likely a volunteer nurse or doctor from the community) for organizing fitness groups.

• **Safe Streets & Spaces** – Goal: Execute at least five safety improvements in the first year: e.g. install proper zebra crossings or speed bumps at two critical spots (one outside a school, one by a busy pedestrian area), repair or install streetlights along at least two presently dark, high-risk footpaths, and fence or fix one playground or court. These projects are small but vital for public safety. Deadline: All five safety projects completed within Year 1, ideally one per quarter.

Responsible: Constituency Council technical officer coordinating with Ministry of Infrastructure (for crossings/lights) and local contractors.

- **Accountable Budget & Fair Share** – Goal: Secure Castries North's full allocation of government community development funds every year, and publicly report all funding received and spent. This means using the Constituency Development Programme (CDP) funds (approximately EC $1 million per year, if evenly divided) fully on Castries North projects, aggressively tapping the Basic Needs Trust Fund (BNTF) for eligible projects, lobbying line ministries for at least 3 major capital investments over the term (e.g. a road re-paving, a school upgrade, a drainage overhaul – things beyond CDP scope), and engaging private or diaspora partnerships for community initiatives. Transparency: Every dollar will be tracked: we will post a quarterly financial summary showing money requested, money received, and money spent, with project names. For example: "Q1: Requested $100k for road repair, received $50k, spent $45k on Pine Drive resurfacing (Contractor: XYZ Co., completed Jan 2026)". If any expected funds don't come (or are withheld), that will be noted and raised publicly – no quietly letting Castries North be starved. Deadline: First budget transparency report by end of first quarter in office; then every 3 months. Responsible: MP (for advocating funds) and Office Financial Clerk (for tracking and publishing reports).

- **Annual "Stop–Start–Scale" Review** – Goal: Institutionalize learning and adaptation by conducting an annual review of all major initiatives. Each year, we will identify at least one practice or project to stop (because it's not working or not a good use of resources), one new idea to start (based on community feedback or emerging needs), and one successful initiative to scale up (expand to reach more people or areas). This could be done via a public town hall or a workshop with community representatives where we go through results – essentially an annual report to constituents followed by decisions for the next year. Deadline: Every December (end of year) starting 2026, with the findings published in a "Year in Review" report. Responsible: MP and an Advisory Panel of community members (which I will form from volunteers, e.g. retired public servants, youth leaders, etc., to provide independent input).

....

Marcellus Bax Stiede – Independent Parliamentary Representative, Castries North (hopefully, by the grace of your vote)

That's the covenant. It's detailed by design – you deserve nothing less. Each bullet is written in plain English, no legalese, so any Lucian can point to a line and ask, "Bax, have you done this yet? If not, why?" My job is to make sure you rarely have to ask why not. This document will be printed large and pinned up in our office lobby. I picture a resident coming in, perhaps skeptical, reading it while they wait, and realizing this is different. It's not a list of excuses or blame; it's a to-do list that we mean to get done.

Importantly, the covenant is not a solo act. I'm the one pledging my name to it, but many parts rely on partnerships – with you, with community groups, with government agencies. To meet these goals, I'll need active Constituency Council members stepping up, volunteers tutoring kids or leading walks, civil servants answering my calls when I push for that road or clinic funding. The covenant basically also serves as their invitation – it names where others will be involved, from the Council's works supervisor to Ministry officials. We'll put actual names next to tasks in our internal tracker (and often on the public board too) so you know, for example, which engineer is overseeing the drain fix or which youth officer is coordinating a scholarship fair. As I often say, nobody climbs alone – and in the same way, nobody governs alone, at least not effectively. This covenant is the rope tying all our hands to the plow in unison.

I want to highlight the boldest part of this for a St. Lucian political context: the radical transparency. "I have pledged something radical for politics here: I will publish what I plan to do, every week; tell you who is doing it, with what money, by when; show when it's done; and if I fail, say so and fix it". That's taken directly from my own campaign messaging and I mean every word. We've had too many MPs who preferred things opaque – budgets hidden in dense reports, decisions made in back rooms, and if nothing happened, well, it just quietly never gets mentioned again. Not under my watch. If I miss a deadline in the covenant, you'll hear it from me first, along with the plan to catch up. I'm effectively tying my reputation and future electability to delivering on these specific items. This is by choice – I want that scoreboard pressure because I "work better with one".

As an independent MP, I won't have a party apparatus to prop me up or spin failures. And I don't want one. My legitimacy must come from visible results, from "results you can point to". One reason I'm confident in making this covenant is that I know Castries North is filled with potential and untapped resources. I often repeat that we have enough talent and community spirit here that "we don't have to be beggars… We have things in our constituency that we can do" to improve our lot. This covenant turns that philosophy into concrete action points. Instead of encouraging dependency (lining up every Wednesday for a handout as if that's all politics offers), we're laying out a path to empowerment. For instance, by focusing on jobs, training, and community projects, we plan to replace the weekly "please help me" visit with "let's work together on this". It's a mutual covenant: I commit to bust a gut to deliver these improvements, and in return I'm asking constituents to participate – show up at meetings, volunteer when you can, hold me accountable always.

I'm not aiming for a ministerial portfolio or some lofty national post; my sole responsibility is the people of Castries North. ... I want to be on the ground from day one working, securing funds for that constituency. If offered a high office that takes me away from this covenant, I'd turn it down. I'd rather be fixing drains and sponsoring school programs here than sitting in an ivory tower elsewhere. Service over status, every time. This covenant is the proof in writing.

In the chapters that follow, I'll break down how, exactly, we will implement the promises embedded in each of these covenant points. You'll read about the Open Dashboards and Open Files that enable transparency, the way we'll Fund What Works and Cut What Doesn't to honour the budget and fairness pledges, and how continuous Learning Loops will ensure we keep improving on education, health, and infrastructure outcomes. Each chapter flows from a section of the covenant. In other words, the covenant is the map; the next chapters are the driving instructions.

I encourage you, as you read on, to flip back to the Castries North Covenant page now and then. Treat it as your reference. See if the details I discuss in the coming pages clearly link to a pledge on that list. If they don't, call me out – because that means I've gone off on some irrelevant tangent. This book, like my service, must stay tethered to those concrete commitments.

One last thing: A covenant is only as good as the integrity of the person who signs it and the vigilance of the people it's made with. I've signed it with conviction. I stand behind it personally. I ask you to hold your end by being vigilant. If you see something, say something. If an issue is being neglected or a promise languishes, bring it up at a town hall or post a comment on our Facebook updates – I won't hide from it. In fact, I'll thank you for the reminder and get back on track. Accountability is not a one-way street; it's a loop between rep and residents. This covenant formalizes my accountability to you, but your engagement is what powers it.

So here we go, Castries North – the covenant is on the wall. Let's make it count, together.

26

Open Dashboards, Open Files

Once we've settled in, you will be able to walk into our constituency office on any given Tuesday and you'll notice something immediately: the walls talk. They talk through the information they carry. On one side, you'll see a large scoreboard listing projects and metrics, with green checkmarks where things are done and dates for upcoming targets. On another, a corkboard displays photocopies of the latest budget breakdown, project bids, and even a monthly report of how we spent our allocation. In the corner, a computer kiosk or tablet will let you scroll through the live Castries North Project Matrix, an interactive spreadsheet of every project big and small, updated in real-time. This is what local transparency looks like – in your face, unfiltered, and useful. In this chapter, I'll explain how open dashboards and open files will transform the relationship between you and your government. No more "mwen pa sav" (I don't know) when you ask what's happening with that road or that grant; we'll be able to pull up the answer together on the spot.

First, let's talk about the ethos behind this: "Information is the new asphalt". I said it earlier: if people feel blindsided, they resist even good projects; but when they're informed and included, they'll help carry blocks and mix cement. Transparency isn't just a moral nicety – it's a practical tool for getting stuff done faster and better. When every constituent can see the plan, the progress, and the problems, two things happen. One, the trust level goes up – folks know you're not hiding anything or favouring anyone in secret. Two, the pressure stays on – I can't slack off or quietly drop a project without it being glaringly obvious. This is why I'm embracing a very public scoreboard you can "hold me against, not a slogan you can sing". I'm effectively hanging my report card in the window for you to grade at will.

THE COMMUNITY SCOREBOARD

Imagine a big sheet or digital screen divided into a few key sections – I call them the four tiles of our community dashboard. These tiles correspond to the main pillars of progress we care about: Local Works, Education & Youth, Health, and Safety & Public Spaces. In the middle of them, we might even have a composite index – an overall "Castries North Progress Score" – but the real value is in the breakout, the specifics. Let me break down what each tile shows, as I've committed earlier:

• **Local Works** – This tile lists the number of jobs (projects) in three categories: Planned, In Progress, and Completed. For example: "Drain/footpath projects – 2 completed / 3 in progress / 4 planned" and "Other small works – 5 completed / 2 in progress / 3 planned." Each significant job has a one-liner next to it: name or location (e.g. "Morne Du Don steps repair"), budget or funding source, the contractor (once selected), and the promised finish date. If it's finished, you'll see a checkmark and the actual completion date (plus maybe a tiny before/after photo pinned nearby). If it's running late, it might be highlighted or have a note why. Essentially, this is the live backlog of infrastructure fixes – you can walk in and literally see if the footpath you complained about is on the list and what's happening with it. If it's not there, you tell us and we'll add it on the spot. The scoreboard ensures no request vanishes into a black hole. As I've said, "If we can't show you the sheet... then we're asking you to trust vibes. And vibes don't pour concrete.". So we'll show you the sheet.

• **Education & Youth** – Here we track things like after-school programs open and active, number of tutors or teachers engaged, how many students attending those programs, plus stats on scholarships or internships facilitated. For instance: "3 homework centres open (Castries Comprehensive, PDJSS, St. Joseph's Convent), serving 120 students this week," and "Scholarships this year: 7 secured, 5 pending." We might also include youth employment or training placements – say, "15 youth in on-the-job training via NICE or other programs." The point is to measure outputs that the public can relate to: is the study space actually open? Are kids actually getting opportunities? If, for example, one of our goals is to double the number of Castries North students winning scholarships, the scoreboard will show the count climbing (or not). Data from the Castries North Data Dossier backs these targets – we know youth unemployment is around 27% nationally in 2023, so these programs are aimed at cutting that number locally, even if by small increments at first.

- **Health** – This tile might show clinic uptime (what percentage of scheduled hours the local health centre was actually open this month), availability of essential medications (perhaps a simple "red/yellow/green" indicator for whether key drugs like insulin, hypertension meds are in stock at the clinic), and community health initiatives status. For example: "Clinic open 95% of scheduled hours in Q1 (closed 4 hours due to nurse shortage)" – if that dips, we know there's a problem to address. Or "Medication stock: Paracetamol – Green, Insulin – Yellow (low stock), Amlodipine (BP med) – Green. Next restock due 5/Nov." We'll also note "Exercise programs running weekly: 2 groups active" (from our seniors' fitness programs) or "Health outreach: mobile screening bus came on Oct 12, served 80 residents." These KPIs tell you and us if health access is improving. If wait times are a major issue, we'll put an average wait time for say, a clinic visit, on there as well. Public visibility of these metrics means if the Ministry of Health isn't keeping our clinic running properly, everyone will see it – and believe me, that motivates officials to fix it. Sunlight is the best disinfectant, even for systemic issues.

- **Safety & Public Spaces** – This covers things like "Parks/courts refurbished: e.g. 1 this quarter (La Clery basketball court lights fixed in Sept) out of 3 planned", or "Streetlights functioning: 98% (2 of 120 reported streetlights awaiting repair)" – yes, we will count and track our streetlights and dark spots. Also, "Neighbourhood watch groups formed: 2 active (e.g. Sunny Acres, Lower Morne Du Don)." This might also include a stat on garbage or cleanup: "Community clean-ups done: 4 year-to-date" or "Drain clearing: on schedule (yes/no)" which ties into both safety and environment. Essentially this tile monitors how liveable and secure our environment is getting. For example, if we pledged to install a new bus shelter at City Gate and we did it, the scoreboard might say "City Gate bus shelter – Completed Jan 2026 ☑". If petty crime or traffic accidents in certain spots are an issue, we could track, say, "Choc Junction accidents last quarter: 2 (down from 5 in same quarter prev. year)" after putting in safety measures.

• **Service & Response** – In earlier drafts I rolled this into other categories, but it deserves its own measure: how well are we responding to you. This includes the average time to return a phone call or message, the average time from a complaint being logged to the first site visit, and from site visit to actual resolution for minor works. For instance, the board could show: "Avg. call-back time: 1 day; Avg. days from report to fix (small issues): 10 days." If those numbers start to slip, everyone can see it and we correct course. Also, a simple count: "Issues reported this week: 12; Issues resolved: 9; Pending: 3." Interestingly, I expect over time the number of new complaints might drop as we clear backlogs – which is a good sign. As I bluntly put it, "A good week is when the 'Completed' column grows and the phone rings less about the same old problem." Right now, people call and call about the same long-running problems (because they were never really fixed). In our future, if we fix things properly, we should hear fewer repeat complaints and more new ideas. That's a metric too.

This scoreboard will be updated weekly. We'll probably choose Friday afternoon or Monday morning as the update time, and it'll be someone's job (with me involved) to gather the data and refresh it. The beauty is most of these numbers aren't hard to get – they come from our own logs and the work we're doing daily. It's a bit of extra discipline, but I'm used to keeping stats from my sports days. I have what I call an "unromantic streak that keeps books" – I see numbers where others might just see anecdotes. As I wrote earlier, I love seeing proof in data: "We can tell these stories with confetti, or we can tell them with receipts that show how a community becomes richer in people you can depend on." For me, this dashboard is a set of receipts for the work of representation.

We'll mirror this scoreboard online for those who can't physically visit the office often. A simple weekly Facebook post or a page on a website can carry the same info. But I insist on the physical version because I want it to confront us when we walk into the office. My staff and I should feel that little jolt of accountability each time we see that red overdue item or that goal not yet met. It's like a constant coach's whistle in the room saying, "What's the status on this? Why isn't it done?" And conversely, when we fill in a green checkmark, we get to celebrate a bit in the open – "Yes, Morne Du Don now has its footbridge, check it off!" Visual progress builds morale.

Let me give you an example scenario of how a citizen might interact with this. Suppose you come in about a concern: say the bridge by your neighbourhood is shaky. Instead of the usual runaround, we walk over to the Local Works section on the wall. Maybe it's already listed as "Planned" because someone reported it last month – you see it there: "Wooden footbridge at X Community – Planned (as of Aug 2025), funding source: CDP, target Q1 2026." You now have immediate info: we haven't ignored it, it's in queue for next round of CDP projects. You might ask, "Why so long?" and we can discuss funding cycles openly. Or if it's not on the list yet, we will write it up and pin it there under "Planned" while you watch, with an estimated timeline. You leave with a ticket number or at least the knowledge that it's visibly logged. This drastically changes the usual dynamic where you'd often be told "we'll see what we can do" and then you'd have to wonder for months. Here, it's tracked in plain sight.

THE OPEN FILES: BUDGETS, CONTRACTS, AND PROJECT MATRIX

Transparency isn't just about the summary stats; it's also about the detailed documents and data behind them. That's where open files come in. I'm essentially adapting the concept of the Public Accounts Committee oversight to the local level – shining a light on every dollar and every deal that touches Castries North. Here's how we'll do it:

Budget Transparency: We will maintain a public budget file for the constituency. This is a document (both on paper at the office and downloadable online) that shows: (1) What funds have been allocated to Castries North from various programs (e.g. "2026-2027 CDP allocation: $1,000,000; received in tranches of $250k quarterly" or "BNTF Project approved: $300,000 for Community Centre upgrades"); (2) What funds have been spent or committed and on which projects ("Q1: $50k spent on ABC Road repair, $10k on drain clearing contracts, $5k on after-school program supplies, $20k pending payment for lights installation… etc."); and (3) pending funding requests ("Proposal submitted to Ministry of Infrastructure for $200k road resurfacing; awaiting response"). Essentially, it's a running ledger of our development money. By publishing this, I answer the question "where our money going?" before it's even asked. It also helps bust the myth that an opposition MP gets nothing – you'll see exactly what we got, or if we truly got nothing, that emptiness will be documented and broadcast (to the government's shame). As noted earlier, PM Pierre publicly promised to fund all constituencies fairly and even launched an EC$18.5 million CDP injection in 2022 that averages ~$1M each. I will "hold the government to that promise", and the budget file will be the evidence. If Castries North only gets a half-share, everyone will know and you better believe I'll be loudly asking why. Conversely, when we do get funds, no one can later claim "we gave Bax money, where did it go?" – it will be documented to the penny.

Contracts and Procurement: Every project involves spending public money, and one area where distrust runs high is who gets the contracts. People always suspect nepotism or waste: a politician's buddy hired for a job, an inflated invoice, materials that "go missing". To counter this, our Open Files board will list key contracts awarded for works in the constituency. For instance: if we bundle five small works into one tender (as I advocate doing) and Contractor XYZ Construction wins the bid for $120,000, we will post: "Contractor: XYZ Construction; Project: CN Community Works 2026 (5 small works package); Value: $120k; Start: Feb 1, 2026; End: Mar 30, 2026.". And once it's done, we'll update the actual amount paid if it differs and any relevant notes ("completed on Mar 15, on time" or "delayed 2 weeks due to heavy rain"). We will not post every single invoice (that would be too granular), but any significant procurement or contract – definitely. Even for things like services or programs: if we hire a bus driver to run a shuttle for elderly folks to clinic, we'll put up "Contract: Senior Shuttle – Driver Jane Doe at $X per trip, operating Tues/Thurs, trial for 3 months." It might seem like overkill, but this level of openness pre-empts gossip and exposes any irregularities immediately. As I promised, "tell you who is doing it, with what money, by when" – that's the rule. We'll abide by the national procurement rules, of course (e.g. 3 quotes for small jobs, etc.), but we'll go a step further and share the outcomes. On a related note, any hiring for the constituency office or contract work funded through our channels will be openly advertised (even if informally on the office door and Facebook) and the selection and pay will be transparent. You won't have to wonder if I've put my cousin on the payroll secretly – if my cousin is crazy enough to apply, you'll know if they got hired and for what.

Project Matrix: This might be my favourite tool – a master spreadsheet that tracks every identified project or need, from the massive to the minute, along with its status and funding source. I mentioned it in the covenant and I'll explain more here. The Castries North Project Matrix is essentially our workflow brain, and I intend to make a version of it accessible to the public (with possibly some internal notes hidden, but 90% of it open). Each row is a project or issue: e.g. "Vide Bouteille Secondary – after-school tutoring program", "La Clery – drain behind the market", "Bisee – new bus shelter", "Youth skills training partnership with NSDC", "Choc – pedestrian crossing by gas station". The columns will include: priority level, brief description, lead person/agency, funding source(s) possible, current status (e.g. "proposal stage", "funding approved", "in procurement", "in construction", "completed"), target start and finish dates, and notes. Crucially, one column will be "Next Action & Who" – meaning what's the very next thing that needs to happen and who's responsible for it. This prevents that classic drift where everyone assumes someone else is handling it. If a project is waiting on me to write a letter to a Minister, the matrix will literally say "Next: MP to write to Min. of Infrastructure re: funding, by 15 Oct." If it's in a Ministry's hands, it might say "Next: MinInfra to approve design, expected by Dec". By maintaining this, "planning and communication" prevent overlaps and gaps. We won't have the left hand not knowing what the right is doing, or two funding streams accidentally both paying for the same thing (double-dipping) because the matrix will have everything in one place.

We'll update the Project Matrix in real-time as things evolve. And I plan to review it in detail weekly with my team – almost like running a company's project portfolio meeting. The public version might be updated less frequently (say, weekly or biweekly), but I want folks to be able to request it anytime. If you come and say, "Can I see the latest project list?" we can print it or email it to you. There is nothing mystical about development work – it's tasks, dates, people.

By demystifying it, we remove the breeding ground for suspicion and also invite collaboration. For example, if a diaspora group sees on our published matrix that we have a "Union playground upgrade – funding needed", they might say "hey, we can contribute to that." Or if a local business sees "Community CCTV camera project – seeking partners", they might chip in. Open data invites partnership.

Another important file is what I'd call the Issue Log or service request log. Similar to the project matrix but for smaller individual issues (pothole reports, individual assistance cases, etc.). It might not be posted on the wall for privacy reasons (we might not want to list people's names and personal issues publicly), but the aggregate numbers will go on the scoreboard as noted. However, I will keep a sanitized version that shows types of issues and resolutions, to spot trends. If 20 people in a month complain about water supply in Hillcrest Gardens, that goes from isolated issue to priority project – perhaps we need to liaise with WASCO (water company) or install a community tank. Open files aren't just for accountability; they're for analysis – to make sure we're not missing a pattern. In fact, the Castries North Data Dossier we compiled is part of this ethos: gather the facts, share them, use them. We'll keep that dossier updated (quarterly mini-updates, annual full updates) and publicly available. By tracking key indicators like unemployment, crime, exam pass rates, etc., we can adjust our local programs accordingly. For example, if next year's data show a spike in youth unemployment in our area beyond the national trend, we might pivot more funds into job training or apprenticeship programs – all of which would be visible on the matrix and scoreboard.

Now, how do we ensure that everyone, not just the digitally savvy or the ones with time to visit the office, benefits from this transparency? We'll have to be creative. Some ideas: a monthly newsletter (printed and PDF) that summarizes the dashboard and key updates – available at the office, sent to community centres, maybe even mailed to those who sign up. Also, utilizing community bulletin boards (like at churches or shops) to post a one-page summary of "This Month in Castries North: X projects done, Y upcoming, key contacts". On radio slots or town halls I can reference the data: "As you can see in our latest report, we completed 8 small projects last quarter... here's how that compares to last year...". Over time, I hope other MPs will copy this approach; it should become the norm that constituencies operate with a local version of an annual report. Perhaps we'll even inspire the government to produce easier-to-read accounts – but I won't wait on that.

Let me give a concrete mini-story of how open files saved the day in a hypothetical scenario. Say we have a project to rebuild a section of sidewalk in Sunny Acres. Mid-way, a resident comes saying, "Hey, I think this project is already budgeted under the Ministry's road program, why are you using CDP funds?" Because our system is open, we quickly cross-check the Project Matrix and indeed see we had marked "Alternate funding: Min. of Infrastructure Road Maintenance 2026" on this project but maybe we didn't hear back and proceeded with CDP. We reach out to the Ministry with that info – turns out, yes, they had plans to do it but hadn't told us. We adjust: if the Ministry confirms they'll handle it next month, we can reallocate our CDP money elsewhere and avoid duplication. If not for openly tracking and inviting that resident's input, we might have double-funded or missed the chance for MinInfra to pay. So openness can prevent both waste and missed opportunities.

Another scenario: suppose someone alleges that I gave a contract to a friend unlawfully. Instead of bluster, I point them to the open contract list: "The contract was awarded after 3 bids, here are the names, and by the way my friend is not among them – check for yourself." Or if my second cousin did win a bid fairly (hey, it could happen), it's all above board: everyone saw the bid notice, and they can see the delivered work quality. Scandals typically need darkness to breed. We're flooding the room with light.

Of course, transparency doesn't guarantee perfection. Mistakes will happen – maybe a data entry error on the dashboard one week, or a projection we announce that doesn't pan out. But the key is we'll correct it in public too. For instance, if we said a project would finish by June and it slips to July, the public log will show the date change and the reason (e.g. "delayed due to supplier issue"). Context is given, not excuses. And if something fails outright – suppose we attempt a new after-school program and nobody shows up – we won't delete it and pretend it never existed. We'll report honestly, "After-school pilot at X school saw low turnout; program under review/reshaped" and it will either move to a revamped status or be marked as stopped. This ties into our learning loops (which I'll expand on in Chapter 28). The point is, an open approach means even failures become lessons out in the open. That's healthier for the community in the long run than brushing things under the rug, because others can chime in with solutions. You'd be surprised – if people see you earnestly trying and openly struggling with an issue, many will step forward to help. It's when officials hide issues or pretend all is well that citizens either get angry or disengage.

One might ask: will there be any downsides to this radical openness? Perhaps a few. It could arm my political opponents with ammunition – they can scrutinize my every shortfall, every delay, every cent spent and try to make hay of it. But you know what? Let them. If an opponent's best strategy is to point out that I promised 10 drains and only 9 are done, that still means 9 drains got done – and I'll own up to the 1 and explain what happened. I prefer that scenario over the usual one where opponents fling allegations in a fog and the public doesn't know who to believe. Here, the record speaks for itself. Also, maintaining all this info is work. Some critics might say, "Will you spend more time updating spreadsheets than actually doing work?" It's a fair concern, but I estimate it's a tiny fraction of effort compared to the benefits. We're talking a couple hours a week to update and post – a task we can schedule and streamline. If I can't carve that out, it means I'm disorganized. Plus, a lot of the tracking will naturally happen as part of doing the work (if you manage projects well, you already have timelines and logs to update internally; we're just making a portion public).

Security of information could be another question – we won't publish private personal data, and anything sensitive (say a security camera placement plan that police prefer not be public until installed) we might summarize rather than detail. But 95% of constituency work is not national security level stuff – it's public by nature. We'll of course comply with any data protection laws, but in general I plan to err on the side of openness.

To ensure our transparency efforts themselves are trustworthy, I might invite third parties to verify or audit some of our reports. For instance, once a year maybe the St. Lucia Accountants Association could glance over our constituency spending report, or an NGO interested in governance could review our open data practices and give feedback. This isn't required by any law – it's just me trying to set a high standard. Who knows, if it works well, perhaps it becomes a model others adopt.

One more aspect of "Open Files" is accessible format. It's not enough to dump a bunch of numbers; it has to be understandable. We'll use plain language and simple charts where helpful. Maybe a giant thermometer chart showing percent of annual projects completed, or a traffic light icon next to each pledge in the covenant (green on track, yellow caution, red behind – like a status report). We'll avoid jargon. If we use an acronym (like CDP or BNTF) on the public board, it'll have a footnote explaining it (because not everyone knows what those mean). The Data Dossier taught me the importance of explaining the data – e.g. we put definitions and sources for each number so people can trust and interpret them correctly. Same for our dashboard: if we say "NEET rate 25%" we'll footnote that NEET means youth not in education, employment, or training. But likely we'll keep such technical stats to the dossier and keep the day-to-day dashboard focused on tangible outputs.

By prying open the files, we also open ourselves to ideas. I fully expect someone from the public will notice something in our data that we didn't. Like they may see from our reports that a particular community keeps having water issues every month and suggest "why not build a community water tank?" Or they'll see the utilization of an after-school program is dipping and suggest a time change or a new volunteer. In this way, transparency begets participation. We move from a world where people only show up to complain after things fail, to one where they're engaged throughout to help things succeed.

In summary, Open Dashboards and Open Files are how we put the "Accountability" in the service-accountability-delivery framework. It's the concrete practice of answering those basic questions I listed in Chapter 1: "Who owns this? When does it finish? Where is the budget? What's next?". Those questions will never go unanswered in Castries North. We will own our answers publicly. When you walk into our office or log onto our page, you'll see exactly what your MP and his team are doing (or not doing). And if an answer is missing, you have every right to point it out and demand it. Frankly, I can't wait for that dynamic – it's going to keep me energized and I hope it keeps you engaged. We're going to replace hush-hush politics with a community-wide conversation backed by facts and figures. This is what "public accounts lens locally" means: treating the constituency like a unit that merits the same scrutiny we give national budgets, but in plain view of the very people it serves.

As we implement this, I anticipate some teething issues. There will be weeks our update is late due to, say, a storm or simply human error. If that happens, we'll be transparent about our transparency (e.g. "Dashboard update delayed this week due to XYZ, will resume by Friday"). The key is to never let the habit slide into neglect. Consistency will build credibility. Over the months and years, these dashboards and files will become a kind of diary of our journey – one that anyone can read. Years from now, whether I'm still in office or not, there will be a record a citizen can follow: "Ah yes, here's what was done in 2026, and what was planned, and how it changed in 2027..." That continuity is often missing in governance; each new rep pretends to start from scratch. Not here. The data will tell the story across administrations. In fact, I will ensure that even if I'm out of office, the files are archived for reference so the next rep (and the people) can see where things left off.

Alright, now that we have the tools of transparency laid out, the next step is making sure we have the resources to act on what we learn. All the openness in the world won't fix a road if there's zero funding or if money is being wasted on the wrong things. The covenant pledges an honest budget and funding what works. So in the next chapter, I'll dive into our plan for marshalling funds from every corner and ruthlessly directing them to effective use. Essentially: how we will fund what works, and cut what doesn't, using the very transparency I've described to guide those decisions. The scoreboard will show the results, and the budget will follow them – not the other way around. Let's explore that.

27

Funding What Works, Cutting What Doesn't

A plan without funding is just a speech. We've laid out what we want to do – now we must tackle how to pay for it, and equally important, how to avoid paying for what doesn't work. Money in public office is always limited, so the surest test of a representative's priorities is where they allocate those precious dollars. In Castries North, every dollar will be a soldier deployed to win a battle against a specific problem – and if a particular battle plan isn't working, we'll redeploy that soldier somewhere else. This chapter is about establishing clear operating rules for our local budget: invest in what delivers results, trim what doesn't, and be creative in finding funds from every legitimate source.

Let me start by debunking an old excuse: "an opposition or independent MP can't get anything done because the government holds the purse strings." That was the convenient alibi of non-performers in the past, and indeed there were times when ruling parties starved opposition constituencies. But times have changed, and frankly I won't accept that mindset. As I noted earlier, in 2022 Prime Minister Pierre publicly committed to allocating development funds to all 17 constituencies, regardless of political stripe, particularly through the Constituency Development Programme (CDP). He even backed it with money from Taiwan – a big EC$18.5 million injection, which is roughly $1 million per constituency. Moreover, he stated that the "revamped CDP" would be transparent, accountable, agile, and accessible to Opposition Parliamentarians. That's on official record; we have the quotes and press releases. So if I'm elected as an independent, you can bet I'll be holding the government to those words every budget cycle.

If any cynics still say, "They'll find ways to starve Castries North if you're not in their party," my answer is twofold: sunlight and persistence. They can try, but the system now has openings I will exploit fully. If they fund everyone, I'm part of that; if they suddenly don't, that's a national scandal I'll raise hell about. Between CDP, BNTF, line ministries, and public pressure, there are enough cracks in the old patronage wall to get the resources we need – provided I act strategically and not passively. And if someone actively tries to shut Castries North out, I'll go public with it – publish the letters, use Parliament, use media – until they relent. One voice may not topple a government, but it can make them very uncomfortable if they're caught punishing an entire community out of spite. No minister wants to be on the evening news accused of denying, say, clinic funds to 10,000 people for political reasons, especially when I can show data on the need.

Now, assuming we do get our fair share of the pie (and I'll scrap tooth-and-nail to ensure we do), how do we use it wisely? I see four major funding streams for local development, and I intend for us to tap all four to the max:

Funding Stream #1: CDP (Constituency Development Programme). Think of CDP as our guaranteed local works bank account. Traditionally, each MP submits a list of small projects under CDP – footpaths, drains, playground repairs, etc. The Ministry of Economic Development (or Infrastructure) manages execution, but the MP identifies and prioritizes the projects. Under past administrations, there were complaints that opposition MPs got frozen out – their project lists sat unfunded. But as discussed, that's supposed to be over, and I will ensure Castries North's list is front and centre and impossible to ignore. We're looking at roughly EC$1 million a year available here (some years more, some less, depending on donor funds and budget).

My approach to CDP funds will be strategic bundling and scheduling. No more ad-hoc scattering of projects like seeds to the wind. For example, rather than submitting 20 tiny projects piecemeal, I'll package several into one procurement so we get economies of scale. If we have, say, five sidewalks and three drains to fix across the constituency, I'd group them into a single "Castries North Community Works 2026" tender. Contractors will bid for the lot. This can reduce overhead costs (mobilize one crew and equipment to handle multiple sites) and shorten timelines (once they're here, they move from one task to the next). It also makes project management more efficient on my end – I chase one contractor or project manager accountable for delivering the bundle, instead of juggling ten different small contractors where something is bound to slip. In practice, if one contractor can't handle all, they might sub-contract pieces or we might award to a couple of firms, but still under one coordinated package. This bundling approach has proven effective elsewhere – local governments combine road patching jobs to get bulk pricing on asphalt, etc.. We will do the same with concrete, labour, and mobilization for our community works.

Let me illustrate: We identify four priority drains (say L'Anse Road, Blackstone, Morne Du Don, and lower Choc) and two sidewalks (Vigie near the beach access, Sunny Acres by the park) that need work. Instead of six separate projects, we tender them together. Maybe a firm wins and does all six for a lump sum, or a couple split it – either way, we cut down duplicated costs. The open contract info (as noted in the previous chapter) will show this clearly: one contract covering multiple fixes. The public benefit is we likely stretch that $1M to cover more ground because we didn't waste it on repeat overhead. I'm basically promising you that one dollar will do the work of two through smart management. And with the scoreboard, you'll see the results – more projects completed per dollar than the old approach.

Another tactic: scheduling by zones or themes. For instance, dedicate Q1 to footpaths and drains, Q2 to road resurfacing (via ministry collab), Q3 to community facilities, etc. This way resources (and the attention of my team) are focused and we get momentum in one area at a time. It's like doing spring cleaning room by room instead of scattering efforts all over the house.

I should note, CDP funds often come from grants like the Taiwan grant or the national budget. They usually have to be used for capital works (not recurrent stuff). I will treat the CDP as the lifeblood for our "small but significant" improvements – those very things residents complain about that are too small for big ministries to prioritize but too large for individual pockets to handle. The footbridge in Ti Rocher I mentioned earlier is a perfect example: a small CDP project that changed daily life for a community. We have dozens of those opportunities ready to roll, thanks to our groundwork identifying them.

Funding Stream #2: BNTF (Basic Needs Trust Fund). BNTF is a gem some constituencies overlook. It's a program funded by the Caribbean Development Bank and managed through the Saint Lucia Social Development Fund (SSDF), focusing on projects that meet basic needs in vulnerable communities. In plain terms, if it improves daily living for a less advantaged group – like water supply, sanitation, access roads, schools, skills training centres – BNTF might fund it. Historically, BNTF has invested around EC$54 million in over 100 projects in Saint Lucia. That's an average of over EC$500k per project, mostly grants. They're into their 11th cycle now and focusing on exactly the stuff we need: community access, drainage, education, livelihood projects.

To me, BNTF money is "on the table for us, if we claim it with good proposals." Not every MP bothers to apply for these, maybe because it's extra work or they lack the data to justify projects. But I do not intend to leave free money unused while Castries North has needs. We will be, if I have my way, the star performer in BNTF participation. We already have a list of ideas: e.g. Morne Du Don slope stabilization and retaining wall (if it's pricey and CDP can't cover, we pitch it as disaster resilience), Bisee back-road footpath for safe student commuting (fits "basic access" perfectly), Community resource centre rehab (if any, though we might not have one yet – maybe turning a vacant building into a skills training hub). The process: I as MP would work with the community and the constituency council to put forward proposals to SSDF/BNTF. If they meet criteria – e.g. serving a poorer area, community involvement, etc. – we can secure funding largely by grants.

One catch: BNTF can be a bit bureaucratic and slow if we're not proactive. But I'm already aware of that and have a plan to mitigate it. The SSDF leadership has noted they're trying to speed up project gestation and encourage early identification with community input. So I'll be "on it from day one – convening with SSDF, identifying projects early, and ensuring proposals are shovel-ready and community-backed". That means by the time a new BNTF cycle or call for projects opens, Castries North will have a polished proposal waiting at the door. No delay. Also, I'll "mainstream discussions with relevant ministries" – basically make sure, for instance, if we're proposing a drain under BNTF, we've checked the Ministry of Infrastructure isn't already doing it or planning it. Coordination prevents duplication and the embarrassment of a project being rejected for not fitting criteria. As I said earlier, running a tight ship: if a drain project is going to BNTF, I coordinate with the Ministry so they don't plan the same drain, and vice versa. This way, every dollar from any source addresses a unique need, and we maximize coverage.

Some might wonder: isn't chasing all these funds complicated? Yes, it is a bit like spinning plates, but that's literally the MP's job as I see it – to be the quarterback coordinating all possible resources. I'd rather have multiple funding streams to manage than sit waiting on one minister's favour. It's more work for me, but yields far more results for the community.

Funding Stream #3: Line Ministry Budgets. Not everything should or can be done via special programs like CDP or BNTF. The government's line ministries (Infrastructure, Education, Health, etc.) have their own budgets for capital works and services. A savvy MP doesn't say "I'll only fix what I can fund directly"; a savvy MP advocates within the national budget process to channel projects to their constituency. This means building relationships, yes, but more importantly making a data-driven case for why Castries North's needs deserve attention. I've already armed myself with the Castries North Data Dossier, which highlights things like flood hotspots, accident-prone roads, infrastructure gaps with evidence. You better believe I'll be citing those stats in every letter and meeting. For example, the dossier notes a flood risk in L'Anse Road/Vide Bouteille – 42.5 mm of rain fell one day in Nov 2022 and caused havoc. The Infrastructure Ministry responded to similar flooding in Corinth, building mitigation works. So I'll say, "Look, you did X in Corinth after that flood; here's the data showing we need similar action in Vide Bouteille." If there's a national Urban Flood Resilience project with World Bank support (which there is), I'll fight tooth and nail to include our ravines and drains in it.

Similarly, if there's a national road improvement plan, I won't sit quiet until an accident happens. I'll point out known trouble spots like the Choc pedestrian crossing where people dash across dangerously, or the Sunny Acres junction lacking signage, armed with accident reports or resident petitions, and insist they be included in the ministry's implementation. And if I get stonewalled, I won't drop it. As noted, I can use Parliament's tools – questions, motions, even the Public Accounts Committee if money is allocated but not used properly – to shine a light if Castries North is being neglected. Many MPs don't bother with these tools because they toe the line; as an independent, my only line is Castries North's interest.

The big stuff – like say a new school building, or a major road resurfacing – will likely have to come from these central budgets. For instance, if Vide Bouteille Road (a major artery) needs complete repaving and drainage, that might exceed CDP resources. So I lobby

Infrastructure for that, reminding them that our roads carry thousands of commuters daily, so fixing them isn't just a local favour, it's in the national interest. I can make a noise as needed: "Castries North's roads aren't just for Castries North people; if you ignore them, you're hurting the whole commuting public." And if I smell pork-barrel politics (like skipping us because I'm not in their party), I will call it out in the House and media.

Now, very importantly: Cutting What Doesn't Work. This phrase means I won't pour money down the drain of an ineffective project just because it exists, and I won't keep funding a program that isn't delivering results for the people. We will have operating rules for that. One rule: every initiative we fund locally must have some performance indicators. If it's an after-school program, how many kids attend regularly? Are their grades improving? If those metrics flatline or decline despite reasonable effort, we either reform the program or reallocate its budget to something else. We won't hesitate to stop doing something that's not yielding benefits, even if it's politically "nice" or someone's pet project.

For example, say we start a monthly job fair workshop for youth and after 6 sessions, only a handful attend and no one's getting jobs out of it. We'll openly evaluate: maybe young people prefer an online job platform or targeted internship drives instead. So we'd stop the lacklustre workshop (save the money on venue, catering, etc.) and start an internship stipend program with that money, which might have higher uptake. Similarly, if we fund a small business grant scheme but find out a year later that half the grantees folded and the other half didn't really create employment, we'll admit it's not working and pivot to maybe funding a business incubator or technical assistance instead of pure grants.

Another scenario: Let's say we tried a community shuttle service to take seniors to clinic weekly. Great idea, but after 3 months only 2 people use it because others have family helping or the timing is off. Rather than stubbornly running an empty bus for four years, we'd cut or redesign it – maybe shift to a call-based transport voucher or coordinate with an existing NGO doing patient transport. The freed-up funds could then scale something that is working, like the seniors exercise class which might be booming. The annual "Stop–Start–Scale" exercise baked into our covenant ensures we systematically make these calls each year. But even within a year, the scoreboard's feedback will hint at what's effective or not, and I won't wait till year-end if a cut is clearly needed.

Crucially, cutting what doesn't work also means no sacred cows in terms of past practices. Just because "we always do an X event every year" doesn't mean we'll keep funding it if it doesn't serve a real need aligned with our mission. For instance, many MPs host annual Christmas parties or give hampers. I'm not against charity for the vulnerable, but if we're spending a large chunk on a public Xmas bash while more structural needs languish, I'd question that. Perhaps the same funds could support a food bank or skills training that has longer-term impact. So we might cut or downsize the party and redirect funds to a more effective relief program. Of course, we'd gauge community sentiment – some traditions matter to people. But overall, expect a more utilitarian approach: measure outcomes, prioritize accordingly.

Let me highlight a positive example of "funding what works": our scholarship pipeline in sports and education. Over the years, I've seen that relatively small investments (organizing camps, paying SAT fees, guiding applications) yield huge returns in terms of full scholarships abroad for youth. This works – we have 20+ success stories to show. So you can bet I will channel funds to scale that up, perhaps establishing a "Castries North Scholarship Fund" to cover SAT prep, application costs, and flights for students who earn opportunities. Conversely, if there's a sports program that historically is a money sink with no progression (say, a tournament that happens but our youth never get further development from it), we'll repurpose those funds into a training program that has clear milestones.

We also have to ensure we're not double-funding or continuing things already done. For instance, once the health centre is finally upgraded (it will happen, I vow), we don't need to keep pouring capital money there – we switch to ensuring it's maintained and staffed. Or if we achieve a high outcome like near-100% after-school coverage for students, maybe we shift marginal funds to another gap, like adult education or community policing.

Funding Stream #4: Community, Diaspora & Private Partnerships. Government money isn't the only money. There's goodwill and resources in our extended community. We have a vibrant diaspora from Castries North – people overseas who still care about their neighbourhoods. Already, I know of ex-residents who pooled funds to repaint a church and fix park benches back home. Let's widen that circle. I propose setting up a "Castries North Community Fund", a transparent account maybe managed by a trusted third party like a credit union or NGO, where diaspora, local businesses, and well-wishers can donate towards specific local projects. Importantly, this is supplementary – not replacing what government should do, but covering nice-to-haves or timing gaps. For example, if we want an extra bus shelter or a set of exercise equipment in a park and government funds are all tied up this year, the Community Fund could chip in. Every dollar would be accounted for publicly just like public funds (we'll apply the same rigor – reports, updates). People are more willing to give when they see exactly how their money is used and that it isn't vanishing into a black box. We could have a little donor honour roll (if they agree) to acknowledge contributions.

Similarly, in-kind contributions from the private sector can stretch our resources. A local hardware might donate paint for a school fence if we publicly thank them (I'll put their logo in our newsletter's thank-you section). A construction company might lend a backhoe for a community clean-up day as part of their corporate social responsibility. These things already happen quietly; I'll actively seek them. No kickbacks, no favouritism – just straightforward "sponsor a bench, sponsor a tree planting" deals that are above board and beneficial to all. Businesses often are happy to help locally if asked properly and shown appreciation.

And of course, community labour – the old cooperative spirit ("koudmen" or "kotchonez" in Kweyol, meaning lend a hand). We used to have neighbourhoods band together for cleanup or to build a neighbour's house in times past. We can revive a bit of that. I will never use volunteer labour to let government off its duties, but for supplemental pride projects, it's fantastic. For example, volunteers could help paint a community centre or plant trees along a new path we built, making it a communal activity. As I noted, if we have materials (which we can buy via CDP or donations), I bet folks will come out to help pour a small concrete step for a disabled neighbour's home. One story I love: in Babonneau, residents once built a wooden footbridge in a day to help kids get to school after floods, before authorities eventually built a permanent one. That interim solution was community-powered and saved months of hardship. I'd encourage that ethic: if something is urgently needed and we can safely do a DIY temporary fix, let's do it, then push the government to follow up with a permanent solution. No one should suffer for months in our community waiting on paperwork if we can organize a quick alleviation. I will empower these micro-initiatives by providing materials or technical advice (like an engineer to guide) as needed. The transparency comes here too – if we mobilize community labour, we'll acknowledge it publicly and make sure it's understood as voluntary and appreciated, not exploited.

Now, bringing these funding streams together is where the magic happens. Often, one source isn't enough on its own, but combined they can accomplish something bigger. I gave a hypothetical earlier – the La Clery River Clean-up & Flood Prevention project. Let me break that multi-faceted approach down, as it exemplifies funding what works from each angle:

• The problem: a choked, flood-prone river that needs heavy cleaning, infrastructure, and community behaviour change. One source alone won't cover all that.

• Ministry of Infrastructure (line ministry) could do the heavy-duty dredging and clearing, since they have budgets for river desilting as routine maintenance. That's a "big ticket" task suited for their equipment.

• CDP funds could build a couple of new concrete drains or outlets in the community to channel runoff better into the river. Small works, fits CDP.

• BNTF could be tapped to fund complementary pieces like proper footpaths or railings along the riverbank, which improve safety and community access. That aligns with BNTF's community focus, and maybe even sanitation angle if it includes waste management features.

• Community & Donors can handle the soft side: we organize annual clean-up drives where locals pick up trash (and we ask a corporate sponsor to donate gloves, garbage bags, refreshments). Maybe an environmental NGO gives a small grant for an awareness campaign about not dumping in the river.

- The result: A multi-pronged solution funded by multiple streams working in concert. The Ministry does what it does best (heavy work), CDP quickly addresses minor infrastructure, BNTF funds community enhancements, and the community tackles behaviour and upkeep. Each piece by itself would only partially solve the problem, but together you reduce flood risk and make the area nicer and involve the people.

This approach of bundling funding streams is something I will practice repeatedly. Another example: for education, maybe the Ministry of Education refurbishes a school science lab (big budget), CDP buys some computers for the lab (small addition), a private donor (alumnus) chips in microscopes, and an NGO provides training workshops for teachers. The synergy yields a modern lab with engaged staff and students.

All this requires coordination – which is my job. We return to the Project Matrix as a crucial tool. In that matrix, every project entry has a "potential funding sources" field, often with multiple sources listed. And we'll update it as funds lock in: if we secure one, we notify others to avoid duplication, as I said. This is program management mentality rather than piecemeal. No more firing off requests blindly; instead, manage it like a program with various inputs.

Another not-to-be-forgotten source: international small grants. Sometimes embassies or international organizations have funds available for community projects – Japan has the GGP (Grant Assistance for Grassroots Projects), the EU and UN have small grant programs, etc. I'll keep an eye on those. Being independent actually might help – I can approach any embassy without party protocol, just as a community rep looking for help. For instance, if we need a rainwater harvesting system at a school (to ensure water during shortages), Japan's GGP might fund it because they've done similar in other constituencies. The

EU might fund a community climate adaptation measure. It's about being creative and proactive; we won't leave any stone unturned.

In deploying funds, I'll also emphasize bundling for impact in a thematic sense. That means if we're tackling an issue, hit it from all angles with all funds in a concentrated period. For example, if youth crime is an issue in a particular area, we might simultaneously: improve lighting and infrastructure (Infrastructure Ministry / CDP), start a late-night basketball or sports program (maybe via Ministry of Youth or donor funding), ramp up after-school tutoring and job training (some via line ministry, some via partners), and organize community policing meetings (no huge cost, just coordination). By bundling those efforts in time and space, you actually create a noticeable change, rather than spreading them thin all over with diluted effect. This is essentially prioritization – do first what yields big results, don't dissipate energy equally on everything at once. The covenant's first bullet list – the 100-day list of small works – is an example of hitting a bunch of obvious wins early. Similarly, in funding terms, if something is clearly high-need and high-impact (like fixing a major water problem), multiple streams can be directed there concurrently to solve it fully, instead of half-fixing ten different things.

Now, let's address a delicate but important aspect: keeping political strings out of funding decisions. Historically, governing parties use funding as a carrot or stick – paving just before elections, or neglecting opposition areas, or only funding projects if a party operative gets the contract, etc. I reject that with every fiber of my being. As I wrote earlier, "Representation is not feudalism… Nowhere in that job description is 'only fix for friends.'". I'm independent precisely so I can serve without permission slips and without these partisan strings. If ever some official suggests, "Cool down on that community, they're not our supporters," my response is to push twice as hard for that community. And frankly, by not being in their party meetings, I won't even be subject to such whispers in the first place. I'll just be doing my thing out in the open.

But let's imagine a worst-case: after I win, the ruling party tries to punish Castries North by dragging feet on every request. They might hope to make me look bad so they can retake the seat. This is where our transparency and persistence fight back. I will document every attempt, go public, rally the community to voice out. It's harder to do the dirty in daylight. Plus, as I laid out, we have multiple streams and I'll pursue them all – they'd have to simultaneously sabotage CDP, BNTF, line ministries, diaspora support, etc., which is a lot of work just to spite one constituency. More likely, if I'm a thorn, they might try to limit discretionary extras, but the basics they promised (like CDP) would still flow or it becomes a national issue. And if indeed our government or any actor starves us, I'll leverage the power of public scrutiny to make it backfire on them. "One independent voice can't sway them? Then I'll make it a chorus" by collaborating with other MPs or the community at large. If something unfair is happening, I won't quietly grumble; I'll bang the drum until it's fixed. This is essentially cutting what doesn't work on a political level – the old politics of spite doesn't work for the people, so I'll do everything to cut it out of the equation.

Let's pivot to some concrete examples of funding decisions I foresee:

• **Example 1: The Vide Bouteille Secondary (PDJSS) After-School Hub.** Say we budget $10,000/year for this program (for tutors, materials, maybe a snack). After Year 1, we see 50 kids attending, and teacher feedback says it improved homework completion and maybe exam scores tick up. Great – it's working. In Year 2, I might increase funding to $15,000 to expand capacity or replicate it at another school (scale what works). Conversely, if only 5 kids come and they're inconsistent, we'd survey why. Perhaps location is fine but timing isn't, or maybe we need to include sports to attract more. We adjust program design rather than kill it prematurely (since it's a needed concept), but if after adjustments it still flops, we'd redeploy that money to maybe a scholarship fund or vocational training which might have better uptake. The scoreboard and monthly education reviews will make that performance visible.

- **Example 2: The Bus Stop that Nobody Uses.** Perhaps we built a nice new bus stop shelter in a spot we thought was needed, using say $8k of CDP funds. But after it's done, we realize buses actually don't stop there often (maybe the route changed) and commuters still stand down the road. Whoops. We won't pour more into that location obviously. It stands as a lesson. Next time, we'd survey bus drivers and commuters before building. But what about the existing structure? Maybe we can relocate it or repurpose it (cut losses smartly). If not, we mark that as a low-impact spend in our annual review and try to avoid such misallocation going forward. Admitting a misstep is important – it builds credibility that we truly focus on what works, not on saving face.

- **Example 3: Sports vs. Other Youth Spending.** I love sports; it's saved lives and opened doors as we've discussed. But I will watch the data: if we pour, say, $20k a year into community sports leagues and it's engaging 200 youth, versus another $20k into ICT training which engages 50 youth, we have to weigh both in terms of depth and breadth of impact. It may be that both "work" in different ways and we keep a balance. However, if one clearly is giving more bang (say the ICT training results in 30 of 50 getting jobs, whereas the sports league engages kids positively but doesn't directly lead to anything further), we might seek additional funding for the ICT to expand while keeping the sports going through maybe more volunteerism or external sponsorship to reduce draw on public funds. It's about optimizing outcomes per dollar, not just sentimental attachments.

- **Example 4: Infrastructure Maintenance.** Everyone loves cutting ribbons on new projects, but maintenance of existing infrastructure often gets ignored until failure. I'll allocate a portion of funds for preventative maintenance (fixing a small road issue before it becomes a big one, cleaning drains regularly, repainting crossings annually etc.). If we see that spending $1 on maintenance saves $5 on major repairs (which is often the case), that's funding what works. Cutting what doesn't might mean cancelling a flashy new project in a year where that money is better used extending the life of what we have. Politically less sexy, but functionally smart. With the scoreboard showing potholes, for instance, if we maintain and the pothole count goes down, people will appreciate that more than a one-off grand project that then deteriorates.

- **Example 5: Legacy Projects vs. Quick Wins.** Sometimes MPs want a "legacy" – like a big community centre with their name on a plaque. I'm less interested in that if it doesn't serve immediate needs. If faced with choosing to build a new community centre for $500k that might be underutilized vs. using that $500k on 10 smaller upgrades across communities (each directly solving a current problem), I'd lean to the latter because it works now for people. Unless the big project truly fills a crucial gap and will be well-used (in which case it would be something that works). We'll scrutinize large capital proposals with a simple question: does it tangibly improve daily life or unlock opportunity? If yes, fund it; if it's more of a vanity or "nice to have eventually" but we have more pressing needs, it waits.

Now, to ensure all this is not just talk, we'll integrate the funding strategy with our transparency tools. The open budget reports I discussed will show spending, and also predicted outcomes. Perhaps we annotate big expenditures with a note of what it achieved ("$50k – 200m of road fixed, serving ~1000 vehicles daily"). In the annual Stop-Start-Scale session, we'll explicitly review: "here's what we spent on Program X, did it achieve Y? If not, do we tweak or drop it?" And those conclusions will be public.

I believe the community will support tough choices if we show the rationale. For example, if we decide to stop funding a long-running festival to redirect money to a new skills workshop, some might initially object ("we loved that festival!"). But if we present, look, only 50 people attended the festival mostly from outside the community, whereas this workshop will train 50 youth every quarter for jobs, many will agree it's a better use. Or maybe the consensus is to keep both and find sponsorship for one – that's fine too, the key is the decision is informed by data and openly debated, not done in a vacuum.

In Lucian politics, cutting things can be risky – every program has its fans. But I'm not here to preserve the status quo; I'm here to deliver results for the people of Castries North. I'll always try to repurpose rather than eliminate – e.g., find a way to maintain a beloved event through volunteers or smaller scale if we can't justify big funding – but I won't shy from redirecting money to where it makes a difference. Because ultimately, the biggest "waste" is not a program that fails – it's a representative who fails to even try. We're going to try lots of things in Castries North, and some will flop, and we'll acknowledge it and move on to the next approach.

Finally, I want to address how funding and accountability intersect with integrity. All the money strategies in the world mean nothing if funds get siphoned by corruption. I have zero tolerance for that. Every dollar that comes to Castries North is going to end up visible either in concrete in the ground or documented service provided – if it doesn't,

I'll be the first to call foul. I intend to work with honest contractors and partners (there are many) and keep the tendering transparent as mentioned. If any impropriety is suspected (say a contractor not delivering but charging in full), we will invoke audit mechanisms, maybe ban them from future bids, possibly even expose them publicly. That might make some uncomfortable – "Bax, you'll make enemies." Well, any enemy of accountability is no friend of Castries North anyway. We have lived for decades under a system where nobody truly gets fired for failing the public. I can't fire a minister, but I can certainly fire a contractor or stop hiring a service provider who doesn't deliver. And I can politically "fire" inefficient programs by defunding them.

This raises an important principle: reward success, not loyalty. If a school's after-school program is thriving, it will get continued or increased support. If another school is doing poorly in using the resources (maybe the principal isn't on board or whatever), we'll reallocate to where it will be used best. Of course, we'll try to fix issues in the lagging case by communicating and troubleshooting, but ultimately I won't pour water into a leaking bucket when there's a sturdy bucket right next to it thirsty for more. I know this sounds a bit cold, but it actually incentivizes folks to step up. Imagine constituency groups realize, "Hey, if we run a good program, Bax will fight to fund it again next year; if we slack off, he might channel the money elsewhere." That encourages a culture of performance at the local level.

One thing I'll ensure: for critical needs of vulnerable groups, "cutting" won't mean abandoning people. If something isn't working for, say, feeding the elderly, we'll replace it with something better, not just eliminate it. The goal is to find what works for them, not to save money at their expense. Efficiency should never become cruelty. It's about effective compassion. Funding what works and cutting what doesn't is ultimately in service of delivering more good per dollar to those who need it.

To wrap up this chapter, think of Castries North's finances as a portfolio of investments. We will invest in roads, in youth, in safety, in health – and we expect returns in the form of smoother commutes, employed youth, safer streets, healthier families. We will constantly evaluate our return on investment. If one stock (project) underperforms, we'll sell it and buy more of a winner. If a new opportunity arises (like a new grant or a new program concept), we'll shift funds to capitalize on it. This agile approach is uncommon in the public sector, but why shouldn't it be? It's your money, after all – it should be used where it makes the most difference.

In the next chapter, we'll delve into the engine that makes this adaptive approach possible: Learning Loops. It's fine to say we'll cut what doesn't work and fund what does, but that presumes we know what's working. How do we know? By measuring, by reviewing frequently, by learning from both success and failure. I've hinted at this with talk of scoreboards and annual reviews. Now I'll formalize how we build a culture of continuous improvement – weekly, monthly, quarterly, yearly cycles where we check the gauges, tune the engine, and sometimes overhaul parts of the machine of governance. That's where the real long-term change happens: not just in one project, but in how we keep getting better at delivering for Castries North. Let's explore those learning loops next.

28

Learning Loops

Walk with me into the future for a moment: It's a Monday morning in Castries North, mid-2027. The constituency office opens at 8:00 a.m. sharp. By 8:15, the new weekly scoreboard is already posted – updated through the weekend after a flurry of Sunday phone calls to confirm which projects finished and which meetings are set for the week. My office assistant is double-checking an online dashboard post, while I'm on the phone with the headmistress of a primary school scheduling a monthly check-in about student reading programs. At 10:00 a.m., I sit with the Constituency Council, and we quickly review last week's completed tasks and any carry-overs; by noon I'm drafting a brief report for an upcoming quarterly infrastructure review meeting. It's routine by now: measure, discuss, adjust, and move. That's the rhythm of what I call Learning Loops – a structured cadence of measurement and improvement that keeps our work from growing stale or veering off track.

Why do we need learning loops? Because no plan survives contact with reality intact. Because human beings have short memories and even shorter attention spans if not prompted. Because a representative's job, like a teacher's or a coach's, is never truly "done" – it's iterative. You don't coach a team in preseason and then just watch quietly all season; you huddle after every game, study the tape, and tweak the playbook. Similarly, community leadership demands constant course correction based on feedback. "The spectacular is just the faithful in fast forward," I wrote in a sports context – meaning those shiny results come from steady, faithful habits repeated. Learning loops are those faithful habits of governance.

I propose to institutionalize loops at four intervals: weekly, monthly, quarterly, and annually. Think of it like this – weekly sprints, monthly checkups, quarterly deep dives, and an annual strategic reset. Each has a purpose and real cases to illustrate their value.

WEEKLY: THE SCOREBOARD SPRINT

Every week is a small cycle of execution and reflection. We start the week with a plan (remember the Monday bulletin? It lists what we aim to do this week). We end the week with outcomes – some tasks done, some in progress, maybe some delayed. Every Friday, my team and I will do a quick review: What got done? What didn't? Why not? Then we update the scoreboard accordingly. This practice means we never go more than 7 days without checking our progress.

This is like a sports team watching game film every week to catch mistakes and improvements. At my basketball camps if the turnover count in a drill hit a certain number, we'd blow the whistle, reset, and teach the error. The scoreboard is a teacher too. That's exactly the attitude here: each week's scoreboard teaches us something. For instance, if two weeks in a row "completed projects" stayed at zero, it raises a red flag – are we bottlenecked somewhere? If complaint response times suddenly lengthen one week, what happened – did staff miss a beat or did we get an influx of issues? The weekly frequency is vital because problems are caught early, when they're easier to fix. It's much better to realize "hey, we slipped on returning calls this week, let's double down next week" than to only notice six months later when a reputation of unresponsiveness has set in.

A real case: Suppose one week the rains were heavy and we had planned to paint a school fence but couldn't. The Friday review notes "Fence painting delayed due to rain – rescheduled for next week, weather permitting." We annotate that, communicate it on the update. This seems minor, but it does two things: it keeps us accountable (we acknowledged the slip and set a new date), and it gives context to the public (so they know it didn't get done and why). The next week, if weather clears, we do it. If it rains again, we might escalate – maybe we need to cover the area or find an indoor task and not keep dragging. The loop forces a decision or adaptation rather than letting tasks languish indefinitely.

Another scenario: On a Friday review, we notice that for three weeks we've had "meet with Ministry about clinic hours" on the plan but it hasn't happened (maybe they rescheduled, etc.). That recurring non-completion will stick out. We then decide – do we try a different route (like send a letter or use a political friend to get that meeting) or escalate (ask a question in Parliament about it)? The weekly check ensures it's not forgotten. In old politics, something like that could slip through cracks, especially if the Ministry was dragging feet intentionally. But if it's on our radar every week, we'll find a way to address it or at least flag publicly that "we've been trying to meet X and it hasn't happened, here's our next step."

We will incorporate feedback into these weekly loops too. If a citizen points out an error on the scoreboard ("hey, that drain is marked completed but it's not actually finished!"), we'll correct it immediately and note what happened (maybe contractor reported done but on inspection, not fully; so we reopen that task). By showing that level of responsiveness, we build trust that the data isn't just window dressing – it's a true working tool.

In many ways, the weekly loop is about reliability. Just like a reliable train schedule, people will know: every week there's an update, every week we adjust course as needed. If I'm out of island or ill one week, the system shouldn't halt – the team will still do an update, even if it's "MP was away at conference, so lower activity this week, but office handled A, B, C." It's important to not break the chain. Because consistency builds momentum. I recall writing about a scholarship student who succeeded through disciplined habit, and I said "we will starve [mistrust] with information" – meaning regular info prevents the silence where rumors grow. Weekly transparency starves mistrust.

MONTHLY: THEMED PERFORMANCE HUDDLES

Every month, I intend to convene at least one focused review meeting on a specific sector or initiative. Think of this as a slightly deeper dive than the quick weekly scan – we gather those involved in that area and discuss progress and problems in detail. For example:

- **Monthly Education & Youth Review:** On the last Thursday of each month, perhaps, I meet with a small "Education Committee" – maybe a couple of principals, a youth rep, my youth development assistant. We look at the education/youth part of the scoreboard and beyond. Are the after-school programs meeting their targets? Did scholarship applications go out on time? What do the school test scores or attendance look like recently (if available)? If one school's after-school program has low attendance, as I imagined earlier, we discuss why – maybe it conflicts with sports practice, so we adjust scheduling. If we see, say, only 2 scholarships this quarter and our goal was 5, we identify bottlenecks (did students not apply? Do we need to push SAT prep harder?). This is the time to share anecdotes too – e.g. a tutor might say "hey, the kids are struggling in math more than expected, maybe get an extra math specialist." That insight goes into next month's plan (maybe hire one via the budget, or get volunteer). We also use data: the Castries North Data Dossier might show, for instance, CSEC (O-level) exam pass rates for our schools vs others. If Castries North schools are behind, that's a flag; we then target interventions and measure again after a year or two. By having a fixed monthly forum, we ensure these topics don't get lost amid daily urgencies.

- **Monthly Health & Well-being Review:** Similarly, say first Monday of each month with health stakeholders – the head nurse at the clinic, maybe a doctor who lives in the area, a rep from the Ministry's local health team. We go over clinic performance: "This month, the clinic was closed 4 hours due to nurse shortage – any fix coming? How are medicine stocks?" (Using our dashboard data: e.g. 90% uptime, a few stockouts). If blood pressure screening turnout is low, perhaps we plan a community health fair next month to boost awareness. We also check on our community exercise groups: are they growing? If the Babonneau Rd walkers group dwindled, find out why (maybe leader fell ill, so assign a new leader). This meeting might note any unusual spikes (e.g. "we saw more Dengue cases this month – maybe coordinate with Vector Unit to fog the area, inform public"). These monthly check-ins allow a quick pivot on public health actions. Maybe at one meeting, a member raises that mental health issues are showing up at the clinic – that could spark starting a support group or getting a counsellor to visit monthly. It's responsive governance in action.

• **Monthly Infrastructure & Safety Check:** Perhaps mid-month with our works supervisor, a police liaison, etc. We examine the state of projects: any contractor issues? Are we on track with the quarter's scheduled works? Did new issues crop up (like a sudden road sinkhole to address)? For safety, discuss crime or accident incidents reported by police or community watch. If break-ins spiked in one neighbourhood, maybe we expedite installing some streetlights or cameras there, or coordinate a town hall with police. This is where the infrastructure scorecards (quarterly, see next section) get prepped, ensuring each month we accumulate data so the quarterly isn't a surprise.

Essentially, monthly loops are sectoral learning loops. They force us to look beyond just completing tasks – we look at outcomes and efficacy on a thematic basis, with input from those on the ground (teachers, nurses, etc.). This aligns with the covenant promises of reviewing scholarships and health regularly. In fact, I explicitly mentioned "monthly scholarship and health reviews" in the task description. By doing these monthly, we catch trends quickly – for example, if one month shows a rise in youth unemployment in our area (if we have that data or even anecdotally more youths asking for work), by next month we might respond with a new training drive or job fair rather than waiting a year.

Let's illustrate with a model case from a hypothetical Year 1:

At the January Youth review, we realize our SAT prep class at one school only has 5 students, all from that school, while another school's students didn't know about it. By February's meeting, we had done outreach to the other school, and now 15 students attend, including 5 from the second school. However, one volunteer tutor can't handle 15 well, so by the March meeting we decide to assign a second tutor (maybe a teacher we pay a small stipend). Scores improve by April. By June, these students take SAT practice and do 10% better than initial test – we celebrate that in the meeting (success, scale or maintain). But maybe we also find out in June that none of our tech/vocational training slots were taken up by girls, only boys. At the July review, we plan a campaign to encourage young women to enrol, and adjust the program to be more appealing (maybe include hospitality skills not just plumbing). By August, we see a couple of young women join. This continuous adjustment is possible because we met every month to notice these details and act.

Without such loops, these fixes might occur too late or not at all. A yearly report might say "20 youth trained, 0 female" and one might go "oh that's unfortunate". But with a loop, you catch it midstream and try to fix it next cycle.

One more monthly mechanism: internal team retrospectives. I will hold a brief staff meeting monthly where we discuss how we are working. Are constituents happy with how we handle walk-ins? Did we meet our own standard of returning calls in 48 hours? (We can check logs – e.g., in our issue log, are most calls returned next day or are some languishing?). If say our data shows we slipped ("average call return was 3 days this month, target is 2"), we ask why – maybe our phone line was down two days, or our receptionist was sick. Then we fix the process (get a backup line or person). We basically practice what I'd call the dignity test on ourselves: are we lifting dignity in how we serve? For instance, I might randomly call a couple of citizens who interacted with the office and ask their experience. If someone says "I reported a broken pipe and never heard back for two weeks," that's a fail – we bring it up, learn from it, and correct the system (maybe a follow-up call was missed).

This mirrors a story I shared: Ms. Joseph and her blocked drain – the "right response" was to log it, schedule fix, and follow-up after to ensure satisfaction. That story sets a standard. Our monthly internal check would ask: are all the "Ms. Josephs" out there getting the right response consistently? If not, why? Maybe one staff needs more training or one procedure needs tweaking (like ensuring we call back after closure of an issue).

QUARTERLY: SCORECARDS AND STRATEGY ADJUSTMENTS

Every quarter (every 3 months), we'll take an even broader view – a "big picture" check on the main categories of our covenant and plans. I envision an Infrastructure Scorecard each quarter, as well as potentially a Social Programs Scorecard. These are more formal summaries that could even be shared with the public in detail, possibly through a town hall or a quarterly report.

The Infrastructure Scorecard would collate all physical projects: which were completed this quarter, which are in progress, which didn't start as planned and why. It will list things like "Roads resurfaced: X out of Y planned, Bridges built: A out of B, Drains cleaned: M out of N, Streetlights fixed: U out of V reported" etc. It might use visual aids: a map with green dots for finished works and red for pending. If we're at Q2 and see only 1 of 5 planned road repairs done, we know we must hustle in Q3/Q4 or adjust goals. These quarterly check-ins also align with financial quarters – we might adjust funding flows accordingly (e.g., push for a BNTF approval by Q3 if we see we're behind on some target and need that boost).

The social programs/ services scorecard might cover education, health, youth engagement metrics: e.g., "After-school program participation rate this quarter vs last; Clinic average wait time; Number of community events held; Crime statistics trend." For instance, if we promised in the covenant to have two extended-hour clinic days a month by mid-year, the Q2 scorecard will explicitly say "Extended hours achieved? Yes/No (how many days so far)". If no, time to press on the Ministry harder or find a workaround. If yes, measure its usage (did people actually come in those early hours? If not many, maybe need better publicity or adjust timing). The quarterly timeline is good for seeing trends without getting lost in weekly fluctuations. Maybe one week clinic was shut due to a freak event, but quarterly it was 95% operational – so that's fine. Or youth crime incidents might vary monthly, but quarterly we can see if the general direction is down or up after interventions.

One real case example to illustrate quarterly learning: road safety improvements. Say at the start of the year we identified 4 dangerous road spots to improve (2 crosswalks, 1 speed bump near a school, 1 mirror on a blind corner). By Q2 scorecard, maybe we've done 2 of 4. We present that: crosswalks done (result: vehicles now slowing down at Vigie, good feedback), speed bump pending because waiting on Ministry material, mirror not installed because of sourcing issues. We then strategize: push Ministry on speed bump before next quarter (maybe allocate CDP funds to it if they delay more), and find another vendor for the mirror or a temporary solution. By Q4, ideally all 4 done, and perhaps accident reports show a reduction in incidents at those spots (we'd love to quantify that: e.g. "Choc junction accidents in second half of year: 1, down from 4 in first half"). If something didn't happen by year-end, the annual review addresses it.

Quarterly meetings can also involve inviting external partners to weigh in. For instance, in a Q3 Youth review maybe invite the head of the National Skills Programme to discuss aligning our local training with their offerings, after reviewing our performance in Q1-2. Or at Q4, invite a rep from Ministry of Infrastructure to our Infrastructure scorecard presentation – show them "here's what we did, here's where we need you – look, our scoreboard shows we completed 15 small fixes, but this big road is still pending your action." That not only informs them but puts a gentle public nudge.

Another tool: a quarterly community forum where we share these scorecards with residents. It doesn't have to be everyone in one place (could be one in each major area or one central plus online stream). In those, we present "Here's what we achieved in the last 3 months, here's where we fell short, here's what's next." And crucially, ask "What are you seeing? What have we missed? How did that new bus shelter work out for you?" Gathering feedback in these intervals means the community also becomes part of the learning loop. Maybe someone stands up to say "that retaining wall you built is great, but water is now diverting to my yard – could you adjust that?" That's invaluable input to take into the next quarter's plan (maybe add a drain extension). Or they might say "we really appreciated the cleanup day, can we do it more often?" – okay, maybe scale it up next quarter.

A prime example of quarterly learning: scholarship outcomes. Let's say at year start we set target to help 10 students get scholarships by year-end. By Q2, only 3 have confirmed placements. In the Q2 review (which might coincide with when acceptance letters come in), we might realize our pipeline needed earlier SAT prep or more aggressive outreach to colleges. So we make an adjustment for Q3:

organize an SAT bootcamp in summer, or personally call coaches/ colleges for a few promising kids (I have that network). By Q4, maybe we end up with 8 instead of 10, but that's better than if we passively waited and ended up with maybe 5. The loop mid-year let us intervene. Perhaps one case like Joel's (a hypothetical student) was borderline and by pushing an extra video or recommendation letter in July, he got in – that's a learning loop success. On the flip side, if we saw by Q2 that a certain approach isn't effective (like a university we were courting isn't responsive), we'd pivot to others for Q3.

Throughout these loops, I'll maintain a habit of logging lessons learned. Maybe a simple table: "Issue – Action – Outcome – Lesson." Example: Issue: Low turnout at first community cleanup; Action: increased promotion and provided snacks next time; Outcome: participation doubled; Lesson: personal invitations via community leaders yield better turnout than generic posters. Accumulating these ensures we don't forget what we learned a year later. Also it helps if others want to replicate or if I get hit by the proverbial bus, the next team has a record of what approaches worked or failed.

ANNUAL: THE STOP–START–SCALE SUMMIT

Finally, the yearly cycle – this is the big one, where we step back and take stock of the whole endeavour and make strategic shifts. I call it the "Stop–Start–Scale" exercise. At the end of each year (likely in December, outside of any election frenzy times), we'll gather a broader group of stakeholders – council members, community leaders, interested citizens who've been active, maybe some subject experts – and review the year's performance across all fronts.

We'll ask three big questions:

1. What do we stop doing next year? (Because it isn't working or isn't a priority anymore.)

2. What new thing do we start doing? (Because a need emerged or we have an idea to address something not covered.)

3. What do we scale up? (Because it worked well and there's demand for more.)

We've touched on scenarios for these decisions in the previous chapter, but here it becomes a formal annual agenda.

Imagine our first year in office:

• Stop: Perhaps we decide to stop the weekly food hamper distribution we inherited. We found that many people coming for hampers could be better helped by longer-term solutions, plus some truly needy were too shy or unable to come. We replace it with a more targeted welfare check-in and an emergency fund for dire cases, plus channel some folks into work programs. So we "stop" the old generic hamper line (thus ending the culture of dependency there) and use those funds/effort for something more empowering. We announce this at the summit, explaining the data: e.g., "Only 30% of hamper recipients were truly vulnerable; many others could work and said they'd prefer jobs. So we're redirecting $X from hampers to a community work program." (This, by the way, echoes my mantra to end the beggar mentality and focus on jobs.)

Or another stop: perhaps we tried a pilot "community shuttle" as earlier mentioned, and it had low usage. Annual review, we decide to stop it and redirect resources to a need identified like a mobile clinic or something more relevant.

• Start: We look at unmet needs or new challenges. For instance, maybe our data dossier or community feedback reveals rising mental health concerns (post-COVID trauma or youth depression). We haven't addressed that yet. So we decide to start a monthly mental health outreach clinic or youth counselling initiative next year. Or start a "business mentorship program" if we realized unemployment still high and entrepreneurs need support. Or maybe start a specific infrastructure project planning – like we say "We will start developing a plan for a community centre at Union" if we see a gap in community space and can aim for funding in future. Starting doesn't always mean executing fully right away; it can mean initiating a process.

We would rank possible new initiatives by impact and feasibility, likely choosing a few key ones. The community's voice is crucial here – what are they asking for that wasn't on our list? For example, maybe throughout the year multiple mothers have asked for a daycare facility. We didn't plan that originally. At the summit, we acknowledge this demand and say, "Alright, in Year 2 we will start efforts toward a community daycare program (maybe lobbying government or partnering with an NGO) because clearly it's needed." That becomes a new stream in our plan.

• Scale: Here we celebrate successes and plan to amplify them. Suppose our after-school program at PDJSS was a runaway success – improvements in grades, high attendance, great feedback. Scale might mean opening similar programs in two more schools or increasing capacity to include lower forms too. If our seniors exercise groups grew popular in 3 communities, maybe we add 2 more communities next year (or increase frequency). If a job apprenticeship pilot placed 10 youths with local businesses and 8 got hired at the end, next year we try to place 30 youths, expanding to more businesses.

We also consider scaling down or adjusting scope where needed: sometimes scale means doing more; sometimes it means expanding focus. For instance, maybe our focus was heavily on sports for youth and it worked for those engaged, but we realize a lot of artistic or less sporty youth were left out. So we "scale" our youth development to include arts – basically broaden the program offerings. The idea is to build on success by either reaching more people or more areas or adding complementary facets.

During this annual review, we'll use both hard data and stories. Hard data: all those metrics we tracked – how did the year-end numbers compare to our initial targets or baseline? Did unemployment in CN drop or rise? (Though that's influenced by national trends, we might look at any local job placements we facilitated.) Did CSEC pass rates in our schools improve? Did reported crimes in CN go down? Did water outages reduce after interventions? Some of these might need one-year-lag or more to see, but we'll gather what we can. For example, if the Census or surveys show our constituency's unemployment is 16% and national 14%, maybe our goal is at least not to let it worsen, and ideally narrow that gap by a point or two – any local actions contributing to that would be noted.

And stories: e.g., highlight five individuals whose lives tangibly improved this year via our programs – the single mother who got a steady job after training, the teenager who went off to university on scholarship, the diabetic senior whose health stabilized because the clinic extended hours and exercise program. These validate the numbers with human faces. They are the feedback loops closed – we did X, person Y benefited in Z way.

We also confront failures openly. If something we pledged didn't happen, we address it: why, and what's the plan – abandon or carry over? For instance, if we promised a particular road fix in 2027 and it didn't get done because Ministry delayed funding, we say so, and renew the push (or figure alternative) for 2028. If it didn't happen because we messed up or underestimated complexity, we own it: "This didn't work out; here's what we learned and how we'll approach such projects differently." People appreciate honesty over cover-ups.

A good example: maybe we aimed to complete 30 small projects but only did 20 by year end. We investigate: out of the 10 undone, perhaps 5 were delayed by procurement, 3 by weather, 2 by oversight. So the lesson: next year, plan procurement earlier (order materials in dry season maybe), pad timelines for rainy months, and improve tracking so none gets forgotten (oversight). We then adjust our planning targets accordingly – maybe we plan 30 again but with those adjustments, or plan 25 more realistically if capacity is a constraint discovered.

The annual summit would also refine our Covenant if needed. The covenant is meant to be somewhat evergreen through the term, but it's not set in stone like scripture. If a pledge becomes obsolete (for a good reason, like it's achieved or circumstances changed), we'll update it. For example, if by year 3 the government finally builds a promised polyclinic, our focus might shift from "advocate for clinic upgrade" to "ensure clinic is well-staffed and used." So the covenant might evolve to reflect that achieved milestone and the new challenge. All changes would be clearly communicated – like "We promised X. It's done, and now we add Y to continue progress."

One of the best parts of an annual loop is the chance to incorporate new ideas and innovations from outside our bubble. Perhaps over the year I attended a conference or read of another town's success or got advice from an expert. The annual strategy session is where we can introduce a novel approach to try out. E.g., maybe I learn about a mobile app that citizens can use to report issues (some cities have that). We could decide, let's pilot that next year (Start). Or I see another constituency started a community farming initiative that provided jobs and produce; maybe we borrow that concept if relevant.

Through all these loops, what we're really doing is fostering a culture: a culture of delivery and improvement. Everyone involved starts expecting that review and adjustment are normal, not signs of failure. We break the old habit of set-and-forget or of only revisiting issues at election time. Instead, it becomes like a continuous class where each test's results lead to adjusting the study plan. This is the antithesis of how many political offices run, where either nothing is measured (so you can always claim "we're working on it") or things are measured but hidden (so the public can't hold you to it).

If your habits are strong, they will cross oceans and still spend. The habits we build with these loops – weekly discipline, monthly focus, quarterly strategy, annual reflection – are habits of strong governance. They will "travel" with us year to year, and hopefully across administrations. Even if parties change or I move on someday, the institutionalized practice in Castries North of tracking and learning would ideally remain, because people will have seen its value.

A quick real-world analogy: In the private sector, companies have quarterly earnings reports and annual general meetings to appease shareholders, and agile teams have weekly sprints. We're adapting those proven cycles to public service. Government often lacks the shareholder forcing function (except elections every 5 years), so we create internal and community-driven ones (scoreboards and citizen feedback). In doing so, we kind of turn the constituents into shareholders in the community enterprise – you get regular reports and can voice satisfaction or concerns regularly, not just once in five years.

Let me share a brief case of a lesson learned mid-course that influenced me. Years ago, in one of my youth programs, we had a rule of very tough physical training. We noticed some kids dropping out. Initially we thought "they're just not disciplined." But after some reflection, we tried tweaking the program to incorporate more mentorship and life-skills discussion days (less physically intense, more engaging differently). The result: retention improved, and those chats actually uncovered issues some kids faced that we could help with (like family troubles). The lesson was that raw intensity wasn't the only way – adaptability and listening improved outcomes. I carry that lesson now: push hard (yes, we will push to deliver), but listen to the feedback and human factors, then adjust the approach for better engagement. The weekly and monthly loops let us detect "drop-outs" or disengagement early and fix the program rather than blame the people.

Another simple lesson: At one of our first scholarship SAT bootcamps, we scheduled it 8am on Saturdays – turnout was low. We found out many students have chores or lessons on Saturday mornings. Next camp we did afternoons – attendance doubled. If we hadn't solicited feedback and tried a change, we might've written off half the interested kids as "not serious" when really our timing was the issue. In governance, similarly, if a community isn't responding to an initiative, maybe the initiative's format is wrong, not that the community doesn't care. Only through iterative tweaking do we find the sweet spot.

Finally, the annual review is also a moment of renewal and motivation. It's like our team's championship off-site, where we celebrate wins, acknowledge MVPs (maybe give a shoutout or award to best community volunteer, best performing staffer, most improved area), and rally everyone for the next year's challenges. People need to see progress to stay energized – our scoreboard and report will show them concretely what changed due to collective effort. I imagine saying, "Last year at this time, that corner had no sidewalk and kids walked in mud; today it's paved and safe – look. Last year, 3 students went off to university; this year it's 8 – here are their names. Last year, our health centre had no evening hours; now it opens late on Wednesdays and 50 working folks got care who otherwise might not. These are our points on the board. Now, where do we aim next?"

By reinforcing that narrative each year – that we set goals, worked, measured, adjusted, and achieved tangible improvements – we build a collective confidence and habit. It becomes normal in Castries North to ask "so what are we starting this year? what are we stopping?" just as one might in a well-run organization. I want our citizens to have that expectation from any representative: show us your plan, show us your progress, show us you can learn and adapt. If I succeed, even my future opponents will have to play on that field, which ultimately benefits governance.

In conclusion, these learning loops close the gap between promises and delivery. They ensure that "delivery" isn't a one-time burst but a continuous, reliable service. It answers a fear many have: that politicians come with energy but then stagnate after a while. With loops in place, stagnation is busted because every cycle naturally injects reflection and impetus for change. If we fall into complacency, the scoreboard's red marks or the community's pointed questions at the quarterly forum quickly snap us out.

As I finish writing this Part VI of Make It Count, I realize how far we've come from the theoretical to the practical. We started with a covenant of clear pledges – that's the "what" and "why". We then established our transparency tools – that's the "with what information and accountability". We strategized funding – that's the "with what resources". And now with learning loops – that's the "how we keep getting better over time". It's a full framework for representation that is service-oriented, data-informed, and relentlessly improving.

None of this is glamorous in the traditional political sense. You won't find much ego-stroking or lofty oratory here (though I hope it inspires in a different way). It is, frankly, a bit boring in its methodical approach – weekly updates, meetings, charts. But as I've often preached: "The spectacular is just the faithful in fast forward." You want big change? Do the small things relentlessly and transparently, and watch change compound. We're turning representation into a craft, one that can be mastered through habit.

I often think about the legacy of this approach. If we do this right in Castries North, even for one term, we will have proven a model. We'll prove that a community can be run in a way that residents feel like active stakeholders, where success is measured not in how loud the political rallies are but in how quiet the problems become (because they got solved). Perhaps other constituencies will adopt a "scoreboard" mindset. Perhaps the national government itself will take cues – imagine a country where ministers publish weekly progress and engage in stop-start-scale annually. It might sound utopian, but someone has to set the example. Why not us? "Quietly, many [MPs] want to act this way – they just need an example and a little cover. We in Castries North can provide that example." I wrote that with conviction, and I intend to make it so.

Let's picture the annual meeting at the end of this term, say 5 years from now. Maybe that elder lady who nodded at my first speech is there in the front row. I can report to her: "We are not beggars, and I did not act like a king. We served, we accounted, we delivered visibly." And I wouldn't just be saying it – I'd point to the scoreboard, the reports, the before-and-after photos around the room. She'd nod again, I hope, in approval this time. And then – in true learning loop fashion – she might raise her hand and say, "That's good, son. Now here's what you need to do next..." Because the work of improving lives doesn't end; it only resets to a new baseline each cycle, asking us to make it count again and again.

With that, Part VI of this book – and this vision – comes to a close. We've laid down the covenant and the system to back it up. What remains is to put it into practice. The tools are ready; the court is marked. It's time to run the plays, measure the score, and keep improving until the final buzzer of our service. Together, let's make every day, every dollar, every decision count for Castries North.

Epilogue – Finish Strong

In sports, they say it's not how you start the game – it's how you finish it. Every drill I ran as a coach, every sprint I pushed through as a player, came with the same reminder: finish strong. Now, as we stand at the end of this playbook – and at the threshold of a new chapter for Castries North – those words have never meant more. Finish strong. This isn't just about concluding a book; it's about carrying its energy into real life, into our streets and schools and clinics. It's about taking everything we've discussed – every small fix, every bold idea – and turning it into action that transforms our community.

I'm writing these final words with a full heart and unwavering resolve. We've walked through the issues and the solutions together in these pages. We've spoken plainly about what needs fixing and how we'll fix it. We've reminded ourselves that representation is a job of service, not a seat of royalty. Through it all runs a single truth: the work ahead is ours, together. The future of Castries North won't be handed down from on high by any minister or party boss. It will be built by the hands of our people – by us – one project, one neighbourhood, one day at a time.

For me, this mission is deeply personal. I'm not coming in from outside to tell you what to do – I am one of you. I was born and raised in Castries North; its lanes and playgrounds are the backdrop of my childhood and the foundation of my values. I went to school in our district. I shot hoops on our community courts. I sat in the same traffic on Manoel Street and walked the same shortcuts through Vide Bouteille. I've felt the pride of this community and I've shared in its frustrations. That's why I'm so passionate about this cause: it's about giving back to the place and the people that raised me. I know our potential firsthand, and I won't rest until that potential is unlocked for everyone who calls Castries North home.

THE WORK IS OURS

The work is ours – those four words carry a powerful truth. This campaign, this plan, this entire effort has never been about one man riding in to save the day. It's about all of us, the people of Castries North, claiming our rightful role in shaping our destiny. I have never pretended to have a magic wand or all the answers alone. What I have is a deep faith in you – in our teachers and coaches, our shopkeepers and nurses, our youth mentors and neighbourhood elders – to be partners in this mission.

For too long, politics made people feel like bystanders or beggars in their own community. We were taught to line up, bow our heads, and wait for handouts, as if we had no agency of our own. That ends now. We are not beggars, and I will never be a king. I am your servant, your representative, and I'm ready to work with you, not above you. The real power to change Castries North has always lived in its people. My job is to organize and amplify that power – not to replace it.

When I say "the work is ours," I mean that every resident can play a part. Maybe you'll volunteer at a homework club or coach a youth team on the weekend. Maybe you'll help us identify which drain floods first when the rains come, or show up at a town hall to voice a concern and a solution. Perhaps you'll join a residents' committee to monitor a project on your street, or offer your professional skills to a community initiative. Each of these actions, big or small, helps drive our community forward.

And when something's not right – when a project stalls or an issue is overlooked – I want you to speak up. Hold me to the promises in this playbook. If a streetlight that was scheduled to be fixed is still dark, let's hear about it. If a scholarship application is languishing, bring it to my office (which will always have its door open to you) and we'll chase it down. In other words, keep me honest and keep each other motivated. Accountability is not a one-way street; it's a loop that connects all of us. I've said it before and I'll say it again: call me out if I slip. That's the energy and vigilance that will keep this movement alive and on track.

Our community has always been strong – sometimes in spite of those in power rather than because of them. We've patched our own potholes, organized our own sports days, cleaned up after storms, and looked after neighbours when official help never arrived. As one mother in La Clery told me during a town hall, "My son doesn't need a welfare hamper, he needs a referee and a chance to play under lights." She wasn't asking for charity; she was asking for opportunity. And then she said what so many of you have echoed in different ways: give us the basics, and we will build the rest.

That simple plea is at the heart of this movement. You're not looking for a politician to do everything; you're looking for a government that does its part so the community can do its part. You want the clinic open and stocked – and you'll take care to use it wisely to keep your family healthy. You want the basketball court maintained and safe – and you'll ensure the youth are there every evening, hustling and learning. You want the streetlights working – and you'll organize the evening neighbourhood walks, keeping everyone active and secure. In short, you want a representative who clears the path, so that you can stride forward.

So let it be known: our success will not be measured by what I build or accomplish, but by what we build and accomplish. When a new sidewalk is poured or a drainage problem fixed, it's going to be our victory as a community – the result of your input, your advocacy, and our collective will. When a young person from Castries North earns a scholarship and boards a plane for college, it's our triumph – family, teachers, mentors, all of us who played a role in that journey.

In the end, the phrase "the work is ours" is both a pledge and a challenge. It's my pledge to always involve you, to never shut you out of your own house of governance. And it's a challenge to each of us to step up and contribute. If we truly embrace the idea that Castries North belongs to its people, then we all share responsibility for its rise. And I have every confidence that we are up to that task – because I have seen what our people are capable of when we come together with purpose.

THE DOOR IS OPEN

Opportunities like this don't come around every day. Right now, the door is open for Castries North to step into a new era of representation. What do I mean by "the door is open"? I mean the barriers that used to keep ordinary citizens out of the process are coming down. The door of the constituency office – both literally and figuratively – will be wide open. Walk in, bring your ideas, your complaints, your aspirations. This is your house. It's the same door that for years might have seemed shut except at election time, or open only to a favoured few. No more. We are throwing it open to sunshine and fresh air, to scrutiny and participation.

This open door symbolizes a government that isn't afraid of its people – it welcomes the people. You will always be greeted as the owners of that office, because you are. Whether you have a problem to log, a proposal to share, or you just want to check the status of a project on the community board, you will be welcomed. And not just to observe, but to shape what happens next. When we hold our "Castries North Accountability Days" and pin those weekly scoreboards and project sheets on the wall, that is your invitation to see everything for yourself. When we publish every budget request and every ministry response, that is your information to use – knowledge that had been locked behind closed doors for too long.

"The door is open" also means that the processes that used to be hidden will be transparent. Think about how things used to be: deals made in back rooms, decisions announced without explanation, funds allocated without clarity – and ordinary folks left in the dark. We're ending that culture. If there's a funding opportunity from central government for community projects, you'll know about it and we'll go after it together. If there's a delay on a planned repair, you'll know why and who's responsible to fix it. We'll post timelines, names, budgets, progress photos – all out in the open. By doing so we are not just opening a door, we're taking the door off its hinges. We're saying that the only way we work from now on is in plain view.

Walking through that door means embracing a totally different relationship between the community and its representative. It means we converse, not dictate; collaborate, not patronize. When I invite you to walk through it with me, I'm inviting you into the room where decisions are being made for Castries North's future. How many times have you heard politicians talk about transparency but never actually let you see the work? Here, we're doing it differently. If we have a planning meeting about fixing a road or improving a school, expect that summary to be shared. If we contact a potential scholarship partner overseas, expect that we'll report the outcome. This open-door approach isn't about publicity – it's about trust. It's about proving that we have nothing to hide and everything to share.

Importantly, this open door is also a door outwards – a gateway for you to step into leadership roles of your own. I truly hope that by seeing how things run, some of you will be inspired to lead community committees, to spearhead projects, even to run for office in the future with the same ethos. When governance is accessible, it nurtures new leaders. A young person sitting in on our youth council meetings or reviewing our public dashboard might realize, "Hey, I can do this. I can serve my community too." If this open style of governance sparks that in even one young man or woman, then we haven't just opened a door – we've opened a path for the next generation.

Castries North has a chance to set a precedent for all of Saint Lucia. There are eyes on us – in other constituencies, in the media, among the broader public – wondering if this little experiment of open, independent, citizen-first representation can really work. I believe it can. In fact, I believe it will become a model for others.

Quietly, I know many good folks inside the parties who are tired of the old ways. They want to serve with the same openness and integrity we talk about here, but they've been waiting for someone to prove that it resonates with the people. If we succeed – when we succeed – we will do more than change Castries North. We'll be opening doors across the country. We'll be saying to every community: demand more, expect transparency, settle for nothing less than true service.

That is the broader civic purpose behind this campaign. Yes, it's about fixing drains and getting scholarships – the nuts and bolts of daily life. But it's also about lighting a small flame that could guide the whole island toward a better style of leadership. It's about demonstrating that when you put people first and treat them as partners, amazing things happen: trust is rebuilt, pride is restored, and progress becomes tangible. We are inviting Saint Lucia to watch Castries North and see a blueprint for a new normal.

The door is wide open now. It's open because you have pushed it open with your insistence on better representation, and because I have thrown my shoulder into it by running as an independent who answers only to you. The old guard might have preferred it stay shut – keeping you as spectators in your own democracy – but that era will be over if we choose to end it. Now it's up to all of us to walk through that door and claim the future that awaits on the other side.

WALKING THROUGH IT TOGETHER

We stand on the doorstep of a new beginning. Everything we need to succeed is already here with us – the ideas in this playbook, the energy of our people, the lessons from our past, and the will to change the way things are done. All that's left is the most important step: walking through that door, together.

I won't pretend that it will always be easy. Real change never is. There will be those who doubt, those who resist, those who say, "This is how it's always been," or "It can't be done." But I ask you: when has anything worth doing ever been easy? Our parents and grandparents built this community through hard work and perseverance, often with scant resources. They didn't quit when times were tough. Neither will we.

I'm reminded of an elder from La Clery who attended one of my early meetings. When I declared "We are not beggars; I am not a king," she didn't cheer or even smile – she just nodded, a slow, resolute nod. It was as if she was saying, "At last, somebody is willing to call a thing by its name." In that small gesture, I saw the accumulated wisdom of years and the quiet hope of a community that has waited too long for real change. I carry that memory with me every day. It reminds me who I'm fighting for–for her generation that has seen promises come and go, and for the next generation that deserves to see promises kept. When I think of walking through this door together, I think of her stepping through with dignity, finally seeing a politics that treats her with the respect she always deserved. And I think of the young people watching, who will say this is how leadership should be.

In fact, we will draw strength from our history of grit and unity. When challenges arise – a funding setback, a stubborn bureaucrat, an unexpected crisis – we will tackle them head-on, just as this community has always done. Together, we'll find another way, push a little harder, and keep moving forward.

Walking through this open door means we enter as one people – united by a shared love for Castries North and a shared commitment to its progress. It doesn't matter which party you supported in the past, what neighbourhood you live in, or what your last name is. If you believe in this vision of honest, accountable, people-centred service, then you are part of this movement. Come on in. I welcome you with open arms. We may not agree on every detail – that's okay. Democracy isn't about unanimous agreement; it's about common purpose. Our common purpose here is clear: to create a constituency where every citizen can say, "I matter, my voice is heard, and my government works for me."

In practical terms, walking together means staying engaged. After you finish this book, I hope you won't set it aside and simply wait to see what happens. I hope you feel fired up to get involved. Talk to your neighbours about what you've read here – about what a difference it would make to have an MP who publishes weekly scoreboards and holds regular town halls that you can actually attend and speak at. Share the idea of the Castries North Covenant – the fact that you could walk into the office and see a list of promises on the wall, and check how many have been met. These ideas light people up when they hear them, because deep down we all crave this kind of transparency and respect. So spread the word. This movement grows one conversation at a time – on a bus, in the market, at your church or your workplace.

And yes, I'm going to ask something very simple of you: when election day comes, make your voice heard. Don't stay home. Don't let anyone tell you your vote doesn't matter or that nothing ever changes. We are proving right here that things can change. Your vote is the weight behind the door, pushing it fully open so it never swings shut again. If you give me the honour of your vote – if you hire me as your public servant – I promise I will work every day to reward that trust. More than that, I promise to keep listening to you after the votes are counted, because that's when the real work begins. Voting is not a favour to a politician; it's a commitment to the vision we share. Cast your vote for independent leadership and then hold me to every word I've said. That is how we will lock in this new era of accountability.

Index